COMPETITION
AND
PUBLIC POLICY

Cases in Antitrust

H. LEE FUSILIER
JEROME C. DARNELL | University of Colorado

PRENTICE-HALL, INC., *Englewood Cliffs, New Jersey*

To ARDINE and PHYLLIS

13–154831–X

Library of Congress Catalog Card No.: 73–144008

Current printing (last digit):

10 9 8 7 6 5 4 3 2 1

631-a

PRENTICE-HALL INTERNATIONAL, INC., *London*
PRENTICE-HALL OF AUSTRALIA, PTY. LTD., *Sydney*
PRENTICE-HALL OF CANADA, LTD., *Toronto*
PRENTICE-HALL OF INDIA PRIVATE LIMITED, *New Delhi*
PRENTICE-HALL OF JAPAN, INC., *Tokyo*

Preface

The purpose of this book is to provide in one convenient volume selections from the leading antitrust cases. For businessmen, economists, public administrators, students of antitrust, and others desiring a clearer understanding of the interrelationship among business practices, economics, and public policy, we believe there is no acceptable substitute for reading the actual decisions.

It is in the antitrust arena where the concept of separation of federal power into three branches with checks and balances is best typified. The Congress has responsibility for enacting the laws, the executive branch is charged with enforcement, and the judiciary interprets the legislative intent. The *law* on antitrust, or any other area of controversy, is ultimately to be found in the court opinions. Thus a study of the court decisions is essential to understanding the law and its attendant public policy.

We believe this book can serve two functions. First, for those who are already conversant with antitrust policy, it can be used independently of other books for in-depth study and comparison of developing public positions as reflected in statutes and decisions. Second, in introductory courses in business and government relations, it can be utilized with the standard texts as supplementary reading. Most courses dealing with public regulation of business will contain fairly extensive treatment of the antitrust statutes and the landmark court interpretations shaping the law. We have excerpted the most important parts from these cases and organized them into groupings with commentaries on the significance of each decision.

We have tried to assist the reader by providing a summary of the major issues raised in each case. This will alert the reader to the points he should look for and will emphasize the contribution of the case to antitrust policy. In each instance we have attempted to include the portions that have proved to be of lasting significance over time.

The large number of cases—a total of seventy-five—provides the user with greater flexibility in choosing those cases he considers most important for discussion. Dissenting opinions were included where appropriate. In several instances these minority opinions have given a preview of the direction antitrust law was to take in the future.

The cases have been organized into two main parts, corresponding roughly to the two major problem areas in antitrust. The first part includes the problems that arise because of industry concentration. These are the problems associated with monopoly and oligopoly power, concentration achieved via external expansion (merging), collusive agreements among competitors, and activities of trade associations. The second major division deals with trade practices that interfere with distribution channels. Included are the issues of price discrimination, delivered pricing, tying contracts and exclusive dealing arrangements, resale price maintenance and refusal to deal, and fraud and deceptive practices. The Appendix contains excerpts from the basic antitrust statutes and thereby eliminates the necessity of going to other references for the wording of these laws.

We have included as many recent cases as possible. In some areas there were no recent decisions, for example, there has been no important Supreme Court decision on price fixing since 1940). On the other hand, the merger issue is one of great currency and there are a number of recent, important decisions. All the Supreme Court decisions rendered to date under the Celler-Kefauver Amendment to Section 7 of the Clayton Act are included.

We have earnestly attempted to provide a volume that will be useful in studying and understanding antitrust policy. We must wait on others to render the final verdict on this issue.

We want to express our gratitude to Professor Ross M. Robertson, Graduate School of Business, Indiana University, for making several useful suggestions for improving the manuscript. Although unaware of the lasting impression he made in a graduate course several years ago, he was primarily responsible for the outline and organization of this book.

Contents

PART TWO   INTERFERENCE WITH DISTRIBUTION CHANNELS

List of Cases

PART ONE

Problems of Concentration
in Industry

1

Economic Power in a Single Firm
—Early Interpretations

The Sherman Antitrust Act was passed in 1890 in response to public outcries to do something about the large business "trusts" that were growing rapidly at that time and gaining control of many consumer-goods industries. This was the first legislative effort designed to influence and oversee the practices of business firms. The major provisions of the Act are contained in the first two sections:[1]

> Sec. 1. Every contract, combination in the form of trust or otherwise, or conspiracy, in restraint of trade or commerce among the several States, or with foreign nations, is hereby declared to be illegal: . . . Every person who shall make any contract or engage in any combination or conspiracy hereby declared to be illegal shall be deemed guilty of a misdemeanor, . . .

> Sec. 2. Every person who shall monopolize, or attempt to monopolize, or combine or conspire with any other person or persons, to monopolize any part of the trade or commerce among the several States, or with foreign nations, shall be deemed guilty of a misdemeanor, . . .

[In reality, the Sherman Act did little more than put the common law in writing since the activities of restraint of trade and monopolization were already considered illegal.] Under the common law violations of this nature were considered matters of private wrong, requiring that the parties seek individual redress against the offender. The Sherman Act made restraint of trade and monopolization violations against the federal government, subject to prosecution by that arm of government, and punishable as a criminal offense by fines and/or imprisonment.

The wording of the Sherman Act, as well as other antitrust legislation, is very broad and general. Congress did not attempt to spell out the precise meaning of those activities considered against the public interest and welfare. Consequently, the courts have the task of interpreting and developing the law as they believe Congress intended it to be.

---

[1] See the Appendix for sections of the Sherman Act and other pertinent antitrust legislation.

What Is Commerce?

In this part we are concerned with the interpretation of what activities are to be included in the phrase "in restraint of trade or commerce." Two cases are included in order to illustrate how the interpretation has changed over a period of years. The Supreme Court was first called upon to interpret the Sherman Act in 1895, and the case revolved around the very question of the meaning of commerce. This was the E. C. *Knight* case, also referred to as the *Sugar Trust* case, in which the American Sugar Refining Company had acquired the stock of the E. C. Knight Company along with three other sugar refiners in the Philadelphia area. The resulting acquisitions raised American Sugar's share of the refining market from 65 per cent to 98 per cent. The government contended that these acquisitions gave American Sugar a monopoly position, which was in restraint of trade. The Supreme Court did recognize that a virtual monopoly had been obtained over the refining of sugar. But whether such activity was proscribed by the Sherman Act depended upon the interpretation of commerce. Was a monopoly of *manufacture* to be considered a monopoly of commerce? Or was manufacture solely an intrastate activity and thus outside the intent of the Act? The Court concluded that sugar refining was an act of manufacture and that manufacturing was not the same as commerce. This conclusion effectively put antitrust questions back in the hands of state jurisdiction.

The decision had another aspect that has had very important consequences during the following years. The Court *implied* that the Sherman Act could not be used to prevent mergers or consolidations carried out by the purchase of property (physical assets). Transfers of properties fall under state jurisdiction, not federal laws. The result was to open the gates for the first great merger movement in United States history, a truly significant movement that lasted some ten years and permanently altered the structure of American industry.

Parts of Justice Harlan's dissent from the majority opinion have been included in which he points out that such a narrow interpretation was both contrary to the will of Congress and destroyed the very body of the Act. He argued that the ultimate purpose of manufacture is to engage in commerce—the movement of goods from the point of origin to point of acquisition—and thereby brings the case within the scope of the Sherman Act.

UNITED STATES v. E. C. KNIGHT COMPANY

156 U.S. 1 (1895)

This was a bill filed by the United States against E. C. Knight Company and others, in the Circuit Court of the United States for the Eastern District of Pennsylvania, charging that the defendants had violated the provisions of an act of Congress approved July 2, 1890 . . . entitled "An act to protect trade and commerce against unlawful restraints and monopolies" . . . "providing that every contract, combination in the form of trust, or otherwise, or conspiracy in restraint of trade and commerce among the several States is illegal, and that persons who shall monopolize or shall attempt to monopolize, or combine or conspire with other persons to monopolize trade and commerce among the several States, shall be guilty of a misdemeanor." The bill alleged that the defendant, the American Sugar Refining Company, was incorporated under and by virtue of the laws of New Jersey, whose certificate of incorporation named the places in New Jersey and New York at which its principal business was to be transacted, and several other States in which it proposed to carry on operations, and stated that the objects for which said company was formed were "the purchase, manufacture, refining, and sale of sugar, molasses, and melada, and all lawful business incidental thereto"; that the defendant, E. C. Knight Company, was incorporated under the laws of Pennsylvania "for the purpose of importing, manufacturing, refining and dealing in sugars and molasses," at the city of Philadelphia; that the defendant, the Franklin Sugar Company, was incorporated under the laws of Pennsylvania "for the purpose of the manufacture of sugar and the purchase of raw material for that purpose," at Philadelphia; that the defendant, Spreckels Sugar Refining Company, was incorporated under the laws of Pennsylvania "for the purpose of refining sugar, which will involve the buying of the raw material therefor and selling the manufactured product, and of doing whatever else shall be incidental to the said business of refining," at the city of Philadelphia; that the defendant, the Delaware Sugar House, was incorporated under the laws of Pennsylvania "for the purpose of the manufacture of sugar and syrups, and preparing the same for market, and the transaction of such work or business as may be necessary or proper for the proper management of the business of manufacture."

It was further averred that the four defendants last named were independently engaged in the manufacture and sale of sugar until on or about March 4, 1892; that the product of their refineries amounted to thirty-three per cent of the sugar refined in the United States; that they were competitors with the American Sugar Refining Company; that the products of their several refineries were distributed among the several States of the United States, and that all the companies were engaged in trade or commerce with the several States and with foreign nations; that the American Sugar Refining Company had, on or prior to March 4, 1892, obtained the control of all the sugar refineries of the United States with the exception of the Revere of Boston, and the refineries of the four defendants above mentioned; that the Revere produced annually about two per cent of the total amount of sugar refined.

The bill then alleged that in order that the American Sugar Refining Company might obtain complete control of the price of sugar in the United States, that company, and John E. Searles, Jr., acting for it, entered into an unlawful and fraudulent scheme to purchase the stock, machinery, and real estate of the other four corporations defendant, by which they attempted to control all the sugar refineries for the purpose of restraining the trade thereof with other States as theretofore carried on independently by said defendants; that in pursuance of this scheme, on or about March 4, 1892, Searles entered into a contract with the defendant Knight Company and individual stockholders named, for the purchase of all the stock of that company, and subsequently delivered to the defendants therefor in exchange shares of the American Sugar Refining Company; that on or about the same date Searles entered into a similar contract with the Spreckels Company and individual stockholders, and with the Franklin Company and stockholders, and with the Delaware Sugar House and stockholders. . . .

The Circuit Court held that the facts did not show a contract, combination, or conspiracy to restrain or monopolize trade or commerce "among the several States or with foreign nations," and dismissed the bill. . . . The cause was taken to the Circuit Court of Appeals for the Third Circuit, and the decree affirmed. . . . This appeal was then prosecuted. . . .

MR. CHIEF JUSTICE FULLER, after stating the case, delivered the opinion of the court.[2]

By the purchase of the stock of the four Philadelphia refineries, with shares of its own stock, the American Sugar Refining Company acquired nearly complete control of the manufacture of refined sugar within the United States. The bill charged that the contracts under which these

---

[2] The citations and footnotes from the opinions of the Court have been, with a few exceptions, omitted from the cases in this chapter.

purchases were made constituted combinations in restraint of trade, and that in entering into them the defendants combined and conspired to restrain the trade and commerce in refined sugar among the several States and with foreign nations, contrary to the act of Congress of July 2, 1890.

The relief sought was the cancellation of the agreements under which the stock was transferred; the redelivery of the stock to the parties respectively; and an injunction against the further performance of the agreements and further violations of the act. . . .

The fundamental question is, whether conceding that the existence of a monopoly in manufacture is established by the evidence, that monopoly can be directly suppressed under the act of Congress in the mode attempted by this bill.

It cannot be denied that the power of a State to protect the lives, health, and property of its citizens, and to preserve good order and the public morals, "the power to govern men and things within the limits of its dominion," is a power originally and always belonging to the States, not surrendered by them to the general government, nor directly restrained by the Constitution of the United States, and essentially exclusive. The relief of the citizens of each State from the burden of monopoly and the evils resulting from the restraint of trade among such citizens was left with the States to deal with, and this court has recognized their possession of that power even to the extent of holding that an employment or business carried on by private individuals, when it becomes a matter of such public interest and importance as to create a common charge or burden upon the citizen; in other words, when it becomes a practical monopoly, to which the citizen is compelled to resort and by means of which a tribute can be exacted from the community, is subject to regulation by state legislative power. On the other hand, the power of Congress to regulate commerce among the several States is also exclusive. The Constitution does not provide that interstate commerce shall be free, but, by the grant of this exclusive power to regulate it, it was left free except as Congress might impose restraints. Therefore it has been determined that the failure of Congress to exercise this exclusive power in any case is an expression of its will that the subject shall be free from restrictions or impositions upon it by the several States, and if a law passed by a State in the exercise of its acknowledged powers comes into conflict with that will, the Congress and the State cannot occupy the position of equal opposing sovereignties, because the Constitution declares its supremacy and that of the laws passed in pursuance thereof; and that which is not supreme must yield to that which is supreme. "Commerce, undoubtedly, is traffic," said Chief Justice Marshall, "but it is something more; it is intercourse. It describes the commercial intercourse between nations and parts of nations in all its branches, and is regulated by prescribing rules for carrying on that intercourse." That which belongs to commerce is within the jurisdiction of the

United States, but that which does not belong to commerce is within the jurisdiction of the police power of the State. . . .

The argument is that the power to control the manufacture of refined sugar is a monopoly over a necessary of life, to the enjoyment of which by a large part of the population of the United States interstate commerce is indispensable, and that, therefore, the general government in the exercise of the power to regulate commerce may repress such monopoly directly and set aside the instruments which have created it. But this argument cannot be confined to necessaries of life merely, and must include all articles of general consumption. Doubtless the power to control the manufacture of a given thing involves in a certain sense the control of its disposition, but this is a secondary and not the primary sense; and although the exercise of that power may result in bringing the operation of commerce into play, it does not control it, and affects it only incidentally and indirectly. Commerce succeeds to manufacture, and is not a part of it. The power to regulate commerce is the power to prescribe the rule by which commerce shall be governed, and is a power independent of the power to suppress monopoly. But it may operate in repression of monopoly whenever that comes within the rules by which commerce is governed or whenever the transaction is itself a monopoly of commerce. . . .

. . . The regulation of commerce applies to the subjects of commerce and not to matters of internal policy. Contracts to buy, sell, or exchange goods to be transported among the several States, the transportation and its instrumentalities, and articles bought, sold, or exchanged for the purposes of such transit among the States, or put in the way of transit, may be regulated, but this is because they form part of interstate trade or commerce. The fact that an article is manufactured for export to another State does not of itself make it an article of interstate commerce, and the intent of the manufacturer does not determine the time when the article or product passes from the control of the State and belongs to commerce. This was so ruled in *Coe v. Errol*, 116 U.S. 517, 525, in which the question before the court was whether certain logs cut at a place in New Hampshire and hauled to a river town for the purpose of transportation to the State of Maine were liable to be taxed like other property in the State of New Hampshire. Mr. Justice Bradley, delivering the opinion of the court, said: "Does the owner's state of mind in relation to the goods, that is, his intent to export them, and his partial preparation to do so, exempt them from taxation? This is the precise question for solution. . . . There must be a point of time when they cease to be governed exclusively by the domestic law and begin to be governed and protected by the national law of commercial regulation, and that moment seems to us to be a legitimate one for this purpose, in which they commence their final movement from the State of their origin to that of their destination."

And again, in *Kidd v. Pearson*, 128 U.S. 1, . . . Mr. Justice Lamar remarked: "No distinction is more popular to the common mind, or more clearly expressed in economic and political literature, than that between manufacture and commerce. Manufacture is transformation—the fashioning of raw materials into a change of form for use. The functions of commerce are different. The buying and selling and the transportation incidental thereto constitute commerce; and the regulation of commerce in the constitutional sense embraces the regulation at least of such transportation. . . . . If it be held that the term includes the regulation of all such manufactures as are intended to be the subject of commercial transactions in the future, it is impossible to deny that it would also include all productive industries that contemplate the same thing. The result would be that Congress would be invested, to the exclusion of the States, with the power to regulate, not only manufactures, but also agriculture, horticulture, stock raising, domestic fisheries, mining—in short, every branch of human industry. For is there one of them that does not contemplate, more or less clearly, an interstate or foreign market? Does not the wheat grower of the Northwest or the cotton planter of the South, plant, cultivate, and harvest his crop with an eye on the prices at Liverpool, New York, and Chicago? The power being vested in Congress and denied to the States, it would follow as an inevitable result that the duty would devolve on Congress to regulate all of these delicate, multiform and vital interests—interests which in their nature are and must be local in all the details of their successful management. . . . The demands of such a supervision would require, not uniform legislation generally applicable throughout the United States, but a swarm of statutes only locally applicable and utterly inconsistent. Any movement toward the establishment of rules of production in this vast country, with its many different climates and opportunities, could only be at the sacrifice of the peculiar advantages of a large part of the localities in it, if not of every one of them. On the other hand, any movement toward the local, detailed and incongruous legislation required by such interpretation would be about the widest possible departure from the declared object of the clause in question. . . . ."

Contracts, combinations, or conspiracies to control domestic enterprise in manufacture, agriculture, mining, production in all its forms, or to raise or lower prices or wages, might unquestionably tend to restrain external as well as domestic trade, but the restraint would be an indirect result, however inevitable and whatever its extent, and such result would not necessarily determine the object of the contract, combination, or conspiracy. . . .

It was in the light of well-settled principles that the act of July 2, 1890, was framed. Congress did not attempt thereby to assert the power to deal with monopoly directly as such; or to limit and restrict the rights of corporations created by the States or the citizens of the States in the acquisition, control, or disposition of property; or to regulate or prescribe the price or prices at which such property or the products thereof should be sold; or to make criminal the acts of persons in the acquisition and control of property which the States of their residence or creation sanctioned or permitted. Aside from the provisions applicable where Congress might exercise municipal power, what the law struck at was combinations, contracts, and conspiracies to monopolize trade and commerce among the several States or with foreign nations; but the contracts and acts of the defendants related exclusively to the acquisition of the Philadelphia refineries and the business of sugar refining in Pennsylvania, and bore no direct relation to commerce between the States or with foreign nations. The object was manifestly private gain in the manufacture of the commodity, but not through the control of interstate or foreign commerce. It is true that the bill alleged that the products of these refineries were sold and distributed among the several States, and that all the companies were engaged in trade or commerce with the several States and with foreign nations; but this was no more than to say that trade and commerce served manufacture to fulfil its function. Sugar was refined for sale, and sales were probably made at Philadelphia for consumption, and undoubtedly for resale by the first purchasers throughout Pennsylvania and other States, and refined sugar was also forwarded by the companies to other States for sale. Nevertheless it does not follow that an attempt to monopolize, or the actual monopoly of, the manufacture was an attempt, whether executory or consummated, to monopolize commerce, even though, in order to dispose of the product, the instrumentality of commerce was necessarily invoked. There was nothing in the proofs to indicate any intention to put a restraint upon trade or commerce, and the fact, as we have seen, that trade or commerce might be indirectly affected was not enough to entitle complainants to a decree. . . .

Decree affirmed.

Mr. Justice Harlan, dissenting. . . .

The court holds it to be vital in our system of government to recognize and give effect to both the commercial power of the nation and the police powers of the States, to the end that the Union be strengthened and the autonomy of the States preserved. In this view I entirely concur. Undoubtedly, the preservation of the just authority of the States is an object of deep concern to every lover of his country. . . .

Congress is invested with power to regulate commerce with foreign nations and among the several States. The power to regulate is the power to prescribe the rule by which the subject regulated is to be governed. It is one that must be exercised whenever necessary throughout the territorial limits of the several States. . . . The power to make these regulations "is complete in itself, may be exercised to its utmost extent, and acknowledges no limitations, other than are prescribed in the Constitution." It is plenary because vested in Congress "as absolutely as it would be in a single government having in its constitution the same restrictions on the exercise of the power as are found in the Constitution of the United States." It may be exercised "whenever the subject exists." *Gibbons* v. *Ogden*, 9 Wheat. 1, . . .

What is commerce among the States? The decisions of this court fully answer the question. "Commerce, undoubtedly, is traffic, but it is something more: it is intercourse. It does not embrace the completely interior traffic of the respective States—that which is "carried on between man and man in a State, or between different parts of the same State and which does not extend to or affect other States"—but it does embrace "every species of commercial intercourse" between the United States and foreign nations and among the States, and, therefore, it includes such traffic or trade, buying, selling, and interchange of commodities, as directly affects or necessarily involves the interests of the People of the United States. "Commerce, as the word is used in the Constitution, is a unit," and "cannot stop at the external boundary line of each State, but may be introduced into the interior." "The genius and character of the whole government seem to be, that its action is to be applied to all the external concerns of the nation, *and to those internal concerns which affect the States generally.*"

These principles were announced in *Gibbons* v. *Ogden*, and have often been approved. It is the settled doctrine of this court that interstate commerce embraces something more than the mere physical transportation of articles of property; and the vehicles or vessels by which such transportation is effected.

. . . In *Kidd* v. *Pearson*, . . . it was said that "the buying and selling, and the transportation *incidental thereto* constitute commerce." Interstate commerce does not, therefore, consist in transportation simply. It includes the purchase and sale of articles that are intended to be transported from one State to another—every species of commercial intercourse among the States and with foreign nations. . . .

It would seem to be indisputable that no *combination* of corporation or individuals can, *of right*, impose unlawful restraints upon *interstate* trade, whether upon transportation or upon such interstate intercourse and traffic as precede transportation, any more than it can, *of right*, impose unreasonable restraints upon the completely internal traffic of a State. The supposition cannot be indulged that this general proposition will be disputed. If it be true that a *combination* of corporations or individuals may, so far as the power of Congress is concerned, subject interstate trade, in any of its stages, to unlawful restraints, the conclusion is inevitable that the Constitution has failed to accomplish one primary object of the Union, which was to place commerce *among the States* under the control of the common government of all the people, and thereby relieve or protect it against burdens or restrictions imposed, by whatever authority, for the benefit of particular localities or special interests. . . .

In my judgment, the citizens of the several States composing the Union are entitled, of right, to buy goods in the State where they are manufactured, or in any other State, without being confronted by an illegal combination whose business extends throughout the whole country, which by the law everywhere is an enemy to the public interests, and which prevents such buying, except at prices arbitrarily fixed by it. I insist that the free course of trade among the States cannot coexist with such combinations. . . .

While the opinion of the court in this case does not declare the act of 1890 to be unconstitutional, it defeats the main object for which it was passed. For it is, in effect, held that the statute would be unconstitutional if interpreted as embracing such unlawful restraints upon the purchasing of goods in one State to be carried to another State as necessarily arise from the *existence* of combinations formed for the purpose and with the effect, not only of monopolizing the ownership of all such goods in every part of the country, but of controlling the prices for them in all the States. This view of the scope of the act leaves the public, so far as national power is concerned, entirely at the mercy of combinations which arbitrarily control the prices of articles purchased to be transported from one State to another State. I cannot assent to that view. . . .

We have before us the case of a combination which absolutely controls, or may, at its discretion, control the price of all refined sugar in this country. Suppose another *combination*, organized for private gain and to control prices, should obtain possession of all the large flour mills in the United States; another, of all the grain elevators; another, of all the oil territory; another, of all the salt-producing regions; another, of all the cotton mills; and another, of all the great establishments for slaughtering animals, and the preparation of meats. What power is competent to protect the people of the United States against such dangers except a national power—one that is capable of exerting its sovereign authority throughout every part of the territory and over all the people of the nation?

To the general government has been committed the control of commercial intercourse among the States, to the end that it may be free at all times from any restraints except such as Congress may impose or permit for the benefit of the whole country. The common government of all the people is the only one that can adequately deal with a matter which directly and injuriously affects the entire commerce of the country, which concerns equally all the people of the Union, and which, it must be confessed, cannot be adequately controlled by any one State. Its authority should not be so weakened by construction that it cannot reach and eradicate evils that, beyond all question, tend to defeat an object which that government is entitled, by the Constitution, to accomplish. . . .

The constitutional basis for the Sherman Act is, of course, the authority of Congress to regulate interstate commerce. Had the narrow interpretation of commerce in the *E. C. Knight* case prevailed, the Act would have been reduced to a toothless tiger. But in subsequent cases, the Supreme Court avoided the *Knight* doctrine by emphasizing the interstate effects of the intrastate activity under review.

For example, the district court had dismissed the government's petition in the case of *Addyston Pipe & Steel Company v. U.S.*, 175 U.S. 211 (1899) on the grounds that the pooling agreements were not directly related to interstate commerce. But the Supreme Court agreed with the circuit court's reversal of the district court, finding, among other things, that the agreements of the manufacturing firms affected contracts to sell and to deliver pipe in interstate commerce.

In 1904 the Court again broadened its interpretation of commerce in *Northern Securities Co. v. U.S.*, 193 U.S. 197. In that case the Supreme Court held that a combination, by means of a holding company, suppressed competition in violation of the Sherman Act. It rejected the argument that the federal government was interfering with intrastate commerce because the holding company was a state corporation acting within its powers granted by state charter.

The leading case establishing once and for all the broad, sweeping scope of the commerce clause is the *Wickard* case. A key issue involved was whether farm production not intended to be placed in commerce but wholly for consumption by the producer could be regulated under the commerce power. The Court held that such farm production did fall within the commerce clause.

WICKARD v. FILBURN

317 U.S. 111 (1942)

MR. JUSTICE JACKSON delivered the opinion of the Court.

The appellee filed his complaint against the Secretary of Agriculture of the United States, three members of the County Agricultural Conservation Committee for Montgomery County, Ohio, and a member of the

State Agricultural Conservation Committee for Ohio. He sought to enjoin enforcement against himself of the marketing penalty imposed by the amendment of May 26, 1941, to the Agricultural Adjustment Act of 1938, upon that part of his 1941 wheat crop which was available for marketing in excess of the marketing quota established for his farm. He also sought a declaratory judgment that the wheat marketing quota provisions of the Act as amended and applicable to him were unconstitutional because not sustainable under the Commerce Clause or consistent with the Due Process Clause of the Fifth Amendment. . . .

The appellee for many years past has owned and operated a small farm in Montgomery County, Ohio, maintaining a herd of dairy cattle, selling milk, raising poultry, and selling poultry and eggs. It has been his practice to raise a small acreage of winter wheat, sown in the Fall and harvested in the following July; to sell a portion of the crop; to feed part to poultry and livestock on the farm, some of which is sold; to use some in making flour for home consumption; and to keep the rest for the following seeding. The intended disposition of the crop here involved has not been expressly stated. . . .

It is urged that under the Commerce Clause of the Constitution, Article I, § 8, clause 3, Congress does not possess the power it has in this instance sought to exercise. The question would merit little consideration since our decision in *United States* v. *Darby*, 312 U.S. 100, sustaining the federal power to regulate production of goods for commerce, except for the fact that this Act extends federal regulation to production not intended in any part for commerce but wholly for consumption on the farm. The Act includes a definition of "market" and its derivatives, so that as related to wheat, in addition to its conventional meaning, it also means to dispose of "by feeding (in any form) to poultry or livestock which, or the products of which, are sold, bartered, or exchanged, or to be so disposed of." Hence, marketing quotas not only embrace all that may be sold without penalty but also what may be consumed on the premises. Wheat produced on excess acreage is designated as "available for marketing" as so defined, and the penalty is imposed thereon. Penalties do not depend upon whether any part of the wheat, either within or without the quota, is sold or intended to be sold. The sum of this is that the Federal Government fixes a quota including all that the farmer may harvest for sale or for his own farm needs, and declares that wheat produced on excess acreage may neither be disposed of nor used except upon payment of the penalty, or except it is stored as required by the Act or delivered to the Secretary of Agriculture.

Appellee says that this is a regulation of production and consumption of wheat. Such activities are, he urges, beyond the reach of Congressional power under the Commerce Clause, since they are local in character, and their effects upon interstate commerce are at most "indirect." In answer the Government argues that the statute regulates neither production nor consumption, but only marketing; and, in the alternative, that if the Act does go beyond the regulation of marketing it is sustainable as a "necessary and proper" implementation of the power of Congress over interstate commerce.

The Government's concern lest the Act be held to be a regulation of production or consumption, rather than of marketing, is attributable to a few dicta and decisions of this Court which might be understood to lay it down that activities such as "production," "manufacturing," and "mining" are strictly "local" and, except in special circumstances which are not present here, cannot be regulated under the commerce power because their effects upon interstate commerce are, as matter of law, only "indirect." Even today, when this power has been held to have great latitude, there is no decision of this Court that such activities may be regulated where no part of the product is intended for interstate commerce or intermingled with the subjects thereof. We believe that a review of the course of decision under the Commerce Clause will make plain, however, that questions of the power of Congress are not to be decided by reference to any formula which would give controlling force to nomenclature such as "production" and "indirect" and foreclose consideration of the actual effects of the activity in question upon interstate commerce. . . .

Whether the subject of the regulation in question was "production," "consumption," or "marketing" is, therefore, not material for purposes of deciding the question of federal power before us. That an activity is of local character may help in a doubtful case to determine whether Congress intended to reach it. The same consideration might help in determining whether in the absence of Congressional action it would be permissible for the state to exert its power on the subject matter, even though in so doing it to some degree affected interstate commerce. But even if appellee's activity be local and though it may not be regarded as commerce, it may still, whatever its nature, be reached by Congress if it exerts a substantial economic effect on interstate commerce, and this irrespective of whether such effect is what might at some earlier time have been defined as "direct" or "indirect." . . .

The effect of consumption of home-grown wheat on interstate commerce is due to the fact that it constitutes the most variable factor in the disappearance of the wheat crop. Consumption on the farm where grown appears to vary in an amount greater than 20 per cent of average production. The total amount of wheat consumed as food varies but relatively little, and use as seed is relatively constant.

The maintenance by government regulation of a price for wheat undoubtedly can be accomplished as effectively by sustaining or increasing the demand as by limiting the supply. The effect of the statute before us is to restrict the amount which may be produced for market and the extent as well to which one may forestall resort to the market by producing to meet his own needs. That appellee's own contribution to the demand for wheat may be trivial by itself is not enough to remove him from the scope of federal regulation where, as here, his contribution, taken together with that of many others similarly situated, is far from trivial. . . .

It is well established by decisions of this Court that the power to regulate commerce includes the power to regulate the prices at which commodities in that commerce are dealt in and practices affecting such prices. One of the primary purposes of the Act in question was to increase the market price of wheat, and to that end to limit the volume thereof that could affect the market. It can hardly be denied that a factor of such volume and variability as home-consumed wheat would have a substantial influence on price and market conditions. This may arise because being in marketable condition such wheat overhangs the market and, if induced by rising prices, tends to flow into the market and check price increases. But if we assume that it is never marketed, it supplies a need of the man who grew it which would otherwise be reflected by purchases in the open market. Home-grown wheat in this sense competes with wheat in commerce. The stimulation of commerce is a use of the regulatory function quite as definitely as prohibitions or restrictions thereon. This record leaves us in no doubt that Congress may properly have considered that wheat consumed on the farm where grown, if wholly outside the scheme of regulation, would have a substantial effect in defeating and obstructing its purpose to stimulate trade therein at increased prices.

It is said, however, that this Act, forcing some farmers into the market to buy what they could provide for themselves, is an unfair promotion of the markets and prices of specializing wheat growers. It is of the essence of regulation that it lays a restraining hand on the self-interest of the regulated and that advantages from the regulation commonly fall to others. The conflicts of economic interest between the regulated and those who advantage by it are wisely left under our system to resolution by the Congress under its more flexible and responsible legislative process. Such conflicts rarely lend themselves to judicial determination. And with the wisdom, workability, or fairness, of the plan of regulation we have nothing to do. . . .

Reversed.

The expansive reach of the commerce clause was further illustrated by the cases of *United States* v. *American Medical Association*, 317 U.S. 519 and *United States* v. *National Association of Real Estate Boards*, 399 U.S. 485. One of the principal defenses in these cases was that the practices of medicine and real estate brokerage were local in nature and thus outside the reach of the antitrust law. The Supreme Court rejected this contention, finding that both these activities were within the meaning of "restraint of trade or commerce."

The Meaning of Restraint of Trade and Monopoly

The cases in this part are devoted to early interpretations of the meaning of restraint of trade and monopoly. The *Northern Securities* case, dealing with the question of what kinds of "combinations" might be held in restraint of trade, is presented first. Following this decision, in chronological order, is the *Standard Oil* case setting forth the "Rule of Reason" and three cases—*United Shoe Machinery Company, United States Steel Corporation,* and *International Harvester Company*—showing how the Sherman Act came to be applied favorably to large firms in substantial control of an industry.

Before the *Northern Securities* decision in 1904, there was little reason to believe that the holding company device, facilitated by a change in the New Jersey general incorporation law, would be considered an illegal combination in restraint of trade. Famous financier J. P. Morgan and his associates had organized the Northern Securities Company in 1901 for the specific purpose of controlling two competing railroads, the Northern Pacific and the Great Northern, by means of stock ownership. The primary argument set forth for allowing the company to exercise its power was that it was a state-chartered corporation, sanctioned by the state of New Jersey, and federal action against it would constitute an interference with the internal commerce of the state of New Jersey. The Supreme Court in a 5–4 decision upheld the government and ordered that the Northern Securities Company be dissolved.[3] This decision not only broadened the interpretation of commerce but also showed clearly that the holding company device was no longer a fool-proof way of achieving concentration in restraint of trade. Furthermore, when significant issues involving interstate commerce were at stake, the laws of a single state, such as New Jersey, would not be permitted to displace the power of the federal government.

[3] An about-face in railroad combination was accomplished in February, 1970, when the Supreme Court granted approval for the Northern Pacific and Great Northern lines to merge with the Chicago, Burlington & Quincy Railroad Company and other small lines. *U.S.* v. *Interstate Commerce Commission,* 396 U.S. 491.

NORTHERN SECURITIES CO. v. UNITED STATES

193 U.S. 197 (1904)

Mr. Justice Harlan announced the affirmance of the decree of the Circuit Court, and delivered the following opinion:

This suit was brought by the United States against the Northern Securities Company, a corporation of New Jersey; the Great Northern Railway Company, a corporation of Minnesota; the Northern Pacific Railway Company, a corporation of Wisconsin; James J. Hill, a citizen of Minnesota; and William P. Clough, D. Willis James, John S. Kennedy, J. Pierpont Morgan, Robert Bacon, George F. Baker and Daniel S. Lamont, citizens of New York.

Its general object was to enforce, as against the defendants, the provisions of the statute of July 2, 1890, commonly known as the Anti-Trust Act, and entitled "An act to protect trade and commerce against unlawful restraints and monopolies." . . . By the decree below the United States was given substantially the relief asked by it in the bill. . . .

Is the case as presented by the pleadings and the evidence one of a combination or a conspiracy in restraint of trade or commerce among the States, or with foreign states? Is it one in which the defendants are properly chargeable with monopolizing or attempting to monopolize any part of such trade or commerce? Let us see what are the facts disclosed by the record.

The Great Northern Railway Company and the Northern Pacific Railway Company owned, controlled and operated separate lines of railway—the former road extending from Superior, and from Duluth and St. Paul, to Everett, Seattle, and Portland, with a branch line to Helena; the latter, extending from Ashland, and from Duluth and St. Paul, to Helena, Spokane, Seattle, Tacoma and Portland. The two lines, main and branches, about 9,000 miles in length, were and are parallel and competing lines across the continent through the northern tier of States between the Great Lakes and the Pacific, and the two companies were engaged in active competition for freight and passenger traffic, each road connecting at its respective terminals with lines of railway, or with lake and river steamers, or with seagoing vessels. . . .

Prior to November 13, 1901, defendant Hill and associate stockholders of the Great Northern Railway Company, and defendant Morgan and associate stockholders of the Northern Pacific Railway Company, entered into a combination to form, under the laws of New Jersey, a *holding* corporation, to be called the Northern Securities Company, with a capital stock of $400,000,000, and to which company, in exchange for its own capital stock upon a certain basis and at a certain rate, was to be turned over the capital stock, or a controlling interest in the capital stock, of each of the constituent railway companies, with power in the holding corporation to vote such stock and in all respects to act as the owner thereof, and to do whatever it might deem necessary in aid of such railway companies or to enhance the value of their stocks. In this manner the interests of individual stockholders in the property and franchises of the two independent and competing railway companies were to be converted into an interest in the property and franchises of the holding corporation. . . .

. . . In our opinion, the recognition of the principles announced in former cases must, under the conceded facts, lead to an affirmance of the decree below, unless the special objections, or some of them, which have been made to the application of the act of Congress to the present case are of a substantial character. We will now consider those objections.

Underlying the argument in behalf of the defendants is the idea that as the Northern Securities Company is a state corporation, and as its acquisition of the stock of the Great Northern and Northern Pacific Railway companies is not inconsistent with the powers conferred by its charter, the enforcement of the act of Congress, as against those corporations, will be an unauthorized interference by the national government with the internal commerce of the States creating those corporations. This suggestion does not at all impress us. There is no reason to suppose that Congress had any purpose to interfere with the internal affairs of the States, nor, in our opinion, is there any ground whatever for the contention that the Anti-Trust Act regulates their domestic commerce. By its very terms the act regulates only commerce among the States and with foreign states. Viewed in that light, the act, if within the powers of Congress, must be respected; . . .

. . . What the Government particularly complains of, indeed, all that it complains of here, is the existence of a combination among the stockholders of competing railroad companies which in violation of the act of Congress restrains interstate and international commerce through the agency of a common corporate trustee designated to act for both companies in repressing free competition between them. Independently of any question of the mere ownership of stock or of the organization of a state corporation, can it in reason be said that such a combination is not embraced by the very terms of the Anti-Trust Act? May not Congress declare that *combination* to be illegal? If Congress legislates for the protection of the public, may it not proceed on the ground that wrongs when effected by a powerful combination are more dangerous and require more stringent supervision than when they are to be effected by a single person? . . .

. . . Indeed, if the contentions of the defendants are sound why may not *all* the railway companies in the United States, that are engaged, under state charters, in interstate and international commerce, enter into a combination such as the one here in question, and by the device of a holding corporation obtain the absolute control throughout the entire country of rates for passengers and freight, beyond the power of Congress to protect the public against their exactions? The argument in behalf of the defendants necessarily leads to such results, and places Congress, although invested by the people of the United States with full authority to regulate interstate and international commerce, in a condition of utter helplessness, so far as the protection of the public against such combinations is concerned. . . .

. . . [We] are confronted with the suggestion that any order or decree of the Federal court which will prevent the Northern Securities Company from exercising the power it acquired in becoming the holder of the stocks of the Great Northern and Northern Pacific Railway companies will be an invasion of the rights of the State under which the Securities Company was chartered, as well as of the rights of the States creating the other companies. In other words, if the State of New Jersey gives a charter to a corporation, and even if the obtaining of such charter is in fact pursuant to a *combination* under which it becomes the holder of the stocks of shareholders in two competing, parallel railroad companies engaged in interstate commerce in other States, whereby competition between the respective roads of those companies is to be destroyed and the enormous commerce carried on over them restrained by suppressing competition, Congress must stay its hands and allow such restraint to continue to the detriment of the public because, forsooth, the corporations concerned or some of them are state corporations. We cannot conceive how it is possible for any one to seriously contend for such a proposition. It means nothing less than that Congress, in regulating interstate commerce, must act in subordination to the will of the States when exerting their power to create corporations. No such view can be entertained for a moment. . . .

. . . In short, the court may make any order necessary to bring about the dissolution or suppression of an illegal combination that restrains interstate commerce. All this can be done without infringing in any degree upon the just authority of the States. The affirmance of the judgment below will only mean that no combination, however powerful, is stronger than the law or will be permitted to avail itself of the pretext that to prevent it doing that which, if done, would defeat a legal enactment of Congress, is to attack the reserved rights of the States. . . .

The judgment of the court is that the decree below be and hereby is affirmed, with liberty to the Circuit Court to proceed in the execution of its decree as the circumstances may require.

Affirmed.

One of the most famous of all antitrust decisions was handed down by the Supreme Court in its *Standard Oil of New Jersey* decision in 1911. Standard Oil was a holding company organized under New Jersey incorporation laws by John D. Rockefeller. By 1899 the firm had effective control over 90 per cent of the business of producing, shipping, refining, and selling petroleum and its products. Because of its overwhelming position in the market, Standard Oil was able to fix the price of crude and refined petroleum and restrain all interstate commerce in these products. The facts brought out in the case showed that it had secured and maintained its monopoly position by resorting to a number of illegal practices. Included among them were preferential rates and rebates extracted from railroads, localized discriminatory pricing intended to drive small firms out of business or force them to become members of the combination, and an enormous number of other predatory practices requiring fifty-seven pages of the trial record just to list them. The Supreme Court concluded that the firm had obtained a monopoly position and there was intent to monopolize. Standard Oil had been engaged in the very activities the Sherman Act was intended to prevent. The decision was to dissolve the holding company and transfer stockholdings back to the original thirty-three companies brought together by the holding company.

Even more important than the fact that Standard Oil was guilty of violating the Sherman Act was the logic and wording used in the majority opinion of Chief Justice White. In an incidental excursion into the development of the law, he noted that while the Sherman Act says *every* contract, combination, etc., in restraint of trade is illegal, the Act was merely intended to capture the original intent of the common law. And the common law had always been interpreted to mean only *unreasonable* or *undue* restraints of trade were illegal. As a result, a "Rule of Reason" must be applied in determining restraint-of-trade cases.

The burden of proof now became much greater for the Justice Department because: (1) the alleged violation must be proved as a restraint of trade, and (2) it must be proved as an unreasonable or undue restraint. The Rule of Reason dictum served to emasculate the Act once again. But, contrary to the *E. C. Knight* decision, this precedent remained the guiding principle until the 1945 *Alcoa* case.[4] As we shall see in the text of the *Alcoa* decision, the emphasis was shifted from abusive use of monopoly power to an examination of how the

[4] See Chapter 2, *U.S. v. Aluminum Co. of America*, 148 F. (2d) 416.

monopoly position was attained. Two of the three cases in this part following the *Standard Oil* case serve to point out how the Rule of Reason came to be applied favorably to firms when challenged because of their dominant position.[5]

Justice Harlan offered an opinion concurring in part and dissenting in part in which he aptly pointed out that the finding of guilty could have been made without any qualification. He observed that the Court has now engaged in "judicial legislation" and amended an act of Congress by inserting the words "unreasonable" or "undue." His criticism proved accurate.

STANDARD OIL COMPANY OF NEW JERSEY v. UNITED STATES

221 U.S. 1 (1911)

MR. CHIEF JUSTICE WHITE delivered the opinion of the court.

The Standard Oil Company of New Jersey and 33 other corporations, John D. Rockefeller, William Rockefeller and five other individual defendants prosecute this appeal to reverse a decree of the court below. . . .

. . . Corporations known as Standard Oil Company of New Jersey, Standard Oil Company of California, Standard Oil Company of Indiana, Standard Oil Company of Iowa, Standard Oil Company of Kansas, Standard Oil Company of Kentucky, Standard Oil Company of Nebraska, Standard Oil Company of New York, Standard Oil Company of Ohio and sixty-two other corporations and partnerships, as also seven individuals were named as defendants. The bill was divided into thirty numbered sections, and sought relief upon the theory that the various defendants were engaged in conspiring "to restrain the trade and commerce in petroleum, commonly called 'crude oil,' in refined oil, and in the other products of petroleum, among the several States and Territories of the United States

---

[5] "Trust busting" enjoyed a banner year in 1911. The American Tobacco Company was another "bad trust" and was ordered broken up. The decision in *American Tobacco* also referred to a Rule of Reason that must be applied in deciding restraint-of-trade cases; Justice Harlan again contributed another ringing dissent (*American Tobacco Co.* v. *U.S.*, 221 U.S. 106). As the years went by, a number of FTC studies repeatedly showed that the four successor companies to the American Tobacco combination followed pricing and buying policies just like those of the old "monopoly." Eventually the firms would make another appearance before the Court on charges of violating the Sherman Act. There may be some virtues in having an oligopoly as opposed to a monopoly, but vigorous price competition is certainly not one of them. For additional interesting comments on the social significance of this case, see Ross M. Robertson, *History of the American Economy*, 2d ed. (New York: Harcourt, Brace & World, Inc., 1964), pp. 423–24.

and the District of Columbia and with foreign nations, and to monopolize the said commerce." The conspiracy was alleged to have been formed in or about the year 1870 by three of the individual defendants, viz: John D. Rockefeller, William Rockefeller and Henry M. Flagler. The detailed averments concerning the alleged conspiracy were arranged with reference to three periods, the first from 1870 to 1882, the second from 1882 to 1899, and the third from 1899 to the time of the filing of the bill. . . .

Duly appreciating the situation just stated, it is certain that only one point of concord between the parties is discernible, which is, that the controversy in every aspect is controlled by a correct conception of the meaning of the first and second sections of the Anti-trust Act. . . .

FIRST. THE TEXT OF THE ACT AND ITS MEANING . . . The debates show that doubt as to whether there was a common law of the United States which governed the subject in the absence of legislation was among the influences leading to the passage of the act. They conclusively show, however, that the main cause which led to the legislation was the thought that it was required by the economic condition of the times, that is, the vast accumulation of wealth in the hands of corporations and individuals, the enormous development of corporate organization, the facility for combination which such organizations afforded, the fact that the facility was being used, and that combinations known as trusts were being multiplied, and the widespread impression that their power had been and would be exerted to oppress individuals and injure the public generally. . . .

There can be no doubt that the sole subject with which the first section deals is restraint of trade as therein contemplated, and that the attempt to monopolize and monopolization is the subject with which the second section is concerned. It is certain that those terms, at least in their rudimentary meaning, took their origin in the common law, and were also familiar in the law of this country prior to and at the time of the adoption of the act in question.

We shall endeavor then, first to seek their meaning, not by indulging in an elaborate and learned analysis of the English law and of the law of this country, but by making a very brief reference to the elementary and indisputable conceptions of both the English and American law on the subject prior to the passage of the Anti-trust Act. . . .

Without going into detail and but very briefly surveying the whole field, it may be with accuracy said that the dread of enhancement of prices and of other wrongs which it was thought would flow from the undue limitation on competitive conditions caused by contracts or other acts of individuals or corporations, led, as a matter of public policy, to the prohibition or treating as illegal all contracts or acts which were unreasonably restrictive of competitive conditions, either from the nature or character of the contract or act or where the surrounding circumstances were such as to justify the conclusion that they had not been entered into or performed with the legitimate purpose of reasonably forwarding personal interest and developing trade, but on the contrary were of such a character as to give rise to the inference or presumption that they had been entered into or done with the intent to do wrong to the general public and to limit the right of individuals, thus restraining the free flow of commerce and tending to bring about the evils, such as enhancement of prices, which were considered to be against public policy. . . .

Undoubtedly, the words "to monopolize" and "monopolize" as used in the section reach every act bringing about the prohibited results. The ambiguity, if any, is involved in determining what is intended by monopolize. But this ambiguity is readily dispelled in the light of the previous history of the law of restraint of trade to which we have referred and the indication which it gives of the practical evolution by which monopoly and the acts which produce the same result as monopoly, that is, an undue restraint of the course of trade, all came to be spoken of as, and to be indeed synonymous with, restraint of trade. In other words, having by the first section forbidden all means of monopolizing trade, that is, unduly restraining it by means of every contract, combination, etc., the second section seeks, if possible, to make the prohibitions of the act all the more complete and perfect by embracing all attempts to reach the end prohibited by the first section, that is, restraints of trade, by any attempt to monopolize, or monopolization thereof, even although the acts by which such results are attempted to be brought about or are brought about be not embraced within the general enumeration of the first section. And, of course, when the second section is thus harmonized with and made as it was intended to be the complement of the first, it becomes obvious that the criteria to be resorted to in any given case for the purpose of ascertaining whether violations of the section have been committed, is the rule of reason guided by the established law and by the plain duty to enforce the prohibitions of the act and thus the public policy which its restrictions were obviously enacted to subserve. And it is worthy of observation, as we have previously remarked concerning the common law, that although the statute by the comprehensiveness of the enumerations embodied in both the first and second sections makes it certain that its purpose was to prevent undue restraints of every kind or nature, nevertheless by the omission of any direct prohibition against monopoly in the concrete it indicates a consciousness that the freedom of the individual right to contract when not unduly or improperly exercised was the most efficient means for the prevention of monopoly, since the operation of the centrifugal and centripetal forces resulting from the right to freely contract was the means by which monopoly would be inevitably prevented if no extraneous or sovereign power imposed it and no right to make unlawful contracts having a monopolistic tendency were permitted. In other words that freedom to contract was the essence of freedom from undue restraint on the right to contract. . . .

SECOND. THE CONTENTIONS OF THE PARTIES AS TO THE MEANING OF THE STATUTE AND THE DECISIONS OF THIS COURT RELIED UPON CONCERNING THOSE CONTENTIONS   In substance, the propositions urged by the Government are reducible to this: That the language of the statute embraces every contract, combination, etc., in restraint of trade, and hence its text leaves no room for the exercise of judgment, but simply imposes the plain duty of applying its prohibitions to every case within its literal language. The error involved lies in assuming the matter to be decided. This is true because as the acts which may come under the classes stated in the first section and the restraint of trade to which that section applies are not specifically enumerated or defined, it is obvious that judgment must in every case be called into play in order to determine whether a particular act is embraced within the statutory classes, and whether if the act is within such classes its nature or effect causes it to be a restraint of trade within the intendment of the act. To hold to the contrary would require the conclusion either that every contract, act or combination of any kind or nature, whether it operated a restraint on trade or not, was within the statute, and thus the statute would be destructive of all right to contract or agree or combine in any respect whatever as to subjects embraced in interstate trade or commerce, or if this conclusion were not reached, then the contention would require it to be held that as the statute did not define the things to which it related and excluded resort to the only means by which the acts to which it relates could be ascertained—the light of reason—the enforcement of the statute was impossible because of its uncertainty. The merely generic enumeration which the statute makes of the acts to which it refers and the absence of any definition of restraint of trade as used in the statute leaves room for but one conclusion, which is, that it was expressly designed not to unduly limit the application of the act by precise definition, but while clearly fixing a standard, that is, by defining the ulterior boundaries which could not be transgressed with impunity, to leave it to be determined by the light of reason, guided by the principles of law and the duty to apply and enforce the public policy embodied in the statute, in every given case whether any particular act or contract was within the contemplation of the statute. . . .

THIRD. THE FACTS AND THE APPLICATION OF THE STATUTE TO THEM   Beyond dispute the proofs establish substantially as alleged in the bill the following facts:

1. The creation of the Standard Oil Company of Ohio;

2. The organization of the Standard Oil Trust of 1882, and also a previous one of 1879, not referred to in the bill, and the proceedings in the Supreme Court of Ohio, culminating in a decree based upon the finding that the company was unlawfully a party to that trust; the transfer by the trustees of stocks in certain of the companies; the contempt proceedings; and, finally, the increase of the capital of the Standard Oil Company of New Jersey and the acquisition by that company of the shares of the stock of the other corporations in exchange for its certificates.

The vast amount of property and the possibilities of far-reaching control which resulted from the facts last stated are shown by the statement which we have previously annexed concerning the parties to the trust agreement of 1882, and the corporations whose stock was held by the trustees under the trust and which came therefore to be held by the New Jersey corporation. . . .

We see no cause to doubt the correctness of these conclusions, . . .

a. Because the unification of power and control over petroleum and its products which was the inevitable result of the combining in the New Jersey corporation by the increase of its stock and the transfer to it of the stocks of so many other corporations, aggregating so vast a capital, gives rise, in and of itself, in the absence of countervailing circumstances, to say the least, to the *prima facie* presumption of intent and purpose to maintain the dominancy over the oil industry, not as a result of normal methods of industrial development, but by new means of combination which were resorted to in order that greater power might be added than would otherwise have arisen had normal methods been followed, the whole with the purpose of excluding others from the trade and thus centralizing in the combination a perpetual control of the movements of petroleum and its products in the channels of interstate commerce.

b. Because the *prima facie* presumption of intent to restrain trade, to monopolize and to bring about monopolization resulting from the act of expanding the stock of the New Jersey corporation and vesting it with such vast control of the oil industry, is made conclusive by considering, 1, the conduct of the persons or corporations who were mainly instrumental in bringing about the extension of power in the New Jersey corporation before the consummation of that result and prior to the formation of the trust agreements of 1879 and 1882; 2, by considering the proof as to what was done under those agreements and the acts which immediately preceded the vesting of power in the New Jersey corporation as well as by weighing the modes in which the power vested in that corporation has been exerted and the results which have arisen from it.

Referring to the acts done by the individuals or corporations who were mainly instrumental in bringing about the expansion of the New Jersey corporation during the period prior to the formation of the trust agreements of 1879 and 1882, including those agreements, not for the purpose of weighing the substantial merit of the numerous charges of wrongdoing made during such period, but solely as an aid for discovering intent and purpose, we think no disinterested mind can survey the period in question without being irresistibly driven to the conclusion that the very genius for commercial development and organization which it would seem was manifested from the beginning soon begot an intent and purpose to exclude others which was frequently manifested by acts and dealings wholly inconsistent with the theory that they were made with the single conception of advancing the development of business power by usual methods, but which on the contrary necessarily involved the intent to drive others from the field and to exclude them from their right to trade and thus accomplish the mastery which was the end in view. And, considering the period from the date of the trust agreements of 1879 and 1882, up to the time of the expansion of the New Jersey corporation, the gradual extension of the power over the commerce in oil which ensued, the decision of the Supreme Court of Ohio, the tardiness or reluctance in conforming to the commands of that decision, the method first adopted and that which finally culminated in the plan of the New Jersey corporation, all additionally serve to make manifest the continued existence of the intent which we have previously indicated and which among other things impelled the expansion of the New Jersey corporation. The exercise of the power which resulted from that organization fortifies the foregoing conclusions, since the development which came, the acquisition here and there which ensued of every efficient means by which competition could have been asserted, the slow but resistless methods which followed by which means of transportation were absorbed and brought under control, the system of marketing which was adopted by which the country was divided into districts and the trade in each district in oil was turned over to a designated corporation within the combination and all others were excluded, all lead the mind up to a conviction of a purpose and intent which we think is so certain as practically to cause the subject not to be within the domain of reasonable contention. . . .

FOURTH. THE REMEDY TO BE ADMINISTERED   It may be conceded that ordinarily where it was found that acts had been done in violation of the statute, adequate measure of relief would result from restraining the doing of such acts in the future. . . . But in a case like this, where the condition which has been brought about in violation of the statute, in and of itself, is not only a continued attempt to monopolize, but also a monopolization, the duty to enforce the statute requires the application of broader and more controlling remedies. As penalties which are not authorized by law may not be inflicted by judicial authority, it follows that to meet the situation with which we are confronted the application of remedies twofold in character becomes essential: 1st. To forbid the doing in the future of acts like those which we have found to have been done in the past which would be violative of the statute. 2d. The exertion of such measure of relief as will effectually dissolve the combination found to exist in violation of the statute, and thus neutralize the extension and continually operating force which the possession of the power unlawfully obtained has brought and will continue to bring about. . . .

So far as the decree held that the ownership of the stock of the New Jersey corporation constituted a combination in violation of the first section and an attempt to create a monopoly or to monopolize under the second section and commanded the dissolution of the combination, the decree was clearly appropriate. And this also is true of §5 of the decree which restrained both the New Jersey corporation and the subsidiary corporations from doing anything which would recognize or give effect to further ownership in the New Jersey corporation of the stocks which were ordered to be retransferred. . . .

. . . Our conclusion is that the decree below was right and should be affirmed, except as to the minor matters concerning which we have indicated the decree should be modified. Our order will therefore be one of affirmance with directions, however, to modify the decree in accordance with this opinion. The court below to retain jurisdiction to the extent necessary to compel compliance in every respect with its decree.

And it is so ordered.

MR. JUSTICE HARLAN concurring in part, and dissenting in part.

A sense of duty constrains me to express the objections which I have to certain declarations in the opinion just delivered on behalf of the court.

I concur in holding that the Standard Oil Company of New Jersey and its subsidiary companies constitute a combination in restraint of interstate commerce, and that they have attempted to monopolize and have monopolized parts of such commerce—all in violation of what is known as the Anti-trust Act of 1890. . . . The evidence in this case overwhelmingly sustained that view and led the Circuit Court, by its final decree, to order the dissolution of the New Jersey corporation and the discontinuance of the illegal combination between that corporation and its subsidiary companies.

In my judgment, the decree below should have been affirmed without qualification. But the court, while affirming the decree, directs some modifications in respect of what it characterizes as "minor matters." It is to be apprehended that those modifications may prove to be mischievous. In saying this, I have particularly in view the statement in the opinion that "it does not necessarily follow that because an illegal restraint of trade or an attempt to monopolize or a monopolization resulted from the combination and the transfer of the stocks of the subsidiary corporations to the New Jersey corporation, that a like restraint of trade or attempt to monopolize or monopolization would necessarily arise from agreements between one or more of the subsidiary corporations after the transfer of the stock by the New Jersey corporation." Taking this language, in connection with other parts of the opinion, the subsidiary companies are thus, in effect, informed—unwisely, I think—that although the New Jersey corporation, being an illegal combination, must go out of existence, *they* may join in an agreement *to restrain commerce* among the States if such restraint be not "undue." . . .

But my brethren, in their wisdom, have deemed it best to pursue a different course. They have now said to those who condemn our former decisions and who object to all legislative prohibitions of contracts, combinations and trusts in restraint of interstate commerce, "You may *now* restrain such commerce, provided you are reasonable about it; only take care that the restraint is not undue." . . .

When Congress prohibited *every* contract, combination or monopoly, in restraint of commerce, it prescribed a simple, definite rule that all could understand, and which could be easily applied by everyone wishing to obey the law, and not to conduct their business in violation of law. But now, it is to be feared, we are to have, in cases without number, the constantly recurring inquiry—difficult to solve by proof—whether the particular contract, combination, or trust involved in each case is or is not an "unreasonable" or "undue" restraint of trade. Congress, in effect, said that there should be *no* restraint of trade, *in any form*, and this court solemnly adjudged many years ago that Congress meant what it thus said in clear and explicit words, and that it *could not* add to the words of the act. . . .

It remains for me to refer, more fully than I have heretofore done, to another, and, in my judgment—if we look to the future—the most important aspect of this case. That aspect concerns the usurpation by the judicial branch of the Government of the functions of the legislative department. The illustrious men who laid the foundations of our institutions, deemed no part of the National Constitution of more consequence or more essential to the permanency of our form of government than the provisions under which were distributed the powers of Government among three separate, equal and coördinate departments—legislative, executive, and judicial. . . .

I said at the outset that the action of the court in this case might well alarm thoughtful men who revered the Constitution. I meant by this that many things are intimated and said in the court's opinion which will not be regarded otherwise than as sanctioning an invasion by the judiciary of the constitutional domain of Congress—an attempt by interpretation to soften or modify what some regard as a harsh public policy. This court, let me repeat, solemnly adjudged many years ago that it could not, except by *"judicial legislation,"* read words into the Anti-trust Act not put there by Congress, and which, being inserted, give it a meaning which the words of the Act, as passed, if properly interpreted, would not justify. . . .

Nevertheless, if I do not misapprehend its opinion, the court has now read into the act of Congress words which are not to be found there, and has thereby done that which it adjudged in 1896 and 1898 could not be done without violating the Constitution, namely, by interpretation of a statute, changed a public policy declared by the legislative department. . . .

The Rule of Reason was not a point of contention in the 1918 *United Shoe Machinery* case. The main question before the Court was whether or not a monopoly position, achieved via a combination of "noncompeting" firms and utilizing patents with tying contracts, should be judged as an unlawful restraint of trade. United Shoe had been organized in 1899 by a combination of seven shoe machinery companies and in later years, according to the Supreme Court's own admission, had attained a monopoly over the shoe machinery industry.

The government was basing its case on the arguments that the original formation of the firm had eliminated competitors, thereby restraining trade, and that the use of restrictive agreements under which patented shoe machinery was leased were violations of the Sherman Act. Justice McKenna's majority opinion states that in determining whether a combination restrains interstate commerce injuriously to the public, the first inquiry must be whether the firms joined by the combination were in fact competitors. On this score the Court agreed with the trial court's finding that the constituent companies had been performing complementary activities in shoemaking and consequently had never been competitors. Second, patent law permits the patentholder to lease machinery only rather than sell it if he so desires. The use of tying agreements to purchase certain of the lessor's supplies and services could not be considered as restraining competition illegally since the leases were entered into by the lessees voluntarily and no coercion was involved.

In this 4–3 decision, the dissenters argued that the "restrictive and prohibitive clauses" of the lease agreements were clearly in restraint of interstate trade, exploitation of these agreements did give United Shoe a dominant position, and the firm did have intent to monopolize the market. The "tying clauses" of the agreements were struck down in a 1922 decision in a case brought under Section 3 of the Clayton Act.[6]

[6] See Chapter 10, *United Shoe Machinery Corp.* v. U.S., 285 U.S. 451.

UNITED STATES v. UNITED SHOE MACHINERY COMPANY OF NEW JERSEY et al.

247 U.S. 32 (1918)

MR. JUSTICE MCKENNA, after stating the case as above, delivered the opinion of the court.

The charge of the bill is that defendants, not being satisfied with the monopoly of their patents and determined to extend it, conceived the idea of acquiring the ownership or control of all concerns engaged in the manufacture of all kinds of shoe machinery. This purpose was achieved, it is charged, and a monopoly acquired, and commerce, interstate and foreign, restrained by the union of competing companies and the acquisition of others. And that leases were exacted which completed and assured the control and monopoly thus acquired.

But this charge of comprehensive trade dominance was modified in the course of the trial. The Government disclaimed the assertion of such extensive culpability and confined its contention to machinery adapted to the bottoming of shoes (attaching soles to uppers), machines called clicking machines (cutting-out machines), and eye-letting machines (sufficiently indicated by name), and declared that if the bill did not so limit the actual monopoly counsel would agree so to limit it. . . .

There are two accusations against the defendants. One is that at the very outset they combined competing companies and subsequently acquired others, §1 of the Act of 1890 being thereby offended. The other is a monopolization of the trade in violation of §2 of that act. And it is charged, as we have said, that certain leases and license agreements are the instruments which consummate both offenses.

The offense of combination was committed, it is contended, February 7, 1899, at which time seven shoe machinery companies were consolidated into the United Shoe Machinery Company of New Jersey, a corporation organized for that purpose. The companies were: Goodyear Shoe Machinery Company, International Goodyear Shoe Machinery Company, Consolidated & McKay Lasting Machine Company, McKay Shoe Machine Company, Davey Pegging Machine Company, Eppler Welt Machine Company and the International Eppler Welt Machine Company. The last two companies were acquired by the new company after its formation, but they may be regarded as constituent companies. The businesses of these companies were conveyed to the new company, the businesses being those of manufacturing, selling and leasing and dealing in shoe machinery, including patents of the United States and other countries. A more particular distinction we do not deem it necessary to to make.

The first question is, Were the companies in competition? It confronts us at the outset; all other considerations are dependent upon it. . . .

We are therefore admonished at once of the complexity of the case and the maze of mechanical technicalities into which we should be plunged in estimating the evidence if we had not the guidance of the opinions of the judges of the trial court. The court found, as we have said, that the companies were not in competition at the time of their union in the United Company, and based the finding not only upon the testimony of witnesses but the uses of the machines of the respective companies and their methods of operation. The testimony was conflicting, it is true, and different judgments might be formed upon it, but from an examination of the record we cannot pronounce that of the trial court to be wrong. Indeed, it seems to us to be supported by the better reason. We should risk misunderstanding and error if we should attempt to pick out that which makes against it and disregard that which makes for it and judge of witnesses from their reported words as against their living presence, the advantage which the trial court had. . . .

The company, indeed, has magnitude, but it is at once the result and cause of efficiency, and the charge that it has been oppressively used is not sustained. Patrons are given the benefits of the improvements made by the company and new machines are substituted for the old ones without disproportionate charge. There has been saving as well in the cost of manufacture of shoes. These are some of the results of the organization of the United Company. Others are testified to and the means of their accomplishment; but time will not permit their statement, and we pass to the leases.

There was complaint of them and the Government attacks them. Complaints, however, may be interested lament; but, on the other hand, they may be the expression of real grievance and demand redress. And which they are should be considered. To the attacks of the Government the defendants reply that the leases are the exercise of their right as patentees and if there is monopoly in them it is the monopoly of the right. . . .

Of course, there is restraint in a patent. Its strength is in the restraint, the right to exclude others from the use of the invention, absolutely or on the terms the patentee chooses to impose. This strength is the compensation which the law grants for the exercise of invention. Its exertion within the field covered by the patent law is not an offense against the Anti-Trust Act. . . .

The question, then, is, Was the patent right lawfully exerted in the leases? Were they anything more than the exercise of the patent monopoly? The word is descriptive and must be used, but it does not imply oppression. . . .

The charge of oppression puts out of view many essential things. We must keep in mind the quality of the right we are considering and that the inventor gets nothing from the law that he did not have before and that the only effect of his patent is to restrain others from dealing with or using its device. . . . Or to put it another way, the inventor does not get from the law a right to a use that he did not have before but he gets the right to an *exclusive* use. Take this from him and you take all that the law gives him and to secure which the public faith is pledged. . . .

What, then, do the leases accomplish? They have clauses called "tying" clauses, so called because, it is said, they tie the use of the machine leased to the use of machines not covered by the particular lease. Their result is, the Government asserts, "to make it in effect a condition of the lease that the lessee shall not use the machines of competitors either to supply a need for additional machines of the kind leased or for machines of other important though wholly different types." . . .

However, we need not dwell further upon the leases. It approaches declamation to say that the lessees were coerced to their making. And, as we have said, there was benefit to the lessee. It is easy to say that the leases are against the policy of the law. But when one tries to be definite one comes back to the rights and obligations of the parties. There is no question in the case of the use of circumstances to compel or restrain; the leases are simply bargains, not different from others, moved upon calculated considerations, and, whether provident or improvident, are entitled nevertheless to the sanctions of the law. We have said this, indeed, with iteration, but sometimes propositions which have become postulates have to be justified to meet objections, which, if they do not deny their existence, tend to bring them into question.

Besides, it is impossible to believe, and the court below refused to find, that the great business of the United Shoe Machinery Company has been built up by the coercion of its customers and that its machinery has been installed in most of the large factories of the country by the exercise of power, even that of patents. The installations could have had no other incentive than the excellence of the machines and the advantage of their use, the conditions imposed having adequate compensation and not being offensive to the letter or the policy of the law.

Decree affirmed.

MR. JUSTICE McREYNOLDS and MR. JUSTICE BRANDEIS took no part in the consideration and decision of the case.

MR. JUSTICE DAY, dissenting. . . .

There are provisions in the so-called leases attacked in this case which in my view are so clearly within the condemnation of the Sherman Anti-Trust Act, that the further enforcement of them and the making of new leases of like character, should be enjoined. The far-reaching character of a decision sustaining a leasing system such as the defendant has developed and uses justifies a statement of the reasons which impel me to this conclusion. . . .

From familiar decisions of this court it may be said to be now well settled that the Sherman Anti-Trust Act condemns all combinations and contracts the effect of which is to unduly restrain the free and natural flow of interstate commerce, or which monopolize or tend to monopolize such trade or commerce in whole or in part. While the act does not reach normal contracts sanctioned by law and sustained by usage, it does reach any and all means and devices by which the purposes of the act to protect the freedom of interstate commerce may be thwarted and monopolies promoted and created. . . .

That these lease restrictions tend to prevent the free flow of interstate commerce, and the natural course of its activities, and at least tend to monopolize an important trade in interstate commerce seems apparent from a mere statement of their terms, having in mind their natural and necessary effect.

For the seventeen years term for which all the leases are drawn, the lessees upon failure to use exclusively the defendant's machines for lasting shoes, or upon failure to purchase needed additional machines from the lessor, or to buy certain supplies from the lessor at prices to be fixed by it, are subject to the right of the lessor to terminate all the leases held by the offending lessee and to take possession of the machines to the utter destruction of the lessee's business. The necessary effect of these prohibitive provisions, in view of the dominating control of the business by the lessor, is to prevent the lessee from using other similar machines, however advantageous to him it may be to do so, unless he is willing to incur the peril of losing machinery essential to his business. It likewise so curtails the field of free customers as to keep others from manufacturing such machinery. Whenever a new machine is acquired by the lessee for the period of seventeen years (the full life of a patent under the statutes of the United States) the chain is forged anew which binds him to the use of the lessor's machines, to the practical exclusion of all others. . . .

The patent statute and the Sherman Act are each valid laws of the

United States. While a patentee should be protected in the exercise of rights secured to the inventor under the patent system enacted into the laws of the United States, there is nothing in the act which gives the patentee a license to violate other statutes of the United States, and certainly not the one now under consideration. In my opinion the restrictive and prohibitive clauses of these leases are within the Sherman Act, as they are clearly in restraint of interstate trade and tend to monopolize in the sense that those terms have been defined in the decisions of this court. . .

MR. JUSTICE PITNEY and MR. JUSTICE CLARKE concur in this dissent.

Two years after the United Shoe decision, with Justice McKenna again writing the 4–3 majority opinion and the same three dissenters as in the United Shoe case, the position of large firms was further insulated against Sherman Act prosecution by a favorable Rule of Reason application in the U.S. Steel case. The United States Steel Corporation had been formed in 1901 as the result of the largest merger up to that time involving some twelve steel manufacturers. The firm had complete vertical and horizontal integration and at the time suit was initiated in 1911 controlled over one-half of the steel industry, having declined from two-thirds control at the time of the merger.

The Court's opinion was based on the following rationale. The fact that the corporation had formerly joined with its competitors to fix and maintain prices—at times successful and at other times unsuccessful—did not warrant a present finding of guilty since the practices were transient in purpose and effect and were abandoned before suit was initiated, because of their futility, not fear of prosecution. Furthermore, there was no evidence to indicate these activities would be resumed. The law is applicable to actual realization of monopoly, not the expectation or futile attempts to achieve it.

The Court recognized the good relationships that the firm had always maintained with its competitors. It had "resorted to none of the brutalities or tyrannies" that had characterized other combinations (for example, Standard Oil and American Tobacco). "It did not have power in and of itself, and the control it exerted was only in and by association with its competitors." The government was contending that the size of the corporation was a potential threat to competition. But the Court disagreed, saying, "The Corporation is undoubtedly of impressive size . . . But we must adhere to the law and the law does not make mere size an offense or the existence of unexerted power an offense." At any rate, the Court could not find an unreasonable restraint of trade in evidence.

Justice Day's dissenting opinion points out that the firm should not be exonerated merely because it had abandoned previously unlawful activities. Certainly, a large part of the dominant position enjoyed by the firm would have to be attributed to its earlier illegal practices, nor was he impressed by the declining relative market share (from about 60 per cent of ingot and basic steel shapes to approximately 50 per cent over a twenty-year period) as a basis for a finding of not guilty.

UNITED STATES v. UNITED STATES STEEL CORPORATION

251 U.S. 417 (1920)

MR. JUSTICE MCKENNA delivered the opinion of the court.

Suit against the Steel Corporation and certain other companies which it directs and controls by reason of the ownership of their stock, it and they being separately and collectively charged as violators of the Sherman Anti-Trust Act. . . .

The Steel Corporation is a holding company only; the other companies are the operating ones, manufacturers in the iron and steel industry, twelve in number. There are, besides, other corporations and individuals more or less connected with the activities of the other defendants that are alleged to be instruments or accomplices in their activities and offendings; and that these activities and offendings (speaking in general terms) extend from 1901 to 1911, when the bill was filed, and have illustrative periods of significant and demonstrated illegality. . . .

The Corporation, it was said, did not at any time abuse the power or ascendency it possessed. It resorted to none of the brutalities or tyrannies that the cases illustrate of other combinations. It did not secure freight rebates; it did not increase its profits by reducing the wages of its employees—whatever it did was not at the expense of labor; it did not increase its profits by lowering the quality of its products, nor create an artificial scarcity of them; it did not oppress or coerce its competitors—its competition, though vigorous, was fair; it did not undersell its competitors in some localities by reducing its prices there below those maintained elsewhere, or require its customers to enter into contracts limiting their purchases or restricting them in resale prices; it did not obtain customers by secret rebates or departures from its published prices; there was no evidence that it attempted to crush its competitors or drive them out of the market, nor did it take customers from its competitors by unfair means, and in its competition it seemed to make no difference between large and small competitors. Indeed it is said in many ways and illustrated that "instead of relying upon its own power to fix and maintain prices, the corporation, at its very beginning sought and obtained the assistance of others." It combined its power with that of its competitors. It did not have power in and of itself, and the control it exerted was only in and by association with its competitors. Its offense, therefore, such as it was, was not different from theirs and was distinguished from theirs "only in the leadership it assumed in promulgating and perfecting the policy." This leadership it gave up, and it had ceased to offend against the law before this suit was brought. It was hence concluded that it should be distinguished from its organizers and that their intent and unsuccessful attempt should not be attributed to it, that it "in and of itself is not now and has never been a monopoly or a combination in restraint of trade," and a decree of dissolution should not be entered against it.

This summary of the opinions, given necessarily in paraphrase, does not adequately represent their ability and strength, but it has value as indicating the contentions of the parties, and the ultimate propositions to which the contentions are addressed. . . .

We state the contentions, we do not have to discuss them, or review the arguments advanced for their acceptance or repulsion. That is done in the opinions of the district judges, and we may well despair to supplement the force of their representation of the conditions antecedent to the formation of the Corporation and in what respect and extent its formation changed them. Of course in that representation and its details there is guidance to decision, but they must be rightly estimated to judge of what they persuade. Our present purpose is not retrospect for itself, however instructive, but practical decision upon existing conditions, that we may not by their disturbance produce, or even risk, consequences of a concern that cannot now be computed. In other words, our consideration should be of not what the Corporation had power to do or did, but what it has now power to do and is doing, and what judgment shall be now pronounced— whether its dissolution, as the Government prays, or the dismissal of the suit, as the Corporation insists?

The alternatives are perplexing—involve conflicting considerations, which, regarded in isolation, have diverse tendencies. We have seen that the judges of the District Court unanimously concurred in the view that the Corporation did not achieve monopoly, and such is our deduction, and it is against monopoly that the statute is directed, not against an expectation of it, but against its realization, and it is certain that it was not realized. The opposing conditions were underestimated. The power attained was much greater than that possessed by any one competitor—it was not greater than that possessed by all of them. Monopoly, therefore, was not achieved, and competitors had to be persuaded by pools, associations, trade meetings, and through the social form of dinners, all of them, it may be, violations of the law, but transient in their purpose and effect. They were scattered through the years from 1901 (the year of the formation of the Corporation), until 1911, but, after instances of success and failure, were abandoned nine months before this suit was brought. There is no evidence that the abandonment was in prophecy of or dread of suit; and the illegal practices have not been resumed, nor is there any evidence of an intention to resume them, and certainly no "dangerous probability" of their resumption, . . . It is our conclusion, therefore, as it was that of the judges below, that the practices were abandoned from a conviction of their futility, from the operation of forces that were not understood or were underestimated, and the case is not peculiar. . . .

But there are other paradoxes. The Government does not hesitate to present contradictions, though only one can be true, such being we were told in our school books the "principle of contradiction." In one competitors (the independents) are represented as oppressed by the superior power of the Corporation; in the other they are represented as ascending to opulence by imitating that power's prices which they could not do if at disadvantage from the other conditions of competition; and yet confederated action is not asserted. If it were this suit would take on another cast. The competitors would cease to be the victims of the Corporation and would become its accomplices. And there is no other alternative. The suggestion that lurks in the Government's contention that the acceptance of the Corporation's prices is the submission of impotence to irresistible power is, in view of the testimony of the competitors, untenable. . . .

We have pointed out that there are several of the Government's contentions which are difficult to represent or measure, and, the one we are now considering, that is the power is "unlawful regardless of purpose," is another of them. It seems to us that it has for its ultimate principle and justification that strength in any producer or seller is a menace to the public interest and illegal because there is potency in it for mischief. The regression is extreme, but short of it the Government cannot stop. The fallacy it conveys is manifest.

The Corporation was formed in 1901, no act of aggression upon its competitors is charged against it, it confederated with them at times in offence against the law, but abandoned that before this suit was brought, and since 1911 no act in violation of law can be established against it except its existence be such an act. This is urged, as we have seen, and that the interest of the public is involved, and that such interest is paramount to corporation or competitors. Granted—though it is difficult to see how there can be restraint of trade when there is no restraint of competitors in the trade nor complaints by customers—how can it be worked out of the situation and through what proposition of law? Of course it calls for nothing other than a right application of the law and to repeat what we have said above, shall we declare the law to be that size is an offense even though it minds its own business because what it does is imitated? The Corporation is undoubtedly of impressive size and it takes an effort of resolution not to be affected by it or to exaggerate its influence. But we must adhere to the law and the law does not make mere size an offence or the existence of unexerted power an offence. It, we repeat, requires overt acts and trusts to its prohibition of them and its power to repress or punish them. It does not compel competition nor require all that is possible.

Admitting, however, that there is pertinent strength in the propositions of the Government, and in connection with them, we recall the distinction we made in the Standard Oil Case . . . between acts done in violation of the statute and a condition brought about which "in and of itself, is not only a continued attempt to monopolize, but also a monopolization." In such case, we declared, "the duty to enforce the statute" required "the application of broader and more controlling" remedies than in the other. And the remedies applied conformed to the declaration; there was prohibition of future acts and there was dissolution of "the combination found to exist in violation of the statute" in order to "neutralize the extension and continually operating force which the possession of the power unlawfully obtained" had "brought" and would "continue to bring about."

Are the case and its precepts applicable here? The Steel Corporation by its formation united under one control competing companies and thus, it is urged, a condition was brought about in violation of the statute, and therefore illegal and became a "continually operating force" with the "possession of power unlawfully obtained."

But there are countervailing considerations. We have seen whatever there was of wrong intent could not be executed, whatever there was of evil effect, was discontinued before this suit was brought; and this, we think, determines the decree. We say this in full realization of the requirements of the law. It is clear in its denunciation of monopolies and equally clear in its direction that the courts of the Nation shall prevent and restrain them (its language is "to prevent and restrain violations of" the act), but the command is necessarily submissive to the conditions which may exist and the usual powers of a court of equity to adapt its remedies to those conditions. In other words, it is not expected to enforce abstractions and do injury thereby, it may be, to the purpose of the law. It is this flexibility of discretion—indeed essential function—that makes its value in our jurisprudence—value in this case as in others. We do not mean to say that the law is not its own measure and that it can be disregarded, but only that the appropriate relief in each instance is remitted to a court of equity to determine, not, and let us be explicit in this, to advance a policy contrary to that of the law, but in submission to the law and its policy, and in execution of both. And it is certainly a matter for consideration that there was no legal attack on the Corporation until 1911, ten years after its formation and the commencement of its career. We do not, however, speak of the delay simply as to its time—that there is estoppel in it because of its time—but on account of what was done during that time—the many millions of dollars spent, the development made, and the enterprises undertaken, the investments by the public that have been invited and are not to be ignored. . . .

But let us see what guide to a procedure of dissolution of the Corporation and the dispersion as well of its subsidiary companies, for they are asserted to be illegal combinations, is prayed. And the fact must not be overlooked or underestimated. The prayer of the Government calls for not only a disruption of present conditions but the restoration of the conditions of twenty years ago, if not literally, substantially. Is there guidance to this in the *Standard Oil Case* and the *Tobacco Case?* . . .

. . . In the *Tobacco Case*, therefore, as in the *Standard Oil Case*, the court had to deal with a persistent and systematic lawbreaker masquerading under legal forms, and which not only had to be stripped of its disguises but arrested in its illegality. A decree of dissolution was the manifest instrumentality and inevitable. We think it would be a work of sheer supererogation to point out that a decree in that case or in the *Standard Oil Case* furnishes no example for a decree in this.

In conclusion we are unable to see that the public interest will be served by yielding to the contention of the Government respecting the dissolution of the company or the separation from it of some of its subsidiaries; and we do see in a contrary conclusion a risk of injury to the public interest, including a material disturbance of, and, it may be serious detriment to, the foreign trade. And in submission to the policy of the law and its fortifying prohibitions the public interest is of paramount regard.

We think, therefore, that the decree of the District Court should be affirmed.

So ordered.

MR. JUSTICE McREYNOLDS and MR. JUSTICE BRANDEIS took no part in the consideration or decision of the case.

MR. JUSTICE DAY dissenting.

This record seems to me to leave no fair room for a doubt that the defendants, the United States Steel Corporation and the several subsidiary corporations which make up that organization, were formed in violation of the Sherman Act. I am unable to accept the conclusion which directs a dismissal of the bill instead of following the well-settled practice, sanctioned by previous decisions of this court, requiring the dissolution of combinations made in direct violation of the law.

It appears to be thoroughly established that the formation of the corporations, here under consideration, constituted combinations between competitors, in violation of law, and intended to remove competition and to directly restrain trade. I agree with the conclusions of Judges Woolley and Hunt, expressed in the court below . . . , that the combinations were not submissions to business conditions but were designed to control them for illegal purposes, regardless of other consequences, and "were made upon a scale that was huge and in a manner that was wild," and "properties were assembled and combined with less regard to their importance as integral parts of an integrated whole than to the advantages expected from the elimination of the competition which theretofore existed between them." . . .

For many years, as the record discloses, this unlawful organization exerted its power to control and maintain prices by pools, associations, trade meetings, and as the result of discussion and agreements at the so-called "Gary Dinners," where the assembled trade opponents secured coöperation and joint action through the machinery of special committees of competing concerns, and by prudent prevision took into account the possibility of defection, and the means of controlling and perpetuating that industrial harmony which arose from the control and maintenance of prices.

It inevitably follows that the corporation violated the law in its formation and by its immediate practices. The power, thus obtained from the combination of resources almost unlimited in the aggregation of competing organizations, had within its control the domination of the trade, and the ability to fix prices and restrain the free flow of commerce upon a scale heretofore unapproached in the history of corporate organization in this country. . . .

I agree that the act offers no objection to the mere size of a corporation, nor to the continued exertion of its lawful power, when that size and power have been obtained by lawful means and developed by natural growth, although its resources, capital and strength may give to such corporation a dominating place in the business and industry with which it is concerned. It is entitled to maintain its size and the power that legitimately goes with it, provided no law has been transgressed in obtaining it. But I understand the reiterated decisions of this court construing the Sherman Act to hold that this power may not legally be derived from conspiracies, combinations, or contracts in restraint of trade. To permit this would be to practically annul the Sherman Law by judicial decree. . . .

Nor can I yield assent to the proposition that this combination has not acquired a dominant position in the trade which enables it to control prices and production when it sees fit to exert its power. Its total assets on December 31, 1913, were in excess of $1,800,000,000; its outstanding capital stock was $868,583,600; its surplus $151,798,428. Its cash on hand ordinarily was $75,000,000; this sum alone exceeded the total capitalization of any of its competitors, and with a single exception, the total capitalization and surplus of any one of them. That such an organization thus fortified and equipped could if it saw fit dominate the trade and control competition would seem to be a business proposition too plain to require extended argument to support it. Its resources, strength and comprehensive ownership of the means of production enable it to adopt measures to do again as it has done in the past, that is, to effectually dominate and control the steel business of the country. From the earliest decisions of this court it has been declared that it was the effective power of such organizations to control and restrain competition and the freedom of trade that Congress intended to limit and control. That the exercise of the power may be withheld, or exerted with forbearing benevolence, does not place such combinations beyond the authority of the statute which was intended to prohibit their formation, and when formed to deprive them of the power unlawfully attained. . . .

It seems to me that if this act is to be given effect, the bill, under the findings of fact made by the court, should not be dismissed, and the cause should be remanded to the District Court, where a plan of effective and final dissolution of the corporations should be enforced by a decree framed for that purpose.

MR. JUSTICE PITNEY and MR. JUSTICE CLARKE concur in this dissent.

The *International Harvester* case, decided in 1927 by a 6–0 vote, was another example of beneficial application of the Rule of Reason to a firm brought to court because of its dominant market position. Although control of two-thirds of the market may involve some restraint of trade, it was not viewed as an "unreasonable" restraint unless a finding of some illegal practice could also be shown.

The facts presented in the case disclosed that International Harvester Company had been formed by a 1902 merger of five makers of agricultural machinery, giving control of 85 per cent of the market. At the time suit was brought, the market share had declined to 64 per cent. But, like U.S. Steel, International Harvester was considered a "good trust," although it was the acknowledged price leader of the industry. In following the *Steel* decision, the Court said: "The law, however, does not make the mere size of a corporation, however impressive, or the existence of unexerted power on its part, an offense, when unaccompanied by unlawful conduct in the exercise of its power." Price leadership does not constitute a violation of the Sherman Act. The Court thus refused to dissolve International Harvester into three independent companies as requested by the government.

UNITED STATES v. INTERNATIONAL HARVESTER COMPANY et al.

274 U.S. 693 (1927)

MR. JUSTICE SANFORD delivered the opinion of the Court.

This is a direct appeal, under §238 of the Judicial Code as amended by the Jurisdictional Act 1925, from a final decree of the District Court . . . dismissing a supplemental petition of the United States to obtain further relief in addition to that granted by an earlier decree in the same case.

In the original petition, which was filed in 1912, the United States alleged that the International Harvester Company—hereinafter referred to as the International Company—and other defendants were engaged in a combination restraining interstate trade and commerce in harvesting machines and other agricultural implements and monopolizing such trade in violation of the Anti-Trust Act; that the International Company had been formed by certain of the other defendants in 1902, with a capital stock of $120,000,000, for the purpose of combining five separate companies then manufacturing and selling harvesting machinery, whose aggregate output exceeded 85 per cent. of such machinery produced and sold in the United States, and thereby eliminating competition between these companies, restraining and monopolizing the interstate trade in such machinery, and promoting a similar monopoly in other agricultural implements; that in pursuance of such purpose the International Company acquired in 1902 the entire property and business of these five companies; that it thereafter acquired the property and business of various competitors and the control of steel, coal and other subsidiary companies, added all other classes of agricultural implements to its lines, used various unfair trade methods and practices to destroy its competitors, closed the opportunities for new competitors in all lines of agricultural implements, and advanced the price of harvesting machinery; and that it was then producing at least 90 per cent.

of the grain binders and 75 per cent. of the mowers produced and sold in the United States, and over 30 per cent. of all agricultural implements other than harvesting machinery. . . .

. . . By the decree as originally entered in August, 1914, it was "adjudged and decreed that said combination and monopoly be forever dissolved and to the end that the business and assets of the International Harvester Company be separated and divided among at least three substantially equal, separate, distinct, and independent corporations with wholly separate owners and stockholders," and that the defendants submit a plan of such separation for the consideration of the court; . . .

The basic contention of the Government here is that the declared purpose of the decree of 1918 was to restore competitive conditions in the harvesting machine industry substantially as they had existed in 1902 before the International Company was formed by the combination of the five original companies, that is, to so increase the amount of competition and the number of competitors as to restore, in a "quantitative" sense, "the free and open competition which existed when the combination was formed"; and that therefore the sole test to be applied in determining whether the decree has accomplished its purpose, is whether it "has had the effect actually to restore in the harvesting machine industry the competitive conditions which obtained prior to 1902." We cannot sustain this contention. This is entirely inconsistent with the purpose of the consent decree, both as appears from its terms and as it was apparently construed by the District Court itself. . . .

Without entering into a detailed statement of the evidence—which is so voluminous as to render this impracticable—we find, from the greater weight of the competent testimony, that competitive conditions in the trade in harvesting machines have been established in compliance with the requirements of the consent decree.

In the course of a general development that had taken place in the agricultural industry since 1902, the International Company and many of its principal competitors had extended their lines from implements used in particular seasons, such as harvesting machines, plows and seeders, and had become in 1918, when the consent decree was entered, "long-line" year-round companies, manufacturing and selling full lines of agricultural implements. This had led to cheaper production and distribution; and, the sale of one line helping to sell the others, had brought about a change in competitive conditions affecting generally all their lines. In distributing their products they had also generally adopted the plan of selling their implements to local retail dealers, who resold them to farmers; and these dealers had become, through their personal efficiency and the good will and the friendly relations which they had established with the farmers, factors of prime importance in distributing the implements of the different companies. Prior to 1912 the International Company had also adopted the general policy, when there was more than one implement dealer in any town, of distributing its various lines, especially its McCormick and Deering harvesting machines, among different dealers; and by means of "exclusive" contracts made with such dealers, its competitors were frequently prevented from acquiring any adequate retail outlet for their implements. This was one of the practices which the Government had assailed in its original petition. . . .

The International Company complied immediately with the single-dealer requirement in clause (a) of the consent decree. This has caused a drastic limitation upon its method of distribution, to which none of its competitors have been subjected. By such compliance it lost the services of almost 5,000 dealers, to whom it had sold in the preceding year implements to the amount of more than $17,000,000. . . .

The International Company also complied with the requirements of clauses (b), (c) and (d) of the consent decree by selling its Champion, Osborne and Milwaukee harvesting lines to independent manufacturers of agricultural implements. . . .

It does not appear that since the entry of the consent decree the International Company has used its capital and resources—which, although much larger than those of any single competitor, are but little larger than the aggregate capital and resources of all its competitors, and are in large part employed in its foreign trade—its subsidiary companies or incidental advantages, for the purpose or with the effect of restraining and suppressing the interstate trade in harvesting machinery; that it has at any time reduced the prices of harvesting machines below cost, for the purpose of driving out its competitors; or that it has at any time controlled and dominated the trade in harvesting machinery by the regulation of prices. It is true that in 1921 and 1922, the period of acute depression in the agricultural implement industry—due chiefly to the depressed agricultural conditions and the diminished purchasing power of the farmers—not only the International Company but its competitors, in a movement initiated by the leading manufacturer of plows, for the purpose primarily of disposing of the surplus stocks which they had accumulated during the war period under high cost conditions, and as a necessary measure of self-protection, made generally material reductions in the prices of harvesting machines and other implements. But the International Company did not at any time reduce its prices below replacement cost; and its reduction in prices was not intended to eliminate competition and has not had that effect. It has not, either during those two years or since, attempted to dominate or in fact controlled or dominated the harvesting machinery industry by the compulsory regulation of prices. The most that can be said as to this, is that many of its competitors have been accustomed, independently and as a matter of business expediency, to follow approximately the prices at which it has sold its harvesting machines; but one of its competitors has habitually sold its machines at somewhat higher prices. The law, however, does not make the mere size of a corporation, however impressive, or the existence of unexerted power on its part, an offense, when unaccompanied by unlawful conduct in the exercise of its power. . . . And the fact that competitors may see proper, in the exercise of their own judgment, to follow the prices of another manufacturer, does not establish any suppression of competition or show any sinister domination. . . .

We further find that while several of the competitors of the International Company in harvesting machines have retired from business since 1911, some during the period of depression commencing in 1921, these retirements were not due to inability to compete with the International Company, but to other causes for which it was in no way responsible; that the place of these retiring competitors has been taken by other and stronger competitors; and that in 1923 it not only had as many competitors in harvesting machines as in 1911, but competitors of greater strength and competitive efficiency.

We also find that the International Company's percentage of the interstate trade in harvesting machinery is not shown to have increased since 1918, as the Government alleged; but, on the contrary, appears to have already decreased. The evidence does not show with any definiteness the percentage of the International Company's trade in such machinery in 1918. This, as alleged in the supplemental petition, had been approximately 77 per cent. in 1911, the year before the original petition was filed. And the Government's own tabulations show that while in 1919, the year after the consent decree was entered, the International Company sold 66.6 per cent. of all the harvesting machines sold in the United States, in 1923 its percentage was only 64.1 per cent. We need not determine the disputed question whether, as the International Company contends, there had been in fact a larger decrease. . . .

We conclude that not only has the International Company complied with the specific requirements of the consent decree, but that competitive conditions have been established in the interstate trade in harvesting machinery bringing about "a situation in harmony with law." The decree of the District Court dismissing the supplemental petition, is therefore

Affirmed.

MR. JUSTICE McREYNOLDS, MR. JUSTICE BRANDEIS, and MR. JUSTICE STONE took no part in the consideration or determination of this cause.

2

Problems of Economic Power
—Recent Interpretations

The cases of the previous chapter were the leading ones during the first three decades of the Sherman Act in setting standards for interpretation of restraint of trade and monopolization. The Supreme Court's position in the *Steel* and *Harvester* cases meant that large firms could acquire and sustain a considerable degree of monopoly power. They had nothing to fear from antitrust prosecution, as long as they were not unreasonable or predatory in their activities. The mere size of the firm or existence of unexerted power would not be grounds for an offense; and the exercise of monopoly power was sanctioned as long as it was not accompanied by "unlawful conduct." This interpretation prevailed until the 1945 *Alcoa* decision. Since that decision effected a change in construing monopoly power and performance, a number of related questions have been raised similar to the one involving the use of monopoly power. Those we shall consider in this chapter include the legality of conscious parallelism, intracorporate conspiracies, vertical integration, and definition of the relevant market.

Monopolization in Practice

A new era of antitrust enforcement was ushered in when Thurman Arnold became head of the Antitrust Division of the Justice Department in 1937. He started a vigorous program of enforcement that has continued through the years. One of his first cases was brought against the Aluminum Company of America, charging them with monopolization in the manufacture of virgin aluminum ingot and in the sale of aluminum products. The final decision upholding the government's position was not rendered until 1945.

The decision of the district court was in Alcoa's favor. The government appealed directly to the Supreme Court, but four of the Justices disqualified themselves because of earlier connections with the case. Thus the Supreme Court lacked the minimum statutory quorum of six Justices. Congress then provided that such cases were to be decided by the three most senior judges of the court of appeals of that circuit in which the case originated or by that court sitting *in banc*. The decision in the *Alcoa* case was written by Judge Learned Hand. Judge Hand's opinion reveals a keen insight into the problem of monopoly and is truly one of the important landmark decisions among all antitrust cases.

Alcoa had originally attained its dominant market position through a basic patent. The company continued its dominant position by the usual business practice of reinvesting earnings in order to expand capacity to meet a growing demand. It further insured its position by stimulating and promoting demand for its product, while making sure it had the capacity to meet such demand. There was thus little opportunity for competitors to enter the market before the essential patents expired, and by that time the optimum size firm necessary to be competitive was too large for entry.

After considering numerous ways of determining the market, the Court concluded that Alcoa controlled more than 90 per cent of the virgin ingot market. Was this market share to be considered a monopoly within the meaning of Section 2 of the Sherman Act? The defense argued that it should not be so construed because profits after taxes on invested capital had averaged only 10 per cent over a period of years. The Court said this contention was irrelevant. Merely because a monopoly has not been used to extract more than a fair profit is not an excuse for "monopolizing." The Court said that Congress "did not condone 'good trusts' and condemn 'bad' ones; it forbad all." Alcoa was judged to have a monopoly within the meaning of Section 2.

Next the Court considered the economic consequences of monopoly. It noted that contracts which fix prices are unconditionally prohibited.[1] When a monopolist sells its products, it must sell at some price, and the "only price at which it could sell is a price which it itself fixed." Since a monopolist has the power to fix prices—even to a greater degree than contracting parties—then it must also be condemned. Judge Hand went on to say: "Indeed it would be absurd to condemn such contracts unconditionally, and not to extend the condemnation to monopolies . . ." Restrictive contracts and monopolies suffer from the same vice of price fixing.

The Court next asked the question: Does it make a difference how the monopoly was attained? Having a monopoly position may not mean that a firm has "monopolized" the industry. Alcoa "may not have achieved monopoly; monopoly may have been thrust upon it." Thus the Court was saying that the origin of the monopoly power may be critical in determining its legality. After considering a number of situations which might "thrust" a firm into a monopoly position, the opinion stated that "the successful competitor, having been urged to compete, must not be turned upon when he wins." But did Alcoa have a monopoly position thrust upon it? The Court concluded that Alcoa was not the "passive beneficiary of a monopoly, following upon an involuntary elimination of competitors by automatically operative economic forces." Alcoa had stimulated new demand for the metal but not without making sure that it could meet this demand. "Nothing compelled it to keep doubling and redoubling its capacity before others entered the field." There can be no more effective

---

[1] See Chapter 6 for the leading cases on price fixing.

exclusion of competitors than to embrace each new opportunity as it comes along, to face every newcomer with sufficient capacity which is "already geared into a great organization, having the advantage of experience, trade connections and the elite of personnel."

The remainder of the decision focuses on a number of practices in which Alcoa had engaged. The firm was found guilty of only one of these, the "price squeeze." An injunction was issued against the resumption of this practice. Finally, there was the question of remedy to be imposed, and on this count the Court could not settle on a satisfactory solution. The government sought dissolution of the company, but Judge Hand rejected this plea. He determined that final action should be postponed until the aluminum plants built by the government during the war could be sold as surplus property. Perhaps with the entry of new firms through this doorway, Alcoa would be faced with competitors. The plants were eventually sold to Reynolds Metals and to Kaiser Aluminum, and Alcoa's share of the market was reduced to less than 60 per cent. Final disposition of the case amounted to no more than a slap on the wrist. The "remedy" was for persons owning stock in both Alcoa and Aluminum, Ltd., the Canadian subsidiary of Alcoa, to dispose of their holdings in one corporation or the other.

The Alcoa decision makes a break with the older cases based on the Rule of Reason and the premise that "mere size is no offense." Size will be an offense when it means control of an industry. In other words, the power to set prices and control entry is the test to be applied. Monopoly must be condemned as price fixing carried out by one party and as a restriction placed upon automatically operating economic forces. Despite this condition, a firm having monopoly thrust upon it is not to be condemned by the courts merely because it was indeed a successful competitor. The source of monopoly power is now emphasized more than the manner in which the position has been used. Thus Section 2 of the Sherman Act was revived as an effective tool against large concentrations of economic power.

UNITED STATES v. ALUMINUM COMPANY OF AMERICA et al.

148 F. 2d 416 (1945)

Before L. HAND, SWAN, and AUGUSTUS N. HAND, Circuit Judges.

L. HAND, Circuit Judge.

This appeal comes to us by virtue of a certificate of the Supreme

Court, under the amendment of 1944 to §29 of 15 U.S.C.A. . . . On June 12, 1944, the Supreme Court, declaring that a quorum of six justices qualified to hear the case was wanting, referred the appeal to this court under §29 of Title 15, already mentioned. . . .[2]

"Alcoa" is a corporation, organized under the laws of Pennsylvania on September 18, 1888; its original name, "Pittsburgh Reduction Company," was changed to its present one on January 1, 1907. It has always been engaged in the production and sale of "ingot" aluminum, and since 1895 also in the fabrication of the metal into many finished and semi-finished articles.

. . . It is undisputed that throughout this period "Alcoa" continued to be the single producer of "virgin" ingot in the United States; and the plaintiff argues that this without more was enough to make it an unlawful monopoly. . . . "Alcoa's" position is that the fact that it alone continued to make "virgin" ingot in this country did not, and does not, give it a monopoly of the market; that it was always subject to the competition of imported "virgin" ingot, and of what is called "secondary" ingot; and that even if it had not been, its monopoly would not have been retained by unlawful means, but would have been the result of a growth which the Act does not forbid, even when it results in a monopoly. We shall first consider the amount and character of this competition; next, how far it established a monopoly; and finally, if it did, whether that monopoly was unlawful under §2 of the Act. . . .

There are various ways of computing "Alcoa's" control of the aluminum market—as distinct from its production—depending upon what one regards as competing in that market. The judge figured its share—during the years 1929–1938, inclusive—as only about thirty-three per cent; to do so he included "secondary," and excluded that part of "Alcoa's" own production which it fabricated and did not therefore sell as ingot. If, on the other hand, "Alcoa's" total production, fabricated and sold, be included, and balanced against the sum of imported "virgin" and "secondary," its share of the market was in the neighborhood of sixty-four per cent for that period. The percentage we have already mentioned—over ninety—results only if we both include all "Alcoa's" production and exclude "secondary." That percentage is enough to constitute a monopoly; it is doubtful whether sixty or sixty-four per cent would be enough; and certainly thirty-three per cent is not. . . .

In the case of a monopoly of any commodity which does not disappear in use and which can be salvaged, the supply seeking sale at any moment will be made up of two components: (1) the part which the

[2] All the footnotes and most of the citations from the opinions of the Court have been omitted from the cases in this chapter.

putative monopolist can immediately produce and sell; and (2) the part which has been, or can be, reclaimed out of what he has produced and sold in the past. . . . Thus, in the case at bar "Alcoa" always knew that the future supply of ingot would be made up in part of what it produced at the time, and, if it was as far-sighted as it proclaims itself, that consideration must have had its share in determining how much to produce. How accurately it could forecast the effect of present production upon the future market is another matter. Experience, no doubt, would help; but it makes no difference that it had to guess; it is enough that it had an inducement to make the best guess it could, and that it would regulate that part of the future supply, so far as it should turn out to have guessed right. The competition of "secondary" must therefore be disregarded, as soon as we consider the position of "Alcoa" over a period of years; it was as much within "Alcoa's" control as was the production of the "virgin" from which it had been derived. . . .

We conclude therefore that "Alcoa's" control over the ingot market must be reckoned at over ninety per cent; that being the proportion which its production bears to imported "virgin" ingot. . . . The producer of so large a proportion of the supply has complete control within certain limits. It is true that, if by raising the price he reduces the amount which can be marketed—as always, or almost always, happens—he may invite the expansion of the small producers who will try to fill the place left open; nevertheless, not only is there an inevitable lag in this, but the large producer is in a strong position to check such competition; and, indeed, if he has retained his old plant and personnel, he can inevitably do so. . . .

. . . [It] is entirely consistent with the evidence that it was the threat of greater foreign imports which kept "Alcoa's" prices where they were, and prevented it from exploiting its advantage as sole domestic producer; indeed, it is hard to resist the conclusion that potential imports did put a "ceiling" upon those prices. Nevertheless, within the limits afforded by the tariff and the cost of transportation, "Alcoa" was free to raise its prices as it chose, since it was free from domestic competition, save as it drew other metals into the market as substitutes. Was this a monopoly within the meaning of §2? The judge found that, over the whole half century of its existence, "Alcoa's" profits upon capital invested, after payment of income taxes, had been only about ten per cent. . . . A profit of ten per cent in such an industry, dependent, in part at any rate, upon continued tariff protection, and subject to the vicissitudes of new demands, to the obsolescence of plant and process—which can never be accurately gauged in advance—to the chance that substitutes may at any moment be discovered which will reduce the demand, and to the other hazards which attend all industry; a profit of ten per cent, so conditioned could hardly be considered extortionate.

Having proved that "Alcoa" had a monopoly of the domestic ingot market, the plaintiff had gone far enough; if it was an excuse, that "Alcoa" had not abused its power, it lay upon "Alcoa" to prove that it had not. But the whole issue is irrelevant anyway, for it is no excuse for "monopolizing" a market that the monopoly has not been used to extract from the consumer more than a "fair" profit. The Act has wider purposes. Indeed, even though we disregarded all but economic considerations, it would by no means follow that such concentration of producing power is to be desired, when it has not been used extortionately. Many people believe that possession of unchallenged economic power deadens initiative, discourages thrift and depresses energy; that immunity from competition is a narcotic, and rivalry is a stimulant, to industrial progress; that the spur of constant stress is necessary to counteract an inevitable disposition to let well enough alone. Such people believe that competitors, versed in the craft as no consumer can be, will be quick to detect opportunities for saving and new shifts in production, and be eager to profit by them. In any event the mere fact that a producer, having command of the domestic market, has not been able to make more than a "fair" profit, is no evidence that a "fair" profit could not have been made at lower prices. . . . True, it might have been thought adequate to condemn only those monopolies which could not show that they had exercised the highest possible ingenuity, had adopted every possible economy, had anticipated every conceivable improvement, stimulated every possible demand. No doubt, that would be one way of dealing with the matter, although it would imply constant scrutiny and constant supervision, such as courts are unable to provide. Be that as it may, that was not the way that Congress chose; it did not condone "good trusts" and condemn "bad" ones; it forbad all. Moreover, in so doing it was not necessarily actuated by economic motives alone. It is possible, because of its indirect social or moral effect, to prefer a system of small producers, each dependent for his success upon his own skill and character, to one in which the great mass of those engaged must accept the direction of a few. These considerations, which we have suggested only as possible purposes of the Act, we think the decisions prove to have been in fact its purposes.

It is settled, at least as to §1, that there are some contracts restricting competition which are unlawful, no matter how beneficent they may be; no industrial exigency will justify them; they are absolutely forbidden. . . . Starting, however, with the authoritative premise that all contracts fixing prices are unconditionally prohibited, the only possible difference between them and a monopoly is that while a monopoly necessarily involves an equal, or even greater, power to fix prices, its mere existence might be thought not to constitute an exercise of that power. That distinction is nevertheless purely formal; it would be valid only so long as the monopoly remained wholly inert; it would disappear as soon as the monopoly began to operate; for, when it did—that is, as soon as it began to sell at all—it must sell at some price and the only price at which it could sell is a price which it itself fixed. Thereafter the power and its exercise must needs coalesce. Indeed it would be absurd to condemn such contracts unconditionally, and not to extend the condemnation to monopolies; for the contracts are only steps toward that entire control which monopoly confers: they are really partial monopolies.

. . . [T]here can be no doubt that the vice of restrictive contracts and of monopoly is really one, it is the denial to commerce of the supposed protection of competition. To repeat, if the earlier stages are proscribed, when they are parts of a plan, the mere projecting of which condemns them unconditionally, the realization of the plan itself must also be proscribed.

We have been speaking only of the economic reasons which forbid monopoly; but, as we have already implied, there are others, based upon the belief that great industrial consolidations are inherently undesirable, regardless of their economic results. . . . Throughout the history of these statutes it has been constantly assumed that one of their purposes was to perpetuate and preserve, for its own sake and in spite of possible cost, an organization of industry in small units which can effectively compete with each other. We hold that "Alcoa's" monopoly of ingot was of the kind covered by §2.

It does not follow because "Alcoa" had such a monopoly, that it "monopolized" the ingot market: it may not have achieved monopoly; monopoly may have been thrust upon it. If it had been a combination of existing smelters which united the whole industry and controlled the production of all aluminum ingot, it would certainly have "monopolized" the market. . . .

. . . We may start therefore with the premise that to have combined ninety per cent of the producers of ingot would have been to "monopolize" the ingot market; and, so far as concerns the public interest, it can make no difference whether an existing competition is put an end to, or whether prospective competition is prevented. . . . Nevertheless, it is unquestionably true that from the very outset the courts have at least kept in reserve the possibility that the origin of a monopoly may be critical in determining its legality.

. . . [P]ersons may unwittingly find themselves in possession of a monopoly, automatically so to say: that is, without having intended either to put an end to existing competition, or to prevent competition from arising when none had existed; they may become monopolists by force of accident. . . . A market may, for example, be so limited that it is impossible to produce at all and meet the cost of production except by a plant large enough to supply the whole demand. . . . A single producer may be the survivor out of a group of active competitors, merely by virtue of his superior skill, foresight and industry. In such cases a strong argument can be made that, although, the result may expose the public to the evils of monopoly, the Act does not mean to condemn the resultant of those very forces which it is its prime object to foster . . . The successful competitor, having been urged to compete, must not be turned upon when he wins. . . .

It would completely misconstrue "Alcoa's" position in 1940 to hold that it was the passive beneficiary of a monopoly, following upon an involuntary elimination of competitors by automatically operative economic forces. . . . this continued and undisturbed control did not fall undesigned into "Alcoa's" lap; obviously it could not have done so. It could only have resulted, as it did result, from a persistent determination to maintain the control, with which it found itself vested in 1912. There were at least one or two abortive attempts to enter the industry, but "Alcoa" effectively anticipated and forestalled all competition, and succeeded in holding the field alone. True, it stimulated demand and opened new uses for the metal, but not without making sure that it could supply what it had evoked. There is no dispute as to this; "Alcoa" avows it as evidence of the skill, energy and initiative with which it has always conducted its business; as a reason why, having won its way by fair means, it should be commended, and not dismembered. We need charge it with no moral derelictions after 1912; we may assume that all it claims for itself is true. The only question is whether it falls within the exception established in favor of those who do not seek, but cannot avoid, the control of a market. It seems to us that that question scarcely survives its statement. It was not inevitable that it should always anticipate increases in the demand for ingot and be prepared to supply them. Nothing compelled it to keep doubling and redoubling its capacity before others entered the field. It insists that it never excluded competitors; but we can think of no more effective exclusion than progressively to embrace each new opportunity as it opened, and to face every newcomer with new capacity already geared into a great organization, having the advantage of experience, trade connections and the elite of personnel. Only in case we interpret "exclusion" as limited to manoeuvres not honestly industrial, but actuated solely by a desire to prevent competition, can such a course, indefatigably pursued, be deemed not "exclusionary." So to limit it would in our judgment emasculate the Act; would permit just such consolidations as it was designed to prevent.

In order to fall within §2, the monopolist must have both the power to monopolize, and the intent to monopolize. To read the passage as demanding any "specific," intent, makes nonsense of it, for no monopolist monopolizes unconscious of what he is doing. So here, "Alcoa" meant to keep, and did keep, that complete and exclusive hold upon the ingot market with which it started. That was to "monopolize" that market, however innocently it otherwise proceeded. So far as the judgment held that it was not within §2, it must be reversed. . . .

As we have said, the plaintiff also sought to convict "Alcoa" of practices in which it engaged, not because they were necessary to the development of its business, but only in order to suppress competitors. Since we are holding that "Alcoa" "monopolized" the ingot market in 1940, regardless of such practices, these issues might be moot, if it inevitably followed from our holding that "Alcoa" must be dissolved. . . . Possibly that would be true, except that conditions have so changed since the case was closed, that, as will appear, it by no means follows, because "Alcoa" had a monopoly in 1940, that it will have one when final judgment is entered after the war. That judgment may leave it intact as a competing unit among other competing units, and the plaintiff might argue, and undoubtedly will, that, if it was in the past guilty of practices, aimed at "monopolizing" the ingot market, it would be proper and necessary to enjoin their resumption, even though it no longer will have a monopoly. For this reason it appears to us that the issues are not altogether moot. In spite of the prolixity of the evidence, the challenged practices can be divided into three classes: (a) the "preemption" of bauxite deposits and water power; (b) the suppression of several efforts by competitors to invade either the ingot market, or some of the markets for fabricated goods; (c) the "domination" of the markets for such goods, and particularly of the markets for "sheet" and "cable." . . .

[The Court found that Alcoa dominated the "sheet" market by the "price squeeze," i.e., selling ingot at so high a price that the "sheet rollers," who could only buy from Alcoa, could not make a living profit out of the price that Alcoa itself sold "sheet."]

Nearly five years have passed since the evidence was closed; during that time the aluminum industry, like most other industries, has been revolutionized by the nation's efforts in a great crisis. That alone would make it impossible to dispose of the action upon the basis of the record as we have it; and so both sides agree. . . .

It is impossible to say what will be "Alcoa's" position in the industry after the war. The [United States] has leased to [Alcoa] all its new plants. . . . No one can now forecast in the remotest way what will be the form of the industry after the [United States] has disposed of these plants . . .

Judgment reversed, and cause remanded for further proceedings not inconsistent with the foregoing.

The *Alcoa* doctrine was re-emphasized in a 1953 lower court case against the United Shoe Machinery Corporation. United Shoe was found guilty of monopolization under Section 2 of the Sherman Act, culminating a forty-year effort on the part of the government to curtail the dominant position of the shoe machinery manufacturer. The decision was appealed but upheld by the Supreme Court in a *per curiam* decision in 1954.

Although Judge Wyzanski followed the *Alcoa* case closely, he tried to probe more deeply into the origin of monopoly power and how it may be used. He found that United Shoe was by far the largest producer of shoemaking equipment, supplying between 75 and 85 per cent of the equipment to nearly fifteen hundred shoe manufacturers in this country. This position was maintained because United Shoe never sold any of its patented machines. It would only lease them on long-term, exclusive contracts. These contracts required that certain supplies to be used in shoemaking be purchased from United Shoe. These practices, when used by such a dominant firm, served as barriers to the entry of competitors.

Judge Wyzanski agreed that monopoly would be lawful if thrust upon the firm. However, it is unlawful if that power results from barriers erected by the use of business methods, not in themselves predatory or immoral, but designed to exclude others. Unless the barriers are exclusively the result of superior skill or products, natural advantages, technological or economic efficiency, scientific research, or other similar conditions, the practices are likely to be struck down. The judge was requiring stricter conduct on the part of a monopolist than would be imposed on a firm with substantial competitors. United Shoe's position, he concluded, could not be attributed to its ". . . economies of scale, research, natural advantages, and adaptation to inevitable economic laws."

The government sought to break up United Shoe into three firms, but the Court refused to grant that remedy. Rather, the remedy granted required United Shoe to sell, as well as lease, its machines; to use shorter-term leases; to grant licenses to use its products; and to divest itself of subsidiaries producing shoemaking supplies. These remedies, like that of *Alcoa*, amounted to no more than a slap on the wrist, although the door was left open for the government to request court review of industry competition in ten years. If the government had been successful in its dissolution request, the cost of shoemaking equipment would have been increased.

UNITED STATES v. UNITED SHOE MACHINERY CORP.

110 F. Supp. 295 (1953)

WYZANSKI, District Judge.

. . . [T]he Government filed a complaint against United Shoe Machinery Corporation[3] . . . in order to restrain alleged violations of §§1 and 2 of [the Sherman Act].

Stripped to its essentials, the 52 page complaint charged, *first*, that since 1912 United had been "monopolizing interstate trade and commerce in the shoe machinery industry of the United States" . . . The *second* principal charge laid by the complaint was that United had been (a) "monopolizing the distribution in interstate commerce of numerous * * * shoe factory supplies" and (b) "attempting to monopolize the distribution in interstate commerce of * * * other such supplies . . . *Third*, the complaint alleged United was "attempting to monopolize and monopolizing the manufacture and distribution in interstate commerce of tanning machinery used in the manufacture of shoe leather" . . .

There are 18 major processes for the manufacturing of shoes by machine. Some machine types are used only in one process, but others are used in several; and the relationship of machine types to one another may be competitive or sequential. The approximately 1460 shoe manufacturers themselves are highly competitive in many respects, including their choice of processes and other technological aspects of production. Their total demand for machine services, apart from those rendered by dry thread sewing machines in the upper-fitting room, constitutes an identifiable market which is a "part of the trade or commerce among the several States." . . .

United, the largest source of supply, is a corporation lineally descended from a combination of constituent companies, adjudged lawful by the Supreme Court of the United States in 1918. . . .

Supplying different aspects of that market are at least 10 other American manufacturers and some foreign manufacturers, whose products are admitted to the United States free of tariff duty. Almost all the operations performed in the 18 processes can be carried out without the use of any of United's machines, and (at least in foreign areas, where patents are

---

[3] Affirmed by the Supreme Court, 347 U.S. 521 (1954).

no obstacle), a complete shoe factory can be efficiently organized without a United machine.

Nonetheless, United at the present time is supplying over 75%, and probably 85%, of the current demand in the American shoe machinery market, as heretofore defined. . . .

United is the only machinery enterprise that produces a long line of machine types, and covers every major process. It is the only concern that has a research laboratory covering all aspects of the needs of shoe manufacturing . . .

Although at the turn of the century, United's patents covered the fundamentals of shoe machinery manufacture, those fundamental patents have expired. Current patents cover for the most part only minor developments, so that it is possible to "invent around" them, to use the words of United's chief competitor. However, the aggregation of patents does to some extent block potential competition. It furnishes a trading advantage. It leads inventors to offer their ideas to United, on the general principle that new complicated machines embody numerous patents. And it serves as a hedge or insurance for United against unforeseen competitive developments. . . .

In supplying its complicated machines to shoe manufacturers, United, like its more important American competitors, has followed the practice of never selling, but only leasing. Leasing has been traditional in the shoe machinery field since the Civil War. So far as this record indicates, there is virtually no expressed dissatisfaction from consumers respecting that system; and Compo, United's principal competitor, endorses and uses it. Under the system, entry into shoe manufacture has been easy. The rates charged for all customers have been uniform. The machines supplied have performed excellently. United has, without separate charge, promptly and efficiently supplied repair service and many kinds of other service useful to shoe manufacturers. . . . The cost to the average shoe manufacturer of its machines and services supplied to him has been less than 2% of the wholesale price of his shoes.

However, United's leases, in the context of the present shoe machinery market, have created barriers to the entry by competitors into the shoe machinery field.

First, the complex of obligations and rights accruing under United's leasing system in operation deter a shoe manufacturer from disposing of a United machine and acquiring a competitor's machine. He is deterred more than if he owned that same United machine, or if he held it on a short lease carrying simple rental provisions and a reasonable charge for cancellation before the end of the term. The lessee is now held closely to United by the combined effect of the 10 year term, the requirement that if he has work available he must use the machine to full capacity, and by the return charge which can in practice, through the right of deduction fund, be reduced to insignificance if he keeps this and other United machines to the end of the periods for which he leased them.

Second, when a lessee desires to replace a United machine, United gives him more favorable terms if the replacement is by another United machine than if it is by a competitive machine.

Third, United's practice of offering to repair, without separate charges, its leased machines, has had the effect that there are no independent service organizations to repair complicated machines. In turn, this has had the effect that the manufacturer of a complicated machine must either offer repair service with his machine, or must face the obstacle of marketing his machine to customers who know that repair service will be difficult to provide. . . .

Although maintaining the same nominal terms for each customer, United has followed, as between machine types, a discriminatory pricing policy. . . . United's own internal documents reveal that these sharp and relatively durable differentials are traceable, at least in large part, to United's policy of fixing a higher rate of return where competition is of minor significance, and a lower rate of return where competition is of major significance. . . .

On the foregoing facts, the issue of law is whether defendant in its shoe machinery business has violated that provision of §2 of the Sherman Act . . .

[In the] recent authorities there are discernible at least three different, but cognate, approaches.

The approach which has the least sweeping implications really antedates the decision in Aluminum. . . .

An enterprise has monopolized in violation of §2 of the Sherman Act if it has acquired or maintained a power to exclude others as a result of using an unreasonable "restraint of trade" in violation of §1 of the Sherman Act. . . .

A more inclusive approach was adopted by Mr. Justice Douglas in United States v. Griffith, 334 U.S. 100, . . . He stated that to prove a violation of §2 it was not always necessary to show a violation of §1. . . . And he concluded that an enterprise has monopolized in violation of §2 if it (a) has the power to exclude competition, and (b) has exercised it, or has the purpose to exercise it. . . .

Indeed the way in which Mr. Justice Douglas used the terms "monopoly power" and "effective market control" . . . and cited Aluminum suggests that he endorses a third and broader approach, which originated with Judge Hand. It will be recalled that Judge Hand said that one who has acquired an overwhelming share of the market "monopolizes" whenever he does business, . . . apparently even if there is no showing that his business involves any exclusionary practice. But, it will also be recalled that this doctrine is softened by Judge Hand's suggestion that the defendant may escape statutory liability if it bears the burden of proving that it owes its monopoly solely to superior skill, superior products, natural advantages, (including accessibility to raw materials or markets), economic or technological efficiency, (including scientific research), low margins of profit maintained permanently and without discrimination, or licenses conferred by, and used within, the limits of law, (including patents on one's own inventions, or franchises granted directly to the enterprise by a public authority).

In the case at bar, the Government contends that the evidence satisfies each of the three approaches to §2 of the Sherman Act, so that it does not matter which one is taken. . . .

This Court finds it unnecessary to choose between the second and third approaches. For, taken as a whole, the evidence satisfies the tests laid down in both Griffith and Aluminum. The facts show that (1) defendant has, and exercises, such overwhelming strength in the shoe machinery market that it controls that market, (2) this strength excludes some potential, and limits some actual, competition, and (3) this strength is not attributable solely to defendant's ability, economies of scale, research, natural advantages, and adaptation to inevitable economic laws.

. . . In the relatively static shoe machinery market where there are no sudden changes in the style of machines or in the volume of demand, United has a network of long-term, complicated leases with over 90% of the shoe factories. These leases assure closer and more frequent contacts between United and its customers than would exist if United were a seller and its customers were buyers. Beyond this general quality, these leases are so drawn and so applied as to strengthen United's power to exclude competitors. Moreover, United offers a long line of machine types, while no competitor offers more than a short line. Since in some parts of its line United faces no important competition, United has the power to discriminate, by wide differentials and over long periods of time, in the rate of return it procures from different machine types. . . .

Not only does the evidence show United has control of the market, but also the evidence does not show that the control is due entirely to excusable causes. The three principal sources of United's power have been the original constitution of the company, the superiority of United's products and services, and the leasing system. The first two of these are plainly beyond reproach. . . .

But United's control does not rest solely on its original constitution, its ability, its research, or its economies of scale. There are other barriers to competition, and these barriers were erected by United's own business policies. Much of United's market power is traceable to the magnetic ties inherent in its system of leasing, and not selling, its more important machines. The lease-only system of distributing complicated machines has many "partnership" aspects, and it has exclusionary features such as the 10-year term, the full capacity clause, the return charges, and the failure to segregate service charges from machine charges. Moreover, the leasing system has aided United in maintaining a pricing system which discriminates between machine types. . . .

Defendant seems to suggest that even if its control of the market is not attributable exclusively to its superior performance, its research, and its economies of scale, nonetheless, United's market control should not be held unlawful, because only through the existence of some monopoly power can the thin shoe machinery market support fundamental research of the first order, and achieve maximum economies of production and distribution.

To this defense the shortest answer is that the law does not allow an enterprise that maintains control of a market through practices not economically inevitable, to justify that control because of its supposed social advantage. . . . It is for Congress, not for private interests, to determine whether a monopoly, not compelled by circumstances, is advantageous. And it is for Congress to decide on what conditions, and subject to what regulations, such a monopoly shall conduct its business. . . .

So far, nothing in this opinion has been said of defendant's *intent* in regard to its power and practices in the shoe machinery market. This point can be readily disposed of by reference once more to Aluminum . . . Defendant intended to engage in the leasing practices and pricing policies which maintained its market power. That is all the intent which the law requires when both the complaint and the judgment rest on a charge of "monopolizing," not merely "attempting to monopolize". Defendant having willed the means, has willed the end.

. . . All that this opinion has ruled is that when control of the market has been obtained in large part by such leases, the market power cannot be said to have been thrust upon its holder through its own skill, energy, and initiative, or through technological conditions of production and distribution, or the inevitable characteristics of the market. In short, the leases themselves are not forbidden; only when they are used as an instrument for seeking market control is the lessor to be charged with using them in an attempt to monopolize. . . .

Where a defendant has monopolized commerce in violation of §2, the principal objects of the decrees are to extirpate practices that have caused or may hereafter cause monopolization, and to restore workable competition in the market.

. . . Concentrations of power, no matter how beneficently they appear to have acted, nor what advantages they seem to possess, are inherently dangerous. Their good behavior in the past may not be continued; and if their strength were hereafter grasped by presumptuous hands, there would be no automatic check and balance from equal forces in the industrial market. . . .

The Government's proposal that the Court dissolve United into three separate manufacturing companies is unrealistic. United conducts all machine manufacture at one plant in Beverly, with one set of jigs and tools, one foundry, one laboratory for machinery problems, one managerial staff, and one labor force. It takes no Solomon to see that this organism cannot be cut into three equal and viable parts. . . .

The Government does not propose that United should cease leasing machines. It does suggest that this Court order defendant to eliminate from the leases those provisions found to be restrictive, to offer for sale every type of machine which it offers for lease, and to make the sales terms somewhat more advantageous to customers, than the lease terms.

The Court agrees that it would be undesirable, at least until milder remedies have been tried, to direct United to abolish leasing forthwith. . . .

Although leasing should not now be abolished by judicial decree, the Court agrees with the Government that the leases should be purged of their restrictive features. . . .

The decree does not prohibit United from rendering service, because, in the Court's view, the rendition of service, if separately charged for, has no exclusionary effects.

The Court also agrees with the Government that if United chooses to continue to lease any machine type, it must offer that type of machine also for sale. . . . The merit of the Government's proposal is in its secondary impact. Insofar as United's machines are sold rather than leased, they will ultimately, in many cases, reach a second-hand market. From that market, United will face a type of substitute competition which will gradually weaken the prohibited market power which it now exercises. . . .

Furthermore, the creation of a sales market together with the purging of the restrictive features of the leases will, in combination, gradually diminish the magnetic hold now exercised by what United properly describes as the partnership features of the leasing system. As United's relationships with its customers grow feebler, competitors will have an enhanced opportunity to market their wares. . . .

One other phase of the decree to which this opinion should expressly advert is the method of handling those subsidiaries and branches which produce supplies in fields which United has monopolized. The clearest examples are nails and tacks, and eyelets for the shoe machinery market. These are large scale monopolizations attributable to the machinery monopoly. And United should be divested of its business of manufacturing and distributing these particular supplies, because this is the kind of dissolution which can be carried out practically, and which will also reduce monopoly power in each of the affected supply fields. . . .

[United Shoe was also required to give nonexclusive licenses at reasonable royalties on any patent now held or which it might acquire from anyone other than its own employees.]

Conscious Parallelism of Action

In a number of earlier cases the Supreme Court had recognized that highly concentrated industries will be characterized by interdependence in the actions of the firms. Similarity or identity of action may in fact occur without any overt conspiracy to do so. But on occasion the Court has inferred unlawful conspiracy on the basis of just circumstantial evidence, the *American Tobacco* case of 1946 being the most outstanding instance.

The government brought a criminal action against the Big Three of the tobacco industry—American Tobacco, Liggett & Myers, and R. J. Reynolds— alleging they had conspired to restrain trade and monopolize the industry. Evidence was produced showing that these firms had nearly identical prices on their cigarettes between 1923 and 1928. After 1928 and continuing through the 1930s, their prices were identical. Starting in the 1930s, the Big Three were confronted with competition from smaller companies selling ten-cent brands. The Big Three then lowered their prices, and when the smaller companies' sales were reduced, the major firms raised prices.

Another tactic used by the Big Three was to buy up the cheaper kind of tobacco leaves used by the smaller companies. The Court found that no explanation was offered as to how or where the cheaper leaves were used; they simply disappeared from the market.

The unique feature of this case was that the government was never able to show with direct evidence that the Big Three had any plan for concerted action. The evidence was wholly circumstantial. The identity of behavior was offered as the determining factor for inferring that a common plan did exist and that the defendants had knowledge of the plan—that is, *conscious parallelism* of action. The identical actions of the firms could not be considered mere coincidence.

The Supreme Court stated: "It is not the form of the combination or the particular means used but the result to be achieved that the statute condemns. . . . No formal agreement is necessary to constitute an unlawful conspiracy." A conspiracy that violates the law may be found from the manner of dealing as well as through an exchange of words. It does not require a proof of exertion of the power to exclude or an actual proof of exclusion of competitors in order to be guilty of monopolization under Section 2. The main consideration in a finding of monopoly is not that prices are raised and competition actually excluded, but that the power does exist to raise prices and exclude competitors whenever it is desirable to do so. Furthermore, the power does not have to be so great as to be able to exclude *all* competitors.

This decision now seems rather harsh from the standpoint of inferring conspiracy merely from identity of activity. Clearly, in concentrated industries there is bound to be a great deal of similarity of policy and action. Recognition of this interdependency of firms in oligopolistic industries has led the courts in subsequent years to retreat from the *American Tobacco* case.

AMERICAN TOBACCO CO. et al. v. UNITED STATES

328 U.S. 781 (1946)

MR. JUSTICE BURTON delivered the opinion of the Court.

The petitioners are The American Tobacco Company, Liggett & Myers Tobacco Company, R. J. Reynolds Tobacco Company, American Suppliers, Inc., a subsidiary of American, and certain officials of the respective companies who were convicted by a jury, in the District Court of the United States for the Eastern District of Kentucky, of violating §§1 and 2 of the Sherman Anti-Trust Act.

Each petitioner was convicted on four counts: (1) conspiracy in restraint of trade, (2) monopolization, (3) attempt to monopolize, and (4) conspiracy to monopolize. Each count related to interstate and foreign trade and commerce in tobacco. No sentence was imposed under the third count as the Court held that that count was merged in the second. Each petitioner was fined $5,000 on each of the other counts, making $15,000 for each petitioner and a total of $255,000. . . .

The Circuit Court of Appeals for the Sixth Circuit, on December 8, 1944, affirmed each conviction. . . . All the grounds urged for review of those judgments were considered here on petitions for certiorari. On March 26, 1945, this Court granted the petitions but each was "limited to the question whether actual exclusion of competitors is necessary to the crime of monopolization under §2 of the Sherman Act." . . .

While the question before us, as briefly stated in the Court's order, makes no express reference to the inclusion, in the crime of "monopolization," of the element of "a combination or conspiracy to acquire and maintain the power to exclude competitors to a substantial extent," yet the trial court . . . described such a combination or conspiracy as an "essential element" and an "indispensable ingredient" of that crime in the present cases. We therefore include that element in determining whether the foregoing instructions correctly stated the law as applied to these cases. In discussing the legal issue we shall assume that such a combination or conspiracy to monopolize has been established. Because of the presence of that element, we do not have here the hypothetical case of parties who themselves have not "achieved" monopoly but have had monopoly "thrust upon" them. . . .

. . . The trial court's instruction did not call for proof of an "actual exclusion" of competitors on the part of the petitioners. For the purposes of this opinion, we shall assume, therefore, that an actual exclusion of competitors by the petitioners was not claimed or established by the prosecution. . . .

Although there is no issue of fact or question as to the sufficiency of the evidence to be discussed here, nevertheless, it is necessary to summarize the principal facts of that conspiracy to monopolize certain trade, which was charged in the fourth count. These facts demonstrate also the vigor and nature of the intent of the petitioners to exclude competitors in order to maintain that monopoly if need or occasion should offer itself to attempt such an exclusion. To support the verdicts it was not necessary to show power and intent to exclude *all* competitors, or to show a conspiracy to exclude *all* competitors. The requirement stated to the jury and contained in the statute was only that the offenders shall "monopolize any part of the trade or commerce among the several States, or with foreign nations." This particular conspiracy may well have derived special vitality, in the eyes of the jury, from the fact that its existence was established, not through the presentation of a formal written agreement, but through the evidence of widespread and effective conduct on the part of petitioners in relation to their existing or potential competitors.

. . . The fact, however, that the purchases of leaf tobacco and the sales of so many products of the tobacco industry have remained largely within the same general group of business organizations for over a generation, inevitably has contributed to the ease with which control over competition within the industry and the mobilization of power to resist new competition can be exercised. A friendly relationship within such a long established industry is, in itself, not only natural but commendable and beneficial, as long as it does not breed illegal activities. Such a community of interest in any industry, however, provides a natural foundation for working policies and understandings favorable to the insiders and unfavorable to outsiders. The verdicts indicate that practices of an informal and flexible nature were adopted and that the results were so uniformly beneficial to the petitioners in protecting their common interests as against those of competitors that, entirely from circumstantial evidence, the jury found that a combination or conspiracy existed among the petitioners from 1937 to 1940, with power and intent to exclude competitors to such a substantial extent as to violate the Sherman Act as interpreted by the trial court.

The position of the petitioners in the cigarette industry from 1931 to 1939 is clear . . . although American, Liggett and Reynolds gradually dropped in their percentage of the national domestic cigarette production from 90.7% in 1931 to 73.3%, 71% and 68%, respectively in 1937, 1938 and 1939, they have accounted at all times for more than 68%, and usually for more than 75%, of the national production. The balance of the cigarette production has come from six other companies. . . .

The further dominance of American, Liggett and Reynolds within their special field of burley blend cigarettes, as compared with the so-called "10 cent cigarettes," is also apparent. In 1939, the 10 cent cigarettes constituted about 14½% of the total domestic cigarette production. Accordingly, the 68% of the total cigarette production enjoyed by American, Liggett and Reynolds amounted to 80% of that production within their special field of cigarettes. . . .

The foregoing demonstrates the basis of the claim of American, Liggett and Reynolds to the title of the "Big Three." . . . Without adverse criticism of it, comparative size on this great scale inevitably increased the power of these three to dominate all phases of their industry. . . .

The verdicts show that the jury found that the petitioners conspired to fix prices and to exclude undesired competition against them in the purchase of the domestic type of flue-cured tobacco and of burley tobacco. . . .

The Government introduced evidence showing that, although there was no written or express agreement discovered among American, Liggett and Reynolds, their practices included a clear course of dealing. This evidently convinced the jury of the existence of a combination or conspiracy to fix and control prices and practices as to domestic leaf tobacco, both in restraint of trade as such, and to establish a substantially impregnable defense against any attempted intrusion by potential competitors into these markets.

It appeared that petitioners refused to purchase tobacco on these markets unless the other petitioners were also represented thereon. There were attempts made by others to open new tobacco markets but none of the petitioners would participate in them unless the other petitioners were present. Consequently, such markets were failures due to the absence of buyers. . . .

The Government presented evidence to support its claim that, before the markets opened, the petitioners placed limitations and restrictions on the prices which their buyers were permitted to pay for tobacco. . . .

. . . Competition also was eliminated between petitioners by the purchase of grades of tobacco in which but one of them was interested. To accomplish this, each company formulated the grades which it alone wished to purchase. The other companies recognized the grades so formulated as distinctive grades and did not compete for them. While the differences between the grades so formulated were distinguishable by the highly trained special buyers, they were in reality so minute as to be inconsequential. . . .

. . . Each company determined in advance what portion of the entire crop it would purchase before the market for that season opened. The petitioners then separately informed their buyers of the percentage of the crop which they wished to purchase and gave instructions that only such a percentage should be purchased on each market. The purchases were spread evenly over the different markets throughout the season. No matter what the size of the crop might be, the petitioners were able to purchase their predetermined percentages thereof within the price limits determined upon by them, thus indicating a stabilized market. . . .

At a time when the manufacturers of lower priced cigarettes were beginning to manufacture them in quantity, the petitioners commenced to make large purchases of the cheaper tobacco leaves used for the manufacture of such lower priced cigarettes. No explanation was offered as to how or where this tobacco was used by petitioners. The compositions of their respective brands of cigarettes calling for the use of more expensive tobaccos remained unchanged during this period of controversy and up to the end of the trial. The Government claimed that such purchases of cheaper tobacco evidenced a combination and a purpose among the petitioners to deprive the manufacturers of cheaper cigarettes of the tobacco necessary for their manufacture, as well as to raise the price of such tobacco to such a point that cigarettes made therefrom could not be sold at a sufficiently low price to compete with the petitioners' more highly advertised brands.

The verdicts show also that the jury found that the petitioners conspired to fix prices and to exclude undesired competition in the distribution and sale of their principal products. . . . The list prices charged and the discounts allowed by petitioners have been practically identical since 1923 and absolutely identical since 1928. Since the latter date, only seven changes have been made by the three companies and those have been identical in amount. . . .

The following record of price changes is circumstantial evidence of the existence of a conspiracy and of a power and intent to exclude competition coming from cheaper grade cigarettes. . . . On June 23, 1931, Reynolds, without previous notification or warning to the trade or public, raised the list price of Camel cigarettes, constituting its leading cigarette brand, from $6.40 to $6.85 a thousand. The same day, American increased the list price for Lucky Strike cigarettes, its leading brand, and Liggett the price for Chesterfield cigarettes, its leading brand, to the identical price of $6.85 a thousand. No economic justification for this raise was demonstrated.

Before 1931, certain smaller companies had manufactured cigarettes retailing at 10 cents a package, which was several cents lower than the retail price for the leading brands of the petitioners. Up to that time, the sales of the 10 cent cigarettes were negligible. However, after the above described increase in list prices of the petitioners in 1931, the 10 cent brands made serious inroads upon the sales of the petitioners. These cheaper brands of cigarettes were sold at a list price of $4.75 a thousand and from 1931 to 1932 the sales of these cigarettes multiplied 30 times, rising from 0.28% of the total cigarette sales of the country in June, 1931, to 22.78% in November, 1932. In response to this threat of competition from the manufacturers of the 10 cent brands, the petitioners, in January, 1933, cut the list price of their three leading brands from $6.85 to $6 a thousand. In February, they cut again to $5.50 a thousand. The evidence tends to show that this cut was directed at the competition of the 10 cent cigarettes. . . . Following the first price cut by petitioners, the sales of the 10 cent brands fell off considerably. After the second cut they fell off to a much greater extent. When the sale of the 10 cent brands had dropped from 22.78% of the total cigarette sales in November, 1932, to 6.43% in May, 1933, the petitioners, in January, 1934, raised the list price of their leading brands from $5.50 back up to $6.10 a thousand. . . . The petitioners, in 1937, again increased the list prices of their above named brands to $6.25 a thousand and in July, 1940, to $6.53 a thousand.

. . . There was evidence that when dealers received an announcement of the price increase from one of the petitioners and attempted to purchase some of the leading brands of cigarettes from the other petitioners at their unchanged prices before announcement of a similar change, the latter refused to fill such orders until their prices were also raised, thus bringing about the same result as if the changes had been precisely simultaneous. . . .

It is not the form of the combination or the particular means used but the result to be achieved that the statute condemns. It is not of importance whether the means used to accomplish the unlawful objective are in themselves lawful or unlawful. Acts done to give effect to the conspiracy may be in themselves wholly innocent acts. Yet, if they are part of the sum of the acts which are relied upon to effectuate the conspiracy which the statute forbids, they come within its prohibition. No formal agreement is necessary to constitute an unlawful conspiracy. . . . The essential combination or conspiracy in violation of the Sherman Act may be found in a course of dealing or other circumstances as well as in an exchange of words. . . . Where the circumstances are such as to warrant a jury in finding that the conspirators had a unity of purpose or a common design and understanding, or a meeting of minds in an unlawful arrangement, the conclusion that a conspiracy is established is justified. Neither proof of exertion of the power to exclude nor proof of actual exclusion of existing or potential competitors is essential to sustain a charge of monopolization under the Sherman Act.

. . . [T]he material consideration in determining whether a monopoly exists is not that prices are raised and that competition actually is excluded but that power exists to raise prices or to exclude competition when it is desired to do so. . . .

In the present cases, the petitioners have been found to have conspired to establish a monopoly and also to have the power and intent to establish and maintain the monopoly. To hold that they do not come within the prohibition of the Sherman Act would destroy the force of that Act. Accordingly, the instructions of the trial court under §2 of the Act are approved and the judgment of the Circuit Court of Appeals is

Affirmed.

Intracorporate Conspiracy and Vertical Integration

Do the decisions in *Alcoa* and *American Tobacco* suggest that the Sherman Act can be used to condemn intracorporate dealings and to attack vertical integration? The *Yellow Cab* case involves the first of these questions, and *Paramount Pictures* the second.

In the *Yellow Cab* case, a manufacturer of taxicabs had acquired control, via stock ownership, of the principal cab operating companies in Chicago, Pittsburgh, New York, and Minneapolis. These companies were then required to purchase their cabs exclusively from the manufacturer, the Checker Cab Manufacturing Corporation.

The United States charged the firms with a combination and conspiracy to restrain and to monopolize commerce in (1) the sale of taxicabs in the four cities, and (2) in the business of furnishing cab services in Chicago and vicinity. The defense argued that these were intracorporate sales within a vertically integrated firm and therefore could not be considered a conspiracy. The Supreme Court observed that a conspiracy in restraint of trade may result as readily "among those who are affiliated or integrated under common owner-ship as from a conspiracy among those who are otherwise independent." It is not the elimination of competition between a parent firm and its subsidiary, or between subsidiaries, that is condemned when common ownership exists. The harm from this type of arrangement arises because members of the corporate family are foreclosed from being customers of outside competing firms.

UNITED STATES v. YELLOW CAB CO. et al.

332 U.S. 218 (1947)

MR. JUSTICE MURPHY delivered the opinion of the Court.

The United States filed a complaint in the federal district court below pursuant to §4 of the Sherman Anti-Trust Act . . . to prevent and restrain the appellees from violating §§1 and 2 of the Act. The complaint alleged that the appellees have been and are engaged in a combination and conspiracy to restrain and to monopolize interstate trade and commerce (1) in the sale of motor vehicles for use as taxicabs to the principal cab operating companies in Chicago, Pittsburgh, New York City and Minne-apolis, and (2) in the business of furnishing cab services for hire in Chicago and vicinity. . . .

It is said that the appellees have agreed to control the operation and purchase of taxicabs by the principal operating companies in Chicago, New York City, Pittsburgh and Minneapolis, insisting that they purchase their cabs exclusively from CCM.[4] This excludes all other manufacturers of taxicabs from 86% of the Chicago market, 15% of the New York City market, 100% of the Pittsburgh market and 58% of the Minneapolis market. At the same time, the trade of the controlled cab companies is restrained since they are prevented from purchasing cabs from manufac-turers other than CCM. The result allegedly is that these companies must pay more for cabs than they would otherwise pay, their other expenditures are increased unnecessarily, and the public is charged high rates for the transportation services rendered.

The commerce which is asserted to be restrained in this manner has a character that is undeniably interstate. The various cab operating com-panies do business in Illinois, New York, Pennsylvania and Minnesota. By virtue of the conspiracy, they must purchase all of their cabs from CCM.

---

4 Checker Cab Manufacturing Corp.

Since CCM's factory is located in Michigan, interstate sales and shipments are inevitable if the conspiracy is to be effectuated. The conspiracy also prevents those operating companies from purchasing cabs from other manufacturers, thus precluding all interstate sales and shipments between each individual cab operating company and manufacturers (other than CCM) located in other states. Interstate trade, in short, is of the very essence of this aspect of the conspiracy.

But the amount of interstate trade thus affected by the conspiracy is immaterial in determining whether a violation of the Sherman Act has been charged in the complaint. Section 1 of the Act outlaws unreasonable restraints on interstate commerce, regardless of the amount of the commerce affected. . . . And §2 of the Act makes it unlawful to conspire to monopolize "any part" of interstate commerce, without specifying how large a part must be affected. Hence it is enough if some appreciable part of interstate commerce is the subject of a monopoly, a restraint or a conspiracy. The complaint in this case deals with interstate purchases of replacements of some 5,000 licensed taxicabs in four cities. That is an appreciable amount of commerce under any standard. . . .

Likewise irrelevant is the importance of the interstate commerce affected in relation to the entire amount of that type of commerce in the United States. The Sherman Act is concerned with more than the large, nation-wide obstacles in the channels of interstate trade. It is designed to sweep away all appreciable obstructions so that the statutory policy of free trade might be effectively achieved. . . . It follows that the complaint in this case is not defective for failure to allege that CCM has a monopoly with reference to the total number of taxicabs manufactured and sold in the United States. Its relative position in the field of cab production has no necessary relation to the ability of the appellees to conspire to monopolize or restrain, in violation of the Act, an appreciable segment of interstate cab sales. . . .

Nor can it be doubted that combinations and conspiracies of the type alleged in this case fall within the ban of the Sherman Act. By excluding all cab manufacturers other than CCM from that part of the market represented by the cab operating companies under their control, the appellees effectively limit the outlets through which cabs may be sold in interstate commerce. . . . In addition, by preventing the cab operating companies under their control from purchasing cabs from manufacturers other than CCM, the appellees deny those companies the opportunity to purchase cabs in a free, competitive market. . . .

The fact that these restraints occur in a setting described by the appellees as a vertically integrated enterprise does not necessarily remove the ban of the Sherman Act. The test of illegality under the Act is the presence or absence of an unreasonable restraint on interstate commerce.

Such a restraint may result as readily from a conspiracy among those who are affiliated or integrated under common ownership as from a conspiracy among those who are otherwise independent. Similarly, any affiliation or integration flowing from an illegal conspiracy cannot insulate the conspirators from the sanctions which Congress has imposed. The corporate interrelationships of the conspirators, in other words, are not determinative of the applicability of the Sherman Act. That statute is aimed at substance rather than form. . . .

And so in this case, the common ownership and control of the various corporate appellees are impotent to liberate the alleged combination and conspiracy from the impact of the Act. . . .

. . . The complaint points out the well-known fact that Chicago is the terminus of a large number of railroads engaged in interstate passenger traffic and that a great majority of the persons making interstate railroad trips which carry them through Chicago must disembark from a train at one railroad station, travel from that station to another some two blocks to two miles distant, and board another train at the latter station. The railroads often contract with the passengers to supply between-station transportation in Chicago. Parmelee then contracts with the railroads and the railroad terminal associations to provide this transportation by special cabs carrying seven to ten passengers. Parmelee's contracts are exclusive in nature.

[The complaint alleged that Yellow and Cab Sales had agreed not to compete with Parmelee for these contracts.]

The transportation of such passengers and their luggage between stations in Chicago is clearly a part of the stream of interstate commerce. When persons or goods move from a point of origin in one state to a point of destination in another, the fact that a part of that journey consists of transportation by an independent agency solely within the boundaries of one state does not make that portion of the trip any less interstate in character. . . .

. . . Only Parmelee is free to attempt to procure such contracts; Yellow and Cab Sales are forbidden to compete for such contracts, despite the fact that they conceivably might provide the same transportation service at lower cost to the railroads. The complaint accordingly states a violation of the Sherman Act in this respect.

Finally, it is said that the appellees have conspired to control the principal taxicab operating companies in Chicago and to exclude others from engaging in the transportation of interstate travelers to and from Chicago railroad stations. . . .

The interstate commerce toward which this aspect of the conspiracy is directed is claimed to arise out of the following facts. Many persons are said to embark upon interstate journeys from their homes, offices and hotels in Chicago by using taxicabs to transport themselves and their luggage to railroad stations in Chicago. Conversely, in making journeys from other states to homes, offices and hotels in Chicago, many persons are said to complete such trips by using taxicabs to transport themselves and their luggage from railroad stations in Chicago to said homes, offices and hotels. Such transportation of persons and their luggage is intermingled with the admittedly local operations of the Chicago taxicabs. But it is that allegedly interstate part of the business upon which rests the validity of the complaint in this particular.

We hold, however, that such transportation is too unrelated to inter-state commerce to constitute a part thereof within the meaning of the Sherman Act. These taxicabs, in transporting passengers and their luggage to and from Chicago railroad stations, admittedly cross no state lines; by ordinance, their service is confined to transportation "between any two points within the corporate limits of the city." None of them serves only railroad passengers, all of them being required to serve "every person" within the limits of Chicago. They have no contractual or other arrange-ment with the interstate railroads. Nor are their fares paid or collected as part of the railroad fares. In short, their relationship to interstate transit is only casual and incidental.

. . . [T]he complaint does state a cause of action under the Act, entitling the United States to a trial on the merits. Since the portion of the complaint [dealing with the alleged exclusion of others from transporting interstate travelers to and from Chicago railroad stations] is defective, appropriate steps should be taken to delete the charges in relation thereto. With that understanding, we reverse the judgment of the District Court and remand the case for further proceedings consistent with this opinion.

Reversed.

In *Paramount Pictures* the government charged that vertical integration was illegal under the Sherman Act. The case was brought against the five major motion picture producers and resulted in one of the largest divestiture decrees ever handed down by the Court.

The five defendants were engaged in producing and distributing motion pictures. They also had control over the exhibition of the films via operation of first-run theaters in major cities and through ownership of a chain of smaller theaters throughout the country. By virtue of this vertical integration, the defendants used their command over the exhibition of films to favor their own houses to the disadvantage of independent producers and exhibitors. Among other things, the smaller exhibitors had to agree to "block booking," charge minimum admission prices, and have extended time intervals between runs of the films.

The Supreme Court said that vertical integration as such is not in violation of the Sherman Act. In determining the legality of the vertical integration, it is essential to define properly the market to be served and the leverage on that market created by the vertical integration. Whereas the lower court found no monopoly power because the market was defined as all motion picture theaters in the country, the Supreme Court indicated the relevant market to be the "first-run" theaters. When defined in this manner, the major producer-distributors controlled nearly two-thirds of the market. Next, the Court considered the purpose or intent of the vertical integration. ". . . the fact that the power created by size was utilized in the past to crush or prevent competition is potent evidence that the requisite purpose or intent attend the presence of monopoly power."

In this case vertical integration was found illegal, although the Court was careful to point out that vertical integration was not to be considered a *per se* violation. The final resolution was to require that the production of motion pictures be separated from distribution and exhibition. By 1952 this divestiture order had been carried out. Separating the two functions of distribution and exhibition of films did not involve any loss of efficiency (that is, higher production costs) for the firms.

UNITED STATES v. PARAMOUNT PICTURES, INC. et al.

334 U.S. 131 (1948)

MR. JUSTICE DOUGLAS delivered the opinion of the Court. . . .

The suit was instituted by the United States under §4 of the Sherman Act to prevent and restrain violations of it. The defendants fall into three groups: (1) Paramount Pictures, Inc., Loew's, Incorporated, Radio-Keith-Orpheum Corporation, Warner Bros. Pictures, Inc., Twentieth Century–Fox Film Corporation, which produce motion pictures, and their respective subsidiaries or affiliates which distribute and exhibit films. These are known as the five major defendants or exhibitor-defendants. (2) Columbia Pictures Corporation and Universal Corporation, which produce motion pictures, and their subsidiaries which distribute films. (3) United Artists Corporation, which is engaged only in the distribution of motion pictures. The five majors, through their subsidiaries or affiliates, own or control theatres; the other defendants do not.

The complaint charged that the producer defendants had attempted to monopolize and had monopolized the production of motion pictures. The District Court found to the contrary and that finding is not challenged here. The complaint charged that all the defendants, as distributors, had conspired to restrain and monopolize and had restrained and monopolized interstate trade in the distribution and exhibition of films by specific practices which we will shortly relate. It also charged that the five major defendants had engaged in a conspiracy to restrain and monopolize, and had restrained and monopolized, interstate trade in the exhibition of motion pictures in most of the larger cities of the country. It charged that the vertical combination of producing, distributing, and exhibiting motion pictures by each of the five major defendants violated §1 and §2 of the Act. It charged that each distributor-defendant had entered into various contracts with exhibitors which unreasonably restrained trade. . . .

First. Restraint of Trade

(1) PRICE FIXING No film is sold to an exhibitor in the distribution of motion pictures. The right to exhibit under copyright is licensed. The District Court found that the defendants in the licenses they issued fixed minimum admission prices which the exhibitors agreed to charge, whether the rental of the film was a flat amount or a percentage of the receipts. It found that substantially uniform minimum prices had been established in the licenses of all defendants. . . .

The District Court found that two price-fixing conspiracies existed— a horizontal one between all the defendants; a vertical one between each distributor-defendant and its licensees. . . .

We start, of course, from the premise that so far as the Sherman Act is concerned, a price-fixing combination is illegal *per se*. . . .

(2) CLEARANCES AND RUNS Clearances are designed to protect a particular run of a film against a subsequent run. The District Court found that all of the distributor-defendants used clearance provisions and that they were stated in several different ways or in combinations: in terms of a given period between designated runs; in terms of admission prices charged by competing theatres; in terms of a given period of clearance over specifically named theatres; in terms of so many days' clearance over specified areas or towns; or in terms of clearances as fixed by other distributors.

The District Court enjoined defendants and their affiliates from agreeing with each other or with any exhibitors or distributors to maintain a system of clearances, or from granting any clearance between theatres not in substantial competition, or from granting or enforcing any clearance against theatres in substantial competition with the theatre receiving the license for exhibition in excess of what is reasonably necessary to protect the licensee in the run granted. In view of the findings this relief was plainly warranted. . . .

(3) POOLING AGREEMENTS; JOINT OWNERSHIP   The District Court found the exhibitor-defendants had agreements with each other and their affiliates by which theatres of two or more of them, normally competitive, were operated as a unit, or managed by a joint committee or by one of the exhibitors, the profits being shared according to prearranged percentages. Some of these agreements provided that the parties might not acquire other competitive theatres without first offering them for inclusion in the pool. The court concluded that the result of these agreements was to eliminate competition *pro tanto* both in exhibition and in distribution of features, since the parties would naturally direct the films to the theatres in whose earnings they were interested.

. . . The District Court required the dissolution of existing pooling agreements and enjoined any future arrangement of that character.

These provisions of the decree will stand. The practices were bald efforts to substitute monopoly for competition and to strengthen the hold of the exhibitor-defendants on the industry by alignment of competitors on their side. Clearer restraints of trade are difficult to imagine. . . .

(4) FORMULA DEALS, MASTER AGREEMENTS, AND FRANCHISES   A formula deal is a licensing agreement with a circuit of theatres in which the license fee of a given feature is measured, for the theatres covered by the agreement, by a specified percentage of the feature's national gross. The District Court found that Paramount and RKO had made formula deals with independent and affiliated circuits. . . . The inclusion of theatres of a circuit into a single agreement gives no opportunity for other theatre owners to bid for the feature in their respective areas . . .

. . . The formula deals and master agreements are unlawful restraints of trade in two respects. In the first place, they eliminate the possibility of bidding for films theatre by theatre. In that way they eliminate the opportunity for the small competitor to obtain the choice first runs, and put a premium on the size of the circuit. They are, therefore, devices for stifling competition and diverting the cream of the business to the large operators. In the second place, the pooling of the purchasing power of an entire circuit in bidding for films is a misuse of monopoly power . . .

(5) BLOCK-BOOKING   Block-booking is the practice of licensing, or offering for license, one feature or group of features on condition that the

exhibitor will also license another feature or group of features released by the distributors during a given period. . . . Block-booking prevents competitors from bidding for single features on their individual merits. . . . The court enjoined defendants from performing or entering into any license in which the right to exhibit one feature is conditioned upon the licensee's taking one or more other features.

We approve that restriction. . . .

(6) DISCRIMINATION   The District Court found that defendants had discriminated against small independent exhibitors and in favor of large affiliated and unaffiliated circuits through various kinds of contract provisions. . . . [T]he competitive advantages of these provisions were so great that their inclusion in contracts with the larger circuits and their exclusion from contracts with the small independents constituted an unreasonable discrimination against the latter. . . .

SECOND. COMPETITIVE BIDDING

The District Court concluded that the only way competition could be introduced into the existing system of fixed prices, clearances and runs was to require that films be licensed on a competitive bidding basis. . . .

. . . But we do not see how, in practical operation, the proposed system of competitive bidding is likely to open up to competition the markets which defendants' unlawful restraints have dominated. Rather real danger seems to us to lie in the opportunities the system affords the exhibitor-defendants and the other large operators to strengthen their hold in the industry. . . . the provisions for competitive bidding. . . . promise little in the way of relief against the real evils of the conspiracy. They implicate the judiciary heavily in the details of business management if supervision is to be effective. They vest powerful control in the exhibitor-defendants over their competitors if close supervision by the court is not undertaken. In light of these considerations we conclude that the competitive bidding provisions of the decree should be eliminated so that a more effective decree may be fashioned. . . .

THIRD. MONOPOLY, EXPANSION OF THEATRE HOLDINGS, DIVESTITURE

. . . [T]he Department of Justice argues vertical integration of producing, distributing and exhibiting motion pictures is illegal *per se*. But the majority of the Court does not take that view. In the opinion of the majority the legality of vertical integration under the Sherman Act turns on (1) the purpose or intent with which it was conceived, or (2) the power it creates and the attendant purpose or intent. First, it runs afoul of the Sherman Act if it was a calculated scheme to gain control over an appreciable segment of the market and to restrain or suppress competition, rather than an expansion to meet legitimate business needs. . . .

Second, a vertically integrated enterprise, like other aggregations of business units . . . will constitute monopoly which, though unexercised, violates the Sherman Act provided a power to exclude competition is coupled with a purpose or intent to do so. . . . And the fact that the power created by size was utilized in the past to crush or prevent competition is potent evidence that the requisite purpose or intent attends the presence of monopoly power. . . . Likewise bearing on the question whether monopoly power is created by the vertical integration, is the nature of the market to be served . . . and the leverage on the market which the particular vertical integration creates or makes possible. . . .

These matters were not considered by the District Court. . . .

The judgment in these cases is affirmed in part and reversed in part, and the cases are remanded to the District Court for proceedings in conformity with this opinion.

So ordered.

Relevant Market for Monopoly Power

In the antitrust cases presented thus far, definition of the *relevant market* was not a pivotal issue in reaching the final verdict. However, in the 1956 *du Pont* case, delineation of the relevant market in which the alleged monopolization had occurred was the most important issue in the decision.

For a number of years the du Pont Company had been the major producer of cellophane in this country, accounting for about 75 per cent of the market during the period in question. Accordingly, in 1947 the Justice Department charged du Pont with monopolizing the market for cellophane. The defense contended that cellophane was not the correct market definition since cellophane was only one of several flexible packaging materials. The relevant market, they argued, should be defined as one encompassing all flexible packaging materials. When the latter market definition was considered, cellophane constituted less than 20 per cent of the total. If the narrow definition—cellophane only—were used, du Pont would be much more likely to be found guilty; if the broad definition were accepted, obviously du Pont would not have a monopoly.

The lower court ruled in favor of the broad definition and, in a 4–3 decision, the Supreme Court upheld this position. The High Court noted that possession of monopoly power means the power to control prices or restrict competition. On the other hand, determination of the relevant competitive market for commodities depends upon their interchangeability, to what extent one can be substituted for another. It does not mean, however, that products must be completely fungible to be considered in the same market. Where there are alternatives that buyers can readily select, it is not proper to say that a product is monopolized merely because it differs from others. Since cellophane is interchangeable with numerous other flexible packaging materials for a number of uses, it should be considered part of the broad market for all flexible packaging materials. Furthermore, just because the price of cellophane was from two to seven times higher than other materials did not mean that du Pont had monopoly control over price or that the other materials were noncompetitors.

Chief Justice Warren, in a dissenting opinion, criticized the majority for failing to give proper consideration to du Pont's discretion over price. He noted that it is difficult to believe that practical businessmen "would have bought cellophane in increasing amounts over a quarter of a century if close substitutes were available at from one-seventh to one-half cellophane's price. That they did so is testimony to cellophane's distinctiveness." Thus the dissent argued for a narrow definition of the market. The position of the dissent prevailed the next year when the *du Pont—General Motors* case came before the Court.[5]

UNITED STATES v. E. I. du PONT de NEMOURS & CO.

351 U.S. 377 (1956)

MR. JUSTICE REED delivered the opinion of the Court.

The United States brought this civil action under §4 of the Sherman Act against E. I. du Pont de Nemours and Company. The complaint, filed December 13, 1947, in the United States District Court for the District of Columbia, charged du Pont with monopolizing, attempting to monopolize and conspiracy to monopolize interstate commerce in cellophane and cellulosic caps and bands in violation of §2 of the Sherman Act. . . .

During the period that is relevant to this action, du Pont produced almost 75% of the cellophane sold in the United States, and cellophane constituted less than 20% of all "flexible packaging material" sales. . . .

[5] See Chapter 3, *U.S. v. E. I. du Pont de Nemours & Co.*, 353 U.S. 586.

The Government contends that, by so dominating cellophane production, du Pont monopolized a "part of the trade or commerce" in violation of §2. Respondent agrees that cellophane is a product which constitutes "a 'part' of commerce within the meaning of Section 2." . . . But it contends that the prohibition of §2 against monopolization is not violated because it does not have the power to control the price of cellophane or to exclude competitors from the market in which cellophane is sold. The court below found that the "relevant market for determining the extent of du Pont's market control is the market for flexible packaging materials," and that competition from those other materials prevented du Pont from possessing monopoly powers in its sales of cellophane.

The Government asserts that cellophane and other wrapping materials are neither substantially fungible nor like priced. For these reasons, it argues that the market for other wrappings is distinct from the market for cellophane and that the competition afforded cellophane by other wrappings is not strong enough to be considered in determining whether du Pont has monopoly powers. Market delimitation is necessary under du Pont's theory to determine whether an alleged monopolist violates §2. The ultimate consideration in such a determination is whether the defendants control the price and competition in the market for such part of trade or commerce as they are charged with monopolizing. Every manufacturer is the sole producer of the particular commodity it makes but its control in the above sense of the relevant market depends upon the availability of alternative commodities for buyers: *i.e.*, whether there is a cross-elasticity of demand between cellophane and the other wrappings. This interchangeability is largely gauged by the purchase of competing products for similar uses considering the price, characteristics and adaptability of the competing commodities. The court below found that the flexible wrappings afforded such alternatives. This Court must determine whether the trial court erred in its estimate of the competition afforded cellophane by other materials. . . .

Two additional questions were raised in the record and decided by the court below. That court found that, even if du Pont did possess monopoly power over sales of cellophane, it was not subject to Sherman Act prosecution, because (1) the acquisition of that power was protected by patents, and (2) that power was acquired solely through du Pont's business expertness. It was thrust upon du Pont. . . .

The Sherman Act and the Courts

The Sherman Act has received long and careful application by this Court to achieve for the Nation the freedom of enterprise from monopoly or restraint envisaged by the Congress that passed the Act in 1890. Because the Act is couched in broad terms, it is adaptable to the changing types of commercial production and distribution that have evolved since its passage. . . .

Judicial construction of antitrust legislation has generally been left unchanged by Congress. This is true of the Rule of Reason. While it is fair to say that the Rule is imprecise, its application in Sherman Act litigation, as directed against enhancement of price or throttling of competition, has given a workable content to antitrust legislation. . . .

. . . It is true that Congress has made exceptions to the generality of monopoly prohibitions, exceptions that spring from the necessities or conveniences of certain industries or business organizations, or from the characteristics of the members of certain groups of citizens. . . . They modify the reach of the Sherman Act but do not change its prohibition of other monopolies. We therefore turn to §2 to determine whether du Pont has violated that section by its dominance in the manufacture of cellophane in the before-stated circumstances.

The Sherman Act, §2—Monopolization

. . . Our cases determine that a party has monopoly power if it has, over "any part of the trade or commerce among the several States," a power of controlling prices or unreasonably restricting competition. . . .

If cellophane is the "market" that du Pont is found to dominate, it may be assumed it does have monopoly power over that "market." Monopoly power is the power to control prices or exclude competition. It seems apparent that du Pont's power to set the price of cellophane has been limited only by the competition afforded by other flexible packaging materials. Moreover, it may be practically impossible for anyone to commence manufacturing cellophane without full access to du Pont's technique. However, du Pont has no power to prevent competition from other wrapping materials. The trial court consequently had to determine whether competition from the other wrappings prevented du Pont from possessing monopoly power in violation of §2. Price and competition are so intimately entwined that any discussion of theory must treat them as one. It is inconceivable that price could be controlled without power over competition or vice versa. This approach to the determination of monopoly power is strengthened by this Court's conclusion in prior cases that, when an alleged monopolist has power over price and competition, an intention to monopolize in a proper case may be assumed. . . .

Determination of the competitive market for commodities depends on how different from one another are the offered commodities in character or use, how far buyers will go to substitute one commodity for another. . . . Whatever the market may be, we hold that control of price or competition establishes the existence of monopoly power under §2. Section 2 requires the application of a reasonable approach in determining the existence of monopoly power just as surely as did §1. This of course does not mean that there can be a reasonable monopoly. . . . Our next step is to determine whether du Pont has monopoly power over cellophane: that is, power over its price in relation to or competition with other commodities. The charge was monopolization of cellophane. The defense, that cellophane was merely a part of the relevant market for flexible packaging materials.

The Relevant Market

When a product is controlled by one interest, without substitutes available in the market, there is monopoly power. Because most products have possible substitutes, we cannot . . . give "that infinite range" to the definition of substitutes. Nor is it a proper interpretation of the Sherman Act to require that products be fungible to be considered in the relevant market. . . .

But where there are market alternatives that buyers may readily use for their purposes, illegal monopoly does not exist merely because the product said to be monopolized differs from others. If it were not so, only physically identical products would be a part of the market. To accept the Government's argument, we would have to conclude that the manufacturers of plain as well as moistureproof cellophane were monopolists, and so with films such as Pliofilm, foil, glassine, polyethylene, and Saran, for each of these wrapping materials is distinguishable. These were all exhibits in the case. New wrappings appear, generally similar to cellophane: is each a monopoly? What is called for is an appraisal of the "cross-elasticity" of demand in the trade. . . . In considering what is the relevant market for determining the control of price and competition, no more definite rule can be declared than that commodities reasonably interchangeable by consumers for the same purposes make up that "part of the trade or commerce," monopolization of which may be illegal. . . .

. . . In determining the market under the Sherman Act, it is the use or uses to which the commodity is put that control. The selling price between commodities with similar uses and different characteristics may vary, so that the cheaper product can drive out the more expensive. Or, the superior quality of higher priced articles may make dominant the more desirable. Cellophane costs more than many competing products and less than a few. But whatever the price, there are various flexible wrapping materials that are bought by manufacturers for packaging their goods in their own plants or are sold to converters who shape and print them for use in the packaging of the commodities to be wrapped. . . .

It may be admitted that cellophane combines the desirable elements of transparency, strength and cheapness more definitely than any of the others. . . .

But, despite cellophane's advantages, it has to meet competition from other materials in every one of its uses. Cellophane's principal uses are analyzed . . . Food products are the chief outlet, with cigarettes next. The Government makes no challenge . . . that cellophane furnishes less than 7% of wrappings for bakery products, 25% for candy, 32% for snacks, 35% for meats and poultry, 27% for crackers and biscuits, 47% for fresh produce, and 34% for frozen foods. Seventy-five to eighty percent of cigarettes are wrapped in cellophane. . . . Thus, cellophane shares the packaging market with others. The over-all result is that cellophane accounts for 17.9% of flexible wrapping materials, measured by the wrapping surface. . . .

An element for consideration as to cross-elasticity of demand between products is the responsiveness of the sales of one product to price changes of the other. If a slight decrease in the price of cellophane causes a considerable number of customers of other flexible wrappings to switch to cellophane, it would be an indication that a high cross-elasticity of demand exists between them; that the products compete in the same market. The court below held that the "[g]reat sensitivity of customers in the flexible packaging markets to price or quality changes" prevented du Pont from possessing monopoly control over price. . . .

We conclude that cellophane's interchangeability with the other materials mentioned suffices to make it a part of this flexible packaging material market.

The Government stresses the fact that the variation in price between cellophane and other materials demonstrates they are noncompetitive. . . . Different producers need different qualities in wrappings and their need may vary from time to time as their products undergo change. But the necessity for flexible wrappings is the central and unchanging demand. We cannot say that these differences in cost gave du Pont monopoly power over prices in view of the findings of fact on that subject. . . .

The facts above considered dispose also of any contention that competitors have been excluded by du Pont from the packaging material market. That market has many producers and there is no proof du Pont ever has possessed power to exclude any of them from the rapidly expanding flexible packaging market. . . .

The "market" which one must study to determine when a producer has monopoly power will vary with the part of commerce under consideration. The tests are constant. That market is composed of products that have reasonable interchangeability for the purposes for which they are produced—price, use and qualities considered. While the application of the tests remains uncertain, it seems to us that du Pont should not be found to monopolize cellophane when that product has the competition and interchangeability with other wrappings that this record shows.

On the findings of the District Court, its judgment is

Affirmed.

MR. CHIEF JUSTICE WARREN, with whom MR. JUSTICE BLACK and MR. JUSTICE DOUGLAS join, dissenting.

This case, like many under the Sherman Act, turns upon the proper definition of the market. In defining the market in which du Pont's economic power is to be measured, the majority virtually emasculate §2 of the Sherman Act. They admit that "cellophane combines the desirable elements of transparency, strength and cheapness more definitely than any of" a host of other packaging materials. Yet they hold that all of those materials are so indistinguishable from cellophane as to warrant their inclusion in the market. We cannot agree that cellophane . . . is the "selfsame product" [as the others].

If the conduct of buyers indicated that glassine, waxed and sulphite papers and aluminum foil were actually "the selfsame products" as cellophane, the qualitative differences demonstrated by the comparison of physical properties . . . would not be conclusive. But the record provides convincing proof that businessmen did not so regard these products. . . . We cannot believe that buyers, practical businessmen, would have bought cellophane in increasing amounts over a quarter of a century if close substitutes were available at from one-seventh to one-half cellophane's price. That they did so is testimony to cellophane's distinctiveness. . . .

Certainly du Pont itself shared our view. From the first, du Pont recognized that it need not concern itself with competition from other packaging materials. For example, when du Pont was contemplating entry into cellophane production, its Development Department reported that glassine "is so inferior that it belongs in an entirely different class and has hardly to be considered as a competitor of cellophane." . . .

The majority opinion purports to reject the theory of "interindustry competition." Brick, steel, wood, cement and stone, it says, are "too different" to be placed in the same market. But cellophane, glassine, wax papers, sulphite papers, greaseproof and vegetable parchment papers, aluminum foil, cellulose acetate, Pliofilm and other films are not "too different," the opinion concludes. The majority approach would apparently enable a monopolist of motion picture exhibition to avoid Sherman Act consequences by showing that motion pictures compete in substantial measure with legitimate theater, television, radio, sporting events and other forms of entertainment.

The foregoing analysis of the record shows conclusively that cellophane is the relevant market. Since du Pont has the lion's share of that market, it must have monopoly power, as the majority concede. This being so, we think it clear that, in the circumstances of this case, du Pont is guilty of "monopolization." The briefest sketch of du Pont's business history precludes it from falling within the "exception to the Sherman Act prohibitions of monopoly power" . . . by successfully asserting that monopoly was "thrust upon" it. Du Pont was not "the passive beneficiary of a monopoly" within the meaning of United States v. Aluminum Co. of America . . . It sought and maintained dominance through illegal agreements dividing the world market, concealing and suppressing technological information, and restricting its licensee's production by prohibitive royalties . . . The public should not be left to rely upon the dispensations of management in order to obtain the benefits which normally accompany competition. Such beneficence is of uncertain tenure. Only actual competition can assure long-run enjoyment of the goals of a free economy. . . .

3

Mergers under the Original Section 7

In recent years mergers of business firms have raised the most important antitrust issues for the courts to settle. Such was not always the case before the Celler-Kefauver Amendment to Section 7 of the Clayton Act. The Sherman Act, of course, has always been applicable to mergers but here the required proof was much greater. A merger must have involved a clear restraint of trade or have produced a monopoly position for the merging firms. Furthermore, the Sherman Act does not have any preventive power; its corrective power can deal with restraint of trade or monopoly only as an accomplished fact.

As originally passed, Section 7 of the Clayton Act was intended to supplement the Sherman Act by incorporating certain preventive measures before monopoly power was fully developed. The test for illegality was to be less stringent; all that was required was the showing of a substantial lessening of competition or a tendency to create a monopoly. The original wording of the key parts of Section 7 was as follows:

> That no corporation engaged in commerce shall acquire, directly or indirectly, the whole or any part of the stock or other share capital of another corporation engaged also in commerce, where the effect of such acquisition may be to substantially lessen competition between the corporation whose stock is so acquired and the corporation making the acquisition, or to restrain such commerce in any section or community, or tend to create a monopoly of any line of commerce.

> No corporation shall acquire, directly or indirectly, the whole or any part of the stock or other share capital of two or more corporations engaged in commerce where the effect of such acquisition, or the use of such stock by the voting or granting of proxies or otherwise, may be to substantially lessen competition between such corporations, or any of them, whose stock or other share capital is so acquired, or to restrain such commerce in any section or community, or tend to create a monopoly of any line of commerce.

Although the language of this section appears to be very inclusive, cases presented in this chapter will point out its ineffectiveness in preventing mergers. First, the Act was not applicable to *asset* acquisition. Before passage, most important mergers had been carried out via the *stock* acquisition route; therefore, it was not considered essential to include those rare mergers performed by asset acquisition. The law also prohibited a company from purchasing stock in two or more competitors when such acquisition would tend to substantially lessen competition, but again saying nothing about asset acquisition. Second, the Act was intended to include only horizontal mergers. A large number of mergers had occurred in previous years that were vertical in nature, but the framers felt that vertical merging would not represent a threat to competition.

The Asset Loophole

In 1926 the Supreme Court rendered decisions in two cases that served to point out the asset loophole in Section 7. The Court ruled in favor of Thatcher Manufacturing Company in one case and Swift & Company in the other, both cases involving almost identical circumstances.

Both Thatcher and Swift had acquired stock in competing firms to bring about a horizontal merger. Before the Federal Trade Commission instituted proceedings to seek divestiture of the stock, control of the stock was used to purchase the assets of the competing firms, thereby converting the merger from a stock acquisition into an asset acquisition. The Supreme Court ruled (5–4) that the FTC was powerless in this situation, even though the purchase of the assets had been carried out by means of an illegal stock acquisition. This ruling meant that Section 7 was applicable only in the case of pure stock mergers, resulting in a convenient loophole for any firm that might be challenged on its stock merger.

THATCHER MANUFACTURING COMPANY v. FEDERAL TRADE COMMISSION
SWIFT & COMPANY v. FEDERAL TRADE COMMISSION

272 U.S. 554 (1926)

CERTIORARI . . . to review decrees of the Circuit Court of Appeals in proceedings taken in that court under the Federal Trade Commission and Clayton Acts.

No. 213 was a petition by the Commission to the court below, to enforce [an] order against Thatcher Manufacturing Company [requiring the company to divest itself of stock of a competing company]. The decree of the court below is here reversed, in so far as it sustained the order.[1]

No. 231 was a petition by Swift & Company to review a similar order. The decree of the court below sustaining the order is here reversed.

[1] All the footnotes and most of the citations from the opinions of the Court have been omitted from the cases in this chapter.

MR. JUSTICE McREYNOLDS delivered the opinion of the Court. . . .

No. 213. The Commission entered complaint against the petitioner, March 1, 1921, and charged that the latter contrary to §7 of the Clayton Act, first acquired the stock of four competing corporations—Lockport Glass Company, Essex Glass Company, Travis Glass Company and Woodbury Glass Company—and thereafter took transfers of all the business and assets of the first three and caused their dissolution . . . the Commission ruled that the acquisitions of all these stocks were unlawful and ordered the petitioner to cease and desist from ownership, operation, management and control of the assets, properties, rights, etc., of the Lockport, Essex and Travis Glass companies secured through such stock ownership, and to divest itself of the assets, properties, rights, etc., formerly held by them. Also, that it should divest itself of the stock of the Woodbury Glass Company.

The court below held that the last-named company was not in competition with petitioner within the meaning of the statute and modified the order accordingly. Therein we agree and to that extent affirm its decree.

The court further ruled, in effect, that as the stocks of the remaining three companies were unlawfully obtained and ownership of the assets came through them, the Commission properly ordered the holder so to dispossess itself of the properties as to restore prior lawful conditions. With this we cannot agree. When the Commission institutes a proceeding based upon the holding of stock contrary to §7 of the Clayton Act, its power is limited by §11 to an order requiring the guilty person to cease and desist from such violation, effectually to divest itself of the stock, and to make no further use of it. The Act has no application to ownership of a competitor's property and business obtained prior to any action by the Commission, even though this was brought about through stock unlawfully held. The purpose of the Act was to prevent continued holding of stock and the peculiar evils incident thereto. If purchase of property has produced an unlawful status a remedy is provided through the courts [under other statutes]. The Commission is without authority under such circumstances.

Affirmed in part; reversed in part.

No. 231. A complaint against petitioner, filed November 24, 1919, charged that in 1917 and 1918 it had unlawfully obtained stock in two competing companies—Moultrie Packing Company and Andalusia Packing Company—and, thereafter, through the use of this, obtained title to their business and physical property. The findings support the charge. The Commission ordered—

That respondent, Swift & Company, within six calendar months from and after the date of the service of a copy of this order upon it, shall:

(1) Cease and desist from further violating Section 7 of the Clayton Act by continuing to own or hold, either directly or indirectly, by itself or by any one for its use and benefit, any of the capital stock of the Moultrie Packing Company and of the Andalusia Packing Company . . .

(2) . . . divest itself of all capital stocks heretofore acquired by respondent, including all the fruits of such acquisitions, in whatever form they now are . . .

(3) In so divesting itself of such capital stocks respondent shall not sell or transfer, either directly or indirectly, any of such capital stocks to any officer, director, stockholder, employe or agent of respondent, or to any person under the control of respondent, or to any partnership or corporation either directly or indirectly owned or controlled by respondent.

The court below denied a petition for review and the matter is here by certiorari. As all property and business of the two competing companies were acquired by the petitioner prior to the filing of the complaint, it is evident that no practical relief could be obtained through an order merely directing petitioner to divest itself of valueless stock. As stated in number 213, we are of opinion that under §§7 and 11 of the Clayton Act the Commission is without authority to require one who has secured actual title and possession of physical property before proceedings were begun against it to dispose of the same, although secured through an unlawful purchase of stock. The courts must administer whatever remedy there may be in such situation. The order of the Commission should have been reviewed and set aside; and judgment to that effect will be entered here.

Reversed.

MR. JUSTICE BRANDEIS, dissenting in part.

In my opinion, the purpose of §7 of the Clayton Act was not, as stated by the Court, merely "to prevent continued holding of the stock and the peculiar evils incident thereto." It was also to prevent the peculiar evils resulting therefrom. The institution of a proceeding before the Commission under §7 does not operate, like an injunction, to restrain a company from acquiring the assets of the controlled corporation by means of the stock held in violation of that section. If, in spite of the commencement of such a proceeding, the company took a transfer of the assets, the Commission could, I assume, require a retransfer of the assets, so as to render effective the order of divestiture of the stock. I see no reason why it should not, likewise, do this although the company succeeded in securing the assets of the controlled corporation before the Commission instituted a proceeding. Support for this conclusion may be found in §11, which provides for action by the Commission whenever it "shall have reason to believe that any person is violating *or has violated* any of the provisions" of the earlier sections. (Italics ours.)

I think that the decrees in Nos. 213 and 231 should be affirmed.

The CHIEF JUSTICE, MR. JUSTICE HOLMES and MR. JUSTICE STONE join in this dissent.

The interpretation of Section 7 contained in the two preceding cases emasculated the Act's power to prevent monopolistic mergers when one firm purchased the assets of a competitor. In the case of *Arrow-Hart & Hegeman Electric Co.*, the Act proved equally ineffective in preventing a holding company from acquiring control of two firms that were competitors. In this case the holding company purchased the stock of the two competing firms. The Federal Trade Commission instituted proceedings, charging violation of Section 7. After commencement of these proceedings, a reorganization was effected that dissolved the holding company. The assets of the former competitors were then acquired by a newly formed company. The FTC ordered dissolution of the new company.

By a 5–4 majority, the Supreme Court ruled that the jurisdiction of the FTC was "ousted" by this maneuver despite recognition by the Court that the reorganization was merely a device to evade Section 7. This ruling meant the FTC had no control over the new corporation and lacked the authority to include it in the proceedings.

ARROW-HART & HEGEMAN ELECTRIC COMPANY v. FEDERAL TRADE COMMISSION

291 U.S. 587 (1934)

MR. JUSTICE ROBERTS delivered the opinion of the Court.

The Circuit Court of Appeals affirmed an order of the Federal Trade Commission issued pursuant to §7 of the Clayton Act. A writ of certiorari was granted upon the claim of petitioner that the formation of a holding company which acquired all the voting shares of two manufacturing corporations was not in violation of the section, or, if it was, the merger of the two manufacturing corporations and dissolution of the holding company after complaint by the Federal Trade Commission deprived the latter of jurisdiction to make any order against the company formed by the merger. . . .

The Arrow Electric Company, hereafter called Arrow, and the Hart & Hegeman Manufacturing Company, hereafter called Hart & Hegeman, were Connecticut corporations engaged in the manufacture and sale in interstate commerce of electric wiring devices. Both were solvent and successful. . . .

. . . Shortly after the death of the principal stockholder, who was also the president, of Hart & Hegeman, the major interests in that company got into touch with those controlling Arrow, and after some negotiation it was agreed that economies could be effected if the business of both were brought under common control. In view, however, of the competition between the goods known by the names of the two manufacturing companies, it was thought that the trade names and the identity of the goods could best be preserved by retaining the separate corporate entities and the sales forces of the two organizations. The plan evolved was, therefore, that of a holding company which should own all of the common shares of both corporations, under the control of which the manufacturing and sales organizations should be kept separate and distinct and in competition with each other as theretofore.

On March 3, 1928, the Federal Trade Commission issued a complaint in which it charged the effect of the holding and voting of all of the common shares of the two operating companies might be to substantially lessen competition between the companies in electrical wiring devices, to restrain commerce in those devices, and to create a monopoly. The holding company filed an answer traversing these allegations. Shortly thereafter counsel advised that the company be dissolved and its assets, consisting of the stock of Arrow and of Hart & Hegeman, be distributed . . . and that thereupon the two latter companies merge into a single corporation under the laws of Connecticut, thus transferring to the new corporation to be formed by merger all of the assets of Arrow and of Hart & Hegeman.

. . . The Commission concluded: The acquisition by the holding company of the shares of the two manufacturing companies might substantially lessen competition between them, restrain interstate commerce, and create a monopoly; the divestment by the holding company was not a compliance with the Clayton Act; the petitioner was organized by the holding company, and its creation was an artifice to evade the provisions of §§7 and 11 of the Clayton Act; and the effect of the organization of the petitioner and "the acquisition by it of the common or voting stocks of" Arrow and Hart & Hegeman has been, is, and may be to suppress competition between the two manufacturing companies, to restrain interstate commerce, and to create a monopoly. . . .

It is unnecessary to discuss or to decide the questions thus raised, for we think the Commission lacked authority to issue any order against the petitioner.

Section 7 of the Clayton Act forbids any corporation to acquire the whole or any part of the share capital of two or more corporations . . . Section 11 specifies the remedy which the Commission may apply, namely, that it may, after hearing, order the violator to divest itself of the stock held contrary to the terms of the Act. The statute does not forbid the acquirement of property, or the merger of corporations pursuant to state laws, nor does it provide any machinery for compelling a divestiture of assets acquired by purchase or otherwise, or the distribution of physical property brought into a single ownership by merger. . . .

Moreover, the holding company could have ousted the Commission's jurisdiction after complaint filed, by divesting itself of the shares, for that was all the Commission could order. And if it had so divested itself the transferees of the shares could immediately have brought about a corporate merger without violating the Clayton Act. We think that is precisely the legal effect of what was done in the present case. The holding company divested itself of the shares, and thereafter the owners of these common shares united with the holders of the preferred shares to bring about a merger. . . .

The argument on behalf of the Commission is that while it is true the petitioner never owned any stock of Arrow or Hart & Hegeman, the holding company, against whom the complaint was originally directed, did hold such stocks in violation of the statute when the proceeding was initiated; and, instead of parting with the shares in good faith, ineffectually attempted to alter the status by initiating and carrying through the merger, the dissolution of which is the aim of the Commission's order.

. . . The Commission is an administrative body possessing only such powers as are granted by statute. It may make only such orders as the Act authorizes; may order a practice to be discontinued and shares held in violation of the Act to be disposed of; but, that accomplished, has not the additional powers of a court of equity to grant other and further relief by ordering property of a different sort to be conveyed or distributed, on the theory that this is necessary to render effective the prescribed statutory remedy.

. . . In the present case the stock which had been acquired contrary to the Act was no longer owned by the holding company when the Commission made its order. Not only so, but the holding company itself had been dissolved. The petitioner, which came into being as a result of merger, was not in existence when the proceeding against the holding company was initiated by the Commission, and never held any stock contrary to the terms of the statute. . . .

The judgment is

Reversed.

MR. JUSTICE STONE, dissenting.

I think the decree should be affirmed.

While this proceeding was pending before the Federal Trade Commission to compel a holding company to divest itself of the controlling common stock of two competing corporations which it had acquired in violation of §7 of the Clayton Act, that stock was used to effectuate a merger of the competing corporations. It is now declared that, however gross the violation of the Clayton Act, however flagrant the flouting of the Commission's authority, the celerity of the offender, in ridding itself of the stock before the Commission could complete its hearings and make an order restoring the independence of the competitors, leaves the Commission powerless to act against the merged corporation. . . .

. . . I am unable to construe so narrowly a statute designed, as I think, to prevent just such suppression of competition as this case exemplifies.

1. It is true that the Clayton Act does not forbid corporate mergers but it does forbid the acquisition by one corporation of the stock of competing corporations so as substantially to lessen competition. It follows that mergers effected, as they commonly are, through such acquisition of stock necessarily involve violations of the Act, as this one did. Only in rare instances would there be hope of a successful merger of independently owned corporations by securing the consent of their stockholders in advance of the acquisition of a working stock control of them. Hence the establishment of such control by the purchase or pooling of the voting stock, often effected in secrecy, is the normal first step toward consolidation.

. . . It seems plain, therefore, that the illegality involved in acquiring the common stock of the competing companies, which was the first step toward the merger, was neither lessened nor condoned by taking the next and final steps in completing it. There is, then, no basis for contending that the Act has not been violated, or that the violation has been excused simply because events were pushed to the very conclusion that §7 was designed to forestall. . . .

That the merged corporation is different from the original offender should lead to no different conclusion. It is but the creature and *alter ego* of the offender, created by the offender's exercise of power over the illegally acquired stock for the very purpose of perpetuating the suppression of competition which the Commission from the start had power to forbid. To declare that an offender, whose cause is pending before the Commission, can effect through its creatures and agents what it may not itself do, nullifies the statute. . . .

The CHIEF JUSTICE, MR. JUSTICE BRANDEIS, and MR. JUSTICE CARDOZO concur in this opinion.

Immunity for Noncompetitors

The wording of Section 7 was designed to prevent stock purchases when the results would be to reduce competition "between the corporation whose stock is so acquired and the corporation making the acquisition . . ." The decision in the 1930 *International Shoe Company* case suggested that only horizontal mergers were affected—that is, the statute was intended to cover only those cases in which the lessening of competition was directly between the combined firms and was not to include a lessening of competition that might occur in the market as a whole.

The International Shoe Company was the largest shoe manufacturer in the country. It purchased the stock of the McElwain Company, a smaller maker of shoes. When charged with violation of Section 7, International argued that McElwain was in a failing position and, furthermore, that there had been no competition between them. The Court agreed that, because of differences in appearance and workmanship, their products appealed to different classes of customers. Although a part of the product of each went into the same geographical areas, by far the major part was sold in separate markets. With respect to 95 per cent of the business, ". . . there was no competition in fact and no contest, . . . in the market for the same purchasers . . ." Since there had been no substantial direct competition between the acquiring and the acquired firms, there could be no substantial lessening of competition.

Because of such limited interpretation of the statute and so many adverse rulings against the government, only twenty-nine cases were ever filed under the old Section 7.

INTERNATIONAL SHOE COMPANY v. FEDERAL TRADE COMMISSION

280 U.S. 291 (1930)

MR. JUSTICE SUTHERLAND delivered the opinion of the Court.

This was a proceeding instituted by complaint of the Federal Trade Commission against petitioner charging a violation of §7 of the Clayton Act . . .

The complaint charges that . . . while petitioner and the W. H. McElwain Company were engaged in commerce in competition with each other, petitioner acquired all, or substantially all, of the capital stock of the McElwain Company and still owns and controls the same; that the effect of such acquisition was to substantially lessen competition between the two companies; to restrain commerce in the shoe business in the localities where both were engaged in business in interstate commerce; and to tend to create a monopoly in interstate commerce in such business. . . .

[C]ommission found, (a) that the capital stock of the McElwain Company had been acquired by the petitioner at the time charged in the complaint, (b) that the two companies were at the time in substantial competition with one another, and (c) that the effect of the acquisition was to substantially lessen competition between them and to restrain commerce. Thereupon the commission put down an order directing petitioner to divest itself of all capital stock of the McElwain Company then held or owned, directly or indirectly, by petitioner, and to cease and desist from the ownership, operation, management and control of all assets acquired from the McElwain Company subsequent to the acquisition of the capital stock, etc., and to divest itself of all such assets, etc. . . .

The principal grounds upon which the order here is assailed are (1) that there never was substantial competition between the two corporations, and, therefore, no foundation for the charge of substantial lessening of competition; (2) that at the time of the acquisition the financial condition of the McElwain Company was such as to necessitate liquidation or sale, and, therefore, the prospect for future competition or restraint was entirely eliminated.

. . . Prior to the acquisition of the capital stock in question the International Shoe Company was engaged in manufacturing leather shoes of various kinds. It had a large number of tanneries and factories and sales houses located in several states. Its business was extensive, and its products were shipped and sold to purchasers practically throughout the United States. The McElwain Company, a Massachusetts corporation with its principal office in Boston, also manufactured shoes and sold and distributed them in several states of the Union. . . .

It is true that both companies were engaged in selling dress shoes to customers for resale within the limits of several of the same states; but the markets reached by the two companies within these states, with slight exceptions hereafter mentioned, were not the same. . . .

. . . The trade policies of the two companies so differed that the McElwain Company generally secured the trade of wholesalers and large retailers; while the International obtained the trade of dealers in the small communities. When requested, the McElwain Company stamped the name of the customer (that is the dealer) upon the shoes, which the International refused to do; and this operated to aid the former company to get, as generally it did get, the trade of the retailers in the larger cities. As an important result of the foregoing circumstances, witnesses estimated that about 95 per cent. of the McElwain sales were in towns and cities having a population of 10,000 or over; while about 95 per cent. of the sales of the International were in towns having a population of 6,000 or less. The bulk of the trade of each company was in different sections of the country, that of the McElwain Company being north of the Ohio River and east of the State of Illinois, while that of the International was in the south and west. . . .

It is plain from the foregoing that the product of the two companies here in question, because of the difference in appearance and workmanship, appealed to the tastes of entirely different classes of consumers; that while a portion of the product of both companies went into the same states, in the main the product of each was in fact sold to a different class of dealers and found its way into distinctly separate markets. Thus it appears that in respect of 95 per cent. of the business there was no competition in fact and no contest, or observed tendency to contest, in the market for the same purchasers; and it is manifest that, when this is eliminated, what remains is of such slight consequence as to deprive the finding that there was substantial competition between the two corporations, of any real support in the evidence. . . .

Mere acquisition by one corporation of the stock of a competitor, even though it result in some lessening of competition, is not forbidden; the act deals only with such acquisitions as probably will result in lessening competition to a substantial degree . . . To hold that the 95 per cent. of the McElwain product, sold in the large centers of population to meet a distinct demand for that particular product, was sold in competition with the 95 per cent. of the International product, sold in the rural sections and the small towns to meet a wholly different demand, is to apply the word "competition" in a highly deceptive sense. . . .

Beginning in 1920 there was a marked falling off in prices and sales of shoes, as there was in other commodities; and, because of excessive commitments which the McElwain Company had made for the purchase of hides as well as the possession of large stocks of shoes and an inability to meet its indebtedness for large sums of borrowed money, the financial condition of the company became such that its officers, after long and careful consideration of the situation, concluded that the company was faced with financial ruin, and that the only alternatives presented were liquidation through a receiver or an outright sale. . . .

The condition of the International Company, on the contrary, notwithstanding these adverse conditions in the shoe trade generally, was excellent. That company had so conducted its affairs that its surplus stock was not excessive, and it was able to reduce prices. Instead of a decrease, it had an increase of business of about 25 per cent. in the number of shoes made and sold. During the early months of 1921, orders exceeded the ability of the company to produce, so that approximately one-third of them were necessarily canceled. In this situation, with demands for its products so much in excess of its ability to fill them, the International was approached by officers of the McElwain Company with a view to a sale of its property. After some negotiation, the purchase was agreed upon. The transaction took the form of a sale of the stock instead of the assets, not, as the evidence clearly establishes, because of any desire or intention to thereby affect competition, but because by that means the personnel and organization of the McElwain factories could be retained, which, for reasons that seem satisfactory, was regarded as vitally important. . . .

Shortly stated, the evidence establishes the case of a corporation in failing circumstances, the recovery of which to a normal condition was, to say the least, in gravest doubt, selling its capital to the only available purchaser in order to avoid what its officers fairly concluded was a more disastrous fate. . . .

In the light of the case thus disclosed of a corporation with resources so depleted and the prospect of rehabilitation so remote that it faced the grave probability of a business failure with resulting loss to its stockholders and injury to the communities where its plants were operated, we hold that the purchase of its capital stock by a competitor (there being no other prospective purchaser), not with a purpose to lessen competition, but to facilitate the accumulated business of the purchaser and with the effect of mitigating seriously injurious consequences otherwise probable, is not in contemplation of law prejudicial to the public and does not substantially lessen competition or restrain commerce within the intent of the Clayton Act. . . .

For the reasons appearing under each of the two foregoing heads of this opinion, the judgment below must be

Reversed.

Application of Sherman Act to Mergers

Recognizing the impotence of the Clayton Act in preventing mergers, the Justice Department tried to secure a conviction under the Sherman Act in the 1948 *Columbia Steel* case. In reality, the Sherman Act was the only route open by which to block this merger since it was to be achieved through asset acquisition. In this case the Justice Department sought to enjoin the United States Steel Corporation from acquiring the assets of the Consolidated Steel Corporation, the largest independent steel fabricator on the West Coast. The acquisition was to be executed by the Columbia Steel Corporation, a wholly owned subsidiary of U.S. Steel and the largest rolled-steel producer on the West Coast.

The government charged that this acquisition would violate Sections 1 and 2 of the Sherman Act, arguing that there would be a restraint of trade for two reasons. One, all manufacturers other than U.S. Steel, via Columbia, would be excluded from supplying Consolidated's requirements for rolled-steel products. Two, the existing competition between Consolidated and U.S. Steel would be eliminated in structural fabricated products. Furthermore, the government argued, in light of the previous acquisitions made by U.S. Steel, this acquisition should be considered as part of an attempt to monopolize the production and sale of fabricated steel products in the West Coast market. Previous acquisitions had included a $200 million ingot plant at Geneva, Utah, which U.S. Steel, with approval of the Attorney General, had purchased from the War Assets Administrator for $47.5 million.

The Supreme Court ruled that the merger did not constitute an unreasonable restraint of trade since the competition between subsidiaries of U.S. Steel and Consolidated was not quantitatively substantial. Nor were Consolidated's purchases of rolled-steel products—3 per cent of the total in that market area—deemed great enough to restrict unduly the opportunities of competitors to market their products. The Court viewed the acquisition as more of a vertical integration step motivated by practical business reasons and not as an attempt to monopolize the market. "It seems clear to us that vertical integration, as such without more, cannot be held violative of the Sherman Act." In determining what constitutes an unreasonable restraint, dollar volume in itself is not of "compelling significance." Consideration must be given to the "percentage of business controlled, the strength of the remaining competition, whether the action springs from business requirements or purpose to monopolize, the

probable development of the industry, consumer demands, and other characteristics of the market." Also, an attempt to monopolize must be accompanied by
a specific intent. Thus the Sherman Act was found no more effective than the
Clayton Act in preventing mergers.

The decision in this case was a close one—5 to 4. The four dissenting
Justices agreed that this case revealed the way of growth to monopoly power.
The dissenting opinion stated, "Here we have the pattern of the evolution of the
great trusts. Little, independent units are gobbled up by the bigger ones. . . .
At other times any number of 'sound business reasons' appear why the sale to
or merger with the trust should be made."

UNITED STATES v. COLUMBIA STEEL CO. et al.

334 U.S. 495 (1948)

Mr. Justice Reed delivered the opinion of the Court.

The United States brings this suit under §4 of the Sherman Act to
enjoin United States Steel Corporation and its subsidiaries from purchasing the assets of the largest independent steel fabricator on the West Coast
on the ground that such acquisition would violate §§1 and 2 of the
Sherman Act. The complaint, filed on February 24, 1947, charged that if
the contract of sale between United States Steel and Consolidated Steel
Corporation were carried out, competition in the sale of rolled steel
products and in fabricated steel products would be restrained, and that the
contract indicated an effort on the part of United States Steel to attempt
to monopolize the market in fabricated steel products.

The steel production involved in this case may be spoken of as being
divided into two stages: the production of rolled steel products and their
fabrication into finished steel products. . . .

. . . United States Steel and its subsidiaries engage in the business of
producing rolled steel products and in structural fabrication, but do no
plate fabrication work. Consolidated Steel, the sale of whose assets the
government seeks to enjoin, is engaged only in structural fabrication and
plate fabrication. United States Steel with its subsidiaries is the largest
producer of rolled steel products in the United States, with a total
investment of more than a billion and a half dollars. During the ten-year
period 1937–1946 United States Steel produced almost exactly a third of all
rolled steel products produced in the United States, and average sales for
that period were nearly a billion and a half dollars. . . . Consolidated, by

contrast, had plants whose depreciated value was less than ten million dollars. During the five-year period 1937–1941, Consolidated had average sales of only twenty million dollars . . .

Columbia Steel, a wholly-owned subsidiary of United States Steel, has been the largest rolled steel producer in the Pacific Coast area since 1930, with plants in Utah and California . . . Consolidated has sold its products during the past ten years in eleven states, referred to hereafter as the Consolidated market: Arizona, California, Idaho, Louisiana, Montana, Nevada, New Mexico, Oregon, Texas, Utah and Washington. It is that market which the government views as significant in determining the extent of competition between United States Steel and Consolidated. . . .

I

The theory of the United States in bringing this suit is that the acquisition of Consolidated constitutes an illegal restraint of interstate commerce because all manufacturers except United States Steel will be excluded from the business of supplying Consolidated's requirements of rolled steel products, and because competition now existing between Consolidated and United States Steel in the sale of structural fabricated products and pipe will be eliminated. In addition, the government alleges that the acquisition of Consolidated, viewed in the light of the previous series of acquisitions by United States Steel, constitutes an attempt to monopolize the production and sale of fabricated steel products in the Consolidated market. The appellees contend that the amount of competition which will be eliminated is so insignificant that the restraint effected is a reasonable restraint not an attempt to monopolize and not prohibited by the Sherman Act. On the record before us and in agreement with the trial court we conclude that the government has failed to prove its contention that the acquisition of Consolidated would unreasonably lessen competition in the three respects charged, and therefore the proposed contract is not forbidden by §1 of the Sherman Act. We further hold that the government has failed to prove an attempt to monopolize in violation of §2.

We read the record as showing that the trial court did not accept the theory that the comparable market was restricted to the demand for plates and shapes in the Consolidated area, but did accept the government's theory that the market was to be restricted to the total demand for rolled steel products in the eleven-state area. On that basis the trial court found that the steel requirements of Consolidated represented "a small part" of the consumption in the Consolidated area, that Consolidated was not a "substantial market" for rolled steel producers selling in competition with

United States Steel, and that the acquisition of Consolidated would not injure any competitor of United States Steel engaged in the production and sale of rolled steel products in the Consolidated market or elsewhere. We recognize the difficulty of laying down a rule as to what areas or products are competitive, one with another. In this case and on this record we have circumstances that strongly indicate to us that rolled steel production and consumption in the Consolidated marketing area is the competitive area and product for consideration.

In analyzing the injury to competition resulting from the withdrawal of Consolidated as a purchaser of rolled steel products, we have been considering the acquisition of Consolidated as a step in the vertical integration of United States Steel. Regarded as a seller of fabricated steel products rather than as a purchaser of rolled steel products, however, the acquisition of Consolidated may be regarded as a step in horizontal integration as well . . .

II

In support of its position that the proposed contract violates §1 of the Sherman Act, the government urges that all the legal conclusions of the district court were erroneous. It is argued that, without regard to the percentages of consumption of rolled steel products by Consolidated just considered, the acquisition by United States Steel of Consolidated violates the Sherman Act. Such an arrangement, it is claimed, excludes other producers of rolled steel products from the Consolidated market and constitutes an illegal restraint *per se* to which the rule of reason is inapplicable. Or, phrasing the argument differently, the government's contention seems to be that the acquisition of facilities which provide a controlled market for the output of the Geneva plant is a process of vertical integration and invalid *per se* under the Sherman Act. . . .

We first lay to one side a possible objection to measuring the injury to competition by reference to a market which is less than nation-wide in area. The Sherman Act is not limited to eliminating restraints whose effects cover the entire United States; we have consistently held that where the relevant competitive market covers only a small area the Sherman Act may be invoked to prevent unreasonable restraints within that area. . . . It is the volume in the area which the alleged restraints affect that is important . . .

We do not construe our holding in the *Yellow Cab* case to make illegal the acquisition by United States Steel of this outlet for its rolled steel without consideration of its effect on the opportunities of other competitor producers to market their rolled steel. In discussing the charge in the *Yellow Cab* case, we said that the fact that the conspirators were integrated did not insulate them from the act, not that corporate integration violated the act. . . .

A subsidiary will in all probability deal only with its parent for goods the parent can furnish. That fact, however, does not make the acquisition invalid. When other elements of Sherman Act violations are present, the fact of corporate relationship is material and can be considered in the determination of whether restraint or attempt to restrain exists. . . .

The legality of the acquisition by United States Steel of a market outlet for its rolled steel through the purchase of the manufacturing facilities of Consolidated depends not merely upon the fact of that acquired control but also upon many other factors. Exclusive dealings for rolled steel between Consolidated and United States Steel, brought about by vertical integration or otherwise, are not illegal, at any rate until the effect of such control is to unreasonably restrict the opportunities of competitors to market their product.

. . . In outlining the factors which we considered to be significant in determining the legality of vertical integration, we emphasized the importance of characterizing the nature of the market to be served, and the leverage on the market which the particular vertical integration creates or makes possible. A second test which we considered important in the *Paramount* case was the purpose or intent with which the combination was conceived. When a combination through its actual operation results in an unreasonable restraint, intent or purpose may be inferred; even though no unreasonable restraint may be achieved, nevertheless a finding of specific intent to accomplish such an unreasonable restraint may render the actor liable under the Sherman Act. . . .

It seems clear to us that vertical integration, as such without more, cannot be held violative of the Sherman Act. . . .

It is not for courts to determine the course of the Nation's economic development. Economists may recommend, the legislative and executive branches may chart legal courses by which the competitive forces of business can seek to reduce costs and increase production so that a higher standard of living may be available to all. The evils and dangers of monopoly and attempts to monopolize that grow out of size and efforts to eliminate others from markets, large or small, have caused Congress and the Executive to regulate commerce and trade in many respects. But no direction has appeared of a public policy that forbids, *per se*, an expansion of facilities of an existing company to meet the needs of new markets of a community, whether that community is nation-wide or county-wide. . . . If businesses are to be forbidden from entering into different stages of production that order must come from Congress, not the courts.

Applying the standards laid down in the *Paramount* case, we conclude that the so-called vertical integration resulting from the acquisition of Consolidated does not unreasonably restrict the opportunities of the competitor producers of rolled steel to market their product. We accept as the relevant competitive market the total demand for rolled steel products in the eleven-state area; over the past ten years Consolidated has accounted for only 3% of that demand . . . Nor can we find a specific intent in the present case to accomplish an unreasonable restraint . . .

We turn now to a discussion of the significance, as to possible violation of the Sherman Act, of the fact that Consolidated has been a competitor of United States Steel in structural steel fabrication and in the manufacture of pipe. The same tests which measure the legality of vertical integration by acquisition are also applicable to the acquisition of competitors in identical or similar lines of merchandise. It is first necessary to delimit the market in which the concerns compete and then determine the extent to which the concerns are in competition in that market. If such acquisition results in or is aimed at unreasonable restraint, then the purchase is forbidden by the Sherman Act. In determining what constitutes unreasonable restraint, we do not think the dollar volume is in itself of compelling significance; we look rather to the percentage of business controlled, the strength of the remaining competition, whether the action springs from business requirements or purpose to monopolize, the probable development of the industry, consumer demands, and other characteristics of the market. We do not undertake to prescribe any set of percentage figures by which to measure the reasonableness of a corporation's enlargement of its activities by the purchase of the assets of a competitor. The relative effect of percentage command of a market varies with the setting in which that factor is placed. . . .

We conclude that in this case the government has failed to prove that the elimination of competition between Consolidated and the structural fabricating subsidiaries of United States Steel constitutes an unreasonable restraint. If we make the doubtful assumption that United States Steel could be expected in the future to sell 13% of the total of structural steel products in the Consolidated trade area and that Consolidated could be expected to sell 11%, we conclude that where we have the present unusual conditions of the western steel industry . . . it can not be said there would be an unreasonable restraint of trade. To hold this does not imply that additional acquisitions of fabricating facilities for structural steel would not become monopolistic.

III

We turn last to the allegation of the government that United States Steel has attempted to monopolize the production and sale of fabricated steel products in the Consolidated market. We think that the trial court applied too narrow a test to this charge; even though the restraint effected may be reasonable under §1, it may constitute an attempt to monopolize forbidden by §2 if a specific intent to monopolize may be shown. To show that specific intent, the government recites the long history of acquisitions of United States Steel, and argues that the present acquisition when viewed in the light of that history demonstrates the existence of a specific intent to monopolize. Although this Court held in 1920 that United States Steel had not violated §2 through the acquisition of 180 formerly independent concerns, we may look to those acquisitions as well as to the eight acquisitions from 1924 to 1943 to determine the intent of United States Steel in acquiring Consolidated.

. . . It only need be added that we have also considered the various items of objection in the aggregate and in the light of the charge of intent to monopolize. But even from that point of view, the government has not persuaded us that the proposed contract violates our public policy as stated in the Sherman Act.

The judgment of the District Court is affirmed.

Mr. Justice Douglas, with whom Mr. Justice Black, Mr. Justice Murphy, and Mr. Justice Rutledge concur, dissenting.

This is the most important antitrust case which has been before the Court in years. It is important because it reveals the way of growth of monopoly power—the precise phenomenon at which the Sherman Act was aimed. Here we have the pattern of the evolution of the great trusts. Little, independent units are gobbled up by bigger ones. At times the independent is driven to the wall and surrenders. At other times any number of "sound business reasons" appear why the sale to or merger with the trust should be made. If the acquisition were the result of predatory practices or restraints of trade, the trust could be required to disgorge. . . . But the impact on future competition and on the economy is the same though the trust was built in more gentlemanly ways.

. . . Control of prices in the steel industry is powerful leverage on our economy. For the price of steel determines the price of hundreds of other articles. Our price level determines in large measure whether we have prosperity or depression—an economy of abundance or scarcity. Size in steel should therefore be jealously watched. In final analysis, size in steel is the measure of the power of a handful of men over our economy. That power can be utilized with lightning speed. It can be benign or it can be dangerous. The philosophy of the Sherman Act is that it should not exist. For all power tends to develop into a government in itself. Power that controls the economy should be in the hands of elected representatives of the people, not in the hands of an industrial oligarchy. Industrial power should be decentralized. It should be scattered into many hands so that the fortunes of the people will not be dependent on the whim or caprice, the political prejudices, the emotional stability of a few self-appointed men. The fact that they are not vicious men but respectable and social-minded is irrelevant. That is the philosophy and the command of the Sherman Act. It is founded on a theory of hostility to the concentration in private hands of power so great that only a government of the people should have it. . . .

This acquisition can be dressed up (perhaps legitimately) in terms of an expansion to meet the demands of a business which is growing as a result of superior and enterprising management. But the test under the Sherman Act strikes deeper. However the acquisition may be rationalized, the effect is plain. It is a purchase for control, a purchase for control of a market for which United States Steel has in the past had to compete but which it no longer wants left to the uncertainties that competition in the West may engender. This in effect it concedes. It states that its purpose in acquiring Consolidated is to insure itself of a market for part of Geneva's production of rolled steel products when demand falls off. . . .

It is unrealistic to measure Consolidated's part of the market by determining its proportion of the national market. There is no safeguarding of competition in the theory that the bigger the national market the less protection will be given those selling to the smaller components thereof. That theory would allow a producer to absorb outlets upon which small enterprises with restricted marketing facilities depend. Those outlets, though statistically unimportant from the point of view of the national market, could be a matter of life and death to small, local enterprises.

The largest market which must be taken for comparison is the market actually reached by the company which is being absorbed. In this case Consolidated's purchases of rolled steel products are a little over 3 per cent of that market. By no standard—United States Steel's or its western competitors—can that percentage be deemed immaterial. . . . a surer test of the effect on competition is the actual business of which competitors will be deprived. We do not know whether they can be sufficiently resourceful to recover from this strengthening of the hold which this giant of the industry now has on their markets. It would be more in keeping with the spirit of the Sherman Act to give the benefits of any doubts to the struggling competitors.

. . . United States Steel has over 51 per cent of the rolled steel or ingot capacity of the Pacific Coast area. This acquisition gives it unquestioned domination there and protects it against growth of the independents in that developing region. That alone is sufficient to condemn the purchase. Its serious impact on competition and the economy is emphasized when it is recalled that United States Steel has one-third of the rolled steel production of the entire country. The least I can say is that a company that has that tremendous leverage on our economy is big enough.

Section 7: A Sleeping Giant

The only important victory won by the government under the old Section 7 came in the 1957 *du Pont–General Motors* case, the next year after the famous cellophane decision. In a peculiar turn of events, the three dissenting Justices in the cellophane case, Chief Justice Warren and Justices Black and Douglas, had argued for a narrow definition of the relevant market. By the next year Justice Brennan had become a member of the Court. He believed that the relevant market should be defined narrowly, thus making a 4–2 majority that ruled in favor of the government.

In 1949 the government brought action against the E. I. du Pont Company, charging violation of Sections 1 and 2 of the Sherman Act and Section 7 of the Clayton Act. Between 1917 and 1919 du Pont had acquired 23 per cent of the stock of the General Motors Corporation and continued to hold it over the years. The government alleged that by means of this close relationship between the two companies du Pont had obtained an illegal preference over competitors in the sale of automotive finishes and fabrics to General Motors. This preference thus tended to "create a monopoly" in a "line of commerce." The district court dismissed the case, and the government appealed.

The Supreme Court stated that merely because the Federal Trade Commission had failed to act under Section 7 against vertical acquisitions this should not be interpreted to mean that Congress did not intend them to come within the purview of the Act. The Court said that *any* acquisition by one corporation of all or part of another was within the scope of Section 7 when there was a reasonable likelihood that the acquisition would "tend to create a monopoly of any line of commerce."

This case makes two important points relevant for future antitrust actions. The first deals with the issue of *what is the relevant market*. The second points up the fact that the government is not restricted in bringing suit to the time when an acquisition or merger actually occurs.

Du Pont argued that the relevant line of commerce should be broadly defined to include *all industrial fabrics and finishes*. Thus defined, du Pont's finish sales to General Motors amounted to only 3.5 per cent of that market. Its fabric sales to General Motors constituted only 1.6 per cent of the industrial fabric market. The Supreme Court concluded that automotive finishes and fabrics have sufficient peculiar characteristics to distinguish them from all other industrial finishes and fabrics. Therefore, they constitute a line of commerce within the meaning of Section 7. Thus narrowly defined, du Pont supplied between 50 to 60 per cent of General Motors' requirements. In turn, General Motors' requirements accounted for almost half of the automotive industry market. Clearly, du Pont had a substantial share of the relevant market by the Court's narrow definition; its "commanding position was promoted by its stock interest and was not gained solely on competitive merit." A stock holding of 23 per cent is sufficient to convey control and secure a captive market. Nor was the acquisition of General Motors stock made "solely for investment."

Finally, and establishing an important precedent, the Court said that the government was not prevented from bringing suit in 1949 just because the acquisition had occurred some thirty years earlier. The option will be left up to the government to proceed at any time there is a reasonable probability that the acquisition contains a threat to restrain commerce or tends to create a monopoly. While the government may not choose to prosecute at the time of the merger, this is no assurance that proceedings will not be initiated in the future if the acquisition should then contain a reasonable threat to competition.

Justice Burton wrote a dissenting opinion in which he observed that some forty years after the enactment of the Clayton Act it "becomes apparent for the first time that Section 7 had been a sleeping giant all along." Little wonder then that every corporation that has acquired an interest in another corporation since 1914, and has had business dealings with it, casts a nervous eye toward the Justice Department because of the "newly discovered teeth of Section 7."

UNITED STATES v. E. I. du PONT de NEMOURS & CO. et al.

353 U.S. 586 (1957)

MR. JUSTICE BRENNAN delivered the opinion of the Court.

This is a direct appeal . . . from a judgment of the District Court for the Northern District of Illinois, dismissing the Government's action . . . The complaint alleged a violation of §7 of the Act resulting from the purchase by E. I. du Pont de Nemours and Company in 1917–1919 of a 23% stock interest in General Motors Corporation. . . .

The primary issue is whether du Pont's commanding position as General Motors' supplier of automotive finishes and fabrics was achieved on competitive merit alone, or because its acquisition of the General Motors' stock, and the consequent close intercompany relationship, led to the insulation of most of the General Motors' market from free competition, with the resultant likelihood, at the time of suit, of the creation of a monopoly of a line of commerce. . . .

Section 7 is designed to arrest in its incipiency not only the substantial lessening of competition from the acquisition by one corporation of the whole or any part of the stock of a competing corporation, but also to arrest in their incipiency restraints or monopolies in a relevant market which, as a reasonable probability, appear at the time of suit likely to result from the acquisition by one corporation of all or any part of the stock of any other corporation. . . .

We are met at the threshold with the argument that §7, before its amendment in 1950, applied only to an acquisition of the stock of a competing corporation, and not to an acquisition by a supplier corporation of the stock of a customer corporation—in other words, that the statute applied only to horizontal and not to vertical acquisitions. . . .

During the 35 years before this action was brought, the Government did not invoke §7 against vertical acquisitions. The Federal Trade Commission has said that the section did not apply to vertical acquisitions. . . .

This Court has the duty to reconcile administrative interpretations with the broad antitrust policies laid down by Congress. . . . The failure of the Commission to act is not a binding administrative interpretation that Congress did not intend vertical acquisitions to come within the purview of the Act. . . .

The first paragraph of §7, written in the disjunctive, plainly is framed to reach not only the corporate acquisition of stock of a competing corporation, where the effect may be substantially to lessen competition between them, but also the corporate acquisition of stock of any corporation, competitor or not, where the effect may be either (1) to restrain commerce in any section or community, or (2) tend to create a monopoly of any line of commerce. The amended complaint does not allege that the effect of du Pont's acquisition may be to restrain commerce in any section or community but alleges that the effect was ". . . to tend to create a monopoly in particular lines of commerce. . . ."

We hold that any acquisition by one corporation of all or any part of the stock of another corporation, competitor or not, is within the reach of the section whenever the reasonable likelihood appears that the acquisition will result in a restraint of commerce or in the creation of a monopoly of any line of commerce. Thus, although du Pont and General Motors are not competitors, a violation of the section has occurred if, as a result of the acquisition, there was at the time of suit a reasonable likelihood of a monopoly of any line of commerce. . . .

Appellees argue that there exists no basis for a finding of a probable restraint or monopoly within the meaning of §7 because the total General Motors market for finishes and fabrics constituted only a negligible percentage of the total market for these materials for all uses, including automative uses. It is stated in the General Motors brief that in 1947 du Pont's finish sales to General Motors constituted 3.5% of all sales of finishes to industrial users, and that its fabrics sales to General Motors comprised 1.6% of the total market for the type of fabric used by the automobile industry.

Determination of the relevant market is a necessary predicate to a finding of a violation of the Clayton Act because the threatened monopoly must be one which will substantially lessen competition "within the area of effective competition." . . . The record shows that automotive finishes and fabrics have sufficient peculiar characteristics and uses to constitute them products sufficiently distinct from all other finishes and fabrics to make them a "line of commerce" within the meaning of the Clayton Act. . . .

The market affected must be substantial. . . . Moreover, in order to establish a violation of §7 the Government must prove a likelihood that competition may be "foreclosed in a substantial share of . . . [that market]." Both requirements are satisfied in this case. The substantiality of a relevant market comprising the automobile industry is undisputed. The substantiality of General Motors' share of that market is fully established in the evidence.

. . . Expressed in percentages, du Pont supplied 67% of General Motors' requirements for finishes in 1946 and 68% in 1947. In fabrics du Pont supplied 52.3% of requirements in 1946, and 38.5% in 1947. Because General Motors accounts for almost one-half of the automobile industry's annual sales, its requirements for automotive finishes and fabrics must represent approximately one-half of the relevant market for these materials. Because the record clearly shows that quantitatively and percentagewise du Pont supplies the largest part of General Motors' requirements, we must conclude that du Pont has a substantial share of the relevant market. . . .

"Incipiency" in this context denotes not the time the stock was acquired, but any time when the acquisition threatens to ripen into a prohibited effect. . . . To accomplish the congressional aim, the Government may proceed at any time that an acquisition may be said with reasonable probability to contain a threat that it may lead to a restraint of commerce or tend to create a monopoly of a line of commerce.

The du Pont Company's commanding position as a General Motors supplier was not achieved until shortly after its purchase of a sizable block of General Motors stock in 1917. At that time its production for the automobile industry and its sales to General Motors were relatively insignificant. General Motors then produced only about 11% of the total automobile production . . .

The Company's interest in buying into General Motors was stimulated by Raskob and Pierre S. du Pont, then du Pont's president, who acquired personal holdings of General Motors stock in 1914. . . .

. . . Raskob broached to Pierre S. du Pont the proposal that part of the fund earmarked for du Pont expansion be used in the purchase of General Motors stock. At this time about $50,000,000 of the $90,000,000 fund was still in hand. Raskob foresaw the success of the automobile industry and the opportunity for great profit in a substantial purchase of General Motors stock. On December 19, 1917, Raskob submitted a Treasurer's Report to the du Pont Finance Committee recommending a purchase of General Motors stock in the amount of $25,000,000. That report makes clear that more than just a profitable investment was contemplated. A major consideration was that an expanding General Motors would provide a substantial market needed by the burgeoning du Pont organization. Raskob's summary of reasons in support of the purchase includes this statement: "Our interest in the General Motors Company will undoubtedly secure for us the entire Fabrikoid, Pyralin [celluloid], paint and varnish business of those companies, *which is a substantial factor*." (Emphasis added.)

This thought, that the purchase would result in du Pont's obtaining a new and substantial market, was echoed in the Company's 1917 and 1918 annual reports to stockholders. . . .

This background of the acquisition, particularly the plain implications of the contemporaneous documents, destroys any basis for a conclusion that the purchase was made "solely for investment." Moreover, immediately after the acquisition, du Pont's influence growing out of it was brought to bear within General Motors to achieve primacy for du Pont as General Motors' supplier of automotive fabrics and finishes.

Two years were to pass before du Pont's total purchases of General Motors stock brought its percentage to 23% of the outstanding stock and its aggregate outlay to $49,000,000. . . . Haskell, du Pont's former sales manager and vice-president, became the General Motors vice-president in charge of the operations committee. The trial judge said that Haskell ". . . was willing to undertake the responsibility of keeping du Pont informed of General Motors affairs during Durant's regime. . . ."

Haskell frankly and openly set about gaining the maximum share of the General Motors market for du Pont. In a contemporaneous 1918 document, he reveals his intention to "pave the way for perhaps a more general adoption of our material," and that he was thinking "how best to get cooperation [from the several General Motors Divisions] whereby makers of such of the low priced cars as it would seem possible and wise to get transferred will be put in the frame of mind necessary for its adoption [du Pont's artificial leather]." . . .

Thus sprung from the barrier, du Pont quickly swept into a commanding lead over its competitors, who were never afterwards in serious contention. . . .

In less than four years, by August 1921, Lammot du Pont, then a du Pont vice-president and later Chairman of the Board of General Motors, in response to a query from Pierre S. du Pont, then Chairman of the Board of both du Pont and General Motors, "whether General Motors was taking its entire requirements of du Pont products from du Pont," was able to reply that four of General Motors' eight operating divisions bought from du Pont their entire requirements of paints and varnishes, five their entire requirements of Fabrikoid, four their entire requirements of rubber cloth, and seven their entire requirements of Pyralin and celluloid. Lammot du Pont quoted du Pont's sales department as feeling that "the condition is improving and that eventually satisfactory conditions will be established in every branch, but they wouldn't mind seeing things going a little faster." . . .

Competitors did obtain higher percentages of the General Motors business in later years, although never high enough at any time substantially to affect the dollar amount of du Pont's sales. Indeed, it appears likely that General Motors probably turned to outside sources of supply at least in part because its requirements outstripped du Pont's production, when General Motors' proportion of total automobile sales grew greater and the company took its place as the sales leader of the automobile industry. . . .

The fact that sticks out in this voluminous record is that the bulk of du Pont's production has always supplied the largest part of the requirements of the one customer in the automobile industry connected to du Pont by a stock interest. The inference is overwhelming that du Pont's commanding position was promoted by its stock interest and was not gained solely on competitive merit.

We agree with the trial court that considerations of price, quality and service were not overlooked by either du Pont or General Motors. Pride in its products and its high financial stake in General Motors' success would naturally lead du Pont to try to supply the best. But the wisdom of this business judgment cannot obscure the fact, plainly revealed by the record, that du Pont purposely employed its stock to pry open the General Motors market to entrench itself as the primary supplier of General Motors' requirements for automotive finishes and fabrics. . . .

. . . We repeat, that the test of a violation of §7 is whether, at the time of suit, there is a reasonable probability that the acquisition is likely to result in the condemned restraints. The conclusion upon this record is inescapable that such likelihood was proved as to this acquisition. The fire that was kindled in 1917 continues to smolder. It burned briskly to forge the ties that bind the General Motors market to du Pont, and if it has quieted down, it remains hot, and, from past performance, is likely at any time to blaze and make the fusion complete.

The judgment must therefore be reversed and the cause remanded to the District Court for a determination, after further hearing, of the equitable relief necessary and appropriate in the public interest to eliminate the effects of the acquisition offensive to the statute.

It is so ordered.

[Justices Clark, Harlan, and Whittaker took no part in the consideration or decision of the case.]

Mr. Justice Burton, whom Mr. Justice Frankfurter joins, dissenting.

. . . In brief it was alleged that, by means of the relationship between du Pont and General Motors, du Pont intended to obtain, and did obtain, an illegal preference over its competitors in the sale to General Motors of its products, and a further illegal preference in the development of chemical discoveries made by General Motors. . . .

. . . District Court found that the Government had failed to prove its case and, specifically, that (a) du Pont did not control General Motors, (b) there had been "no limitation or restraint upon General Motors' freedom to deal freely and fully with competitors of du Pont" or upon its "freedom . . . to deal with its chemical discoveries," and (c) after 30 years in which no such restraint had resulted, there was no "basis for a finding that there is or has been any reasonable probability of such a restraint within the meaning of the Clayton Act." . . .

This Court, ignoring the Sherman Act issues which have been the focal point of eight years of litigation, now holds that du Pont's acquisition of a 23% stock interest in General Motors during the years 1917–1919 violates §7 of the Clayton Act because "at the time of suit [in 1949] there [was] a reasonable probability that the acquisition [was] likely to result in the condemned restraints." . . . In reaching this conclusion, the Court holds (1) that §7 of the Clayton Act applies to vertical as well as horizontal stock acquisitions; (2) that in determining whether the effect of the stock acquisition is such as to constitute a restraint within §7, the time chosen by the Government in bringing the action is controlling rather than the time of the acquisition itself; and (3) that §7 is violated when, at the time of suit, there is a reasonable probability that the stock acquisition is likely to result in the foreclosure of competitors of the acquiring corporation from a substantial share of the relevant market.

The Court's decision is far reaching. Although §7 of the Clayton Act was enacted in 1914—over 40 years ago—this is the first case in which the United States or the Federal Trade Commission has sought to apply it to a vertical integration. . . . All that is required, if this case is to be our guide, is that some court in some future year be persuaded that a "reasonable probability" then exists that an advantage over competitors in a narrowly construed market may be obtained as a result of the stock interest. Thus, over 40 years after the enactment of the Clayton Act, it now becomes apparent for the first time that §7 has been a sleeping giant all along. Every corporation which has acquired a stock interest in another corporation after the enactment of the Clayton Act in 1914, and which has had business dealings with that corporation is exposed, retroactively, to the bite of the newly discovered teeth of §7. . . .

4

Mergers under the
Amended Section 7—I

The cases in the previous chapter illustrate the ineffectiveness and loopholes of the original Section 7 of the Clayton Act. Mergers achieved via asset acquisitions were legal, and the Act did not prohibit either vertical or conglomerate mergers. This chapter and the following one contain cases that have been decided since the 1950 Celler-Kefauver amendment to Section 7. Although the Sherman Act is still applicable to mergers,[1] the new Section 7 is now the more relevant statute for challenging mergers. In order to see what changes the amendment made, a comparison is given below between the old and new wording (words in italics were added by the amendment; those in brackets were deleted):

> No corporation engaged in commerce shall acquire, directly or indirectly, the whole or any part of the stock or other share capital *and no corporation [subject to the jurisdiction of the Federal Trade Commission shall acquire the whole* or *any part of the assets]* of another corporation engaged also in commerce where *in any line of commerce in any section of the country,* the effect of such acquisition may be [to] substantially *to* lessen competition [between the corporation whose stock is so acquired and the corporation making the acquisition, or to restrain such commerce in any section or community] or *to* tend to create a monopoly [of any line of commerce].

The cases reveal that the amendment did indeed make very substantial changes in the merger law. The important interpretations of the Supreme Court, in addition to one court of appeals decision, handed down under the new Section 7 are included in these two chapters. *Horizontal* and *vertical mergers,* discussed in the first section, are combined in one grouping because to date there has not been a case that could be labeled strictly as a vertical merger. The second section includes mergers in regulated industries. We give separate treatment to these mergers because they must be approved by the appropriate regulatory agency before the Justice Department contests the case.

Horizontal and Vertical Mergers

The Supreme Court was not called upon to interpret the Celler-Kefauver amendment until the *Brown Shoe* case in 1962. This decision, a unanimous one,

---

[1] A Sherman Act violation was charged and upheld by the Supreme Court in *U.S. v. First National Bank of Lexington,* 376 U.S. 665 (1964).

has proved to be a landmark interpretation. The Court recognized the importance of the precedent being set and did not hesitate to explore fully all ramifications of the intent of Congress with regard to the direction future merger policy should assume.

The case combined both horizontal and vertical aspects of merging since the two merging parties, Brown Shoe Company and G. R. Kinney Company, were each engaged in both the manufacturing and retailing of shoes. The first part of the decision is devoted to reviewing the facts and noting that neither of the firms had dominant market positions in terms of percentage market shares. At the time of the merger in 1956, Brown was manufacturing 4 per cent of the national output of shoes and was the third largest retailer. Kinney was also a "large manufacturer of shoes" and the eighth leading retailer. Nearly a thousand firms manufactured shoes, and retailing was carried on by some seventy thousand stores. By any measure used, the shoe business was not highly concentrated, nor would this merger be one that resulted in significantly increased concentration in and of itself.

Recognizing the importance of the case before it, the Court reviewed in detail the intent of Congress in passing the 1950 amendment. A series of eight points were listed as crucial to the interpretation of congressional intent. Among these were specific recognition that the law would now apply to all mergers—vertical and conglomerate as well as horizontal. Congress did intend to plug the assets loophole while at the same time stopping short of making mergers *per se* violations. The Court believed Congress was motivated primarily by the fear of what was considered a "rising tide of economic concentration" and desired to erect a barrier against the tide by granting authority to the courts to arrest mergers while the trend toward lessening of competition "was still in its incipiency."

The Court went on to examine the merger before them in terms of its vertical aspects by looking at the effect on the product market, the geographic market, and the probable impact on competition. The Court's conviction was that the anticompetitive effects of vertical mergers come from the foreclosing of a substantial share of the market to competitors "without producing any countervailing competitive, economic, or social advantages." The ultimate result of this merger would be to put Brown shoes in Kinney stores and exclude competitors from these outlets. The horizontal aspects of the merger, occurring at both the manufacturing and retailing level, must be viewed in terms of the same three criteria, but the relative market share now becomes more important. And even on this score the fact that Brown's share of shoe manufacturing was increased from 4 to 5 per cent was not given as much weight as the noticeable shoe industry trend toward concentration. The Court believed the merger, in both its vertical and horizontal characteristics, was contrary to the intent of Congress.

Another important facet of the case involved standards for determining the relevant market. A number of guidelines were established, including one that a line of commerce generally considered shoes may be further subdivided into men's, women's, and children's—that is, sub-lines within a line of commerce may exist. Thus a merger may be ruled illegal if there is any substantial lessening of competition in a sub-line of a broader product line.

It is obvious from this case and those that follow it that the hand of the Justice Department has been greatly strengthened in merger cases. The government can now select a definition of the relevant market from a number of very broad or very narrow alternative measures, the primary restriction being that it must be a credible one that the Court will accept. Since the market may be viewed from a number of vantage points, the defendants must be prepared to argue their case by using the weapons chosen by the opposition.

BROWN SHOE COMPANY v. UNITED STATES

370 U.S. 294 (1962)

MR. CHIEF JUSTICE WARREN delivered the opinion of the Court.[2]

I

This suit was initiated in November 1955 when the Government filed a civil action in the United States District Court for the Eastern District of Missouri alleging that a contemplated merger between the G. R. Kinney Company, Inc. (Kinney), and the Brown Shoe Company, Inc. (Brown), through an exchange of Kinney for Brown stock, would violate §7 of the Clayton Act, . . .

A motion by the Government for a preliminary injunction *pendente lite* was denied, and the companies were permitted to merge provided, however, that their businesses be operated separately and that their assets be kept separately identifiable. The merger was then effected on May 1, 1956.

In the District Court, the Government contended that the effect of the merger of Brown—the third largest seller of shoes by dollar volume in the United States, a leading manufacturer of men's, women's, and children's shoes, and a retailer with over 1,230 owned, operated or controlled retail outlets—and Kinney—the eighth largest company, by dollar volume,

[2] The citations and footnotes from the opinions of the Court have been, with a few exceptions, omitted from the cases in this chapter.

among those primarily engaged in selling shoes, itself a large manufacturer of shoes, and a retailer with over 350 retail outlets—"may be substantially to lessen competition or to tend to create a monopoly" by eliminating actual or potential competition in the production of shoes for the national wholesale shoe market and in the sale of shoes at retail in the Nation, by foreclosing competition from "a market represented by Kinney's retail outlets whose annual sales exceed $42,000,000," and by enhancing Brown's competitive advantage over other producers, distributors and sellers of shoes. The Government argued that the "line of commerce" affected by this merger is "footwear," or alternatively, that the "line[s]" are "men's," "women's," and "children's" shoes, separately considered, and that the "section of the country," within which the anticompetitive effect of the merger is to be judged, is the Nation as a whole, or alternatively, each separate city or city and its immediate surrounding area in which the parties sell shoes at retail. . . .

THE INDUSTRY The District Court found that although domestic shoe production was scattered among a large number of manufacturers, a small number of large companies occupied a commanding position. Thus, while the 24 largest manufacturers produced about 35% of the Nation's shoes, the top 4—International, Endicott-Johnson, Brown (including Kinney) and General Shoe—alone produced approximately 23% of the Nation's shoes or 65% of the production of the top 24.

In 1955, domestic production of nonrubber shoes was 509.2 million pairs, of which about 103.6 million pairs were men's shoes, about 271 million pairs were women's shoes, and about 134.6 million pairs were children's shoes. The District Court found that men's, women's, and children's shoes are normally produced in separate factories.

The public buys these shoes through about 70,000 retail outlets, only 22,000 of which, however, derive 50% or more of their gross receipts from the sale of shoes and are classified as "shoe stores" by the Census Bureau. These 22,000 shoe stores were found generally to sell (1) men's shoes only, (2) women's shoes only, (3) women's and children's shoes, or (4) men's, women's, and children's shoes. . . .

BROWN SHOE Brown Shoe was found not only to have been a participant, but also a moving factor, in these industry trends. . . . Between 1952 and 1955 Brown made a number of smaller acquisitions: Wetherby-Kayser Shoe Company (three retail stores), Barnes & Company (two stores), Reilly Shoe Company (two leased shoe departments), Richardson Shoe Store (one store), and Wohl Shoe Company of Dallas (not connected with Wohl) (leased shoe departments in Dallas). In 1954, Brown made another major acquisition: Regal Shoe Corporation which, at the time, operated one manufacturing plant producing men's shoes and 110 retail outlets. . . .

During the same period of time, Brown also acquired the stock or assets of seven companies engaged solely in shoe manufacturing. As a result, in 1955, Brown was the fourth largest shoe manufacturer in the country, producing about 25.6 million pairs of shoes or about 4% of the Nation's total footwear production.

KINNEY   Kinney is principally engaged in operating the largest family-style shoe store chain in the United States. At the time of trial, Kinney was found to be operating over 400 such stores in more than 270 cities. These stores were found to make about 1.2% of all national retail shoe sales by dollar volume. . . .

In addition to this extensive retail activity, Kinney owned and operated four plants which manufactured men's, women's, and children's shoes and whose combined output was 0.5% of the national shoe production in 1955, making Kinney the twelfth largest shoe manufacturer in the United States.

Kinney stores were found to obtain about 20% of their shoes from Kinney's own manufacturing plants. At the time of the merger, Kinney bought no shoes from Brown; however, in line with Brown's conceded reasons for acquiring Kinney, Brown had, by 1957, become the largest outside supplier of Kinney's shoes, supplying 7.9% of all Kinney's needs.

It is in this setting that the merger was considered and held to violate §7 of the Clayton Act. The District Court ordered Brown to divest itself completely of all stock, share capital, assets or other interests it held in Kinney, to operate Kinney to the greatest degree possible as an independent concern pending complete divestiture, to refrain thereafter from acquiring or having any interest in Kinney's business or assets, and to file with the court within 90 days a plan for carrying into effect the divestiture decreed. The District Court also stated it would retain jurisdiction over the cause to enable the parties to apply for such further relief as might be necessary to enforce and apply the judgment. Prior to its submission of a divestiture plan, Brown filed a notice of appeal in the District Court. . . .

III LEGISLATIVE HISTORY

This case is one of the first to come before us in which the Government's complaint is based upon allegations that the appellant has violated §7 of the Clayton Act, as that section was amended in 1950. The amendments adopted in 1950 culminated extensive efforts over a number of years, on the parts of both the Federal Trade Commission and some members of Congress, to secure revision of a section of the antitrust laws considered by many observers to be ineffective in its then existing form. . . . In the light of this extensive legislative attention to the measure, and the broad, general language finally selected by Congress for the expression of its will, we think it appropriate to review the history of the amended Act in determining whether the judgment of the court below was consistent with the intent of the legislature. . . .

As enacted in 1914, §7 of the original Clayton Act prohibited the acquisition by one corporation of the *stock* of another corporation when such acquisition would result in a substantial lessening of competition *between the acquiring and the acquired* companies, or tend to create a monopoly in any line of commerce. The Act did not, by its explicit terms, or as construed by this Court, bar the acquisition by one corporation of the *assets* of another. Nor did it appear to preclude the acquisition of stock in any corporation other than a direct competitor. . . .

It was, however, not long before the Federal Trade Commission recognized deficiencies in the Act as first enacted. Its Annual Reports frequently suggested amendments, principally along two lines: first, to "plug the loophole" exempting asset acquisitions from coverage under the Act, and second, to require companies proposing a merger to give the Commission prior notification of their plans. . . .

The dominant theme pervading congressional consideration of the 1950 amendments was a fear of what was considered to be a rising tide of economic concentration in the American economy. . . . Throughout the recorded discussion may be found examples of Congress' fear not only of accelerated concentration of economic power on economic grounds, but also of the threat to other values a trend toward concentration was thought to pose.

What were some of the factors, relevant to a judgment as to the validity of a given merger, specifically discussed by Congress in redrafting §7?

First, there is no doubt that Congress did wish to "plug the loophole" and to include within the coverage of the Act the acquisition of assets no less than the acquisition of stock.

Second, by the deletion of the "acquiring-acquired" language in the original text, it hoped to make plain that §7 applied not only to mergers between actual competitors, but also to vertical and conglomerate mergers whose effect may tend to lessen competition in any line of commerce in any section of the country.

Third, it is apparent that a keystone in the erection of a barrier to what Congress saw was the rising tide of economic concentration, was its

provision of authority for arresting mergers at a time when the trend to a lessening of competition in a line of commerce was still in its incipiency.
. . .

Fourth, and closely related to the third, Congress rejected, as inappropriate to the problem it sought to remedy, the application to §7 cases of the standards for judging the legality of business combinations adopted by the courts in dealing with cases arising under the Sherman Act, and which may have been applied to some early cases arising under original §7.

Fifth, at the same time that it sought to create an effective tool for preventing all mergers having demonstrable anticompetitive effects, Congress recognized the stimulation to competition that might flow from particular mergers. When concern as to the Act's breadth was expressed, supporters of the amendments indicated that it would not impede, for example, a merger between two small companies to enable the combination to compete more effectively with larger corporations dominating the relevant market, nor a merger between a corporation which is financially healthy and a failing one which no longer can be a vital competitive factor in the market. The deletion of the word "community" in the original Act's description of the relevant geographic market is another illustration of Congress' desire to indicate that its concern was with the adverse effects of a given merger on competition only in an economically significant "section" of the country. Taken as a whole, the legislative history illuminates congressional concern with the protection of *competition*, not *competitors*, and its desire to restrain mergers only to the extent that such combinations may tend to lessen competition.

Sixth, Congress neither adopted nor rejected specifically any particular tests for measuring the relevant markets, either as defined in terms of product or in terms of geographic locus of competition, within which the anti-competitive effects of a merger were to be judged. Nor did it adopt a definition of the word "substantially " whether in quantitative terms of sales or assets or market shares or in designated qualitative terms, by which a merger's effects on competition were to be measured.[3]

Seventh, while providing no definite quantitative or qualitative tests

---

[3] The House Report on H.R. 2734 stated that two tests of illegality were included in the proposed Act: whether the merger substantially lessened competition or tended to create a monopoly. It stated that such effects could be perceived through findings, for example, that a whole or material part of the competitive activity of an enterprise, which had been a substantial factor in competition, had been eliminated; that the relative size of the acquiring corporation had increased to such a point that its advantage over competitors threatened to be "decisive"; that an "undue" number of competing enterprises had seen eliminated; or that buyers and sellers in the relevant market had established relationships depriving their rivals of a fair opportunity to compete. H.R. Rep. No. 1191, 81st Cong., 1st Sess. 8. Each of these standards, couched in general language, reflects a conscious avoidance of exclusively mathematical tests . . .

by which enforcement agencies could gauge the effects of a given merger to determine whether it may "substantially" lessen competition or tend toward monopoly, Congress indicated plainly that a merger had to be functionally viewed, in the context of its particular industry. That is, whether the consolidation was to take place in an industry that was fragmented rather than concentrated, that had seen a recent trend toward domination by a few leaders or had remained fairly consistent in its distribution of market shares among the participating companies, that had experienced easy access to markets by suppliers and easy access to suppliers by buyers or had witnessed foreclosure of business, that had witnessed the ready entry of new competition or the erection of barriers to prospective entrants, all were aspects, varying in importance with the merger under consideration, which would properly be taken into account.

Eighth, Congress used the words "*may be* substantially to lessen competition" (emphasis supplied), to indicate that its concern was with probabilities, not certainties. . . .

IV The Vertical Aspects of the Merger

Economic arrangements between companies standing in a supplier-customer relationship are characterized as "vertical." The primary vice of a vertical merger or other arrangement tying a customer to a supplier is that, by foreclosing the competitors of either party from a segment of the market otherwise open to them, the arrangement may act as a "clog on competition," *Standard Oil Co. of California* v. *United States*, . . . which "deprive[s] . . . rivals of a fair opportunity to compete." . . . The "area of effective competition" must be determined by reference to a product market (the "line of commerce") and a geographic market (the "section of the country").

THE PRODUCT MARKET   The outer boundaries of a product market are determined by the reasonable interchangeability of use or the cross-elasticity of demand between the product itself and substitutes for it. However, within this broad market, well-defined submarkets may exist which in themselves, constitute product markets for antitrust purposes. . . . The boundaries of such a submarket may be determined by examining such practical indicia as industry or public recognition of the submarket as a separate economic entity, the product's peculiar characteristics and uses, unique production facilities, distinct customers, distinct prices, sensitivity to price changes, and specialized vendors. Because §7 of the Clayton Act prohibits any merger which may substantially lessen competition "in *any* line of commerce" (emphasis supplied), it is necessary to examine the effects of a merger in each such economically significant submarket to determine if there is a reasonable probability that the merger will substantially lessen competition. If such a probability is found to exist, the merger is proscribed.

Applying these considerations to the present case, we conclude that the record supports the District Court's finding that the relevant lines of commerce are men's, women's, and children's shoes. These product lines are recognized by the public; each line is manufactured in separate plants; each has characteristics peculiar to itself rendering it generally noncompetitive with the others; and each is, of course, directed toward a distinct class of customers. . . .

THE GEOGRAPHIC MARKET   We agree with the parties and the District Court that insofar as the vertical aspect of this merger is concerned, the relevant geographic market is the entire Nation. The relationships of product value, bulk, weight and consumer demand enable manufacturers to distribute their shoes on a nationwide basis, as Brown and Kinney in fact, do. The anticompetitive effects of the merger are to be measured within this range of distribution.

THE PROBABLE EFFECT OF THE MERGER   Once the area of effective competition affected by a vertical arrangement has been defined, an analysis must be made to determine if the effect of the arrangement "may be substantially to lessen competition, or to tend to create a monopoly" in this market.

Since the diminution of the vigor of competition which may stem from a vertical arrangement results primarily from a foreclosure of a share of the market otherwise open to competitors, an important consideration in determining whether the effect of a vertical arrangement "may be substantially to lessen competition, or to tend to create a monopoly" is the size of the share of the market foreclosed. . . .

A most important such factor to examine is the very nature and purpose of the arrangement. Congress not only indicated that "the tests of illegality [under §7] are intended to be similar to those which the courts have applied in interpreting the same language as used in other sections of the Clayton Act," but also chose for §7 language virtually identical to that of §3 of the Clayton Act, . . . which had been interpreted by this Court to require an examination of the interdependence of the market share foreclosed by, and the economic purpose of, the vertical arrangement. . . .

. . . Congress foresaw that the merger of two large companies or a large and a small company might violate the Clayton Act while the merger of two small companies might not, although the share of the market foreclosed be identical, if the purpose of the small companies is to enable them in combination to compete with larger corporations dominating the market. . . .

The District Court's findings, and the record facts, many of them set forth in Part I of this opinion, convince us that the shoe industry is being subjected to just such a cumulative series of vertical mergers which, if left unchecked, will be likely "substantially to lessen competition."

We reach this conclusion because the trend toward vertical integration in the shoe industry, when combined with Brown's avowed policy of forcing its own shoes upon its retail subsidiaries may foreclose competition from a substantial share of the markets for men's, women's, and children's shoes, without producing any countervailing competitive, economic, or social advantages.

V The Horizontal Aspects
of the Merger

An economic arrangement between companies performing similar functions in the production or sale of comparable goods or services is characterized as "horizontal." The effect on competition of such an arrangement depends, of course, upon its character and scope. Thus, its validity in the face of the antitrust laws will depend upon such factors as: the relative size and number of the parties to the arrangement; whether it allocates shares of the market among the parties; whether it fixes prices at which the parties will sell their product; or whether it absorbs or insulates competitors. . . .

THE PRODUCT MARKET   Shoes are sold in the United States in retail shoe stores and in shoe departments of general stores. These outlets sell: (1) men's shoes, (2) women's shoes, (3) women's or children's shoes, or (4) men's, women's or children's shoes. Prior to the merger, both Brown and Kinney sold their shoes in competition with one another through the enumerated kinds of outlets characteristic of the industry.

In Part IV of this opinion we hold that the District Court correctly defined men's, women's, and children's shoes as the relevant lines of commerce in which to analyze the vertical aspects of the merger. For the reasons there stated we also hold that the same lines of commerce are appropriate for considering the horizontal aspects of the merger.

THE GEOGRAPHIC MARKET   The criteria to be used in determining the appropriate geographic market are essentially similar to those used to determine the relevant product market. . . . Moreover, just as a product submarket may have §7 significance as the proper "line of commerce," so may a geographic submarket be considered the appropriate "section of the country." . . . Congress prescribed a pragmatic, factual approach to the definition of the relevant market and not a formal, legalistic one. The geographic market selected must, therefore both "correspond to the commercial realities" of the industry and be economically significant. Thus, although the geographic market in some instances may encompass the entire Nation, under other circumtances it may be as small as a single metropolitan area. . . .

The parties do not dispute the findings of the District Court that the Nation as a whole is the relevant geographic market for measuring the anticompetitive effects of the merger viewed vertically or of the horizontal merger of Brown's and Kinney's manufacturing facilities. As to the retail level, however, they disagree.

The District Court found that the effects of this aspect of the merger must be analyzed in every city with a population exceeding 10,000 and its immediate contiguous surrounding territory in which both Brown and Kinney sold shoes at retail through stores they either owned or controlled. By this definition of the geographic market, less than one-half of all the cities in which either Brown or Kinney sold shoes through such outlets are represented. The appellant recognizes that if the District Court's characterization of the relevant market is proper, the number of markets in which both Brown and Kinney have outlets is sufficiently numerous so that the validity of the entire merger is properly judged by testing its effects in those markets. However, it is appellant's contention that the areas of effective competition in shoe retailing were improperly defined by the District Court. It claims that such areas should, in some cases, be defined so as to include only the central business districts of large cities, and in others, so as to encompass the "standard metropolitan areas" within which smaller communities are found. It argues that any test failing to distinguish between these competitive situations is improper.

We believe, however, that the record fully supports the District Court's findings that shoe stores in the outskirts of cities compete effectively with stores in central downtown areas, and that while there is undoubtedly some commercial intercourse between smaller communities within a single "standard metropolitan area," the most intense and important competition in retail sales will be confined to stores within the particular communities in such an area and their immediate environs.[4]

We therefore agree that the District Court properly defined the relevant geographic markets . . .

---

[4] The District Court limited its findings to cities having a population of at least 10,000 persons, since Kinney operated only in such areas.

THE PROBABLE EFFECT OF THE MERGER   Having delineated the product and geographic markets within which the effects of this merger are to be measured, we turn to an examination of the District Court's finding that as a result of the merger competition in the retailing of men's, women's and children's shoes may be lessened substantially in those cities in which both Brown and Kinney stores are located. . . .

In the case before us, not only was a fair sample used to demonstrate the soundness of the District Court's conclusions, but evidence of record fully substantiates those findings as to each relevant market. An analysis of undisputed statistics of sales of shoes in the cities in which both Brown and Kinney sell shoes at retail, separated into the appropriate lines of commerce, provides a persuasive factual foundation upon which the required prognosis of the merger's effects may be built. . . . They show, for example, that during 1955 in 32 separate cities, ranging in size and location from Topeka, Kansas, to Batavia, New York, and Hobbs, New Mexico, the combined share of Brown and Kinney sales of women's shoes (by unit volume) exceeded 20%. In 31 cities—some the same as those used in measuring the effect of the merger in the women's line—the combined share of children's shoes sales exceeded 20%; in 6 cities their share exceeded 40%. In Dodge City, Kansas, their combined share of the market for women's shoes was over 57%; their share of the children's shoe market in that city was 49%. In the 7 cities in which Brown's and Kinney's combined shares of the market for women's shoes were greatest (ranging from 33% to 57%) each of the parties alone, prior to the merger, had captured substantial portions of those markets (ranging from 13% to 34%); the merger intensified this existing concentration. In 118 separate cities the combined shares of the market of Brown and Kinney in the sale of one of the relevant lines of commerce exceeded 5%. In 47 cities, their share exceeded 5% in all three lines.

The market share which companies may control by merging is one of the most important factors to be considered when determining the probable effects of the combination on effective competition in the relevant market. In an industry as fragmented as shoe retailing, the control of substantial shares of the trade in a city may have important effects on competition. If a merger achieving 5% control were now approved, we might be required to approve future merger efforts by Brown's competitors seeking similar market shares. The oligopoly Congress sought to avoid would then be furthered and it would be difficult to dissolve the combinations previously approved. . . .

Other factors to be considered in evaluating the probable effects of a merger in the relevant market lend additional support to the District Court's conclusion that this merger may substantially lessen competition. One such factor is the history of tendency toward concentration in the industry.[5] As we have previously pointed out, the shoe industry has, in recent years, been a prime example of such a trend. Most combinations have been between manufacturers and retailers, as each of the larger producers has sought to capture an increasing number of assured outlets for its wares. Although these mergers have been primarily vertical in their aim and effect, to the extent that they have brought ever greater numbers of retail outlets within fewer and fewer hands, they have had an additional important impact on the horizontal plane. By the merger in this case, the largest single group of retail stores still independent of one of the large manufacturers was absorbed into an already substantial aggregation of more or less controlled retail outlets. As a result of this merger, Brown moved into second place nationally in terms of retail stores directly owned. Including the stores on its franchise plan, the merger placed under Brown's control almost 1,600 shoe outlets, or about 7.2% of the Nation's retail "shoe stores" as defined by the Census Bureau, and 2.3% of the Nation's total retail shoe outlets. We cannot avoid the mandate of Congress that tendencies toward concentration in industry are to be curbed in their incipiency, particularly when those tendencies are being accelerated through giant steps striding across a hundred cities at a time. In the light of the trends in this industry we agree with the Government and the court below that this is an appropriate place at which to call a halt.

At the same time appellant has presented no mitigating factors, such as the business failure or the inadequate resources of one of the parties that may have prevented it from maintaining its competitive position, nor a demonstrated need for combination to enable small companies to enter into a more meaningful competition with those dominating the relevant markets. On the basis of the record before us, we believe the Government sustained its burden of proof. We hold that the District Court was correct in concluding that this merger may tend to lessen competition substantially in the retail sale of men's, women's, and children's shoes in the overwhelming majority of those cities and their environs in which both Brown and Kinney sell through owned or controlled outlets.

The judgment is

Affirmed.

[5] . . . A company's history of expansion through mergers presents a different economic picture than a history of expansion through unilateral growth. Internal expansion is more likely to be the result of increased demand for the company's products and is more likely to provide increased investment in plants, more jobs and greater output. Conversely, expansion through merger is more likely to reduce available consumer choice while providing no increase in industry capacity, jobs or output. It was for these reasons, among others, Congress expressed its disapproval of successive acquisitions. Section 7 was enacted to prevent even small mergers that added to concentration in an industry. . . .

MR. JUSTICE FRANKFURTER took no part in the decision of this case.

MR. JUSTICE WHITE took no part in the consideration or decision of this case.

The significance of the merger case involving the Aluminum Company of America and the Rome Cable Corporation is to be found in the Supreme Court's interpretation of the "relevant market" in which the alleged substantial lessening of competition was to take place. In this instance the relevant line of commerce was judged to be very narrow, consisting of a "line within a line" as established by the guidelines of the Brown Shoe case.

In 1959 Alcoa acquired the stock and assets of Rome, primarily a manufacturer of insulated copper products. In the year before the acquisition, Rome produced 0.3 per cent of the industry's output of bare aluminum conductor, 4.7 per cent of insulated aluminum conductor, and 1.3 per cent of the two lines combined. On the other hand, Alcoa did not produce any copper conductor, and its total share of the bare and insulated aluminum conductor market was 27.8 per cent. All these conductors are used in the transmission of electrical power—overhead lines consisting mainly of aluminum conductor and underground lines relying essentially on copper.

The district court separated aluminum conductor into its two varieties—bare and insulated. It held that bare conductor was one line of commerce while insulated copper and aluminum form a separate line of commerce. By this grouping the lower court could find no substantial lessening of competition. The Supreme Court, however, noted that each type of conductor has developed distinctive end uses, and there is a substantial price differential between the two. Hence bare and insulated aluminum should properly form one line of commerce distinct from that of copper. After this determination was made, there was little chance for the merger to stand. Although the acquisition of Rome added only 1.3 per cent to Alcoa's number one position in the aluminum conductor business, the industry was already dominated by a few large firms and the number of independent firms was small and diminishing. This kind of merger should be proscribed because "Rome seems to us the prototype of the small independent that Congress aimed to preserve by Section 7."

UNITED STATES v. ALUMINUM CO. OF AMERICA et al.

377 U.S. 271 (1964)

MR. JUSTICE DOUGLAS delivered the opinion of the Court.

The question is whether the 1959 acquisition by the Aluminum Company of America (Alcoa) of the stock and assets of the Rome Cable Corporation (Rome) "may be substantially to lessen competition, or to tend to create a monopoly" in the production and sale of various wire and cable products and accessories within the meaning of §7 of the Clayton Act. The United States, claiming that §7 had been violated, instituted this civil suit and prayed for divestiture. The District Court, after a trial, held that there was no violation and dismissed the complaint.

I

The initial question concerns the identification of the "line of commerce," as the term is used in §7.

Aluminum wire and cable (aluminum conductor) is a composite of bare aluminum wire and cable (bare aluminum conductor) and insulated or covered wire and cable (insulated aluminum conductor). These products are designed almost exclusively for use by electric utilities in carrying electric power from generating plants to consumers throughout the country. Copper conductor wire and cable (copper conductor) is the only other product utilized commercially for the same general purpose. Rome produced both copper conductor and aluminum conductor. In 1958—the year prior to the merger—it produced 0.3% of total industry production of bare aluminum conductor, 4.7% of insulated aluminum conductor, and 1.3% of the broader aluminum conductor line.

Alcoa produced no copper conductor. In 1958 it produced 32.5% of the bare aluminum conductor, 11.6% of insulated aluminum conductor, and 27.8% of aluminum conductor.

These products, as noted, are most often used by operating electrical utilities. Transmission and distribution lines are usually strung above ground, except in heavily congested areas, such as city centers, where they are run underground. Overhead, where the lines are bare or not heavily insulated, aluminum has virtually displaced copper, except in seacoast areas, as shown by the following table:

Percent of Aluminum Conductor in Gross Additions to Overhead
Utility Lines

	1950	1955	1959
Transmission Lines (All Bare Conductor)	74.4%	91.0%	94.4%
Distribution Lines:			
Bare Conductor	35.5	64.4	79.0
Insulated Conductor	6.5	51.6	77.2
Total, Transmission and Distribution Lines	25.0	60.9	80.1

Underground, where the conductor must be heavily insulated, copper is virtually the only conductor used. In sum, while aluminum conductor dominates the overhead field, copper remains virtually unrivaled in all other conductor applications.

The parties agree, and the District Court found, that bare aluminum conductor is a separate line of commerce. The District Court, however, denied that status to the broader aluminum conductor line because it found that insulated aluminum conductor is not an appropriate line of commerce separate and distinct from its copper counterpart. The court said the broad product group cannot result in a line of commerce, since a line of commerce cannot be composed of two parts, one of which independently qualifies as a line of commerce and one of which does not. . . .

Insulated aluminum conductor is so intrinsically inferior to insulated copper conductor that in most applications it has little consumer acceptance. But in the field of overhead distribution it enjoys decisive advantages—its share of total annual installations increasing from 6.5% in 1950 to 77.2% in 1959. In the field of overhead distribution the competition of copper is rapidly decreasing. As the record shows, utilizing a high-cost metal, fabricators of insulated copper conductor are powerless to eliminate the price disadvantage under which they labor and thus can do little to make their product competitive, unless they enter the aluminum field. The price of most insulated aluminum conductors is indeed only 50% to 65% of the price of their copper counterparts; and the comparative installed costs are also generally less. As the District Court found, aluminum and copper conductor prices do not respond to one another.

Separation of insulated aluminum conductor from insulated copper conductor and placing it in another submarket is, therefore, proper. It is not inseparable from its copper equivalent though the class of customers is the same. The choice between copper and aluminum for overhead distribution does not usually turn on the quality of the respective products, for each does the job equally well. The vital factors are economic considerations. . . .

The combination of bare and insulated aluminum conductor products into one market or line of commerce seems to us proper.[6] Both types are used for the purpose of conducting electricity and are sold to the same customers, electrical utilities. While the copper conductor does compete with aluminum conductor, each has developed distinctive end uses— aluminum as an overhead conductor and copper for underground and indoor wiring, applications in which aluminum's brittleness and larger size render it impractical. And, as we have seen, the price differential further sets them apart.

Thus, contrary to the District Court, we conclude (1) that aluminum conductor and copper conductor are separable for the purpose of analyzing the competitive effect of the merger and (2) that aluminum conductor (bare and insulated) is therefore a submarket and for purposes of §7 a "line of commerce."

II

Taking aluminum conductor as an appropriate "line of commerce" we conclude that the merger violated §7.

Alcoa is a leader in markets in which economic power is highly concentrated. Prior to the end of World War II it was the sole producer of primary aluminum and the sole fabricator of aluminum conductor. It was held in 1945 to have monopolized the aluminum industry in violation of §2 of the Sherman Act. . . .

In 1958—the year prior to the merger—Alcoa was the leading producer of aluminum conductor, with 27.8% of the market; in bare aluminum conductor, it also led the industry, with 32.5%. Alcoa plus Kaiser controlled 50% of the aluminum conductor market and, with its three leading competitors, more than 76%. Only nine concerns (including Rome with 1.3%) accounted for 95.7% of the output of aluminum conductor. In the narrower market of insulated aluminum conductor, Alcoa was third with 11.6% and Rome was eighth with 4.7%. Five companies controlled 65.4% and four smaller ones, including Rome, added another 22.8%.

In other words, the line of commerce showed highly concentrated

---

[6] The dissent criticizes this grouping of bare and insulated aluminum conductor into one line of commerce. This overlooks the fact that the parties agree, and the District Court found, that bare aluminum conductor and conductor generally (aluminum and copper, bare and insulated) constitute separate lines of commerce. Having concluded above that insulated aluminum conductor and insulated copper conductor are separable even though some interproduct competition exists, the conclusion that aluminum conductor (bare and insulated) is a line of commerce is a logical extension of the District Court's findings.

markets, dominated by a few companies but served also by a small, though diminishing, group of independents. Such decentralization as had occurred resulted from the establishment of a few new companies through federal intervention, not from normal, competitive decentralizing forces. . . .

The acquisition of Rome added, it is said, only 1.3% to Alcoa's control of the aluminum conductor market. But in this setting that seems to us reasonably likely to produce a substantial lessening of competition within the meaning of §7. . . . Preservation of Rome, rather than its absorption by one of the giants, will keep it "as an important competitive factor," to use the words of S. Rep. No. 1775, . . . Rome seems to us the prototype of the small independent that Congress aimed to preserve by §7.

The judgment is reversed and since there must be divestiture, the case is remanded to the District Court for proceedings in conformity with this opinion.

Reversed and remanded.

MR. JUSTICE STEWART, whom MR. JUSTICE HARLAN and MR. JUSTICE GOLDBERG join, dissenting.

The definition of the relevant line of commerce where a merger may substantially lessen competition was broadened considerably in another 1964 Supreme Court decision handed down shortly after the *Alcoa* ruling. In 1956 Continental Can Corporation, the second largest producer of metal containers, acquired the assets of Hazel-Atlas Glass Company, the third largest producer of glass containers. The merger was held illegal since it would eliminate "inter-industry competition" between glass and metal containers.

The Court observed that competition between glass and metal containers had been "insistent, continuous, effective and quantitywise very substantial." Even though the interchangeability of use may not be as complete and the cross elasticity of demand as immediate as in the case of an intraindustry merger, the long-run results do bring the competition between the industries within the scope of Section 7. "Where the area of effective competition cuts across industry lines, so must the relevant line of commerce; otherwise an adequate determination of the merger's true impact cannot be made."

The product market of the combined glass and metal container industries was dominated by six firms, Continental Can ranking second and Hazel-Atlas sixth. The merged firms would account for 25 per cent of this market. Where a merger is of such magnitude as this, detailed market analysis and proof of anticompetitive effects were not required since the purpose of Section 7 is to prevent undue concentration. Coupled with these findings was recognition of a pronounced trend toward concentration among firms producing glass and metal containers.

Justice Harlan offered his customary vigorous dissent. He stated: ". . . the Court's conclusions are, to say the least, remarkable." The market consisting of glass and metal containers forms "a distinct line of commerce only in the mind of this Court." He concluded his dissent by pointing out that the Court's ruling, in effect, makes mergers between two large firms in related industries a *per se* violation. "I have no idea where Section 7 goes from here, nor will businessmen or the antitrust bar."

UNITED STATES v. CONTINENTAL CAN CO. et al.

378 U.S. 441 (1964)

MR. JUSTICE WHITE delivered the opinion of the Court.

In 1956, Continental Can Company, the Nation's second largest producer of metal containers, acquired all of the assets, business and good will of Hazel-Atlas Glass Company, the Nation's third largest producer of glass containers, in exchange for 999,140 shares of Continental's common stock and the assumption by Continental of all the liabilities of Hazel-Atlas. The Government brought this action seeking a judgment that the acquisition violated §7 of the Clayton Act and requesting an appropriate divestiture order. Trying the case without a jury, the District Court found that the Government had failed to prove reasonable probability of anti-competitive effect in any line of commerce, and accordingly dismissed the complaint at the close of the Government's case. . . . We reverse the decision of the District Court.

I

The industries with which this case is principally concerned are, as found by the trial court, the metal can industry, the glass container industry and the plastic container industry, each producing one basic type of container made of metal, glass, and plastic, respectively.

Continental Can is a New York corporation organized in 1913 to acquire all the assets of three metal container manufacturers. Since 1913 Continental has acquired 21 domestic metal container companies as well as numerous others engaged in the packaging business, including producers of flexible packaging; a manufacturer of polyethylene bottles and similar plastic containers; 14 producers of paper containers and paperboard; four companies making closures for glass containers; and one—Hazel-Atlas—producing glass containers. In 1955, the year prior to the present merger, Continental, with assets of $382 million, was the second largest company in the metal container field, shipping approximately 33% of all such containers sold in the United States. It and the largest producer, American Can Company, accounted for approximately 71% of all metal container shipments. National Can Company, the third largest, shipped approximately 5%, with the remaining 24% of the market being divided among 75 to 90 other firms.

During 1956, Continental acquired not only the Hazel-Atlas Company but also Robert Gair Company, Inc.—a leading manufacturer of paper and paperboard products—and White Cap Company—a leading producer of vacuum-type metal closures for glass food containers—so that Continental's assets rose from $382 million in 1955 to more than $633 million in 1956, and its net sales and operating revenues during that time increased from $666 million to more than $1 billion.

Hazel-Atlas was a West Virginia corporation which in 1955 had net sales in excess of $79 million and assets of more than $37 million. Prior to the absorption of Hazel-Atlas into Continental the pattern of dominance among a few firms in the glass container industry was similar to that which prevailed in the metal container field. Hazel-Atlas, with approximately 9.6% of the glass container shipments in 1955, was third. Owens-Illinois Glass Company had 34.2% and Anchor-Hocking Glass Company 11.6%, with the remaining 44.6% being divided among at least 39 other firms. . . .

II

We deal first with the relevant market. It is not disputed here, and the District Court held, that the geographical market is the entire United States. As for the product market, the court found, as was conceded by the parties, that the can industry and the glass container industry were relevant lines of commerce. Beyond these two product markets, however, the Government urged the recognition of various other lines of commerce, some of them defined in terms of the end uses for which tin and glass containers were in substantial competition. These end-use claims were containers for the beer industry, containers for the soft drink industry, containers for the canning industry, containers for the toiletry and cosmetic industry, containers for the medicine and health industry, and containers for the household and chemical industry. . . .

It is quite true that glass and metal containers have different characteristics which may disqualify one or the other, at least in their present form, from this or that particular use; that the machinery necessary to pack in glass is different from that employed when cans are used; that a particular user of cans or glass may pack in only one or the other container and does not shift back and forth from day to day as price and other factors might make desirable; and that the competition between metal and glass containers is different from the competition between the can companies themselves or between the products of the different glass companies. These are relevant and important considerations but they are not sufficient to obscure the competitive relationships which this record so compellingly reveals. . . .

Interchangeability of use and cross-elasticity of demand are not to be used to obscure competition but to "recognize competition where, in fact, compeition exists." *Brown Shoe Co.* v. *United States,* . . . In our view there is and has been a rather general confrontation between metal and glass containers and competition between them for the same end uses which is insistent, continuous, effective and quantitywise very substantial. Metal has replaced glass and glass has replaced metal as the leading container for some important uses; both are used for other purposes; each is trying to expand its share of the market at the expense of the other; and each is attempting to preempt for itself every use for which its product is physically suitable, even though some such uses have traditionally been regarded as the exclusive domain of the competing industry. In differing degrees for different end uses manufacturers in each industry take into consideration the price of the containers of the opposing industry in formulating their own pricing policy. Thus, though the interchangeability of use may not be so complete and the cross-elasticity of demand not so immediate as in the case of most intraindustry mergers, there is over the long run the kind of customer response to innovation and other competitive stimuli that brings the competition between these two industries within §7's competition-preserving proscriptions.

Moreover, price is only one factor in a user's choice between one container or the other. That there are price differentials between the two products or that the demand for one is not particularly or immediately responsive to changes in the price of the other are relevant matters but not determinative of the product market issue. Whether a packager will use glass or cans may depend not only on the price of the package but also upon other equally important considerations. The consumer, for example, may begin to prefer one type of container over the other and the manufacturer of baby food cans may therefore find that his problem is the housewife rather than the packer or the price of his cans. This may not be price competition but it is nevertheless meaningful competition between interchangeable containers. . . .

Glass and metal containers were recognized to be two separate lines of commerce. But given the area of effective competition between these lines, there is necessarily implied one or more other lines of commerce embracing both industries. Since the purpose of delineating a line of commerce is to provide an adequate basis for measuring the effects of a given acquisition, its contours must, as nearly as possible, conform to competitive reality. Where the area of effective competition cuts across industry lines, so must the relevant line of commerce; otherwise an adequate determination of the merger's true impact cannot be made.

Based on the evidence thus far revealed by this record we hold that the interindustry competition between glass and metal containers is sufficient to warrant treating as a relevant product market the combined glass and metal container industries and all end uses for which they compete. . . .

III

We approach the ultimate judgment under §7 having in mind the teachings of *Brown Shoe,* supplemented by their application and elaboration in *United States* v. *Philadelphia National Bank,* . . . and *United States* v. *El Paso Natural Gas Co.,* . . . The issue is whether the merger between Continental and Hazel-Atlas will have probable anticompetitive effect within the relevant line of commerce. Market shares are the primary indicia of market power but a judgment under §7 is not to be made by any single qualitative or quantitative test. The merger must be viewed functionally in the context of the particular market involved, its structure, history and probable future. Where a merger is of such a size as to be inherently suspect, elaborate proof of market structure, market behavior and probable anticompetitive effects may be dispensed with in view of §7's design to prevent undue concentration. Moreover, the competition with which §7 deals includes not only existing competition but that which is sufficiently probable and imminent. . . .

When Continental acquired Hazel-Atlas it added significantly to its position in the relevant line of commerce. Hazel-Atlas was the third largest glass container manufacturer in an industry in which the three top companies controlled 55.4% of the total shipments of glass containers. Hazel-Atlas' share was 9.6%, which amounted to 1,857,000,000 glass containers out of a total of 19⅓ billion industrial total. Its annual sales amounted to $79 million, its assets exceeded $37 million and it had 13 plants variously located in the United States. In terms of total containers shipped, Hazel-Atlas ranked sixth in the relevant line of commerce, its almost 2 billion containers being 3.1% of the product market total.

The evidence so far presented leads us to conclude that the merger between Continental and Hazel-Atlas is in violation of §7. The product market embracing the combined metal and glass container industries was dominated by six firms having a total of 70.1% of the business. Continental, with 21.9% of the shipments, ranked second within this product market, and Hazel-Atlas, with 3.1%, ranked sixth. Thus, of this vast market—amounting at the time of the merger to almost $3 billion in annual sales—a large percentage already belonged to Continental before the merger. By the acquisition of Hazel-Atlas stock Continental not only increased its own share more than 14% from 21.9% to 25%, but also reduced from five to four the most significant competitors who might have threatened its dominant position. . . .

We think our holding is consonant with the purpose of §7 to arrest anticompetitive arrangements in their incipiency. Some product lines are offered in both metal and glass containers by the same packer. In such areas the interchangeability of use and immediate interindustry sensitivity to price changes would approach that which exists between products of the same industry. In other lines, as where one packer's products move in one type container while his competitor's move in another, there are inherent deterrents to customer diversion of the same type that might occur between brands of cans or bottles. But the possibility of such transfers over the long run acts as a deterrent against attempts by the dominant members of either industry to reap the possible benefits of their position by raising prices above the competitive level or engaging in other comparable practices. And even though certain lines are today regarded as safely within the domain of one or the other of these industries, this pattern may be altered, as it has been in the past. From the point of view not only of the static competitive situation but also the dynamic long-run potential, we think that the Government has discharged its burden of proving prima facie anticompetitive effect. Accordingly the judgment is reversed and the case remanded for further proceedings consistent with this opinion.

Reversed.

Mr. Justice Harlan, whom Mr. Justice Stewart joins, dissenting.

Measured by any antitrust yardsticks with which I am familiar, the Court's conclusions are, to say the least, remarkable. Before the merger which is the subject of this case, Continental Can manufactured metal containers and Hazel-Atlas manufactured glass containers. The District Court found, with ample support in the record, that the Government had wholly failed to prove that the merger of these two companies would adversely affect competition in the metal container industry, in the glass container industry, or between the metal container industry and the glass container industry. Yet this Court manages to strike down the merger under §7 of the Clayton Act, because, in the Court's view, it is anticompetitive. With all respect, the Court's conclusion is based on erroneous analysis, which makes an abrupt and unwise departure from established antitrust law. . . .

In fairness to the District Court it should be said that it did not err in failing to consider the "line of commerce" on which this Court now relies. For the Government did not even suggest that such a line of commerce existed until it got to this Court. And it does not seriously suggest even now that such a line of commerce exists. The truth is that "glass and metal containers" form a distinct line of commerce only in the mind of this Court. . . .

The Court's spurious market-share analysis should not obscure the fact that the Court is, in effect, laying down a *"per se"* rule that mergers between two large companies in related industries are presumptively unlawful under §7. Had the Court based this new rule on a conclusion that such mergers are inherently likely to dampen interindustry competition or that so few mergers of this kind would fail to have that effect that a *"per se"* rule is justified, I could at least understand the thought process which lay behind its decision. . . .

In any event, the Court does not take this tack. It chooses instead to invent a line of commerce the existence of which no one, not even the Government, has imagined; for which businessmen and economists will look in vain; a line of commerce which sprang into existence only when the merger took place and will cease to exist when the merger is undone. I have no idea where §7 goes from here, nor will businessmen or the antitrust bar. Hitherto, it has been thought that the validity of a merger was to be tested by examining its effect in identifiable, "well-defined" . . . markets. Hereafter, however slight (or even nonexistent) the competitive impact of a merger on any actual market, businessmen must rest uneasy lest the Court create some "market," in which the merger presumptively dampens competition, out of bits and pieces of real ones. No one could say that such a fear is unfounded, since the Court's creative powers in this respect are declared to be as extensive as the competitive relationships between industries. This is said to be recognizing "meaningful competition where it is found to exist." It is in fact imagining effects on competition where none has been shown.

I would affirm the judgment of the District Court.

The *Alcoa* and *Continental Can* cases focused attention on the relevant line of commerce and concluded that it may be very narrow or very broad. The last two cases in this section look at two different aspects of antimerger law: (1)

appropriate "section of the country," and (2) market share required to constitute a "substantial lessening of competition."

In 1958 Pabst Brewing Company, the tenth largest brewer, acquired Blatz Brewing Company, the eighteenth largest, and thus became number five with 4.5 per cent of the nation's beer sales. The combined share of the two companies in 1957 amounted to 24 per cent in Wisconsin and 11 per cent in the three-state area of Wisconsin, Illinois, and Michigan. The district court dismissed the case, finding that the government had not shown either the Wisconsin or the three-state area to be the relevant geographic section of the country. And 4.5 per cent of the national market did not constitute a substantial lessening of competition.

The Supreme Court held that the wording of "any section of the country" is inclusive enough to encompass a state, a regional, or nationwide market. Proof of the *relevant* section of the country where the anticompetitive effects take place is "subsidiary to the crucial question . . . which is whether a merger may substantially lessen competition anywhere in the United States." The combined market shares of the two firms were sufficiently ample to sustain a conviction regardless of whether Wisconsin, the three-state area, or the entire country were used as the relevant section of the country. The Court had now, by unanimous opinion, moved down the market-share scale to strike down a merger that involved only 4.5 per cent of a national market.

Justice Douglas included a concurring opinion which consists of a not-so-funny squib on the ultimate course of business mergers.

UNITED STATES v. PABST BREWING CO. et al.

384 U.S. 546 (1966)

MR. JUSTICE BLACK delivered the opinion of the Court.

In 1958 Pabst Brewing Company, the Nation's tenth largest brewer, acquired the Blatz Brewing Company, the eighteenth largest. In 1959 the Government brought this action charging that the acquisition violated §7 of the Clayton Act as amended by the Celler-Kefauver Anti-Merger amendment. . . .

At the close of the Government's case, the District Court dismissed the case . . . holding that the Government's proof had not shown that either Wisconsin or the three-state area of Wisconsin, Michigan and Illinois was a "relevant geographic market within which the probable effect of the acquisition of Blatz by Pabst should be tested." The District Court also ruled that the Government had not shown that "the effect of the acquisition . . . may be substantially to lessen competition or to tend to create a monopoly in the beer industry in the continental United States, the only relevant geographic market." . . .

I

We first take up the court's dismissal based on its conclusion that the Government failed to prove either Wisconsin or the three-state area constituted "a relevant section of the country within the meaning of Section 7." Apparently the District Court thought that in order to show a violation of §7 it was essential for the Government to show a "relevant geographic market" in the same way the corpus delicti must be proved to establish a crime. But when the Government brings an action under §7 it must, according to the language of the statute, prove no more than that there has been a merger between two corporations engaged in commerce and that the effect of the merger may be substantially to lessen competition or tend to create a monopoly in any line of commerce *"in any section of the country."* (Emphasis supplied.) The language of this section requires merely that the Government prove the merger may have a substantial anticompetitive effect somewhere in the United States—"in *any* section" of the United States. This phrase does not call for the delineation of a "section of the country" by metes and bounds as a surveyor would lay off a plot of ground. The Government may introduce evidence which shows that as a result of a merger competition may be substantially lessened throughout the country, or on the other hand it may prove that competition may be substantially lessened only in one or more sections of the country. In either event a violation of §7 would be proved. Certainly the failure of the Government to prove by an army of expert witnesses what constitutes a relevant "economic" or "geographic" market is not an adequate ground on which to dismiss a §7 case. . . . Congress did not seem to be troubled about the exact spot where competition might be lessened; it simply intended to outlaw mergers which threatened competition in any or all parts of the country. Proof of the section of the country where the anticompetitive effect exists is entirely subsidiary to the crucial question in this and every §7 case which is whether a merger may substantially lessen competition anywhere in the United States.

II

The Government's evidence, consisting of documents, statistics, official records, depositions, and affidavits by witnesses, related principally to the competitive position of Pabst and Blatz in the beer industry throughout the Nation, in the three-state area of Wisconsin, Illinois, and Michigan, and in the State of Wisconsin. The record in this case, including admissions by Pabst in its formal answer to the Government's complaint, the evidence introduced by the Government, the findings of fact and opinion of the District Judge, shows among others the following facts. In 1958, the year of the merger, Pabst was the tenth largest brewer in the Nation and Blatz ranked eighteenth. The merger made Pabst the Nation's fifth largest brewer with 4.49% of the industry's total sales. By 1961, three years after the merger, Pabst had increased its share of the beer market to 5.83% and had become the third largest brewer in the country. In the State of Wisconsin, before the merger, Blatz was the leading seller of beer and Pabst ranked fourth. The merger made Pabst the largest seller in the State with 23.95% of all the sales made there. By 1961 Pabst's share of the market had increased to 27.41%. This merger took place in an industry marked by a steady trend toward economic concentration. According to the District Court the number of breweries operating in the United States declined from 714 in 1934 to 229 in 1961, and the total number of different competitors selling beer has fallen from 206 in 1957 to 162 in 1961. . . .

As was true in the beer industry throughout the Nation, there was a trend toward concentration in the three-state area. From 1957 to 1961 the number of major brewers selling there dropped from 104 to 86 and during the same period the eight leading sellers increased their combined shares of beer sales from 58.93% to 67.65%.

These facts show a very marked thirty-year decline in the number of brewers and a sharp rise in recent years in the percentage share of the market controlled by the leading brewers. If not stopped, this decline in the number of separate competitors and this rise in the share of the market controlled by the larger beer manufacturers are bound to lead to greater and greater concentration of the beer industry into fewer and fewer hands. The merger of Pabst and Blatz brought together two very large brewers competing against each other in 40 States. In 1957 these two companies had combined sales which accounted for 23.95% of the beer sales in Wisconsin, 11.32% of the sales in the three-state area of Wisconsin, Illinois, and Michigan, and 4.49% of the sales throughout the country. In accord with our prior cases, we hold that the evidence as to the probable effect of the merger on competition in Wisconsin, in the three-state area, and in the entire country was sufficient to show a violation of §7 in each and all of these three areas. . . .

. . . We hold that a trend toward concentration in an industry, whatever its causes, is a highly relevant factor in deciding how substantial the anticompetitive effect of a merger may be.

Reversed and remanded.

Mr. Justice Douglas, concurring.

While I join the Court's opinion, I add only a word in support of the Court's description of the anatomy of the "relevant geographic market" for purposes of the Clayton Act. The alternative leads to a form of concentration whose ultimate *reductio ad absurdum* is described in the Appendix to this opinion.

Appendix to Concurring Opinion of Mr. Justice Douglas

Every time you pick up the newspaper you read about one company merging with another company. Of course, we have laws to protect competition in the United States, but one can't help thinking that, if the trend continues, the whole country will soon be merged into one large company.

It is 1978 and by this time every company west of the Mississippi will have merged into one giant corporation known as Samson Securities. Every company east of the Mississippi will have merged under an umbrella corporation known as the Delilah Company.

It is inevitable that one day the chairman of the board of Samson and the president of Delilah would meet and discuss merging their two companies.

"If we could get together," the president of Delilah said, "we would be able to finance your projects and you would be able to finance ours."

"Exactly what I was thinking," the chairman of Samson said.

"That's a great idea and it certainly makes everyone's life less complicated."

The men shook on it and then they sought out approval from the Anti-Trust Division of the Justice Department.

At first the head of the Anti-Trust Division indicated that he might have reservations about allowing the only two companies left in the United States to merge.

"Our department," he said, "will take a close look at this proposed merger. It is our job to further competition in private business and industry, and if we allow Samson and Delilah to merge we may be doing the consumer a disservice."

The chairman of Samson protested vigorously that merging with Delilah would not stifle competition, but would help it. "The public will be the true beneficiary of this merger," he said. "The larger we are, the more services we can perform, and the lower prices we can charge."

The president of Delilah backed him up. "In the Communist system the people don't have a choice. They must buy from the state. In our capitalistic society the people can buy from either the Samson Company or the Delilah Company."

"But if you merge," someone pointed out, "there will be only *one* company left in the United States."

"Exactly," said the president of Delilah. "Thank God for the free enterprise system."

The Anti-Trust Division of the Justice Department studied the merger for months. Finally the Attorney General made this ruling. "While we find some drawbacks to only one company being left in the United States, we feel the advantages to the public far outweigh the disadvantages.

"Therefore, we're making an exception in this case and allowing Samson and Delilah to merge.

"I would like to announce that the Samson and Delilah Company is now negotiating at the White House with the President to buy the United States. The Justice Department will naturally study this merger to see if it violates any of our strong anti-trust laws."

ART BUCHWALD, *Washington Post*, June 2, 1966, p. A21.

In *Von's Grocery Company,* the High Court for the first time outlawed a merger between two firms operating exclusively in a market consisting only of a city's metropolitan area. Von's Grocery acquired the stock and assets of the Shopping Bag Food Stores in 1960. Before the merger, Von's was the third leading retail grocer and Shopping Bag was number six in the Los Angeles area. Their combined market share in 1960 was 7.5 per cent of the grocery sales. Both firms were "highly successful, expanding and aggressive competitors." Their merger created the second largest grocery chain in the area.

Noting that the market exhibited a marked trend toward concentration, the Court found that it was becoming more and more difficult for small grocery stores to compete. Justice Black wrote in his majority opinion that "Congress sought to preserve competition among many small businesses by arresting a trend toward concentration in its incipiency. . . . The facts in this case present exactly the trend toward concentration which Congress wanted to halt." The *Von's Grocery* ruling means that Section 7 is now fully applicable to mergers between firms that control only a *small* share (7.5 per cent) of a *small* geographic market.

UNITED STATES v. VON'S GROCERY CO. et al.

384 U.S. 270 (1966)

MR. JUSTICE BLACK delivered the opinion of the Court.

On March 25, 1960, the United States brought this action charging that the acquisition by Von's Grocery Company of its direct competitor Shopping Bag Food Stores, both large retail grocery companies in Los Angeles, California, violated §7 of the Clayton Act . . . as amended in 1950 by the Celler-Kefauver Anti-Merger Act, . . . On March 28, 1960, three days later, the District Court refused to grant the Government's motion for a temporary restraining order and immediately Von's took over all of Shopping Bag's capital stock and assets including 36 grocery stores in the Los Angeles area. After hearing evidence on both sides, the District Court made findings of fact and concluded as a matter of law that there was "not a reasonable probability" that the merger would tend "substantially to lessen competition" or "create a monopoly" in violation of §7. For this reason the District Court entered judgment for the defendants. . . . The sole question here is whether the District Court properly concluded on the facts before it that the Government had failed to prove a violation of §7.

The record shows the following facts relevant to our decision. The market involved here is the retail grocery market in the Los Angeles area. In 1958 Von's retail sales ranked third in the area and Shopping Bag's ranked sixth. In 1960 their sales together were 7.5% of the total two and one-half billion dollars of retail groceries sold in the Los Angeles market each year. For many years before the merger both companies had enjoyed great success as rapidly growing companies. From 1948 to 1958 the number of Von's stores in the Los Angeles area practically doubled from 14 to 27, while at the same time the number of Shopping Bag's stores jumped from 15 to 34. During that same decade, Von's sales increased fourfold and its share of the market almost doubled while Shopping Bag's sales multiplied seven times and its share of the market tripled. The merger of these two highly successful, expanding and aggressive competitors created the second largest grocery chain in Los Angeles with sales of almost $172,488,000 annually. In addition the findings of the District Court show that the number of owners operating single stores in the Los Angeles retail grocery market decreased from 5,365 in 1950 to 3,818 in 1961. By 1963, three years after the merger, the number of single-store owners had dropped still further to 3,590. . . . These facts alone are enough to cause us to conclude contrary to the District Court that the Von's-Shopping Bag merger did violate §7. Accordingly, we reverse. . . . As we said in *Brown Shoe Co.* v. *United States*, . . . "The dominant theme pervading congressional consideration of the 1950 amendments was a fear of what was considered to be a rising tide of economic concentration in the American economy." To arrest this "rising tide" toward concentration into too few hands and to halt the gradual demise of the small businessman, Congress decided to clamp down with vigor on mergers. It both revitalized §7 of the Clayton Act by "plugging its loophole" and broadened its scope so as not only to prohibit mergers between competitors, the effect of which "may be substantially to lessen competition, or to tend to create a monopoly" but to prohibit all mergers having that effect. By using these terms in §7 which look not merely to the actual present effect of a merger but instead to its effect upon future competition, Congress sought to preserve competition among many small businesses by arresting a trend toward concentration in its incipiency before that trend developed to the point that a market was left in the grip of a few big companies. Thus, where concentration is gaining momentum in a market, we must be alert to carry out Congress' intent to protect competition against ever-increasing concentration through mergers.

The facts of this case present exactly the threatening trend toward concentration which Congress wanted to halt. The number of small grocery companies in the Los Angeles retail grocery market had been declining rapidly before the merger and continued to decline rapidly afterwards. This rapid decline in the number of grocery store owners moved hand in hand with a large number of significant absorptions of the small companies by the larger ones. In the midst of this steadfast trend toward concentration, Von's and Shopping Bag, two of the most successful and largest companies in the area, jointly owning 66 grocery stores merged to become the second largest chain in Los Angeles. This merger cannot be defended on the ground that one of the companies was about to fail or that the two had to merge to save themselves from destruction by some larger and more powerful competitor. What we have on the contrary is simply the case of two already powerful companies merging in a way which makes them even more powerful than they were before. If ever such a merger would not violate §7, certainly it does when it takes place in a market characterized by a long and continuous trend toward fewer and fewer owner-competitors which is exactly the sort of trend which Congress, with power to do so, declared must be arrested.

Appellees' primary argument is that the merger between Von's and Shopping Bag is not prohibited by §7 because the Los Angeles grocery market was competitive before the merger, has been since, and may continue to be in the future. . . . It is enough for us that Congress feared that a market marked at the same time by both a continuous decline in the number of small businesses and a large number of mergers would slowly but inevitably gravitate from a market of many small competitors to one dominated by one or a few giants, and competition would thereby be destroyed. Congress passed the Celler-Kefauver Act to prevent such a destruction of competition. Our cases since the passage of that Act have faithfully endeavored to enforce this congressional command. We adhere to them now. . . .

Reversed and remanded.

Mr. Justice Fortas took no part in the consideration or decision of this case.

Mergers in Regulated Industries

The *Philadelphia National Bank* case of 1963 was another landmark decision for reasons different from those of *Brown Shoe*. First, the decision marked the first time that the antimerger statute had been extended to include commercial banks, thereby casting serious doubt upon the true meaning of the 1960 Bank Merger Act. Second, the decision overturned the ruling of a regulatory agency, the Comptroller of Currency, which had apparently been given responsibility for ruling on mergers of national banks by the 1960 law.

The merger would have joined the second largest bank in the Philadelphia metropolitan area, Philadelphia National Bank, with the third largest, Girard Trust Corn Exchange Bank, making the new bank the largest with 36 per cent of the area's deposits and assets. The concentration of banking facilities accounted for by the two largest banks would have been increased by more than a third, rising from 44 per cent to 59 per cent. This increase "in concentration must be regarded as significant."

Defining the line of commerce and section of the country presented few problems in this case. The relevant line of commerce was declared to be commercial banking in all its various forms. Likewise, the relevant section of the country was settled upon as the metropolitan area consisting of Philadelphia and its three contiguous countries.

The Supreme Court noted that the 1950 amendment to the Clayton Act did not intend to exclude bank mergers. Next, the Court said that the Bank Merger Act of 1960 did not immunize mergers approved by regulatory agencies from the federal antitrust laws, nor does the doctrine of "primary jurisdiction" hold in this case. The fact that commercial banking is already subjected to a high degree of government regulation and that it deals with "intangibles of credit and services rather than in the manufacture and sale of tangible commodities" does not remove the case from antitrust jurisdiction.

The Court then rejected the three defenses used to justify the merger. First, the proposed consolidation could not be justified on the theory that only through mergers can banks follow their customers to the suburbs since this can be accomplished by new branches in the suburbs. Second, the merger could not be allowed on the grounds that the lending limit would be increased and thereby enable the merged bank to compete better with large New York banks. "If anticompetitive effects in one market could be justified by procompetitive consequences in another, the logical upshot would be that every firm in an industry could, without violating Section 7, embark on a series of mergers that would make it in the end as large as the industry leader." Third, the Court also rejected the plea that Philadelphia needs a larger bank than it now has in order to bring new business into the area. "Congress determined to preserve our traditionally competitive economy. It therefore proscribed anticompetitive mergers, the benign and the malignant alike, . . ."

Justice Harlan argued strenuously in his dissenting opinion that the Court was engaging in judicial legislation by overturning the 1960 Bank Merger Act. He argued that the majority opinion, making the antimerger act superior to the banking act, reduces the latter act to "an exorbitant waste of congressional time and energy."

UNITED STATES v. PHILADELPHIA NATIONAL BANK et al.

374 U.S. 321 (1963)

Mr. Justice Brennan delivered the opinion of the Court.

The United States, appellant here, brought this civil action in the United States District Court for the Eastern District of Pennsylvania under §4 of the Sherman Act, . . . and §15 of the Clayton Act, . . . to enjoin a proposed merger of The Philadelphia National Bank (PNB) and Girard Trust Corn Exchange Bank (Girard), appellees here. The complaint charged violations of §1 of the Sherman Act, and §7 of the Clayton Act, . . . We reverse the judgment of the District Court. We hold that the merger of appellees is forbidden by §7 of the Clayton Act and so must be enjoined; we need not, and therefore do not, reach the further question of alleged violation of §1 of the Sherman Act.

The Facts and Proceedings Below

THE BACKGROUND: COMMERCIAL BANKING IN THE UNITED STATES   Because this is the first case which has required this Court to consider the application of the antitrust laws to the commercial banking industry, and because aspects of the industry and of the degree of governmental regulation of it will recur throughout our discussion, we deem it appropriate to begin with a brief background description.

Commercial banking in this country is primarily unit banking. That is, control of commercial banking is diffused throughout a very large number of independent, local banks—13,460 of them in 1960—rather than concentrated in a handful of nationwide banks, as, for example, in England and Germany. There are, to be sure, in addition to the independent banks, some 10,000 branch banks; but branching, which is controlled largely by state law—and prohibited altogether by some States—enables a bank to extend itself only to state lines and often not that far. It is also the case, of course, that many banks place loans and solicit deposits outside their home area. But with these qualifications, it remains true that ours is essentially a decentralized system of community banks. Recent years, however, have witnessed a definite trend toward concentration. . . .

THE PROPOSED MERGER OF PNB AND GIRARD   The Philadelphia National Bank and Girard Trust Corn Exchange Bank are, respectively, the second and third largest of the 42 commercial banks with head offices in the Philadelphia metropolitan area, which consists of the City of Philadelphia and its three contiguous counties in Pennsylvania. The home county of both banks is the city itself; Pennsylvania law, however, permits branching into the counties contiguous to the home county, . . . and both banks have offices throughout the four-county area. PNB, a national bank, has assets of over $1,000,000,000, making it (as of 1959) the twenty-first largest bank in the Nation. Girard, a state bank, is a member of the FRS and is insured by the FDIC; it has assets of about $750,000,000. Were the proposed merger to be consummated, the resulting bank would be the largest in the four-county area, with (approximately) 36% of the area banks' total assets, 36% of deposits, and 34% of net loans. It and the second largest (First Pennsylvania Bank and Trust Company, now the largest) would have between them 59% of the total assets, 58% of deposits, and 58% of the net loans, while after the merger the four largest banks in the area would have 78% of total assest, 77% of deposits, and 78% of net loans.

The present size of both PNB and Girard is in part the result of mergers. Indeed, the trend toward concentration is noticeable in the Philadelphia area generally, in which the number of commercial banks has declined from 108 in 1947 to the present 42. Since 1950, PNB has acquired nine formerly independent banks and Girard six; and these acquisitions have accounted for 59% and 85% of the respective banks' asset growth during the period, 63% and 91% of their deposit growth, and 12% and 37% of their loan growth. During this period, the seven largest banks in the area increased their combined share of the area's total commercial bank resources from about 61% to about 90%.

In November 1960 the boards of directors of the two banks approved a proposed agreement for their consolidation under the PNB charter. . . . But under the Banker Merger Act of 1960, . . . , the Comptroller may not give his approval until he has received reports from the other two banking agencies and the Attorney General respecting the probable effects of the proposed transaction on competition. All three reports advised that the proposed merger would have substantial anticompetitive effects in the Philadelphia metropolitan area. However, on February 24, 1961, the Comptroller approved the merger. No opinion was rendered at that time. But as required by §1828 (c), the Comptroller explained the basis for his decision to approve the merger in a statement to be included in his annual report to Congress. As to effect upon competition, he reasoned that "[s]ince there will remain an adequate number of alternative sources of banking service in Philadelphia, and in view of the beneficial effects of this consolidation upon international and national competition it was concluded that the over-all effect upon competition would not be unfavorable." He also stated that the consolidated bank "would be far better able to serve the convenience and needs of its community by being of material assistance to its city and state in their efforts to attract new industry and to retain existing industry." The day after the Comptroller approved the merger, the United States commenced the present action. No steps have been taken to consummate the merger pending the outcome of this litigation.

THE TRIAL AND THE DISTRICT COURT'S DECISION The Government's case in the District Court relied chiefly on statistical evidence bearing upon market structure and on testimony by economists and bankers to the effect that, notwithstanding the intensive governmental regulation of banking, there was a substantial area for the free play of competitive forces; that concentration of commercial banking, which the proposed merger would increase, was inimical to that free play; that the principal anticompetitive effect of the merger would be felt in the area in which the banks had their offices, thus making the four-county metropolitan area the relevant geographical market; and that commercial banking was the relevant product market. The defendants, in addition to offering contrary evidence on these points, attempted to show business justifications for the merger. They conceded that both banks were economically strong and had sound management, but offered the testimony of bankers to show that the resulting bank, with its greater prestige and increased lending limit, would be better able to compete with large out-of-state (particularly New York) banks, would attract new business to Philadelphia, and in general would promote the economic development of the metropolitan area.

Upon this record, the District Court held that: (1) the passage of the Bank Merger Act of 1960 did not repeal by implication the antitrust laws insofar as they may apply to bank mergers; (2) §7 of the Clayton Act is inapplicable to bank mergers because banks are not corporations "subject to the jurisdiction of the Federal Trade Commission"; (3) but assuming that §7 is applicable, the four-county Philadelphia metropolitan area is not the relevant geographical market because PNB and Girard actively compete with other banks for bank business throughout the greater part of the northeastern United States; (4) but even assuming that §7 is applicable and that the four-county area is the relevant market, there is no reasonable probability that competition among commercial banks in the area will be substantially lessened as the result of the merger; (5) since the merger does not violate §7 of the Clayton Act, *a fortiori* it does not violate §1 of the Sherman Act; (6) the merger will benefit the Philadelphia metropolitan area economically. The District Court also ruled that for the purposes of §7, commercial banking is a line of commerce; the appellees do not contest this ruling.

The Applicability of Section 7 of the Clayton Act to Bank Mergers

the original section and the 1950 amendment   By its terms, the present §7 reaches acquisitions of corporate stock or share capital by any corporation engaged in commerce, but it reaches acquisitions of corporate assets only by corporations "subject to the jurisdiction of the Federal Trade Commission." The FTC, under §5 of the Federal Trade Commission Act, has no jurisdiction over banks. . . . Therefore, if the proposed merger be deemed an assets acquisition, it is not within §7. Appellant argues vigorously that a merger is crucially different from a pure assets acquisition, and appellees argue with equal vigor that it is crucially different from a pure stock acquisition. Both positions, we think, have merit; a merger fits neither category neatly. Since the literal terms of §7 thus do not dispose of our question, we must determine whether a congressional design to embrace bank mergers is revealed in the history of the statute. The question appears to be one of first impression; we have been directed to no previous case in which a merger or consolidation was challenged under §7 of the Clayton Act, as amended, where the acquiring corporation was not subject to the FTC's jurisdiction.

When it was first enacted in 1914, §7 referred only to corporate acquisitions of stock and share capital; it was silent as to assets acquisitions . . .

. . . Congress contemplated that the 1950 amendment would give §7 a reach which would bring the entire range of corporate amalgamations, from pure stock acquisitions to pure assets acquisitions, within the scope of §7. Thus, the stock-acquisition and assets-acquisition provisions, *read together*, reach mergers, which fit neither category perfectly but lie somewhere between the two ends of the spectrum. . . .

This construction is supported by a number of specific considerations.

First. Any other construction would be illogical and disrespectful of the plain congressional purpose in amending §7, because it would create a large loophole in a statute designed to close a loophole. . . .

Second. The Congress which debated the bill to amend §7 was fully aware of the important differences between a merger and a pure purchase of assets. . . .

Plainly, acquisition of "assets" as used in amended §7 was not meant to be a simple equivalent of acquisition by meager, but was intended rather to ensure against the blunting of the antimerger thrust of the section by evasive transactions such as had rendered the original section ineffectual.

Third. The legislative history shows that the objective of including the phrase "corporation subject to the jurisdiction of the Federal Trade Commission" in §7 was not to limit the amalgamations to be covered by the amended statute but to make explicit the role of the FTC in administering the section. . . .

Fourth. It is settled law that "[i]mmunity from the antitrust laws is not lightly implied." *California* v. *Federal Power Comm'n*, 369 U.S. 482, 485. . . . This canon of construction, which reflects the felt indispensable role of antitrust policy in the maintenance of a free economy, is controlling here. For there is no indication in the legislative history to the 1950 amendment of §7 that Congress wished to confer a special dispensation upon the banking industry; if Congress had so wished, moreover, surely it would have exempted the industry from the stock-acquisition as well as the assets-acquisition provision. . . .

THE EFFECT OF THE BANK MERGER ACT OF 1960 Appellees contended below that the Bank Merger Act, by directing the banking agencies to consider competitive factors before approving mergers, . . . immunizes approved mergers from challenge under the federal antitrust laws. We think the District Court was correct in rejecting this contention. No express immunity is conferred by the Act. Repeals of the antitrust laws by implication from a regulatory statute are strongly disfavored, and have only been found in cases of plain repugnancy between the antitrust and regulatory provisions. . . .

. . . Although the Comptroller was required to consider effect upon competition in passing upon appellees' merger application, he was not required to give this factor any particular weight; he was not even required to (and did not) hold a hearing before approving the application; and there is no specific provision for judicial review of his decision. . . .

Nor did Congress, in passing the Bank Merger Act, embrace the view that federal regulation of banking is so comprehensive that enforcement of the antitrust laws would be either unnecessary, in light of the completeness of the regulatory structure, or disruptive of that structure. On the contrary, the legislative history of the Act seems clearly to refute any suggestion that applicability of the antitrust laws was to be affected. . . .

We note, finally, that the doctrine of "primary jurisdiction" is not applicable here. That doctrine requires judicial abstention in cases where protection of the integrity of a regulatory scheme dictates preliminary resort to the agency which administers the scheme. . . .

It should be unnecessary to add that in holding as we do that the Bank Merger Act of 1960 does not preclude application of §7 of the Clayton Act to bank mergers, we deprive the later statute of none of its intended force. Congress plainly did not intend the 1960 Act to extinguish other sources of federal restraint of bank acquisitions having anticompetitive effects. . . .

The Lawfulness of the Proposed Merger Under Section 7

The statutory test is whether the effect of the merger "may be substantially to lessen competition" "in any line of commerce in any section of the country." We analyzed the test in detail in *Brown Shoe Co. v. United States,* . . . , and that analysis need not be repeated or extended here, for the instant case presents only a straightforward problem of application to particular facts.

We have no difficulty in determining the "line of commerce" (relevant product or services market) and "section of the country" (relevant geographical market) in which to appraise the probable competitive effects of appellees' proposed merger. We agree with the District Court that the cluster of products (various kinds of credit) and services (such as checking accounts and trust administration) denoted by the term "commercial banking," . . . composes a distinct line of commerce. . . .

We part company with the District Court on the determination of the appropriate "section of the country." The proper question to be asked in this case is not where the parties to the merger do business or even where they compete, but where, within the area of competitive overlap, the effect of the merger on competition will be direct and immediate. . . .

The merger of appellees will result in a single bank's controlling at least 30% of the commercial banking business in the four-county Philadelphia metropolitan area. Without attempting to specify the smallest market share which would still be considered to threaten undue concentration, we are clear that 30% presents that threat. Further, whereas presently the two largest banks in the area (First Pennsylvania and PNB) control between them approximately 44% of the area's commercial banking business, the two largest after the merger (PNB-Girard and First Pennsylvania) will control 59%. Plainly, we think, this increase of more than 33% in concentration must be regarded as significant.

Our conclusion that these percentages raise an inference that the effect of the contemplated merger of appellees may be substantially to lessen competition is not an arbitrary one, although neither the terms of §7 nor the legislative history suggests that any particular percentage share was deemed critical. . . .

So also, we reject the position that commercial banking, because it is subject to a high degree of governmental regulation, or because it deals in the intangibles of credit and services rather than in the manufacture or sale of tangible commodities, is somehow immune from the anticompetitive effects of undue concentration. Competition among banks exists at every level—price, variety of credit arrangements, convenience of location, attractiveness of physical surroundings, credit information, investment advice, service charges, personal accommodations, advertising, miscellaneous special and extra services—and it is keen; on this appellees' own witnesses were emphatic. There is no reason to think that concentration is less inimical to the free play of competition in banking than in other service industries. On the contrary, it is in all probability more inimical. For example, banks compete to fill the credit needs of businessmen. Small businessmen especially are, as a practical matter, confined to their locality for the satisfaction of their credit needs. . . . If the number of banks in the locality is reduced, the vigor of competition for filling the marginal small business borrower's needs is likely to diminish. At the same time, his concomitantly greater difficulty in obtaining credit is likely to put him at a disadvantage *vis-à-vis* larger businesses with which he competes. In this fashion, concentration in banking accelerates concentration generally.

We turn now to three affirmative justifications which appellees offer for the proposed merger. The first is that only through mergers can banks follow their customers to the suburbs and retain their business. This justification does not seem particularly related to the instant merger, but in any event it has no merit. There is an alternative to the merger route: the opening of new branches in the areas to which the customers have moved—so-called *de novo* branching. Appellees do not contend that they are unable to expand thus, by opening new offices rather than acquiring existing ones, and surely one premise of an antimerger statute such as §7 is that corporate growth by internal expansion is socially preferable to growth by acquisition.

Second, it is suggested that the increased lending limit of the resulting bank will enable it to compete with the large out-of-state banks, particularly the New York banks, for very large loans. We reject this application of the concept of "countervailing power." . . . If anticompetitive effects in one market could be justified by procompetitive consequences in another, the logical upshot would be that every firm in an industry could, without violating §7, embark on a series of mergers that would make it in the end as large as the industry leader. For if all the commercial banks in the Philadelphia area merged into one, it would be smaller than the largest bank in New York City. This is not a case, plainly, where two small firms in a market propose to merge in order to be able to compete more successfully with the leading firms in that market. Nor is it a case in which lack of adequate banking facilities is causing hardships to individuals or businesses in the community. The present two largest banks in Philadelphia have lending limits of $8,000,000 each. The only businesses located in the Philadelphia area which find such limits inadequate are large enough readily to obtain bank credit in other cities.

This brings us to appellees' final contention, that Philadelphia needs a bank larger than it now has in order to bring business to the area and stimulate its economic development. . . . We are clear, however, that a merger the effect of which "may be substantially to lessen competition" is not saved because, on some ultimate reckoning of social or economic debits and credits, it may be deemed beneficial. A value choice of such magnitude is beyond the ordinary limits of judicial competence, and in any event has been made for us already, by Congress when it enacted the amended §7. Congress determined to preserve our traditionally competitive economy. It therefore proscribed anticompetitive mergers, the benign and the malignant alike, fully aware, we must assume, that some price might have to be paid. . . .

The judgment of the District Court is reversed and the case remanded with direction to enter judgment enjoining the proposed merger.

It is so ordered.

Mr. Justice White took no part in the consideration or decision of this case.

MR. JUSTICE HARLAN, whom MR. JUSTICE STEWART joins, dissenting.

I suspect that no one will be more surprised than the Government to find that the Clayton Act has carried the day for its case in this Court.
. . .

The key to this case is found in the special position occupied by commercial banking in the economy of this country. With respect to both the nature of the operations performed and the degree of governmental supervision involved, it is fundamentally different from ordinary manufacturing and mercantile business. . . .

The inapplicability of §7 to bank mergers was also an explicit basis on which Congress acted in passing the Bank Merger Act of 1960. The Senate Report on S. 1062, the bill that was finally enacted, stated:

> Since bank mergers are customarily, if not invariably, carried out by asset acquisitions, they are exempt from section 7 of the Clayton Act. (Stock acquisitions by bank holding companies, as distinguished from mergers and consolidations, are subject to both the Bank Holding Company Act of 1956 and sec. 7 of the Clayton Act.) . . .
>
> In 1950 (64 Stat. 1125) section 7 of the Clayton Act was amended to correct these deficiencies. Acquisitions of assets were included within the section, in addition to stock acquisitions, but only in the case of corporations subject to the jurisdiction of the Federal Trade Commission (banks, being subject to the jurisdiction of the Federal Reserve Board for purposes of the Clayton Act by virtue of section 11 of that act, were not affected). . . .

During the floor debates Representative Spence, the Chairman of the House Committee on Banking and Currency, recognized the same difficulty: "The Clayton Act is ineffective as to bank mergers because in the case of banks it covers only stock acquisitions and bank mergers are not accomplished that way." . . .

But instead of extending the scope of §7 to cover bank mergers, as numerous proposed amendments to that section were designed to accomplish, Congress made the deliberate policy judgment that "it is impossible to subject bank mergers to the simple rule of section 7 of the Clayton Act. Under that act, a merger would be barred if it might tend substantially to lessen competition, regardless of the effects on the public interest."
. . . (remarks of Senator Robertson, a sponsor of S. 1062). Because of the peculiar nature of the commercial banking industry, its crucial role in the economy, and its intimate connection with the fiscal and monetary operations of the Government, Congress rejected the notion that the general

economic and business premises of the Clayton Act should be the only considerations applicable to this field. . . .

I am unable to conceive of a more inappropriate case in which to overturn the considered opinion of all concerned as to the reach of prior legislation. For 10 years everyone—the department responsible for antitrust law enforcement, the banking industry, the Congress, and the bar— proceeded on the assumption that the 1950 amendment of the Clayton Act did not affect bank mergers. This assumption provided a major impetus to the enactment of remedial legislation, and Congress, when it finally settled on what it thought was the solution to the problem at hand, emphatically rejected the remedy now brought to life by the Court.

The result is, of course, that the Bank Merger Act is almost completely nullified; its enactment turns out to have been a exorbitant waste of congressional time and energy. As the present case illustrates, the Attorney General's report to the designated banking agency is no longer truly advisory, for if the agency's decision is not satisfactory a §7 suit may be commenced immediately. . . .

In order to insure complete coverage of mergers, let us interrupt the chronological order of cases in this section and include three other recent Section 7 bank merger cases to come before the Supreme Court. The first of these was the *First City National Bank of Houston* case,[7] a unanimous decision in 1967, and basically contained an interpretation of the procedural process relating the Bank Merger Act of 1966[8] to Section 7. If a regulatory approval of a bank merger is challenged by the Justice Department, the challenge is brought under the *antitrust* laws and not the Bank Merger Act. If the government sustains its allegation that the merger has anticompetitive effects in violation of Section 7 standards, the Bank Merger Act provides a defense that the merging banks can use to justify the merger. It permits them to prove to the courts that the anticompetitive effects of the merger are "clearly outweighed" in the public interest by meeting the convenience and needs of the community. The Court emphasized that the burden of proof will be on the merging parties to show anticompetitive effects are "clearly outweighed." Furthermore, it is still the function of the courts, not the administrative agencies, to decide the legality of a bank merger when anticompetitive effects are present.

The second recent bank merger decision was handed down in 1968, a

---

[7] U.S. v. *First City National Bank of Houston*, 386 U.S. 361.

[8] 80 Stat. 7, 12 U.S. Code 1828(c). Among other provisions, the Act now stipulates that the Justice Department has only thirty days in which to file an appeal to regulatory approvals of mergers.

merger joining the second and fourth largest banks in the Nashville, Tennessee, area. The banks had merged in 1964 with the approval of the Comptroller of Currency, and the Justice Department brought suit on the grounds that Section 7 was violated. This merger was performed before passage of the Bank Merger Act of 1966, but the intent of Congress was to leave all mergers carried out after the 1963 *Philadelphia National Bank* decision (and for which litigation was pending) subject to continued liability because the merging parties were alerted that their action did run the risk of an eventual order to dissolve.

The Bank Merger Act adopted the language of Section 7 and did not change the antitrust standards for bank cases. Contrary to the lower court findings, the Supreme Court experienced no difficulty in judging that the merger would substantially lessen competition in the Nashville banking market. However, could this anticompetitive effect be offset by the convenience-and-needs justification of the Bank Merger Act? Because the district court reached an erroneous conclusion on anticompetitive effects, the High Court found that the lower court misunderstood the conditions under which "convenience and needs of the community" clearly outweigh the anticompetitive effects of the merger. The lower court did observe some beneficial services arising from the merger, such as an increased lending limit, but attached no particular weight to these conditions. The defendants argued there was a management-succession problem with the smaller bank. The Court found, however, that it was not in a failing condition, and no real effort had been put forth to solve the problem. Nor was an increased lending limit sufficient to offset detrimental factors. No attempt had been made to satisfy the convenience and needs of the community without having a merger. Thus the case was remanded to the lower court to reconsider the alternatives to merging.

UNITED STATES v. THIRD NATIONAL BANK IN NASHVILLE et al.

390 U.S. 171 (1968)

MR. JUSTICE WHITE delivered the opinion of the Court.

In this case the United States appeals from a District Court decision upholding the merger of Third National Bank in Nashville and Nashville Bank and Trust Company against challenge under §7 of the Clayton Act. The court below concluded that the merger, which joined the second largest and the fourth largest banks in Davidson County, Tennessee, into a bank which immediately after the merger was the county's largest bank but since has become the second largest, would not tend substantially to lessen competition and also that any anticompetitive effect would be outweighed by the "convenience and needs of the community to be served." We disagree with the District Court on both issues. We hold that the United States established that this merger would tend to lessen competition, and also that the District Court did not point to community benefits in terms of "convenience and needs" sufficient to outweigh the anticompetitive impact. . . .

The legislative history of the Bank Merger Act of 1966 leaves no doubt that the Act was passed to make substantial changes in the law applicable to bank mergers. Congress was evidently dissatisfied with the 1960 Bank Merger Act as that Act was interpreted in *United States* v. *Philadelphia National Bank,* . . . and in *United States* v. *First National Bank & Trust Co. of Lexington,* . . . and wished to alter both the procedures by which the Justice Department challenges bank mergers and the legal standard which courts apply in judging those mergers. The resulting statute, however, as some members of Congress recognized, was more clear and more specific in prescribing new procedures for testing mergers than in expounding the new standard by which they should be judged.

Last Term, in *United States* v. *First City National Bank of Houston,* . . . this Court interpreted the procedural provisions of the 1966 Act, holding that the Bank Merger Act provided for continued scrutiny of bank mergers under the Sherman Act and the Clayton Act, but had created a new defense, with the merging banks having the burden of proving that defense. The task of the district courts was to inquire *de novo* into the validity of a bank merger approved by the relevant bank regulatory agency to determine, first, whether the merger offended the antitrust laws and, second, if it did, whether the banks had established that the merger was nonetheless justified by "the convenience and needs of the community to be served." . . .

The District Court asserted that one effect of the Bank Merger Act of 1966 was to alter the standards used in determining whether a merger is in violation of §7 of the Clayton Act and §1 of the Sherman Act. . . . We find in the 1966 Act, which adopted precisely that §7 Clayton Act phrase, as well as the "restraint of trade" language of Sherman Act §1, no intention to adopt an "antitrust standard" for bank cases different from that used generally in the law. Only one conclusion can be drawn from the exhaustive legislative deliberations that preceded passage of the Act: Congress intended bank mergers first to be subject to the usual antitrust analysis; if a merger failed that scrutiny, it was to be permissible only if the merging banks could establish that the merger's benefits to the community would outweigh its anticompetitive disadvantages. . . .

We therefore hold that the District Court employed an erroneous standard in applying §7 of the Clayton Act to the merger. In addition we hold that, appraised by the test enunciated in recent Clayton Act cases, the tendency of the merger substantially to lessen competition is apparent. Nashville had three large banks and one of middle size. In this merger the bank of middle size was absorbed by the second largest of the big banks. By the merger the market share of the three largest banks rose from 93% to 98%; the merged bank alone had almost 40% of the Nashville banking business. In addition, the record is replete with evidence that Nashville Bank and Trust was in fact an important competitive element in certain, though not in all, facets of Nashville banking. It offered somewhat different services, at somewhat different rates, from those offered by other banks, and some customers found those services desirable. Although Nashville Bank failed to increase its percentage share of the Nashville banking market after 1960, the absolute size of its business increased steadily from 1956, when it entered seriously into the commercial banking market, to the date of the merger. Throughout this period it was profitable. The record permits no conclusion that Nashville Bank was in any way a "failing" company. . . . On these facts, the conclusion is inescapable that the merger of Third National Bank in Nashville with Nashville Bank and Trust Co. tended to lessen competition in the Nashville commercial banking market. . . .

Because the District Court erroneously concluded that the merger would not tend to lessen competition, its conclusion upon weighing the competitive effect against the asserted benefits to the community is suspect. To weigh adequately one of these factors against the other requires a proper conclusion as to each. Having decided that the court below erred in assessing competitive impact, we should remand, so that the District Court can perform again the balancing process mandated by the Act.

There is, however, an additional reason to remand. In our view, the District Court misapprehended the meaning of the phrase "convenience and needs of the community"; it misunderstood the weight to be given the relevant factors when seeking to determine whether the anticompetitive effects of a merger are "clearly outweighed in the public interest by the probable effect of the transaction in meeting the convenience and needs of the community to be served."

The purpose of the Bank Merger Act was to permit certain bank mergers even though they tended to lessen competition in the relevant market. Congress felt that the role of banks in a community's economic life was such that the public interest would sometimes be served by a bank merger even though the merger lessened competition. The public interest was the ultimate test imposed. . . .

It is plain that Congress considered both competition in commercial banking and satisfaction of "the convenience and needs of the community" to be in the public interest. It concluded that a merger should be judged in terms of its overall effect upon the public interest. If a merger

posed a choice between preserving competition and satisfying the requirements of convenience and need, the injury and benefit were to be weighed
and decision was to rest on which alternative better served the public
interest.

The necessity of choosing is most clearly posed where the proposed
merger would create an institution with capabilities for serving the public
interest not possessed by either of the two merging institutions alone and
where the potential could be realized only through merger. Thus, it might
be claimed, as it is in this case, that a combined bank would have a greater
lending capacity and hence be better equipped to serve the financial needs
of the community. . . . Expressions in Congress during consideration
of the 1966 Act suggest that one purpose of that Act was to give this factor,
not previously relevant in appraising bank mergers, suitable weight in
judging their validity. In the case before us the District Court's findings of
fact suggest that the new bank, with a 20% greater lending limit than
Third National Bank previously had, was able to make larger loans, for
which Nashville area companies had previously to go to Chicago or New
York. . . .

Congress was also concerned about banks in danger of collapse—
banks not so deeply in trouble as to call forth the traditional "failing
company" defense, but nonetheless in danger of becoming before long
financially unsound institutions. Congress seems to have felt that a bank
failure is a much greater community catastrophe than the failure of an
industrial or retail enterprise, and that a much smaller risk of failure than
that required by the failing company doctrine should be sufficient to justify
the rather radical preventive step of an anticompetitive merger. . . .

The District Court, it appears, considered the merger beneficial to
the community because Nashville Bank and Trust had only one branch,
because it had no program of correspondent banking, because its operations were not computerized, because it emphasized real estate loans rather
than commercial loans, because its management was old and unable to
render sound business advice to borrowers, because it was not recruiting
new talent, and because its salary scale was low. . . .

Undeniably, Nashville Bank and Trust had significant problems of
the kind outlined in the findings of the District Court, problems which
were primarily rooted in unsatisfactory and backward management. Just as
surely, securing better banking service for the community is a proper
element for consideration in weighing convenience and need against the
loss of competition. Nor is there any doubt on this record that merger with
Third National would very probably end the managerial problems of
Nashville Bank and Trust and secure the better use of its assets in the
public interest. Thus if the gains in better service outweighed the anticompetitive detriment and the merger was essential to secure this net gain
to the public interest, the merger should be approved.

But this analysis puts aside possible ways of satisfying the requirement of convenience and need without resort to merger. If the injury to the public interest flowing from the loss of competition could be avoided and the convenience and needs of the community benefited in ways short of merger but within the competence of reasonably able businessmen, the situation is radically different. In such circumstances, we seriously doubt that Congress intended a merger to be authorized by either the banking agencies or the courts. . . . Otherwise, the benefits of competition, acknowledged by Congress, would be sacrificed needlessly. For the same reasons, we think it was incumbent upon those seeking to merge in this case to demonstrate that they made reasonable efforts to solve the management dilemma of Nashville Bank short of merger with a major competitor but failed in these attempts, or that any such efforts would have been unlikely to succeed. . . .

The question we therefore face is whether the findings of the District Court sufficiently or reliably establish the unavailability of alternative solutions to the woes of Nashville Bank and Trust Company. In our view, they do not. The District Court described the nature and extent of the bank's managerial shortcomings. . . .

. . . The District Court did not ask whether the Weaver group had made concrete efforts to recruit new management, especially a chief executive officer, who was needed most. The record seems clear that they made no proposals to any individual prospects in or outside of Nashville, save one rather casual letter to a banking acquaintance in New York, and that they neither sought nor cared to seek the help of firms specializing in finding or furnishing new management. The court made no reference to the possibility that the new owners themselves might have taken active charge of the bank. . . .

The burden of showing that an anticompetitive bank merger would be in the public interest because of the benefits it would bring to the convenience and needs of the community to be served rests on the merging banks. *Houston Bank, supra.* A showing that one bank needed more lively and efficient management, absent a showing that the alternative means for securing such management without a merger would present unusually severe difficulties, cannot be considered to satisfy that burden.

We therefore conclude that the District Court was in error in holding that the factors it cited as ways in which this merger benefited the Nashville community were sufficient to outweigh the anticompetitive effects of the merger. . . . The judgment below is reversed and the case is remanded for proceedings consistent with this opinion.

It is so ordered.

MR. JUSTICE FORTAS and MR. JUSTICE MARSHALL took no part in the consideration or decision of this case.

MR. JUSTICE HARLAN, whom MR. JUSTICE STEWART joins, concurring in part and dissenting in part. . . .

The most recent bank merger decision came in June, 1970, and for the first time extended the law down to two small banks operating in a small metropolitan area. The banks involved were the Phillipsburg National Bank & Trust Co. and the Second National Bank, both located in Phillipsburg, New Jersey. Each had less than $25 million in assets, and they ranked as the first and second largest of three Phillipsburg banks. The geographical setting is such that Easton, Pennsylvania, lies directly across a river and the two cities are considered "one town." The merging banks ranked third and fifth in assets among seven banks in "one town." The banks were acknowledged to be direct competitors and accounted for about 25 per cent of the area's deposits.

The Supreme Court ruled that mergers of directly competing small banks are subject to antitrust review no less than mergers of large banks. Customers of small banks are no less entitled to the preservation of competition in banking. Indeed, the need for antitrust protection may be greater in small communities where a large array of financial services is not available. Since anticompetitive effects were observed, the two-step decision process required a determination to see if the convenience and needs of the community "clearly outweighed" the adverse impact on competition. The Court could not make such a finding.

Justice Harlan expressed amazement that the Justice Department would be using its scarce resources to attack such a small merger. His question was: "With tigers still at large in our competitive jungle, why should the Department be taking aim at such small game?" We must conclude that the government's intent was to establish a precedent that would clearly encompass all bank mergers in the future, including those between small banks in small towns. The long-run effect may well be a saving of scarce resources.

UNITED STATES v. PHILLIPSBURG NATIONAL BANK & TRUST CO. et al.
399 U.S. 350 (1970)

MR. JUSTICE BRENNAN delivered the opinion of the Court.

This direct appeal under the Expediting Act, . . . is taken by the United States from a judgment of the District Court for the District of

New Jersey dismissing, after full hearing, the Government's complaint seeking to enjoin as a violation of §7 of the Clayton Act, . . . the proposed merger of appellees, Phillipsburg National Bank and Trust Co. (PNB) and the Second National Bank of Phillipsburg (SNB), both located in Phillipsburg, New Jersey. The Comptroller of the Currency, also an appellee here, approved the merger in December 1967 and intervened in this action to defend it, as he was authorized to do by the Bank Merger Act of 1966, . . . The Bank Merger Act required that the District Court engage in a two-step process, *United States* v. *First City National Bank of Houston*, . . . *United States* v. *Third National Bank in Nashville*, . . . the first of which was to decide whether the merger would violate the antitrust prohibitions of §7 of the Clayton Act. If the court found that §7 would be violated, then the Bank Merger Act required that the District Court decide whether "the anticompetitive effects of the proposed transaction are clearly outweighed in the public interest by the probable effect of the transaction in meeting the convenience and needs of the community to be served." . . . The District Court found that the United States "failed to establish by a preponderance of the evidence that the proposed merger would have any anticompetitive effect and, further, that even if there were *de minimis* anticompetitive effect in the narrowly drawn market proposed by the government, such effect is clearly outweighed by the convenience and needs of the community to be served by the merged bank." . . . We reverse. We have concluded from our examination of the record that the District Court erred in its definitions of the relevant product and geographic markets and that these errors invalidate the court's determination that the merger would have no significant anticompetitive effects.

The Factual Setting

Phillipsburg is a small industrial city on the Delaware River in the southwestern corner of Warren County, New Jersey. Its population was 18,500 in 1960, 28,500 counting the population of its bordering suburbs. Although the population of the suburbs is and has been increasing, Phillipsburg itself has not grown. Easton, Pennsylvania, lies directly across the river. It had a population of 32,000 in 1960, 60,000 counting its bordering suburbs. Its population growth pattern has paralleled that of Phillipsburg. The cities are linked by two bridges and the testimony was that they are "in effect . . . one town."

This "one town" has seven commercial banks, four in Easton and three in Phillipsburg. PNB and SNB are respectively the third and fifth largest in overall banking business. All seven fall within the category of small banks, their assets in 1967 ranging from $13,200,000 to $75,600,000. PNB, with assets then of approximately $23,900,000, and SNB with assets of approximately $17,300,000, are the first and second largest of the three Phillipsburg banks. The merger would produce a bank with assets of over $41,100,000, second in size of the six remaining commercial banks in "one town."

PNB and SNB are direct competitors. Their main offices are opposite one another on the same downtown street. SNB's only branch is across a suburban highway from one of PNB's two branches. Both banks offer the wide range of services and products available at commercial banks, including, for instance, demand deposits, savings and time deposits, consumer loans, commercial and industrial loans, real estate mortgages, trust services, safe deposit boxes, and escrow services. . . .

Both banks serve predominantly Phillipsburg residents. In 1967, although 91.6% of PNB's and 92% of SNB's depositors were residents of "one town," only 5.3% of PNB's and 9% of SNB's depositors lived in Easton. And, although 78.6% of PNB's and 87.2% of SNB's number of loans were made to residents of "one town," only 14.8% and 11.6% respectively went to persons living in Easton. A witness testified that all of the approximately 8,500 Phillipsburg families deal with one or another of the three commercial banks in that city. The town's businessmen prefer to do the same. . . .

The merger would reduce the number of commercial banks in "one town" from seven to six, and from three to two in Phillipsburg. The merged bank would have five of the seven banking offices in Phillipsburg and its environs and would be three times as large as the other Phillipsburg bank; it would have 75.8% of the city's banking assets, 76.1% of its deposits, and 84.1% of its loans. Within Phillipsburg-Easton PNB-SNB would become the second largest commercial bank, having 19.3% of the total assets, 23.4% of total deposits, 19.2% of demand deposits, and 27.3% of total loans. This increased concentration would give the two largest banks 54.8% of the "one town" banking assets, 64.8% of its total deposits, 63.3% of demand deposits, 63% of total loans, and 10 of the 16 banking offices.

We entertain no doubt that this factual pattern requires a determination whether the merger passes muster under the antitrust standards of *United States* v. *Philadelphia National Bank*, . . . which were preserved in the Bank Merger Act of 1966. . . . Mergers of directly competing small commercial banks in small communities, no less than those of large banks in large communities, are subject to scrutiny under these standards. Indeed, competitive commercial banks, with their cluster of products and services, play a particularly significant role in a small community unable to support a large variety of alternative financial institutions. Thus, if any-

thing, it is even more true in the small town than in the large city that "if the businessman is denied credit because his banking alternatives have been eliminated by mergers, the whole edifice of an enterpreneurial system is threatened; if the costs of banking services and credit are allowed to become excessive by the absence of competitive pressures, virtually all costs, in our credit economy, will be affected. . . ." *Philadelphia Bank,*
. . .

The Product Market

In *Philadelphia Bank* we said that the "cluster of products (various kinds of credit) and services (such as checking accounts and trust administration) denoted by the term 'commercial banking' . . . composes a distinct line of commerce." . . . As indicated, PNB and SNB offer the wide range of products and services customarily provided by commercial banks. The District Court made no contrary finding, and, in its actual evaluation of the effect of the merger upon competition, the court looked only to commercial banking as the relevant product market. . . .

Philadelphia Bank emphasized that it is the *cluster* of products and services that full-service banks offer that as a matter of trade reality makes commercial banking a distinct line of commerce. Commercial banks are the only financial institutions in which a wide variety of financial products and services—some unique to commercial banking and others not—are gathered together in one place. The clustering of financial products and services in banks facilitates convenient access to them for all banking customers. . . .

Customers of small banks need and use this cluster of services and products no less than customers of large banks. A customer who uses one service usually looks to his bank for others as well, and is encouraged by the bank to do so. . . .

Moreover, if commercial banking were rejected as the line of commerce for banks with the same or similar ratios of business as those of the appellee banks, the effect would likely be to deny customers of small banks—and thus residents of many small towns—the antitrust protection to which they are no less entitled than customers of large city banks. Indeed, the need for that protection may be greater in the small town since, as we have already stated, commercial banks offering full-service banking in one institution may be peculiarly significant to the economy of communities whose population is too small to support a large array of differentiated savings and credit businesses.

The Relevant Geographic Market

. . .

The District Court selected as the relevant geographic market an area approximately four times as large as Phillipsburg-Easton, with a 1960 population of 216,000 and 18 banks. The area included the city of Bethlehem, Pennsylvania. . . . The court explicitly rejected the claim of the United States that Phillipsburg-Easton constitutes the relevant market. We hold that the District Court erred.

Commercial realities in the banking industry make clear that banks generally have a very localized business. . . . In locating "the market area in which the seller operates," it is important to consider the places from which it draws its business, the location of its offices, and where it seeks business. As indicated, the appellee banks' deposit and loan statistics show that in 1967 they drew over 85% of their business from the Phillipsburg-Easton area and, of that, only about 10% from Easton. It has been noted that nearly every family in Phillipsburg deals with one of the city's three banks, and the town's businessmen prefer to do the same. . . .

The localization of business typical of the banking industry is particularly pronounced when small customers are involved. . . . Small depositors have little reason to deal with a bank other than the one most geographically convenient to them. For such persons, geographic convenience can be a more powerful influence than the availability of a higher rate of interest at a more distant, though still nearby, bank. The small borrower, if he is to have his needs met, must often depend upon his community reputation and upon his relationship with the local banker.

. . .

. . . We find that the evidence shows that Phillipsburg-Easton constitutes a geographic market in which the proposed merger's effect would be "direct and immediate." It is the market area in which PNB and SNB operate, and, as a practical matter, it is the area in which most of the merging banks' customers must, or will, do their banking. Thus, we hold that the District Court mistakenly rejected the Government's contention that Phillipsburg-Easton is an appropriate "section of the country" under §7.

Appellee banks argue that Phillipsburg-Easton "cannot conceivably be considered a 'market' for antitrust purposes," on the ground that it is not an "economically significant section of the country." . . . In *Brown Shoe*, however, we found "relevant geographic markets" in cities "with a population exceeding 10,000 and their environs." . . . Phillipsburg-Easton and their immediate environs had a population of almost 90,000 in 1960.

Seven banks compete for their business. This market is clearly an economically significant section of the country for the purposes of §7.

THE ANTICOMPETITIVE EFFECTS
OF THE MERGER

We turn now to the ultimate question under §7: whether the effect of the proposed merger "may be substantially to lessen competition." . . . In *Philadelphia Bank*, . . . we held that "[t]his intense congressional concern with the trend toward concentration warrants dispensing, in certain cases, with elaborate proof of market structure, market behavior, or probable anticompetitive effects. Specifically, we think that a merger which produces a firm controlling an undue percentage share of the relevant market, and results in a significant increase in the concentration of firms in that market, is so inherently likely to lessen competition substantially that it must be enjoined in the absence of evidence clearly showing that the merger is not likely to have such anti-competitive effects." That principle is applicable to this case.

The commercial banking market in Phillipsburg-Easton is already concentrated. Of its seven banks, the two largest in 1967—Easton National Bank and Lafayette Trust Co.—had 49% of its total banking assets, 56% of its total deposits, 49% of its total loans and seven of its 16 banking offices. Easton National is itself the product of the merger of two smaller banks in 1959. The union of PNB-SNB would, in turn, significantly increase commercial banking concentration in "one town." The combined bank would become the second largest in the area, with assets of over $41,100,-000 (19.3% of the area's assets), total deposits of $38,400,000 (23.4%), and total loans of $24,900,000 (27.3%). . . . In Phillipsburg alone, of course, the impact would be much greater: banking alternatives would be reduced from three to two; the resultant bank would be three times larger than the only other remaining bank, and all but two of the banking offices in the city would be controlled by one firm. Thus, we find on this record that the proposed merger, if consummated, "is . . . inherently likely to lessen competition substantially." . . .

Appellee banks argue that they are presently so small that they lack the personnel and resources to serve their community effectively and to compete vigorously. Thus, they contend that the proposed merger could have procompetitive effects: by enhancing their competitive position, it would stimulate other small banks in the area to become more aggressive in meeting the needs of the area and it would enable PNB-SNB to meet an alleged competitive challenge from large, outside banks. Although such considerations are certainly relevant in determining the "convenience and needs of the community" under the Bank Merger Act, they are not persuasive in the context of the Clayton Act. . . .

MEETING THE CONVENIENCE AND NEEDS
OF THE COMMUNITY

The District Court's errors necessarily require reexamination of its conclusion that any anticompetitive effects caused by the proposed merger would be outweighed by the merger's contribution to the community's convenience and needs. The District Court's conclusion, moreover, is undermined by the court's erroneous application of the convenience-and-needs standard. . . .

The District Court misapplied the convenience-and-needs standard by assessing the competitive effect of the proposed merger in the broad, multi-community area which it adopted as the relevant geographic market, while assessing the merger's contribution to community convenience and needs in Phillipsburg alone. . . . We hold, however, that evaluation must be in terms of the convenience and needs of Phillipsburg-Easton as a whole. . . .

The judgment of the District Court is reversed and the case is remanded for further proceedings consistent with this opinion. No costs shall be assessed against appellee banks.

It is so ordered.

MR. JUSTICE STEWART took no part in the decision of this case, and MR. JUSTICE BLACKMUN took no part in its consideration or decision.

MR. JUSTICE HARLAN, with whom THE CHIEF JUSTICE joins, concurring in part and dissenting in part.

My first reaction to this case, from the vantage point of what is depicted in the record and briefs, was wonderment that the Department of Justice had bothered to sue. How could that agency of government, I asked myself, be efficiently allocating its own scarce resources if it chose to attack a merger between two banks as small as those involved in this case? . . . With tigers still at large in our competitive jungle, why should the Department be taking aim at such small game?

. . . After today's opinion the legality of every merger of two directly competing banks—no matter how small—is placed in doubt if a court, through what has become an exercise in "antitrust numerology," *United States v. First National Bank & Trust Co. of Lexington,* . . . (HARLAN, J., dissenting), concludes that the merger "produces a firm controlling an undue percentage share of the relevant market," . . .

For the first stage of the analysis, the Court appears to decide whether the effect of this proposed merger "may be substantially to lessen competition" by the following process: First, the Court defines the relevant product market as commercial banking. Second, it defines the geographic market as Phillipsburg-Easton. The Court next calculates the percentage share of this market that would be held by the proposed merged bank, and the resulting changes in "concentration," as measured by the percent of market held by the two largest and three largest banks. It appears that from the magnitude of these figures alone, the Court concludes that the proposed merger would "significantly increase commercial banking concentration" in an "already concentrated" market. On the basis of the magnitude of these figures alone the Court concludes that this merger would violate §7 of the Clayton Act. . . .

The *El Paso Natural Gas* case was another example of a merger between two firms in a regulated industry in which the regulatory agency gave its approval, but the Justice Department entered a challenge and won the case. In 1956 El Paso Natural Gas was the only out-of-state supplier of natural gas for the lucrative California market, accounting for over 50 per cent of the gas consumed in the state. The Pacific Northwest Pipeline Corporation, also a supplier of natural gas but operating primarily in the three upper northwestern states, tried to enter the rapidly growing California market. In order to forestall this entry, El Paso purchased the stock of Pacific Northwest. Immediately the Justice Department filed suit to void the merger, whereupon El Paso promptly requested permission from the Federal Power Commission to purchase the assets of Pacific Northwest. The Commission gave its approval and the merger was finally completed on December 31, 1959.

The Supreme Court found that the production, transportation, and sale of natural gas was a line of commerce with the meaning of Section 7, and California was the relevant section of the country wherein the impact of the merger must be judged. Although the acquired company had never achieved actual entry into the California market, its effect as a potential supplier made it a substantial competitive factor in the market. "Unsuccessful bidders are no less competitors than the successful one."

While he concurred with the opinion of the Court, Justice Harlan offered the observation that the dual system of regulation should be re-examined to avoid the "unsatisfactoriness of the existing bifurcated system of antitrust and other regulation in various fields."

UNITED STATES v. EL PASO NATURAL GAS CO. et al.

376 U.S. 651 (1964)

Opinion of the Court by MR. JUSTICE DOUGLAS, announced by MR. JUSTICE CLARK.

This is a civil suit charging a violation of §7 of the Clayton Act, by reason of the acquisition of the stock and assets of Pacific Northwest Pipeline Corp. (Pacific Northwest) by El Paso Natural Gas Co. (El Paso). The District Court dismissed the complaint after trial, making findings of fact and conclusions of law, but not writing an opinion. . . .

The ultimate issue revolves around the question whether the acquisition substantially lessened competition in the sale of natural gas in California—a market of which El Paso was the sole out-of-state supplier at the time of the acquisition. . . .

In 1954 Pacific Northwest entered into two gas exchange contracts with El Paso—one to deliver 250 million cubic feet per day to El Paso in Idaho for transportation to California via Nevada, the other to gather gas jointly in the San Juan Basin for five-year period. Under the latter agreement El Paso loaned gas to Pacific Northwest from its wells in the San Juan Basin; to avoid duplication of facilities, Pacific Northwest agreed to gather gas with its own facilities from El Paso's wells in the eastern portion of the basin, and El Paso agreed to perform the same service for Pacific Northwest in the western portion. At the same time Pacific Northwest undertook to purchase 300 million cubic feet per day from Westcoast Transmission Co., Ltd., a Canadian pipeline. . . .

El Paso had been interested in acquiring Pacific Northwest since 1954. The first offer from El Paso was in December 1955—an offer Pacific Northwest rejected. Negotiations were resumed by El Paso in the summer of 1956, while Pacific Northwest was trying to obtain a California outlet. The exchange of El Paso shares for Pacific shares was accepted by Pacific Northwest's directors in November 1956, and by May 1957 El Paso had acquired 99.8% of Pacific Northwest's outstanding stock. In July 1957 the Department of Justice filed its suit charging that the acquisition violated

§7 of the Clayton Act. In August 1957 El Paso applied to the Federal Power Commission for permission to acquire the assets of Pacific Northwest. On December 23, 1959, the Commission approved and the merger was effected on December 31, 1959. In 1962 we set aside the Commission's order, holding that it should not have acted until the District Court had passed on the Clayton Act issues. . . . Meanwhile (in October 1960) the United States amended its complaint so as to include the asset acquisition in the charged violation of the Clayton Act. . . .

. . . On review of the record—which is composed largely of undisputed evidence—we conclude that "the effect of such acquisition may be substantially to lessen competition" within the meaning of §7 of the Clayton Act.

There can be no doubt that the production, transportation, and sale of natural gas is a "line of commerce" within the meaning of §7. There can also be no doubt that California is a "section of the country" as that phrase is used in §7. The sole question, therefore, is whether on undisputed facts the acquisition had a sufficient tendency to lessen competition or is saved by the findings that Pacific Northwest, as an independent entity, could not have obtained a contract from the California distributors, could not have received the gas supplies or financing for a pipeline project to California, or could not have put together a project acceptable to the regulatory agencies. Those findings are irrelevant. . . .

Pacific Northwest, though it had no pipeline into California, is shown by this record to have been a substantial factor in the California market at the time it was acquired by El Paso. . . .

Edison's search for a firm supply of natural gas in California, when it had El Paso gas only on an "interruptible" basis, illustrates what effect Pacific Northwest had merely as a potential competitor in the California market. Edison took its problem to Pacific Northwest and, as we have seen, a tentative agreement was reached for Edison to obtain Pacific Northwest gas. El Paso responded, offering Edison a firm supply of gas and substantial price concessions. We would have to wear blinders not to see that the mere efforts of Pacific Northwest to get into the California market, though unsuccessful, had a powerful influence on El Paso's business attitudes within the State. . . .

This is not a field where merchants are in a continuous daily struggle to hold old customers and to win new ones over from their rivals. In this regulated industry a natural gas company (unless it has excess capacity) must compete for, enter into, and then obtain Commission approval of sale contracts in advance of constructing the pipeline facilities. In the natural gas industry pipelines are very expensive; and to be justified they need long-term contracts for sale of the gas that will travel them. Those transactions with distributors are few in number. For example, in California there are only two significant wholesale purchasers—Pacific Gas & Electric in the north and the Southern Companies in the south. Once the Commission grants authorization to construct facilities or to transport gas in interstate commerce, once the distributing contracts are made, a particular market is withdrawn from competition. *The competition then is for the new increments of demand that may emerge with an expanding population and with an expanding industrial or household use of gas.*

The effect on competition in a particular market through acquisition of another company is determined by the nature or extent of that market and by the nearness of the absorbed company to it, that company's eagerness to enter that market, its resourcefulness, and so on. Pacific Northwest's position as a competitive factor in California was not disproved by the fact that it had never sold gas there. Nor is it conclusive that Pacific Northwest's attempt to sell to Edison failed. That might be weighty if a market presently saturated showed signs of petering out. But it is irrelevant in a market like California, where incremental needs are booming. That is underscored in the case by a memorandum dated October 18, 1956, which summarized a meeting at which terms of the acquisition were negotiated. . . .

Unsuccessful bidders are no less competitors than the successful one. The presence of two or more suppliers gives buyers a choice. Pacific Northwest was no feeble, failing company; nor was it inexperienced and lacking in resourcefulness. . . .

Since appellees have been on notice of the antitrust charge from almost the beginning—indeed before El Paso sought Commission approval of the merger—we not only reverse the judgment below but direct the District Court to order divestiture without delay.

Reversed.

Mr. Justice White took no part in the consideration or decision of this case.

Mr. Justice Harlan, concurring in part and dissenting in part. . . .

. . . This case affords another example of the unsatisfactoriness of the existing bifurcated system of antitrust and other regulation in various fields. In this case, the Federal Power Commission had indicated its approval of this merger as being in the public interest. The Department of Justice, however, considered the merger to be violative of the antitrust laws and, for that reason alone, against the public interest. This Court, under the present scheme of things has no choice on this record but to sustain the position of the Department of Justice, as indeed it has felt constrained to do, albeit in my view with less justification, in other recent cases involving dual regulation. . . . It would be unrealistic not to recognize that this state of affairs has the effect of placing the Department of Justice in the driver's seat even though Congress has lodged primary regulatory authority elsewhere.

It does seem to me that the time has come when this duplicative and, I venture to say, anachronistic system of dual regulation should be re-examined. . . .

5

Mergers under the Amended
Section 7—II

This chapter continues with cases that have been handed down under the amended Section 7 of the Clayton Act. The focus is on two different kinds of merger problems that have evolved and how the law may influence these situations. The interpretation and application of Section 7 to conglomerate mergers is considered in the first section, and the question of joint ventures is presented in the second section.

Conglomerate Mergers

The most unsettled area of merger law is that dealing with conglomerate mergers. Although the *Brown Shoe* case said clearly that the intent of Congress was to include conglomerate mergers within the purview of the Celler-Kefauver amendment, the Supreme Court has not yet been called upon to make direct application of the law in a true conglomerate case. The *conglomerate merger* may be defined in a variety of ways, but all would be characterized by one common theme. That is, these mergers bring together firms in noncompeting lines of endeavor; they have no apparent horizontal or vertical economic relationships. The outstanding feature of the current merger wave, in progress since the mid-1950s, has been this drive to achieve diversification into a number of unrelated fields via the external expansion route.

Because of the dearth of rulings on true conglomerates, the three cases presented in this section are not as revealing on the future fate of conglomerates as one might wish. Nevertheless, these cases have been referred to as conglomerate mergers at one time or another, and they do give hints on the direction that future decisions may take.

The first was decided by the Supreme Court in 1965 in a suit brought by the Federal Trade Commission against Consolidated Foods Corporation, a large, diversified food processor, wholesaler, and retailer. Consolidated had acquired Gentry, Inc., a manufacturer of dehydrated onion and garlic, controlling 32 per cent of that market before the merger in 1951. This merger has sometimes been labeled a *"product extension"* merger.

After acquisition, Consolidated attempted to use its market position to induce the buying of Gentry's products by the processor/suppliers of Consolidated, simultaneously excluding competitors from the market for these products.

This tactic of "reciprocity" was not particularly successful because nearly a decade later the market share of Gentry had been raised only to 35 per cent. Perhaps the real success was merely in holding and increasing slightly the market share since Gentry's president "freely and repeatedly admitted" that the product of the leading competitor was superior to Gentry's.

This case, then, did not revolve around the questions of relevant line of commerce or section of the country. The real issue was whether or not the strategy of reciprocal buying employed by a large, diversified food company as the logical consequence of a product extension merger would result in a probable lessening of competition. The court of appeals, looking mainly at post-acquisition experience and noting the relatively insignificant increase in Gentry's market share after ten years, decided there was no violation of Section 7. The High Court reversed this decision and said that reciprocity made possible by an acquisition such as this was contrary to the law. "The practice results in 'an irrelevant and alien factor' . . . intruding into the choice among competing products, . . ." The evidence was sufficient to confirm a finding of probable anticompetitive effects.

FEDERAL TRADE COMMISSION v. CONSOLIDATED FOODS CORP.

380 U.S. 592 (1965)

MR. JUSTICE DOUGLAS delivered the opinion of the Court.[1]

The question presented involves an important construction and application of §7 of the Clayton Act, . . . Consolidated Foods Corp.—which owns food processing plants and a network of wholesale and retail food stores—acquired Gentry, Inc., in 1951. Gentry manufactures principally dehydrated onion and garlic. The Federal Trade Commission held that the acquisition violated §7 because it gave respondent the advantage of a mixed threat and lure of reciprocal buying in its competition for business and "the power to foreclose competition from a substantial share of the markets for dehydrated onion and garlic." It concluded, in other words, that the effect of the acquisition "may be substantially to lessen competition" within the meaning of §7, and it ordered divestiture and gave other relief. . . . The Court of Appeals, relying mainly on 10 years of post-acquisition experience, held that the Commission had failed to show a

---

[1] All the footnotes and most of the citations from the opinions of the Court have been omitted from the casese in this chapter.

probability that the acquisition would substantially lessen competition.
. . .

We hold at the outset that the "reciprocity" made possible by such
an acquisition is one of the congeries of anticompetitive practices at which
the antitrust laws are aimed. The practice results in "an irrelevant and
alien factor," . . . intruding into the choice among competing products,
creating at the least "a priority on the business at equal prices." *International Salt Co. v. United States*, . . . Reciprocal trading may ensue not
from bludgeoning or coercion but from more subtle arrangements. A
threatened withdrawal of orders if products of an affiliate cease being
bought, as well as a conditioning of future purchases on the receipt of
orders for products of that affiliate, is an anticompetitive practice. Section 7
of the Clayton Act is concerned "with probabilities, not certainties."
Brown Shoe Co. v. United States, . . . Reciprocity in trading as a result of
an acquisition violates §7, if the probability of a lessening of competition is
shown. We turn then to that, the principal, aspect of the present case.

Consolidated is a substantial purchaser of the products of food
processors who in turn purchase dehydrated onion and garlic for use in
preparing and packaging their food. Gentry, which as noted is principally
engaged in the manufacture of dehydrated onion and garlic, had in 1950,
immediately prior to its acquisition by Consolidated, about 32% of the
total sales of the dehydrated garlic and onion industry and, together with
its principal competitor, Basic Vegetable Products, Inc., accounted for
almost 90% of the total industry sales. The remaining 10% was divided
between two other firms. By 1958 the total industry output of both
products had doubled, Gentry's share rising to 35% and the combined
share of Gentry and Basic remaining at about 90%.

After the acquisition Consolidated (though later disclaiming adherence to any policy of reciprocity) did undertake to assist Gentry in
selling. . . .

Food processors who sold to Consolidated stated they would give
their onion and garlic business to Gentry for reciprocity reasons if it could
meet the price and quality of its competitors' products. . . .

The Commission found, however, that "merely as a result of its
connection with Consolidated, and without any action on the latter's part,
Gentry would have an unfair advantage over competitors enabling it to
make sales that otherwise might not have been made." . . .

Moreover, the post-acquisition evidence here tends to confirm, rather
than cast doubt upon, the probable anticompetitive effect which the
Commission found the merger would have. The Commission found that
Basic's product was superior to Gentry's—as Gentry's president freely and
repeatedly admitted. Yet Gentry, in a rapidly expanding market, was able
to increase its share of onion sales by 7% and to hold its losses in garlic to a

12% decrease. Thus the Commission was surely on safe ground in reaching the following conclusion:

> If reciprocal buying creates for Gentry a protected market, which others cannot penetrate despite superiority of price, quality, or service, competition is lessened whether or not Gentry can expand its market share. It is for this reason that we reject respondent's argument that the decline in its share of the garlic market proves the ineffectiveness of reciprocity. We do not know that its share would not have fallen still farther, had it not been for the influence of reciprocal buying. This loss of sales fails to refute the likelihood that Consolidated's reciprocity power, which it has shown a willingness to exploit to the full, will not immunize a substantial segment of the garlic market from normal quality, price, and service competition. . . .

But the Court of Appeals ignored the Commission's findings as to the inferiority of Gentry's product; . . .

We conclude that there is substantial evidence to sustain that conclusion and that the order of the Commission should not have been denied enforcement. The judgment of the Court of Appeals is accordingly

Reversed.

Mr. Justice Harlan, concurring in the judgment. . . .

Mr. Justice Stewart, concurring in the judgment.

The Federal Trade Commission, in invalidating a merger between Consolidated Foods and Gentry, Inc., has espoused a novel theory to bring the facts of this case within the scope of §7 of the Clayton Act. Its resolution of the issue has been much debated and much disputed. . . . We must decide the applicability of the Act to the facts of this case, but we should also provide guidance to the Commission and to the courts which will have to grapple in the future with the potentialities of reciprocal buying in §7 cases. While I agree with the result that the Court has reached, I am persuaded to file this separate statement of my views regarding the issues involved.

Clearly the opportunity for reciprocity is not alone enough to invalidate a merger under §7. The Clayton Act was not passed to outlaw diversification. Yet large scale diversity of industrial interests almost always presents the possibility of some reciprocal relationships. Often the purpose of diversification is to acquire companies whose present management can benefit from the technical skills and sales acumen of the acquiring corporation. Without more, §7 of the Clayton Act does not prohibit mergers whose sole effect is to introduce into an arena of "soft" competition the experience and skills of a more aggressive organization.

It obviously requires more than this kind of bare potential for reciprocal buying to bring a merger within the ban of §7. Before a merger may be properly outlawed under §7 on the basis solely of reciprocal buying potentials, the law requires a more closely textured economic analysis. . . .

. . . Certainly the mere effort at reciprocity cannot be the basis for finding the probability of a significant alteration in the market structure. Section 7 does not punish intent. No matter how bent on reciprocity Consolidated might have been, if its activities would not have the requisite probable impact on competition, it cannot be held to have violated this law. . . .

The record in this case is sorely incomplete, and a reviewing court is given little guidance in determining why this merger should be voided, if reciprocity-creating mergers are not *per se* invalid. Yet our responsibility to the Commission—to respect its findings where there is evidence to support them—requires close scrutiny of the record before its conclusions are upset. I think the record contains just enough to support invalidation of the merger, but because of evidence not referred to in the Court's opinion. . . .

Another Federal Trade Commission ruling against a conglomerate, or product extension, merger was upheld unanimously by the Supreme Court in 1967. Ten years before Proctor & Gamble Company—the large, well-known, and diversified maker of household cleansing items—acquired the assets of Clorox Chemical Company, the leading manufacturer of household liquid bleach. At the time of the merger, Clorox had 49 per cent of the national market for liquid bleach and the top four firms accounted for almost 80 per cent. The FTC found that the substitution of P. & G. for Clorox would dissuade new entrants into the liquid bleach field, discourage active competition from already existing firms because of fear of retaliation by P. & G., and diminish potential competition because P. & G., the most likely new entrant, was now eliminated. The appellate court reversed this decision by finding that the FTC ruling was based on "treacherous conjecture" and suspicion.

The Supreme Court looked at the problem differently. Mergers, whether horizontal, vertical, conglomerate, or product extension, must be tested against the Section 7 standard—that is, whether they may substantially lessen competition. This test requires a prediction of the merger's impact on present and future competition. In the view of the Court, this merger would have anticompetitive effects for the following reasons: First, in this oligopolistic industry the substitution of the powerful acquiring firm for the smaller but dominant firm might substantially reduce the competitive structure of the industry by dissuading smaller firms from competing aggressively. Second, barriers to entry became more rigid because of the reluctance of new entrants to face the huge P. & G. Third, the FTC finding that the acquisition eliminated P. & G. as a potential competitor was amply supported by the evidence. Fourth, P. & G.'s economies of scale in advertising—advertising is a major competitive weapon in marketing bleach—would tend to close the field to new entrants.

Justice Harlan offered a concurring opinion, criticizing the majority for making such a feeble effort to formulate standards for applying Section 7 to conglomerate cases. He felt that the majority decision did very little to show the FTC, lawyers, and businessmen what was to be expected from them in future cases.

FEDERAL TRADE COMMISSION v. PROCTER & GAMBLE CO.

386 U.S. 568 (1967)

Mr. Justice Douglas delivered the opinion of the Court.

This is a proceeding initiated by the Federal Trade Commission charging that respondent, Procter & Gamble Co., had acquired the assets of Clorox Chemical Co. in violation of §7 of the Clayton Act, . . . , as amended by the Celler-Kefauver Act, . . . The charge was that Procter's acquisition of Clorox might substantially lessen competiton or tend to create a monopoly in the production and sale of household liquid bleaches. . . .

As indicated by the Commission in its painstaking and illuminating report, it does not particularly aid analysis to talk of this merger in conventional terms, namely, horizontal or vertical or conglomerate. This merger may most appropriately be described as a "product-extension merger," as the Commission stated. The facts are not disputed, and a summary will demonstrate the correctness of the Commission's decision.

At the time of the merger, in 1957, Clorox was the leading manufacturer in the heavily concentrated household liquid bleach industry. It is agreed that household liquid bleach is the relevant line of commerce. The product is used in the home as a germicide and disinfectant, and, more importantly, as a whitening agent in washing clothes and fabrics. It is a distinctive product with no close substitutes. Liquid bleach is a low-price, high-turnover consumer product sold mainly through grocery stores and supermarkets. The relevant geographical market is the Nation and a series of regional markets. Because of high shipping costs and low sales price, it is not feasible to ship the product more than 300 miles from its point of manufacture. Most manufacturers are limited to competition within a single region since they have but one plant. Clorox is the only firm selling nationally; it has 13 plants distributed throughout the Nation. Purex, Clorox's closest competitor in size, does not distribute its bleach in the northeast or mid-Atlantic States; in 1957, Purex's bleach was available in less than 50% of the national market.

At the time of the acquisition, Clorox was the leading manufacturer of household liquid bleach, with 48.8% of the national sales—annual sales of slightly less than $40,000,000. Its market share had been steadily increasing for the five years prior to the merger. Its nearest rival was Purex, which manufactures a number of products other than household liquid bleaches, including abrasive cleaners, toilet soap, and detergents. Purex accounted for 15.7% of the household liquid bleach market. The industry is highly concentrated; in 1957, Clorox and Purex accounted for almost 65% of the Nation's household liquid bleach sales, and, together with four other firms, for almost 80%. The remaining 20% was divided among over 200 small producers. Clorox had total assets of $12,000,000; only eight producers had assets in excess of $1,000,000 and very few had assets of more than $75,000. . . .

Since all liquid bleach is chemically identical, advertising and sales promotion are vital. In 1957 Clorox spent almost $3,700,000 on advertising, imprinting the value of its bleach in the mind of the consumer. In addition, it spent $1,700,000 for other promotional activities. The Commission found that these heavy expenditures went far to explain why Clorox maintained so high a market share despite the fact that its brand, though chemically indistinguishable from rival brands, retailed for a price equal to or, in many instances, higher than its competitors.

Procter is a large, diversified manufacturer of low-price, high-turnover household products sold through grocery, drug, and department stores. Prior to its acquisition of Clorox, it did not produce household liquid bleach. Its 1957 sales were in excess of $1,100,000,000 from which it realized profits of more than $67,000,000; its assets were over $500,000,000. Procter has been marked by rapid growth and diversification. It has successfully developed and introduced a number of new products. Its primary activity is in the general area of soaps, detergents, and cleansers; in 1957, of total domestic sales, more than one-half (over $500,000,000) were in this field. Procter was the dominant factor in this area. It accounted for

54.4% of all packaged detergent sales. The industry is heavily concentrated—Procter and its nearest competitors, Colgate-Palmolive and Lever Brothers, account for 80% of the market.

In the marketing of soaps, detergents, and cleansers, as in the marketing of household liquid bleach, advertising and sales promotion are vital. In 1957, Procter was the Nation's largest advertiser, spending more than $80,000,000 on advertising and an additional $47,000,000 on sales promotion. Due to its tremendous volume, Procter receives substantial discounts from the media. As a multiproduct producer Procter enjoys substantial advantages in advertising and sales promotion. Thus, it can and does feature several products in its promotions, reducing the printing, mailing, and other costs for each product. It also purchases network programs on behalf of several products, enabling it to give each product network exposure at a fraction of the cost per product that a firm with only one product to advertise would incur.

Prior to the acquisition, Procter was in the course of diversifying into product lines related to its basic detergent-soap-cleanser business. Liquid bleach was a distinct possibility since packaged detergents—Procter's primary product line—and liquid bleach are used complementarily in washing clothes and fabrics, and in general household cleaning. . . .

The Commission found that the acquisition might substantially lessen competition. The findings and reasoning of the Commission need be only briefly summarized. The Commission found that the substitution of Procter with its huge assets and advertising advantages for the already dominant Clorox would dissuade new entrants and discourage active competition from the firms already in the industry due to fear of retaliation by Procter. The Commission thought it relevant that retailers might be induced to give Clorox preferred shelf space since it would be manufactured by Procter, which also produced a number of other products marketed by the retailers. There was also the danger that Procter might underprice Clorox in order to drive out competition, and subsidize the underpricing with revenue from other products. The Commission carefully reviewed the effect of the acquisition on the structure of the industry, noting that "[t]he practical tendency of the . . . merger . . . is to transform the liquid bleach industry into an arena of big business competition only, with the few small firms that have not disappeared through merger eventually falling by the wayside, unable to compete with their giant rivals." . . . Further, the merger would seriously diminish potential competition by eliminating Procter as a potential entrant into the industry. Prior to the merger, the Commission found, Procter was the most likely prospective entrant, and absent the merger would have remained on the periphery, restraining Clorox from exercising its market power. If Procter had actually entered, Clorox's dominant position would have been eroded and the concentration of the industry reduced. The Commission stated that it had not placed reliance on post-acquisition evidence in holding the merger unlawful.

The Court of Appeals said that the Commission's finding of illegality had been based on "treacherous conjecture," mere possibility and suspicion. . . . It dismissed the finding that Procter, with its huge resources and prowess, would have more leverage than Clorox with the statement that it was Clorox which had the "knowhow" in the industry, and that Clorox's finances were adequate for its purposes. . . .

The anticompetitive effects with which this product-extension merger is fraught can easily be seen: (1) the substitution of the powerful acquiring firm for the smaller, but already dominant, firm may substantially reduce the competitive structure of the industry by raising entry barriers and by dissuading the smaller firms from aggressively competing; (2) the acquisition eliminates the potential competition of the acquiring firm. . . .

The acquisition may also have the tendency of raising the barriers to new entry. The major competitive weapon in the successful marketing of bleach is advertising. Clorox was limited in this area by its relatively small budget and its inability to obtain substantial discounts. By contrast, Procter's budget was much larger; and, although it would not devote its entire budget to advertising Clorox, it could divert a large portion to meet the short-term threat of a new entrant. Procter would be able to use its volume discounts to advantage in advertising Clorox. Thus, a new entrant would be much more reluctant to face the giant Procter than it would have been to face the smaller Clorox.

Possible economies cannot be used as a defense to illegality. Congress was aware that some mergers which lessen competition may also result in economies but it struck the balance in favor of protecting competition. . . .

The Commission also found that the acquisition of Clorox by Procter eliminated Procter as a potential competitor. The Court of Appeals declared that this finding was not supported by evidence because there was no evidence that Procter's management had ever intended to enter the industry independently and that Procter had never attempted to enter. The evidence, however, clearly shows that Procter was the most likely entrant. . . .

It is clear that the existence of Procter at the edge of the industry exerted considerable influence on the market. First, the market behavior of the liquid bleach industry was influenced by each firm's predictions of the market behavior of its competitors, actual and potential. Second, the barriers to entry by a firm of Procter's size and with its advantages were not significant. There is no indication that the barriers were so high that the price Procter would have to charge would be above the price that would maximize the profits of the existing firms. Third, the number of potential entrants was not so large that the elimination of one would be insignificant. Few firms would have the temerity to challenge a firm as solidly entrenched as Clorox. Fourth, Procter was found by the Commission to be the most likely entrant. These findings of the Commission were amply supported by the evidence.

The judgment of the Court of Appeals is reversed and remanded with instructions to affirm and enforce the Commission's order.

It is so ordered.

Mr. Justice Stewart and Mr. Justice Fortas took no part in the consideration or decision of this case.

Mr. Justice Harlan, concurring.

I agree that the Commission's order should be sustained, but I do not share the majority opinion's view that a mere "summary will demonstrate the correctness of the Commission's decision" nor that "[t]he anticompetitive effects with which this product-extension merger is fraught can easily be seen." I consider the case difficult within its own four corners, and beyond that, its portents for future administrative and judicial application of §7 of the Clayton Act to this kind of merger important and far-reaching. From both standpoints more refined analysis is required before putting the stamp of approval on what the Commission has done in this case. It is regrettable to see this Court as it enters this comparatively new field of economic adjudication starting off with what has almost become a kind of *res ipsa loquitur* approach to antitrust cases.

The type of merger represented by the transaction before us is becoming increasingly important as large corporations seek to diversify their operations, . . .

I thus believe that it is incumbent upon us to make a careful study of the facts and opinions below in this case, and at least to embark upon the formulation of standards for the application of §7 to mergers which are neither horizontal nor vertical and which previously have not been considered in depth by this Court. I consider this especially important in light of the divisions which have arisen in the Commission itself in similar cases decided subsequent to this one. See *General Foods Corp.*, . . . My prime difficulty with the Court's opinion is that it makes no effort in this direction at all, and leaves the Commission, lawyers, and businessmen at large as to what is to be expected of them in future cases of this kind. . . .

The final conglomerate decision, a court of appeals ruling in the *General Foods* case which the Supreme Court refused to review,[2] corresponded very closely to the *Proctor & Gamble* "precedent." The circumstances surrounding the two mergers were very similar; therefore, the appellate court followed the recent ruling of *P. & G.*

In 1957 the General Foods Corporation, one of the largest manufacturers and distributors of packaged food, acquired the S.O.S. Company, one of two companies dominating the household steel wool cleansing pad market. The Federal Trade Commission challenged the merger under Section 7, ruling in 1964 that there was a violation. On appeal, the Commission's findings were upheld. General Foods argued the acquisition was legal because the relevant market was a broad one encompassing some forty other household cleaning devices which compete with steel wool pads. The Commission ruled that steel wool pads should be the relevant market for a number of reasons: First, a definite steel wool market is recognized as an identifiable industry. Second, steel wool pads have peculiar characteristics and uses. Third, steel wool products are sold at distinct prices and display no sensitivity to price changes in nonsteel products. Fourth, steel wool products use unique production facilities.

If steel wool products are accepted as the relevant market, was there sufficient evidence to find a probable lessening of competition in this product extension merger? Like the *Proctor* case, a large, multiproduct firm was acting to add a new product to its line by acquiring a company controlling over 50 per cent of its market. The Commission found that General Foods used its large promotional resources to increase the position of S.O.S. vis-à-vis its number one competitor, Brillo. The dominance of S.O.S. was so enhanced that new competition would refuse to enter the industry. The Commission's ruling, therefore, was that the acquisition "raised to virtually insurmountable heights entry barriers which were already high."

GENERAL FOODS CORPORATION v. FEDERAL TRADE COMMISSION

386 F. 2d 936 (1967)

Opinion of the Court

STALEY, Chief Judge.

Appellant, General Foods Corporation (hereinafter "G. F."), seeks to have reviewed and set aside a final order of the Federal Trade Commission.

---

[2] Certiorari denied, 391 U.S. 919.

The Commission's order required G.F. to divest itself of all S.O.S. assets acquired in violation of §7 of the Clayton Act, . . .

G.F. is one of the largest producers and distributors of packaged food in the United States. All its products are low-priced high-turnover household consumer commodities sold to customers through the same grocery and supermarket outlets as are S.O.S. steel wool soap pads. Between 1955 and 1964, its net sales rose from $825 million to $1.3 billion, and its net assets from $279 million to $436 million, an increase of 57.6% and 56.2% respectively. . . .

Prior to the acquisition, the steel wool industry had been an almost perfectly balanced duopoly. But in terms of regional, as distinguished from national sales, S.O.S. managed to achieve a monopoly position in many areas. G.F., however, was not satisfied with the market position of the company it acquired. Soon after the acquisition, appellant concluded that the entire marketing and advertising approach of S.O.S. needed rejuvenation. This task was entrusted to an advertising agency then handling other G.F. products. The new agency succeeded in enhancing the S.O.S. image by skillfully emphasizing different aspects of the product than had previously been featured and by persuading G.F.'s management that they should place an almost total reliance on television advertising.

A survey of sales' statistics for the household steel wool industry reveals the dramatic change that G.F. was able to effect. During the period from 1955 to 1957 total sales in the industry rose from $24.2 million to $28.6 million, a market expansion of over 18%. The sales of S.O.S., however, increased by only 14.5% from $12.7 million in 1955 to $14.6 million in 1957. S.O.S. thus failed to keep pace with the expanding market, its share falling from 52.8% in 1955 to 51% in 1957. . . .

Beginning in 1960, with the post-acquisition period coming to a close, the advantages derived from G.F.'s great competitive strength began to make themselves evident, and the fortunes of S.O.S. took an upward turn. Sales began to accelerate sharply and at a much faster pace than those for the total industry. Between 1959 and 1962, the sales of S.O.S. rose from $15.2 million to $19.2 million, a gain of 26.5%. Total industry sales, however, increased by only 11.5%, from $30.7 million to $34.2 million. Sales of S.O.S., therefore, expanded at more than twice the rate of the household steel wool market, and the market share of S.O.S. grew from 49.4% in 1959 to 56% in 1962.

In the face of this remarkable comeback by S.O.S., Brillo's position deteriorated rapidly. Even though industry household steel wool sales increased by 11.5%, Brillo's sales actually decreased from $14.9 million in 1959 to $14.3 million in 1962, a decline of 4.2% in an expanding market. Confronted with steadily falling sales, a dangerously declining market share, and mounting advertising and promotional expenses, Brillo, in December 1963, ceased operations as an independent company and merged with Purex Corporation, Ltd.

I

Section 7 of the Clayton Act prohibits any merger which may substantially lessen competition or tend toward monopoly "in any line of commerce." Prohibition of a merger depends, not upon the form it assumes, but upon the realities of the market in which the merged companies operate. . . .

In the present case, the Commission followed, as far as possible, the guidelines laid down in *Brown Shoe*. It found that the appropriate line of commerce or relevant product market within which to test the impact of the G.F.–S.O.S. merger was household steel wool. Appellant challenges this finding, accusing the Commission of "untenable gerrymandering" because of its failure to include in the relevant market numerous nonsteel wool household aids that G.F. introduced into the record. Appellant further argues that even if the market definition was technically tenable, the Commission nevertheless erred in assessing the impact of the merger by treating nonsteel wool scouring devices as though they did not exist. . . .

We now return to G.F.'s contention that the Commission erroneously found many of the crucial facts in this case. As mentioned earlier, we think this argument is without merit. The Commission found that there was a definite *industry recognition of the household steel wool submarket as a separate economic entity*. This finding is supported by testimony of several household steel wool producers stating that they only looked to other steel wool producers in setting prices and in reaching marketing decisions with respect to their products. As far as these producers were concerned, their only serious competition was with those companies in the industry who manufactured household steel wool. Little or no attention was paid to producers of materials other than steel wool. Indeed, G.F. itself recognized that competition offered by nonsteel wool products is at best "indirect." . . .

The Commission further found that steel wool pads have *peculiar characteristics and uses*. Testimony and exhibits relating to the physical composition, operational characteristics, and stated uses for household steel wool substantiate this finding. Nonsteel wool products assume variant forms bearing little resemblance to steel wool and their compositions range from plastic, to copper, to abrasive-surface sponges. But appellant argues that these products are functionally similar to the steel wool soap pad. An attempt is made to support this argument by pointing to advertising claims made by some of the allegedly direct competitors. The attempt is unsuccessful. Advertising puffs will not be considered by this court as evidence of that which could not be proved below. We prefer to place reliance on testimony given by both the former general manager of appellant's Kool-Aid Division and the pre-acquisition president of S.O.S. These gentlemen stated that, to the best of their knowledge, there was no available device that would perform as well as the steel wool soap pad for the purposes advertised on the S.O.S. box. . . .

Adhering to the *Brown Shoe* guidelines, the Commission next compared the retail sales price of steel wool soap pads with the prices of allegedly competing products. After carefully computing and contrasting the prices of all the products in both categories, the Commission concluded that *household steel wool products are sold at distinct prices.* . . .

Almost no evidence was introduced on behalf of the Commission concerning consumer sensitivity to price changes. There is, however, sufficient evidence to support the finding that the *prices of household steel wool products display no sensitivity to prices of nonsteel products.* Without exception, the smaller steel wool manufacturers testified that they disregarded the pricing structure of the nonsteel wool devices. These manufacturers stated that they looked only to prices established by S.O.S. and Brillo when making pricing decisions. . . .

Finally, the Commission found that the equipment used for the production of steel wool is distinct from, and lacks any similarity to, the facilities required to manufacture the other cleaning devices that appellant contends should be included in the relevant market. It seems to us that this finding is self-evident and unimpeachable. Steel wool producing machinery is not available on the open market, but must be custom made to specification. It cannot practically be used to manufacture other products. To argue that S.O.S. did not utilize *unique production facilities* would be to ignore the obvious.

To summarize, we think that there is substantial evidence in the record to support the Commission's finding that the relevant product market is household steel wool. It has been shown that household steel wool products constitute an economically significant market and that this market is sufficiently inclusive to be meaningful in terms of trade realities. . . .

We therefore reject appellant's contention that non-steel wool cleaning devices constitute part of the relevant market and hold that there is substantial evidence in the record to support the Commission's finding that household steel wool constitutes a relevant market within the meaning of Section 7.

II

The essential issue remains whether the Commission had substantial evidence to support its finding that the acquisition of S.O.S. by G.F. would have a substantial anticompetitive effect in the household steel wool market. In evaluating the record before us, we are mindful that the facts must show more than a "mere possibility" of an anticompetitive effect. . . . On the basis of our review of the record, the Commission's opinion, and the recent holding in *Clorox, supra,* we will affirm the Commission's order.

In general business parlance, the instant acquisition would be classified as a conglomerate merger. A merger is considered conglomerate when the relationship of the merging companies before the merger was not one of buyer and seller (a vertical merger) or direct competitor (horizontal merger). The fact that a given merger is of a conglomerate nature has no effect per se on the antitrust consequences of the union: "All mergers are within the reach of §7, and all must be tested by the same standard, whether they are classified as horizontal, vertical, conglomerate or other." *Clorox,* . . .

Agreeing as we do with this characterization of the merger, it is still necessary to determine whether the Commission had substantial evidence to support its prediction that the merger would probably substantially lessen competition. This determination is necessary because we do not read *Clorox* as proscribing, per se, all mergers labeled "product extension mergers."

As summarized by the Commission, the conclusion that G.F.'s acquisition of S.O.S. would in fact substantially lessen competition in the steel wool soap pad market was based on its

> . . . finding that respondent's acquisition of S.O.S. has raised to virtually insurmountable heights entry barriers which were already high, that the presence of General Foods in the market has changed the steel wool pad market which prior to the merger consisted of two substantially equal-sized companies and several smaller firms to one in which S.O.S. is now dominant, and finally that the substitution of General Foods for S.O.S. will depress rather than enhance the competitive vitality of the market and will paralyze any incentive to compete which might otherwise have existed. The fact that these high entry barriers to potential entrants and the impairment of the competitive vitality of the market arises in part because of the impact which General Foods' advertising, promotional and distributional resources had on potential and actual competitors in this market did not make its acquisition any less anticompetitive.

Although G.F. asserts that its acquisition of S.O.S. did not raise entry barriers, the Commission could reasonably conclude the contrary on the basis of the record before it. The Commission found that before the merger, the steel soap pad market was highly concentrated, and although the products of the competitors were functionally identical, consumer preference for the S.O.S. and Brillo products had been generated through extensive advertising and a long history of industry dominance. Thus the smaller companies producing less well-known brands and potential producers of new brands could not make significant market penetrations without engaging in heavy expenditures for advertising and promotions. After the merger of S.O.S. and G.F., the existing competitors and such potential competitors as existed faced an even more formidable opponent. G.F. was able to advertise and promote S.O.S. less expensively than the pre-merger S.O.S. Company, especially because of the television discounts available to G.F. Moreover, after the merger, S.O.S. could and did induce potential customers to purchase its soap pads by offering them discounts based on pooled purchases from various divisions of G.F. The Commission also reasonably concluded that G.F. was in a position vis-à-vis the retailers that made it highly likely that G.F. would be able to obtain advantages in the display or marketing of S.O.S. which were not available to the pre-merger company, nor then available to S.O.S.' competitors. These factors are adequate to support the Commission's finding that factual and psychological barriers to entry were substantially heightened by this merger.

The Commission also found that the merger had an adverse impact on the structure of the soap pad industry. Comparing the situation with that presented in *Clorox*, the Commission found that the impact of G.F.'s acquisition of S.O.S. was of greater competitive significance than Procter & Gamble's acquisition of Clorox since G.F.'s entrance into the soap pad market had a more pronounced effect on the competitive structure of the industry. . . .

Moreover, the Commission could reasonably conclude that the potential competition was adversely affected by G.F.'s entrance into the market through the acquisition of S.O.S. because the entry of such a large, well-financed, aggressive competitor would necessarily hamper whatever effect potential competition had in the pre-merger market. This result follows because the threat of entrance into a given market by potential competitors is reduced to the extent that entry barriers are raised. Thus the Commission's finding that potential competition was reduced by the instant merger is based on its finding that the substitution of G.F. for the smaller S.O.S. Company increased the difficulty of entering the market, and the reduction of potential competition was a predictable consequence.

The Commission could reasonably conclude that the entry of G.F. would have a depressing effect on the quality of competition in the market.

As in *Clorox*, the degree of market power enjoyed by G.F., including the power to take retaliatory action against any aggressive competition by smaller competitors, made it likely that the market would become an even more rigid oligopoly. It is no answer to contend that the market was oligopolistic before the entrance of G.F. because the Commission could reasonably conclude that under G.F.'s eventual dominance, the market would become even less competitive. Moreover, the immediate post-acquisition flurry of competition between Brillo and S.O.S.—which apparently lead to S.O.S.' eventual emergence with a greater market share, and the merger of Brillo with Purex—certainly does not compel the conclusion that the market will become competitive.

Thus we conclude that the Commission was justified in finding that G.F.'s acquisition of the S.O.S. Company would substantially lessen competition in the steel wool soap pad market, and in adopting the order entered by the hearing examiner requiring G.F. to divest itself of the S.O.S. assets found to have been acquired in violation of §7. . . .

The order of the Commission will be affirmed and enforced.

Joint Ventures

A different application of Section 7 than the ordinary ones involving horizontal, vertical, and conglomerate mergers was made in the *Penn-Olin* decision of 1964. The case involved a fifty-fifty joint venture on the part of the Pennsalt Chemicals Corporation and Olin Mathieson Company. In 1960 these two firms agreed to form the Penn-Olin Chemical Company for the purpose of producing sodium chlorate, which neither of the parent companies produced.

The Supreme Court, by a 6–3 vote, ruled that Section 7 does apply to joint ventures. The *effect on competition* is the standard for testing, and a joint venture does substantially lessen competition between the parents. This would be true whether the competition between the joint venturers was actual or potential, or whether the new company was formed for an entirely new enterprise, because the new company would be established to engage in commerce and to further the business of its parents. "Realistically, the parents would not compete with their progeny." The same considerations apply to joint ventures as to outright mergers and actual restraint need not be proved, only a reasonable likelihood of a substantial lessening of competition.

The trial court believed that the test for illegality was whether as a matter of probability *both* companies would have entered the market as individual competitors if Penn-Olin had not been formed. The High Court stated that the appropriate test is to determine if only *one* of the parent companies would probably have entered alone and also if the joint venture served to eliminate the potential competition of the company that might have stayed at the edge of the market threatening to enter. The case was then remanded to the district court to make these determinations.

Justice Douglas dissented from this opinion on the grounds that agreements among competitors to divide markets are *per se* violations of the Sherman Act. A joint venture is, in terms of competitive consequences, the same as an agreement to divide the market. The case could have been disposed of in this manner because: "What may not be done by two companies who decide to divide a market surely cannot be done by the convenient creation of a legal umbrella—whether joint venture or common ownership and control . . ."

UNITED STATES v. PENN-OLIN CHEMICAL CO. et al.

378 U.S. 158 (1964)

Mr. Justice Clark delivered the opinion of the Court.

Pennsalt Chemicals Corporation and Olin Mathieson Chemical Corporation jointly formed Penn-Olin Chemical Company to produce and sell sodium chlorate in the southeastern United States. The Government seeks to dissolve this joint venture as violative of both §7 of the Clayton Act and §1 of the Sherman Act. This direct appeal, . . . , raises two questions. First, whether §7 of the Clayton Act is applicable where two corporations form a third to engage in a new enterprise; and, second, if this question is answered in the affirmative, whether there is a violation of §1 or §7 under the facts of this case. The trial court found that the joint venture, on this record violated neither of these sections and found it unnecessary to reach the first question. . . . We have concluded that a joint venture as organized here would be subject to the regulation of §7 of the Clayton Act and, reaching the merits, we hold that while on the present record there is no violation of §1 of the Sherman Act, the District Court erred in dismissing the complaint as to §7 of the Clayton Act. Accordingly, the judgment is vacated and remanded for further consideration.

Line of Commerce, Relevant Market, etc.

At the outset it is well to note that some of the troublesome questions ordinarily found in antitrust cases have been eliminated by the parties. First, the line of commerce is a chemical known as sodium chlorate. . . . Next, the relevant market is not disputed. It is the south-eastern part of the United States. Nor is the fact that Olin has never engaged in the commercial production of sodium chlorate contested. . . .

The Companies Involved

Pennsalt is engaged solely in the production and sale of chemicals and chemical products throughout the United States. Its assets are around a hundred million dollars and its sales are about the same amount. Its sodium chlorate production is located at Portland, Oregon, with a capacity of some 15,000 tons as of 1959. It occupied 57.8% of the market west of the Rocky Mountains. It has marketed sodium chlorate in the southeastern United States to some extent since 1957. Its shipments into that territory in 1960 were 4,186 tons of which Olin sold 3,202 tons on its sales agency contract.

Olin is a large diversified corporation, the result of a merger of Olin Industries, Inc., and Mathieson Chemical Corporation in 1954. One of its seven divisions operates plants in 15 States and produces a wide range of chemicals and chemical products accounting for about 30% of Olin's revenues. Olin's sales in 1960 grossed some $690,000,000 and its total assets were $860,000,000.

Penn-Olin was organized in 1960 as a joint venture of Olin and Pennsalt. Each owns 50% of its stock and the officers and directors are divided equally between the parents. Its plant at Calvert City, Kentucky, was built by equal contribution of the two parents and cost $6,500,000. It has a capacity to produce 26,500 tons of sodium chlorate annually and began operations in 1961. Pennsalt operates the plant and Olin handles the sales. Penn-Olin deals in no other chemicals.

Background and Statistics of the Industry

Prior to 1961 the sodium chlorate industry in the United States was made up of three producing companies. The largest producer, Hooker Chemical Corporation, entered the industry in 1956 when it acquired Oldbury Electro Chemical Company, which had been producing sodium chlorate for over half a century. . . . Hooker has assets of almost $200,-000,000. American Potash & Chemical Corporation entered the industry in 1955 by the acquisition of Western Electro Chemical Company. . . . Its assets are almost $100,000,000. The trial court found that these two corporations "had a virtual monopoly" in the relevant southeast market, holding over 90% of the market.

A third company in the industry was Pennsalt which had a 15,392-ton plant at Portland, Oregon. It entered seriously into the relevant marketing area through a sales arrangement with Olin dated December 1957 and finalized in 1958, which was aimed at testing the availability of the southeastern market. . . . In 1960, 4,186 tons of sodium chlorate were marketed in the relevant market with the aid of this agreement. This accounted for 8.9% of the sales in that market. . . .

The sales arrangement between Pennsalt and Olin, previously mentioned, was superseded by the joint venture agreement on February 11, 1960, and the Penn-Olin plant operations at Calvert City, Kentucky, began in 1961. . . .

The Setting From Which the Joint Venture Emerged

As early as 1951 Pennsalt had considered building a plant at Calvert City and starting in 1955 it initiated several cost and market studies for a sodium chlorate plant in the southeast. Three different proposals from within its own organization were rejected prior to 1957, apparently because the rate of return was so unattractive that "the expense of refining these figures further would be unwarranted." When Hooker announced in December 1956 that it was going to increase the capacity of its Columbus plant, the interest of Pennsalt management was reactivated. It appointed a "task force" to evaluate the company's future in the eastern market; it retained management consultants to study that market and its chief engineer prepared cost estimates. However, in December 1957 the management decided that the estimated rate of return was unattractive and considered it "unlikely" that Pennsalt would go it alone. It was suggested that Olin would be a "logical partner" in a joint venture . . .

During this same period—beginning slightly earlier—Olin began investigating the possibility of entering the sodium chlorate industry. It had never produced sodium chlorate commercially, although its predecessor had done so years before. However, the electrolytic process used in making sodium chlorate is intimately related to other operations of Olin and required the same general knowledge. . . .

Olin's engineering supervisor concluded that entry into sodium chlorate production was "an attractive venture" . . .

The staff, however, did not agree with the engineering supervisor or the "Whither Report" and concluded "that they didn't feel that this particular project showed any merit worthy of serious consideration by the corporation at that time." They were dubious of the cost estimates and felt the need to temper their scientists' enthusiasm for new products with the uncertainties of plant construction and operation. But, as the trial court found, the testimony indicated that Olin's decision to enter the joint venture was made without determining that Olin could not or would not be an independent competitor. That question, the president of Penn-Olin testified, "never reached the point of final decision."

This led the District Court to find that "[t]he possibility of individual entry into the southeastern market had not been completely rejected by either Pennsalt or Olin before they decided upon the joint venture." . . .

SECTION 7 OF THE CLAYTON ACT APPLIES TO "JOINT VENTURES"

Appellees argue that §7 applies only where the acquired company is "engaged" in commerce and that it would not apply to a newly formed corporation, such as Penn-Olin. The test, they say, is whether the enterprise to be acquired is engaged in commerce—not whether a corporation formed as the instrumentality for the acquisition is itself engaged in commerce at the moment of its formation. We believe that this logic fails in the light of the wording of the section and its legislative background. The test of the section is the effect of the acquisition. Certainly the formation of a joint venture and purchase by the organizers of its stock would substantially lessen competition—indeed foreclose it—as between them, both being engaged in commerce. This would be true whether they were in actual or potential competition with each other and even though the new corporation was formed to create a wholly new enterprise. Realistically, the parents would not compete with their progeny. Moreover, in this case the progeny was organized to further the business of its parents, already in commerce, and the fact that it was organized specifically to engage in commerce should bring it within the coverage of §7. . . .

THE APPLICATION OF THE MERGER DOCTRINE

This is the first case reaching this Court and on which we have written that directly involves the validity under §7 of the joint participation of two corporations in the creation of a third as a new domestic producing organization. We are, therefore, plowing new ground. . . .

The joint venture, like the "merger" and the "conglomeration," often creates anticompetitive dangers. It is the chosen competitive instrument of two or more corporations previously acting independently and usually competitively with one another. The result is "a triumvirate of associated corporations." If the parent companies are in competition, or might compete absent the joint venture, it may be assumed that neither will compete with the progeny in its line of commerce. Inevitably, the operations of the joint venture will be frozen to those lines of commerce with will not bring it into competition with the parents, and the latter, by the same token will be foreclosed from the joint venture's market.

This is not to say that the joint venture is controlled by the same criteria as the merger or conglomeration. The merger eliminates one of the participating corporations from the market while a joint venture creates a new competitive force therein. . . .

Overall, the same considerations apply to joint ventures as to mergers, for in each instance we are but expounding a national policy enunciated by the Congress to preserve and promote a free competitive economy. . . . The grand design of the original §7, as to stock acquisitions, as well as the Celler-Kefauver Amendment, as to the acquisition of assets, was to arrest incipient threats to competition which the Sherman Act did not ordinarily reach. It follows that actual restraints need not be proved. The requirements of the amendment are satisfied when a "tendency" toward monopoly or the "reasonable likelihood" of a substantial lessening of competition in the relevant market is shown. Congress made it plain that the validity of such arrangements was to be gauged on a broader scale by using the words "may be substantially to lessen competition" which "indicate that its concern was with probabilities, not certainties." *Brown Shoe Co.* v. *United States,* . . .

THE CRITERIA GOVERNING § 7 CASES

We apply the light of these considerations in the merger cases to the problem confronting us here. The District Court found that "Pennsalt and Olin each possessed the resources and general capability needed to build its own plant in the southeast and to compete with Hooker and [American Potash] in that market. Each could have done so if it had wished." . . . In addition, the District Court found that, contrary to the position of the management of Olin and Pennsalt, "the forecasts of each company indicated that a plant could be operated with profit." . . .

The District Court held, however, that these considerations had no controlling significance, except "as a factor in determining whether as a matter of probability *both* companies would have entered the market as individual competitors if Penn-Olin had not been formed. Only in this event would potential competition between the two companies have been foreclosed by the joint venture." . . . In this regard the court found it "impossible to conclude that as a matter of reasonable probability *both* Pennsalt and Olin would have build plants in the southeast if Penn-Olin had not been created." . . . The court made no decision concerning the probability that one would have built "while the other continued to ponder." It found that this "hypothesized situation affords no basis for concluding that Penn-Olin had the effect of substantially lessening competition." . . . That would depend, the court said, "upon the competitive impact which Penn-Olin will have as against that which might have resulted if Pennsalt or Olin had been an individual market entrant." . . . The court found that this impact could not be determined from the record in this case. "Solely as a matter of theory," it said, ". . . no reason exists to suppose that Penn-Olin will be a less effective competitor than Pennsalt or Olin would have been. The contrary conclusion is the more reasonable." . . .

We believe that the court erred in this regard. Certainly the sole test would not be the probability that *both* companies would have entered the market. Nor would the consideration be limited to the probability that one entered alone. There still remained for consideration the fact that Penn-Olin eliminated the potential competition of the corporation that might have remained at the edge of the market, continually threatening to enter. Just as a merger eliminates actual competition, this joint venture may well foreclose any prospect of competition between Olin and Pennsalt in the relevant sodium chlorate market. The difference, of course, is that the merger's foreclosure is present while the joint venture's is prospective. . . . The existence of an aggressive, well equipped and well financed corporation engaged in the same or related lines of commerce waiting anxiously to enter an oligopolistic market would be a substantial incentive to competition which cannot be underestimated. Witness the expansion undertaken by Hooker and American Potash as soon as they heard of the interest of Olin Mathieson and of Pennsalt in southeast territory. This same situation might well have come about had either Olin or Pennsalt entered the relevant market alone and the other remained aloof watching developments.

The Problem of Proof

Here the evidence shows beyond question that the industry was rapidly expanding; the relevant southeast market was requiring about one-half of the national production of sodium chlorate; few corporations had the inclination, resources and know-how to enter this market; both parent corporations of Penn-Olin had great resources; each had long been identified with the industry, one owning valuable patent rights while the other had engaged in sodium chlorate production for years; each had other chemicals, the production of which required the use of sodium chlorate;

right up to the creation of Penn-Olin, each had evidenced a long-sustained and strong interest in entering the relevant market area; each enjoyed good reputation and business connections with the major consumers of sodium chlorate in the relevant market, *i.e.*, the pulp and paper mills; and, finally, each had the know-how and the capacity to enter that market and could have done so individually at a reasonable profit. Moreover, each company had compelling reasons for entering the southeast market. Pennsalt needed to expand its sales to the southeast, which it could not do economically without a plant in that area. Olin was motivated by "the fact that [it was] already buying and using a fair quantity [of sodium chlorate] for the production of sodium chlorite and that [it was] promoting the Mathieson process of the generation of chlorine dioxide which uses sodium chlorate." Unless we are going to require subjective evidence, this array of probability certainly reaches the prima facie stage. As we have indicated, to require more would be to read the statutory requirement of reasonable probability into a requirement of certainty. This we will not do.

However, despite these strong circumstances, we are not disposed to disturb the court's finding that there was not a reasonable probability that both Pennsalt and Olin would have built a plant in the relevant market area. But we have concluded that a finding should have been made as to the reasonable probability that either one of the corporations would have entered the market by building a plant, while the other would have remained a significant potential competitor. The trial court said that this question "need not be decided." It is not clear whether this conclusion was based on the erroneous assumption that the Government could not show a lessening of competition even if such a situation existed, or upon the theory (which the court found erroneous in its final opinion) that the Government need not show the impact of such an event on competition in the relevant market as compared with the entry of Penn-Olin. The court may also have concluded that there was no evidence in the record on which to base such a finding. In any event, we prefer that the trial court pass upon this question and we venture no opinion thereon. Since the trial court might have been concerned over whether there was evidence on this point, we reiterate that it is impossible to demonstrate the *precise* competitive effects of the elimination of either Pennsalt or Olin as a potential competitor. . . . We note generally the following criteria which the trial court might take into account in assessing the probability of a substantial lessening of competition: the number and power of the competitors in the relevant market; the background of their growth; the power of the joint venturers; the relationship of their lines of commerce; the competition existing between them and the power of each in dealing with the competitors of the other; the setting in which the joint venture was created; the reasons and necessities for its existence; the joint venture's line of com-

merce and the relationship thereof to that of its parents; the adaptibility of
its line of commerce to noncompetitive practices; the potential power of
the joint venture in the relevant market; an appraisal of what the competition in the relevant market would have been if one of the joint venturers
had entered it alone instead of through Penn-Olin; the effect, in the event
of this occurrence, of the other joint venturer's potential competition; and
such other factors as might indicate potential risk to competition in the
relevant market. In weighing these factors the court should remember that
the mandate of the Congress is in terms of the probability of a lessening
of substantial competition, not in terms of tangible present restraint.

The judgment is therefore vacated and the case is remanded for
further proceedings in conformity with this opinion.

Vacated and remanded.

Mr. Justice White dissents.

Mr. Justice Douglas, with whom Mr. Justice Black agrees, dissenting.

Agreements among competitors to divide markets are *per se* violations of the Sherman Act. . . .

During the years when Pennsalt and Olin were considering independent entry into the southeast market, they were also discussing joint entry.
In order to test the southeast market the two agreed in December of 1957
that Pennsalt would make available to Olin, as exclusive seller, 2,000 tons
of sodium chlorate per year for two or three years, Olin agreeing to sell the
chemical only to pulp and paper companies in the southeast, except for
one company which Pennsalt reserved the right to serve directly. Another
agreement entered into in February 1958 provided that neither of the two
companies would "move in the chlorate or perchlorate field without
keeping the other party informed." . . .

So what we have in substance is two major companies who on the eve
of competitive projects in the southeastern market join forces. In principle
the case is no different from one where Pennsalt and Olin decide to divide
the southeastern market as was done in *Addyston Pipe* and in the other
division-of-markets cases already summarized. Through the "joint venture"
they do indeed divide it fifty-fifty. That division through the device of the
"joint venture" is as plain and precise as though made in more formal
agreements. As we saw in the *Timken* case, "agreements between legally
separate persons and companies to suppress competition among themselves
and others" cannot be justified "by labeling the project a 'joint venture.'"
341 U.S., at 598. . . . What may not be done by two companies who
decide to divide a market surely cannot be done by the convenient creation

of a legal umbrella—whether joint venture or common ownership and control . . . under which they achieve the same objective by moving in unison.

An actual division of the market through the device of "joint venture" has, I think, the effect "substantially to lessen competition" within the meaning of §7 of the Clayton Act. . . .

We do not, of course, know for certain what would have happened if the "joint venture" had not materialized. But we do know that §7 deals only with probabilities, not certainties. We know that the interest of each company in the project was lively, that one if not both of them would probably have entered that market, and that even if only one had entered at the beginning the presence of the other on the periphery would in all likelihood have been a potent competitive factor. . . .

MR. JUSTICE HARLAN, dissenting. . . .

Final disposition of the *Penn-Olin* case came in 1967.[3] The district court ruled that the Justice Department failed to prove that either of the parents would have entered the market in the absence of the joint venture. The Supreme Court divided 4–4 on appeal; thus the lower court ruling automatically stands.

[3] *U.S.* v. *Penn-Olin Chemical Corp.*, 246 F. Supp. 917, affirmed by a 4–4 vote, 389 U.S. 308.

6

Economic Power Achieved by Collusion

A number of sections of the antitrust statutes have been subject to variation in court interpretation through the years. The same is true for business practices included within the scope of the law. Sometimes these variations have arisen because of the personalities sitting on the Court bench; other times it was because of greater understanding of the economic consequences of specified activities. For example, once interstate commerce was viewed narrowly so as to exclude manufacturing. Now commerce is viewed broadly, encompassing all phases of economic activity.

While this general flux has persisted from the very beginning with regard to most activities covered by antitrust law, one interpretation—with a single important exception—has remained steady and unswerving. That is the interpretation dealing with collusive agreements designed to fix prices, control production, and/or share markets.

The courts have steadfastly maintained that collusive agreements which tamper with the free play of economic forces are *per se* violations of the Sherman Act. Once it has been proven that there was manipulation of prices, production, or market share, there is no defense open to the violators, such as a plea of reasonableness or no harm to competitors.

Interpretations of Section 1 and 2 of the Sherman Act, under which collusive actions fall, have sometimes been subject to criticism because of the alleged double standard that has prevailed. Contracts, agreements, or simple conspiracies among individual competitors that restrain trade by interfering with price, production, or marketing territory are condemned outright. On the other hand, the combination of individual competitors through merger, or the monopolization of an industry due to natural advantages, technological efficiencies, patents, and so on are usually permitted because they are "reasonable." To permit firms to achieve market power over an industry by either external or internal growth while absolutely prohibiting agreements which generally result in less market power does seem somewhat inconsistent.

The cases presented in this chapter are the leading ones which have established the law as it applies to collusive agreements.

Early Price-Fixing and Market-Sharing Cases

The second case to reach the Supreme Court after passage of the Sherman Act revolved around the legality of rate agreements adopted by a group of railroads. A group of some eighteen competing railroads operating in the West and Southwest had formed the Trans-Missouri Freight Association in 1889. The main purpose of the association was to introduce some organization and consistency into the rates the railroads were charging, eventually developing a common set of rules whereby the competing railroads were fixing and enforcing the same freight rates. The association sought and received approval for the rates to be used from the Interstate Commerce Commission, an agency established in 1887 for the purpose of regulating railroads and approving freight rates.

The defendants used two main arguments to justify their actions. First, they said that the ICC had approved their rates and, therefore, the Sherman Act was inapplicable. The Court dismissed this contention by saying that the Commission's approval did not place the agreement beyond reach of the Sherman Act. Their second argument was that the rates fixed were "reasonable." The Court countered this position by observing that the purpose of the agreements was to restrain trade. And the Act was intended to prevent "every restraint of trade." Therefore, "reasonableness" of the rates could not be used as the basis for justification. Thus, from the very earliest interpretation, price-fixing agreements were considered per se violations, and no inquiry was necessary or allowed into the reasonableness of the prices fixed.

UNITED STATES v. TRANS-MISSOURI FREIGHT ASSOCIATION

166 U.S. 290 (1897)

MR. JUSTICE PECKHAM, after stating the facts, delivered the opinion of the court.[1]

The defendants object to the hearing of this appeal, and ask that it be dismissed on the ground that the Trans-Missouri Freight Association has been dissolved by a vote of its members . . .

The prayer of the bill filed in this suit asks not only for the dissolution of the association, but, among other things, that the defendants should be restrained from continuing in a like combination, and that they should be enjoined from further conspiring, agreeing or combining and acting together to maintain rules and regulations and rates for carrying freight upon their several lines, etc. The mere dissolution of the association

---

[1] All the footnotes and most of the citations from the opinions of the Court have been omitted from the cases in this chapter.

is not the most important object of this litigation. The judgment of the court is sought upon the question of the legality of the agreement itself for the carrying out of which the association was formed, and if such agreement be declared to be illegal, the court is asked not only to dissolve the association named in the bill, but that the defendants should be enjoined for the future.

. . . If the mere dissolution of the association worked an abatement of the suit as to all the defendants, as is the claim made on their part, it is plain that they have thus discovered an effectual means to prevent the judgment of this court being given upon the question really involved in the case. The defendants having succeeded in the court below, it would only be necessary thereafter to dissolve their association and instantly form another of a similar kind, and the fact of the dissolution would prevent an appeal to this court or procure its dismissal if taken. This result does not and ought not to follow. . . .

The bill shows here an agreement entered into (as stated in the agreement itself) for the purpose of maintaining reasonable rates to be received by each company executing the agreement . . . This agreement so made, the Government alleges, is illegal as being in restraint of trade, and was entered into between the companies for the purpose of enhancing the freight rates. The companies, while denying the illegality of the agreement or its purpose to be other than to maintain reasonable rates, yet allege that without some such agreement the competition between them for traffic would be so severe as to cause great losses to each defendant and possibly ruin the companies represented in the agreement. Such a result, it is claimed, is avoided by reason of the agreement. Upon the existence, therefore, of this or some similar agreement directly depends (as is alleged) the prosperity, if not the life, of each company. . . .

Coming to the merits of the suit, there are two important questions which demand our examination. They are, first, whether the above-cited act of Congress (called herein the Trust Act) applies to and covers common carriers by railroad; and, if so, second, does the agreement set forth in the bill violate any provision of that act?

As to the first question:

The language of the act includes *every* contract, combination in the form of trust or otherwise, or conspiracy, in restraint of trade or commerce among the several States or with foreign nations. So far as the very terms of the statute go, they apply to any contract of the nature described. A contract therefore that is in restraint of trade or commerce is by the strict language of the act prohibited even though such contract is entered into between competing common carriers by railroad, and only for the purposes of thereby affecting traffic rates for the transportation of persons and property. If such an agreement restrain trade or commerce, it is prohibited by the statute, unless it can be said that an agreement, no matter what its terms, relating only to transportation cannot restrain trade or commerce. We see no escape from the conclusion that if any agreement of such a nature does restrain it, the agreement is condemned by this act. It cannot be denied that those who are engaged in the transportation of persons or property from one State to another are engaged in interstate commerce, and it would seem to follow that if such persons enter into agreements between themselves in regard to the compensation to be secured from the owners of the articles transported, such agreement would at least relate to the business of commerce, and might more or less restrain it. The point urged on the defendants' part is that the statute was not really intended to reach that kind of an agreement relating only to traffic rates entered into by competing common carriers by railroad; that it was intended to reach only those who were engaged in the manufacture or sale of articles of commerce, and who by means of trusts, combinations and conspiracies were engaged in affecting the supply or the price or the place of manufacture of such articles. The terms of the act do not bear out such construction. Railroad companies are instruments of commerce, and their business is commerce itself.

But it is maintained that an agreement like the one in question on the part of the railroad companies is authorized by the Commerce Act, which is a special statute applicable only to railroads, and that a construction of the Trust Act (which is a general act) so as to include within its provisions the case of railroads, carries with it the repeal by implication of so much of the Commerce Act as authorized the agreement. It is added that there is no language in the Trust Act which is sufficiently plain to indicate a purpose to repeal those provisions of the Commerce Act which permit the agreement . . .

The first answer to this argument is that, in our opinion, the Commerce Act does not authorize an agreement of this nature. . . . The provisions of that act look to the prevention of discrimination, to the furnishing of equal facilities for the interchange of traffic, to the rate of compensation for what is termed the long and the short haul, to the attainment of a continuous passage from the point of shipment to the point of destination, at a known and published schedule, . . . The act was not directed to the securing of uniformity of rates to be charged by competing companies, nor was there any provision therein as to a maximum or minimum of rates. Competing and non-connecting roads are not authorized by this statute to make an agreement like this one. . . .

Second. The next question to be discussed is as to what is the true construction of the statute, assuming that it applies to common carriers by railroad. What is the meaning of the language as used in the statute, that "every contract, combination in the form of trust or otherwise, or conspiracy in restraint of trade or commerce among the several States or with foreign nations, is hereby declared to be illegal"? Is it confined to a contract or combination which is only in unreasonable restraint of trade or commerce, or does it include what the language of the act plainly and in terms covers, all contracts of that nature? . . .

It is now with much amplification of argument urged that the statute, in declaring illegal every combination in the form of trust or otherwise, or conspiracy in restraint of trade or commerce, does not mean what the language used therein plainly imports, but that it only means to declare illegal any such contract which is in *unreasonable* restraint of trade, . . .

There is another side to this question, however, . . . If only that kind of contract which is in unreasonable restraint of trade be within the meaning of the statute, and declared therein to be illegal, it is at once apparent that the subject of what is a reasonable rate is attended with great uncertainty. What is a proper standard by which to judge the fact of reasonable rates? Must the rate be so high as to enable the return for the whole business done to amount to a sum sufficient to afford the shareholder a fair and reasonable profit upon his investment? If so, what is a fair and reasonable profit? That depends sometimes upon the risk incurred, and the rate itself differs in different localities: which is the one to which reference is to be made as the standard? . . . It is quite apparent, therefore, that it is exceedingly difficult to formulate even the terms of the rule itself which should govern in the matter of determining what would be reasonable rates for transportation. While even after the standard should be determined there is such an infinite variety of facts entering into the question of what is a reasonable rate, no matter what standard is adopted . . . To say, therefore, that the act excludes agreements which are not in unreasonable restraint of trade, and which tend simply to keep up reasonable rates for transportation, is substantially to leave the question of reasonableness to the companies themselves.

. . . Does the agreement restrain trade or commerce in any way so as to be a violation of the act? We have no doubt that it does. The agreement on its face recites that it is entered into "for the purpose of mutual protection by establishing and maintaining reasonable rates, rules and regulations on all freight traffic, both through and local." To that end the association is formed and a body created which is to adopt rates, which, when agreed to, are to be the governing rates for all the companies . . . there can be no doubt that its direct, immediate and necessary effect is to put a restraint upon trade or commerce as described in the act.

For these reasons the suit of the Government can be maintained without proof of the allegation that the agreement was entered into for the purpose of restraining trade or commerce or for maintaining rates above what was reasonable. The necessary effect of the agreement is to restrain trade or commerce, no matter what the intent was on the part of those who signed it. . . .

Reversed, and the case remanded to the Circuit Court for further proceedings in conformity with this opinion.

Mr. Justice White, with whom concurred Mr. Justice Field, Mr. Justice Gray and Mr. Justice Shiras, dissenting.

A decision similar to that of the *Trans-Missouri Freight* case was rendered by the Supreme Court in *Addyston Pipe & Steel.* That case was decided two years later in 1899 and was the fourth Sherman Act case to reach the high tribunal. In this instance, six manufacturers of cast iron pipe, controlling about one-third of the total production, agreed to assign certain geographical markets to each member of their group. They also agreed to eliminate competitive bidding for contracts. The avowed purpose of the agreement was to eliminate the ruinous competition that had existed, thereby enabling member firms to secure prices which were fair and reasonable to themselves and to the public.

As in the *Trans-Missouri* case, the defense contended that the prices established were fair, and that the restraint imposed by the market division was reasonable. The Court said the reasonableness of prices or restraint was not a point for discussion. When the direct, immediate, and intended effect of a contract among dealers of a commodity is to enhance its price and destroy competition, it amounts to a restraint of trade which the Sherman Act forbids. Circuit Judge Taft, in his opinion condemning the agreement, did not believe "there is any question of reasonableness open to the courts with reference to such a contract." The Supreme Court agreed with his position.

ADDYSTON PIPE AND STEEL COMPANY v. UNITED STATES

175 U.S. 211 (1899)

This proceeding was commenced in behalf of the United States, under the so-called anti-trust act of Congress . . . for the purpose of obtaining an injunction perpetually enjoining the six corporations, who were made defendants, and who were engaged in the manufacture, sale and transportation of iron pipe at their respective places of business in the States of their residence, from further acting under or carrying on the combination alleged in the petition to have been entered into between them, and which was stated to be an illegal and unlawful one, under the act above mentioned, because it was in restraint of trade and commerce among the States, etc.

The trial court dismissed the petition, . . . but upon appeal to the Circuit Court of Appeals the judgment of the court below was reversed with instructions to enter a decree for the United States perpetually enjoining defendants from maintaining the combination in cast-iron pipe as described in the petition, and from doing any business under such combination. . . .

. . . [T]he defendants . . . admitted the existence of an association between them for the purpose of avoiding the great losses they would otherwise sustain, due to ruinous competition between defendants, but denied that their association was in restraint of trade, state or interstate, or that it was organized to create a monopoly, and denied that it was a violation of the anti-trust act of Congress. . . .

The States for sale in which bonuses had to be paid into the association were called "pay" territory as distinguished from "free" territory in which defendants were at liberty to make sales without restriction and without paying any bonus. . . .

The system of bonuses as a means of restricting competition and maintaining prices was not successful. A change was therefore made by which prices were to be fixed for each contract by the association, and except in reserved cities, the bidder was determined by competitive bidding of the members, the one agreeing to give the highest bonus for division among the others getting the contract. The plan was embodied in a resolution passed May 27, 1895, in the words following:

"Whereas, the system now in operation in this association of having a fixed bonus on the several States has not in its operation resulted *in the advancement in the prices of pipe as was anticipated, except in reserved cities,* and some further action is imperatively necessary in order to accomplish the ends for which this association was formed: Therefore, be it resolved, that from and after the first day of June, that all competition on the pipe lettings shall take place among the various pipe shops prior to the said letting. To accomplish this purpose it is proposed that the six competitive shops have a representative board located at some central city to whom all inquiries for pipe shall be referred, and said board shall fix the price at which said pipe shall be sold, and bids taken from the respective shops for the privilege of handling the order, and the party securing the order shall have the protection of all the other shops."

An illustration of the manner in which "reserved" cities were dealt with may be seen in the case of a public letting at St. Louis. On February 4, 1896, the water department of that city let bids for 2800 tons of pipe. St. Louis was "reserved" to the Howard-Harrison Company of Bessemer, Alabama. The price was fixed by the association at $24 a ton, and the bonus at $6.50. . . .

It appears quite clearly from the prices at which the Chattanooga and the South Pittsburg Companies offered pipe in "free" territory that any price which would net them from $13 to $15 a ton at their foundries would give them a profit. Pipe was freely offered by the defendants in "free" territory more than five hundred miles from their foundries at less prices than their representative boards fixed prices for jobs let in cities in "pay" territory nearer to defendants' foundries by three hundred miles or more. . . .

MR. JUSTICE PECKHAM, after stating the case, delivered the opinion of the court. . . .

We are thus brought to the question whether the contract or combination proved in this case is one which is either a direct restraint or a regulation of commerce among the several States or with foreign nations contrary to the act of Congress. It is objected on the part of the appellants that even if it affected interstate commerce the contract or combination was only a reasonable restraint upon a ruinous competition among themselves, and was formed only for the purpose of protecting the parties thereto in securing prices for their product that were fair and reasonable to themselves and the public. It is further objected that the agreement does not come within the act because it is not one which amounts to a regulation of interstate commerce, as it has no direct bearing upon or relation to that commerce . . .

. . . [W]e are of opinion that the agreement or combination was not one which simply secured for its members fair and reasonable prices for the article dealt in by them. . . . we agree with the Circuit Court of Appeals in its statement of the special facts upon this branch of the case and with its opinion thereon as set forth by Circuit Judge Taft, as follows:

"The defendants being manufacturers and vendors of cast-iron pipe entered into a a combination to raise the prices for pipe for all the States west and south of New York, Pennsylvania and Virginia, constituting considerably more than three quarters of the territory of the United States, and significantly called by the associates 'pay' territory. . . .

"The defendants were by their combination therefore able to deprive the public in a large territory of the advantages otherwise accruing to them from the proximity of defendants' pipe factories and, by keeping prices just low enough to prevent competition by Eastern manufacturers, to compel the public to pay an increase over what the price would have been if fixed by competition between defendants, nearly equal to the advantage in freight rates enjoyed by defendants over Eastern competitiors. . . .

"It has been earnestly pressed upon us that the prices at which the cast-iron pipe was sold in 'pay' territory were reasonable. . . . We do not think the issue an important one, because, as already stated, we do not think that at common law there is any question of reasonableness open to the courts with reference to such a contract. Its tendency was certainly to give defendants the power to charge unreasonable prices, had they chosen to do so. . . ."

We are also of opinion that the direct effect of the agreement or combination is to regulate interstate commerce . . .

While no particular contract regarding the furnishing of pipe and the price for which it should be furnished was in the contemplation of the parties to the combination at the time of its formation, yet it was their intention, as it was the purpose of the combination, to directly and by means of such combination increase the price for which all contracts for the delivery of pipe within the territory above described should be made, and the latter result was to be achieved by abolishing all competition between the parties to the combination. . . .

The combination thus had a direct, immediate and intended relation to and effect upon the subsequent contract to sell and deliver the pipe. It was to obtain that particular and specific result that the combination was formed, and but for the restriction the resulting high prices for the pipe would not have been obtained. It is useless for the defendants to say they did not intend to regulate or affect interstate commerce. They intended to make the very combination and agreement which they in fact did make, and they must be held to have intended (if in such case intention is of the least importance) the necessary and direct result of their agreement. . . .

The views above expressed lead generally to an affirmance of the judgment of the Court of Appeals. In one aspect, however, that judgment is too broad in its terms—the injunction is too absolute in its directions—as it may be construed as applying equally to commerce wholly within a State as well as to that which is interstate or international only. This was probably an inadvertence merely. Although the jurisdiction of Congress over commerce among the States is full and complete, it is not questioned that it has none over that which is wholly within a State, and therefore none over combinations or agreements so far as they relate to a restraint of such trade or commerce. . . .

To the extent that the present decree includes in its scope the enjoining of defendants thus situated from combining in regard to contracts for selling pipe in their own State, it is modified, and limited to that portion of the combination or agreement which is interstate in its character. As thus modified, the decree is

Affirmed.

Price Fixing in Recent Years

Contracts fixing prices and sharing markets continued as unquestioned *per se* violations for many years until the Rule of Reason gained such favorable application in the *U.S. Steel* case. Consequently, this raised the possibility that the Court might now apply a Rule of Reason to price-fixing cases. The Supreme Court laid to rest any doubts in the *Trenton Potteries* decision of 1927 by condemning once again *all* collusive agreements fixing prices.

Twenty-three firms had formed a trade association known as the Sanitary Potters' Association. These firms were producing 82 per cent of the vitreous pottery fixtures used in bathrooms and lavatories. The trade association was created for the specific purpose of fixing prices and limiting sales in interstate commerce to certain jobbers. The government charged that this was a violation of Section 1 of the Sherman Act, a contract and conspiracy in restraint of trade. The respondents did not dispute this contention; their defense rested on the argument that the prices they had fixed were reasonable. The association believed the essence of the law was injury to the public. Not every restraint of trade involves injury to the public. Since their prices were reasonable, the agreement should not be condemned because there had been no public injury.

The Supreme Court would not accept this view. In holding all price-fixing agreements illegal, the Court said: "Reasonableness is not a concept of definite and unchanging content. . . . The aim and result of every price-fixing agreement, if effective, is the elimination of one form of competition. The power to fix prices, whether reasonably exercised or not, involves power to control the market and to fix arbitrary and unreasonable prices. The reasonable price fixed today may through economic and business changes become the unreasonable price of tomorrow." The government should not have the burden of ascertaining on a daily basis whether a price has become unreasonable because of variation in economic conditions. Agreements which create such power will be considered unlawful restraints in and of themselves. Once more the Court had struck down all price-fixing agreements.

UNITED STATES v. TRENTON POTTERIES COMPANY et al.

273 U.S. 392 (1927)

MR. JUSTICE STONE delivered the opinion of the Court.

Respondents, twenty individuals and twenty-three corporations, were convicted in the district court for southern New York of violating the Sherman Anti-Trust Law, . . . The indictment was in two counts. The first charged a combination to fix and maintain uniform prices for the sale of sanitary pottery, in restraint of interstate commerce; the second, a combination to restrain interstate commerce by limiting sales of pottery to a special group known to respondents as "legitimate jobbers." . . .

Respondents, engaged in the manufacture or distribution of 82 per cent. of the vitreous pottery fixtures produced in the United States for use in bathrooms and lavatories, were members of a trade organization known as the Sanitary Potters' Association. . . .

There is no contention here that the verdict was not supported by sufficient evidence that respondents, controlling some 82 per cent. of the business of manufacturing and distributing in the United States vitreous pottery of the type described, combined to fix prices and to limit sales in interstate commerce to jobbers. . . .

The trial court charged, in submitting the case to the jury, that if it found the agreements or combination complained of, it might return a verdict of guilty without regard to the reasonableness of the prices fixed, or the good intentions of the combining units, whether prices were actually lowered or raised or whether sales were restricted to the special jobbers, since both agreements of themselves were unreasonable restraints. . . .

That only those restraints upon interstate commerce which are unreasonable are prohibited by the Sherman Law was the rule laid down by the opinions of this Court in the *Standard Oil* and *Tobacco* cases. But it does not follow that agreements to fix or maintain prices are reasonable restraints and therefore permitted by the statute, merely because the prices themselves are reasonable. Reasonableness is not a concept of definite and unchanging content. Its meaning necessarily varies in the different fields of the law, because it is used as a convenient summary of the dominant considerations which control in the application of legal doctrines. Our view of what is a reasonable restraint of commerce is controlled by the recognized purpose of the Sherman Law itself. Whether this type of restraint is reasonable or not must be judged in part at least in the light of its effect on competition, for whatever difference of opinion there may be among economists as to the social and economic desirability of an unrestrained competitive system, it cannot be doubted that the Sherman Law and the judicial decisions interpreting it are based upon the assumption that the public interest is best protected from the evils of monopoly and price control by the maintenance of competition. . . .

The aim and result of every price-fixing agreement, if effective, is the elimination of one form of competition. The power to fix prices, whether reasonably exercised or not, involves power to control the market and to fix arbitrary and unreasonable prices. The reasonable price fixed today may through economic and business changes become the unreasonable price of tomorrow. Once established, it may be maintained unchanged because of the absence of competition secured by the agreement for a price reasonable when fixed. Agreements which create such potential power may well be held to be in themselves unreasonable or unlawful restraints, without the necessity of minute inquiry whether a particular price is reasonable or unreasonable as fixed and without placing on the government in enforcing the Sherman Law the burden of ascertaining from day to day whether it has become unreasonable through the mere variation of economic conditions. Moreover, in the absence of express legislation requiring it, we should hestitate to adopt a construction making the difference between legal and illegal conduct in the field of business relations depend upon so uncertain a test as whether prices are reasonable—a determination which can be satisfactorily made only after a complete survey of our economic organization and a choice between rival philosophies. . . .

The charge of the trial court, viewed as a whole, fairly submitted to the jury the question whether a price-fixing agreement as described in the first count was entered into by the respondents. Whether the prices actually agreed upon were reasonable or unreasonable was immaterial in the circumstances charged in the indictment and necessarily found by the verdict. . . .

It follows that the judgment of the circuit court of appeals must be reversed and the judgment of the district court reinstated.

Reversed.

MR. JUSTICE VAN DEVANTER, MR. JUSTICE SUTHERLAND and MR. JUSTICE BUTLER dissent.

MR. JUSTICE BRANDEIS took no part in the consideration or decision of this case.

As previously noted, there has been only one important deviation in the Supreme Court's holding that all price-fixing, production control, and market-sharing agreements are illegal regardless of reasonableness. This exception was handed down in the 1933 *Appalachian Coals* case.[2] In this case the Court adopted a lenient attitude and said that industry conditions dictated the use of a Rule of Reason. Later on the Court would return to the position that price fixing is illegal *per se*.

Appalachian Coals, Inc. was formed as an exclusive selling agency with the authority to set prices for 137 bituminous coal producers operating in the Appalachian territory. They accounted for 12 per cent of the soft coal mined east of the Mississippi River and as much as 75 per cent of the coal produced in the Appalachian territory. The primary reason for creating the agency was because the industry was in grave distress as a result of overexpansion, rela-tively diminishing consumption, and injurious marketing practices among its members. The members of the organization sought, through the agency, to eliminate those practices, to promote the sale of their coal, and to sell as much of it as possible. Although they controlled a large part of the coal produced in their region, they actually produced a very small part of the vast volume available for total consumption. As a consequence, they argued there was no basis for concluding that competition or the public would be affected injuriously by the operation of their plan.

In view of the recognized conditions in the industry, the Court felt that a cooperative endeavor, otherwise free from harmful effects and creating no monopolistic menace, should not be condemned merely because it might bring a change in marketing conditions, where the change would improve competi-tive conditions. Just because competition was eliminated between parties to an agreement was not enough to condemn it. The real question was one of intent and effect, and this could not be determined by mechanical or artificial rules. Given the economic conditions of the coal industry and the reason for forming the agency, the public interest would be better served by allowing it to continue.

It must be kept in mind that this decision was rendered during the depths of the Great Depression. At that time steps were being taken to restrict competi-tion and restrain price cutting by implementing the National Industrial Recovery Act. The Supreme Court was merely responding in an acceptable manner to the general philosophy prevailing during this period.

[2] Another possible exception occurred in the case of *National Assn. of Window Glass Manufacturers et al. v. U.S.*, 263 U.S. 403 (1923), involving an agreement be-tween all manufacturers of hand-blown glass and the union which in essence limited production. The Supreme Court, speaking through Justice Holmes, treated the agree-ment solely as a union labor contract.

APPALACHIAN COALS, INC., et al. v. UNITED STATES

288 U.S. 344 (1933)

MR. CHIEF JUSTICE HUGHES delivered the opinion of the Court.

This suit was brought to enjoin a combination alleged to be in restraint of interstate commerce in bituminous coal and in attempted monopolization of part of that commerce, in violation of §§1 and 2 of the Sherman Anti-Trust Act . . .

Defendants, other than Appalachian Coals, Inc., are 137 producers of bituminous coal in eight districts (called for convenience Appalachian territory) lying in Virginia, West Virginia, Kentucky and Tennessee. . . . In 1929 (the last year for which complete statistics were available) the total production of bituminous coal east of the Mississippi river was 484,786,000 tons, of which defendants mined 58,011,367 tons, or 11.96 per cent. In the so-called Appalachian territory and the immediately surrounding area, the total production was 107,008,209 tons, of which defendants' production was 54.21 per cent, or 64 per cent if the output of 'captive' mines (16,455,001 tons) be deducted. . . .

The challenged combination lies in the creation by the defendant producers of an exclusive selling agency. This agency is the defendant Appalachian Coals, Inc., which may be designated as the Company. Defendant producers own all its capital stock, their holdings being in proportion to their production. The majority of the common stock, which has exclusive voting right, is held by seventeen defendants. By uniform contracts, separately made, each defendant producer constitutes the Company an exclusive agent for the sale of all coal . . . The Company agrees to establish standard classifications, to sell all the coal of all its principals at the best prices obtainable and, if all cannot be sold, to apportion orders upon a stated basis. The plan contemplates that prices are to be fixed by the officers of the Company at its central office . . .

The Government's contention, which the District Court sustained, is that the plan violates the Sherman Anti-Trust Act,—in the view that it eliminates competition among the defendants themselves and also gives the selling agency power substantially to affect and control the price of bituminous coal in many interstate markets. On the latter point the District Court made the general finding that "this elimination of competition and concerted action will affect market conditions, and have a tendency to stabilize prices and to raise prices to a higher level than would prevail under conditions of free competition." . . .

Defendants insist that the primary purpose of the formation of the selling agency was to increase the sale, and thus the production, of Appalachian coal through better methods of distribution, intensive advertising and research; to achieve economies in marketing, and to eliminate abnormal, deceptive and destructive trade practices. . . . Defendants contend that the evidence establishes that the selling agency will not have the power to dominate or fix the price of coal in any consuming market; that the price of coal will continue to be set in an open competitive market; and that their plan by increasing the sale of bituminous coal from Appalachian territory will promote, rather than restrain, interstate commerce.

FIRST   There is no question as to the test to be applied in determining the legality of the defendants' conduct. The purpose of the Sherman Anti-Trust Act is to prevent undue restraints of interstate commerce, to maintain its appropriate freedom in the public interest, to afford protection from the subversive or coercive influences of monopolistic endeavor. . . .

In applying this test, a close and objective scrutiny of particular conditions and purposes is necessary in each case. Realities must dominate the judgment. The mere fact that the parties to an agreement eliminate competition between themselves is not enough to condemn it. "The legality of an agreement or regulation cannot be determined by so simple a test, as whether it restrains competition. Every agreement concerning trade, every regulation of trade, restrains." . . . The question of the application of the statute is one of intent and effect, and is not to be determined by arbitrary assumptions. It is therefore necessary in this instance to consider the economic conditions peculiar to the coal industry, the practices which have obtained, the nature of defendant's plan of making sales, the reasons which led to its adoption, and the probable consequences of the carrying out of that plan in relation to market prices and other matters affecting the public interest in interstate commerce in bituminous coal.

SECOND   The findings of the District Court, upon abundant evidence, leave no room for doubt as to the economic condition of the coal industry. That condition, as the District Court states, "for many years has been indeed deplorable." Due largely to the expansion under the stimulus of the Great War, "the bituminous mines of the country have a developed capacity exceeding 700,000,000 tons" to meet a demand "of less than 500,000,000 tons." And in a graphic summary of the economic situation, the court found that "numerous producing companies have gone into bankruptcy or into the hands of receivers, many mines have been shut down, the number of days of operation per week have been greatly curtailed, wages to labor have been substantially lessened, and the States in which coal producing companies are located have found it increasingly difficult to collect taxes."

THIRD   The findings also fully disclose the proceedings of the defendants in formulating their plan and the reasons for its adoption. The serious economic conditions had led to discussions among coal operators and state and national officials, seeking improvement of the industry. Governors of States had held meetings with coal producers. . . . The District Court found that "the evidence tended to show that other selling agencies with a control of at least 70 per cent of the production in their respective districts will be organized if the petition in this case is dismissed"; that in that event "there will result an organization in most of the districts whose coal is or may be competitive with Appalachian coal; but the testimony tends to show that there will still be substantial, active competition in the sale of coal in all markets in which Appalachian coal is sold."

Defendants refer to the statement of purposes in their published plan of organization,—that it was intended to bring about "a better and more orderly marketing of the coals from the region to be served by this company (the selling agency) and better to enable the producers in this region, through the larger and more economic facilities of such selling agency, more equally to compete in the general markets for a fair share of the available coal business." . . .

No attempt was made to limit production. The producers decided that it could not legally be limited and, in any event, it could not be limited practically. The finding is that "it was designed that the producer should produce and the selling agent should sell as much coal as possible." The importance of increasing sales is said to lie in the fact that the cost of production is directly related to the actual running time of the mines.

FOURTH   Voluminous evidence was received with respect to the effect of defendants' plan upon market prices. As the plan has not gone into operation, there are no actual results upon which to base conclusions. The question is necessarily one of prediction. The court below found that, as between defendants themselves, competition would be eliminated. This was deemed to be the necessary consequence of a common selling agency with power to fix the prices at which it would make sales for its principals. . . .

The more serious question relates to the effect of the plan upon competition between defendants and other producers. . . . Elaborate statistics were introduced with respect to the production and distribution of bituminous coal and the transportation rates from the different producing sections to the consuming markets, as bearing upon defendants' competitive position, together with evidence as to the requirements of various sections and consumers and the relative advantages possessed by reason of the different qualities and uses of the coals produced. It would be impossible to make even a condensed statement of this evidence, (which has been carefully analyzed by both parties,) but an examination of it fails to disclose an adequate basis for the conclusion that the operation of the defendants' plan would produce an injurious effect upon competitive conditions, in view of the vast volume of coal available, the conditions of production, and the network of transportation facilities at immediate command. . . .

FIFTH We think that the evidence requires the following conclusions:

(1). With respect to defendant's purposes, we find no warrant for determining that they were other than those they declared. Good intentions will not save a plan otherwise objectionable, but knowledge of actual intent is an aid in the interpretation of facts and prediction of consequences. . . .

(2). The question thus presented chiefly concerns the effect upon prices. The evidence as to the conditions of the production and distribution of bituminous coal, the available facilities for its transportation, the extent of developed mining capacity, and the vast potential undeveloped capacity, makes it impossible to conclude that defendants through the operation of their plan will be able to fix the price of coal in the consuming markets.

. . . [T]he facts found do not establish, and the evidence fails to show, that any effect will be produced which in the circumstances of this industry will be detrimental to fair competition. A coöperative enterprise, otherwise free from objection, which carries with it no monopolistic menace, is not to be condemned as an undue restraint merely because it may effect a change in market conditions, where the change would be in mitigation of recognized evils and would not impair, but rather foster, fair competitive opportunities. . . .

(3). The question remains whether, despite the foregoing conclusions, the fact that the defendants' plan eliminates competition between themselves is alone sufficient to condemn it. Emphasis is placed upon defendants' control of about 73 per cent of the commercial production in Appalachian territory. But only a small percentage of that production is sold in that territory. . . . We agree that there is no ground for holding defendants' plan illegal merely because they have not integrated their properties and have chosen to maintain their independent plants, seeking not to limit but rather to facilitate production. We know of no public policy, and none is suggested by the terms of the Sherman Act, that, in order to comply with the law, those engaged in industry should be driven to unify their properties and businesses, in order to correct abuses which may be corrected by less drastic measures. . . .

The decree will be reversed and the cause will be remanded to the District Court with instructions to enter a decree dismissing the bill of complaint . . .

Reversed and remanded.

Mr. Justice McReynolds thinks that the court below reached the proper conclusion and that its decree should be affirmed.

The doctrine of *Trenton Potteries* was re-established firmly in a landmark decision of 1940 in the *Socony-Vacuum Oil* case. This case is the most recent Supreme Court pronouncement that details the evils of price fixing.

The Socony-Vacuum Oil Company was one of twelve large oil firms that conspired to raise and maintain spot market prices of gasoline and prices to jobbers and consumers in eleven midwestern states by buying the surplus or "distress" supplies of small, independent refiners. There was evidence to prove that the defendants did intend to raise and maintain the price of gasoline by carrying on an organized program of regularly ascertaining the amount of surplus gasoline produced by the independents, by assigning members of the group to buy surplus quantities from specified independents (euphemistically referred to as "dancing partners"), and by this process did remove a part of the market supply which resulted in an increase in prices.

The defendants offered a number of justifications for their actions. They argued that *complete* control of the market did not exist, therefore competition was not eliminated. Justice Douglas, in writing the majority opinion, stated that even though there was not complete control of the market, when prices are raised, lowered, or stabilized, they "would be directly interfering with the free play of market forces." The defendants argued that their plan had been initiated under the National Industrial Recovery Act and had been given tacit approval. The Court replied that any activity contrary to the Sherman Act automatically became unlawful when continued after the expiration of the Recovery Act.

Finally, the defendants argued that the prices established were fair and reasonable. The Court overruled, holding that any combination tampering with price is engaged in an unlawful activity. Justice Douglas repeated once again that "a combination formed for the purpose and with the effect of raising, depressing, fixing, pegging, or stabilizing the price of a commodity in interstate or foreign commerce is illegal *per se*." There can be no economic justification or an inquiry into reasonableness. They are banned because they represent a threat to the "central nervous system" of the economy.

The Court felt no inconsistency between the *Appalachian Coals* and *Socony-Vacuum Oil* cases. The *Coals* case involved firms operating in a depressed industry, affected only a small part of the total, and did not control the market price. The oil firms were dominant and intended to control the market. In addition, the National Industrial Recovery Act had been declared unconstitutional and a different philosophy regarding price fixing as a cure for depression now prevailed. The general attitude of the country had changed, as had the composition of the Court, and by 1940 there was some semblance of a return to prosperity. Certainly the *Coals* case has to be considered a temporary deviation from the general rule that all collusive agreements are illegal.

UNITED STATES v. SOCONY-VACUUM OIL CO. *et al.*

310 U.S. 150 (1940)

Mr. Justice Douglas delivered the opinion of the Court.

Respondents were convicted by a jury . . . under an indictment charging violations of §1 of the Sherman Anti-Trust Act . . .

The indictment was returned in December 1936 in the United States District Court for the Western District of Wisconsin. It charges that certain major oil companies, selling gasoline in the Mid-Western area (which includes the Western District of Wisconsin), (1) "combined and conspired together for the purpose of artificially raising and fixing the tank car prices of gasoline" in the "spot markets" in the East Texas and Mid-Continent fields: (2) "have artificially raised and fixed said spot market tank car prices of gasoline and have maintained said prices at artificially high and non-competitive levels, and at levels agreed upon among them and have thereby intentionally increased and fixed the tank car prices of gasoline contracted to be sold and sold in interstate commerce as aforesaid in the Mid-Western area"; (3) "have arbitrarily," by reason of the provisions of the prevailing form of jobber contracts which made the price to the jobber dependent on the average spot market price, "exacted large sums of money from thousands of jobbers with whom they have had such contracts in said Mid-Western area"; and (4) "in turn have intentionally raised the general level of retail prices prevailing in said Mid-Western area."

The *manner* and *means* of effectuating such conspiracy are alleged in substance as follows: Defendants, from February 1935 to December 1936 "have knowingly and unlawfully engaged and participated in two concerted gasoline buying programs" for the purchase "from independent refiners in spot transactions of large quantities of gasoline in the East Texas and Mid-Continent fields at uniform, high, and at times progressively increased prices." . . . It is alleged that the purchases in this buying program amounted to nearly 50% of all gasoline sold by those independents. As respects both the East Texas and the Mid-Continent buying programs, it is alleged that the purchases of gasoline were in excess of the amounts which defendants would have purchased but for those programs; that at the instance of certain defendants these independent refiners curtailed their production of gasoline. . . .

The *methods of marketing and selling gasoline* in the Mid-Western area are set forth in the indictment in some detail. Since we hereafter develop the facts concerning them, it will suffice at this point to summarize them briefly. Each defendant major oil company owns, operates or leases retail service stations in this area. It supplies those stations, as well as independent retail stations, with gasoline from its bulk storage plants. All but one sell large quantities of gasoline to jobbers in tank car lots under term contracts. In this area these jobbers exceed 4,000 in number and distribute about 50% of all gasoline distributed to retail service stations therein, the bulk of the jobbers' purchases being made from the defendant companies. The price to the jobbers under those contracts with defendant companies is made dependent on the spot market price, pursuant to a formula hereinafter discussed. And the spot market tank car prices of gasoline directly and substantially influence the retail prices in the area. In sum, it is alleged that defendants by raising and fixing the tank car prices of gasoline in these spot markets could and did increase the tank car prices and the retail prices of gasoline sold in the Mid-Western area. . . .

The first meeting of the Tank Car Committee was held February 5, 1935, and the second on February 11, 1935. At these meetings the alleged conspiracy was formed, the substance of which, so far as it pertained to the Mid-Continent phase, was as follows:

It was estimated that there would be between 600 and 700 tank cars of distress gasoline produced in the Mid-Continent oil field every month by about 17 independent refiners. These refiners, not having regular outlets for the gasoline, would be unable to dispose of it except at distress prices. Accordingly, it was proposed and decided that certain major companies (including the corporate respondents) would purchase gasoline from these refiners. The Committee would assemble each month information as to the quantity and location of this distress gasoline. Each of the major companies was to select one (or more) of the independent refiners having distress gasoline as its "dancing partner," and would assume responsibility for purchasing its distress supply. In this manner buying power would be coördinated, purchases would be effectively placed, and the results would be much superior to the previous haphazard purchasing. There were to be no formal contractual commitments to purchase this gasoline, either between the major companies or between the majors and the independents. Rather it was an informal gentlemen's agreement or understanding whereby each undertook to perform his share of the joint undertaking. Purchases were to be made at the "fair going market price."

. . . As we have said, there does not appear to have been any binding commitment to purchase; the plan was wholly voluntary; there is nothing in the record to indicate that a participant would be penalized for failure to coöperate. But though the arrangement was informal, it was nonetheless effective, as we shall see. And, as stated by the Circuit Court of Appeals, there did appear to be at least a moral obligation to purchase the amounts specified at the fair market prices "recommended." That alone would seem to explain why some of the major companies cancelled or declined to enter into profitable deals for the exchange of gasoline with other companies in order to participate in this buying program. . . .

. . . On May 27, 1935, this Court held in *Schechter Poultry Corp.* v. *United States*, 295 U.S. 495, that the code-making authority conferred by the National Industrial Recovery Act was an unconstitutional delegation of legislative power. Shortly thereafter the Tank Car Stabilization Committee held a meeting to discuss their future course of action. It was decided that the buying program should continue. Accordingly, that Committee continued to meet each month through February 1936. The procedure at these meetings was essentially the same as at the earlier ones. Gradually the buying program worked almost automatically, as contacts between buyer and seller became well established. The Mechanical Sub-Committee met at irregular intervals until December 1935. Thereafter it conducted its work on the telephone. . . .

In the meetings when the Mid-Continent buying program was being formulated it was recognized that it would be necessary or desirable to take the East Texas surplus gasoline off the market so that it would not be a "disturbing influence in the Standard of Indiana territory." . . .

Early in 1935 the East Texas Refiners' Marketing Association was formed to dispose of the surplus gasoline manufactured by the East Texas refiners. . . .

As a result of these buying programs it was hoped and intended that both the tank car and the retail markets would improve. The conclusion is irresistible that defendants' purpose was not merely to raise the spot market prices but, as the real and ultimate end, to raise the price of gasoline in their sales to jobbers and consumers in the Mid-Western area. Their agreement or plan embraced not only buying on the spot markets but also, at least by clear implication, an understanding to maintain such improvements in Mid-Western prices as would result from those purchases of distress gasoline. The latter obviously would be achieved by selling at the increased prices, not by price cutting. Any other understanding would have been wholly inconsistent with and contrary to the philosophy of the broad stabilization efforts which were under way. In essence the raising and maintenance of the spot market prices were but the means adopted for raising and maintaining prices to jobbers and consumers. . . . Certainly there was enough evidence to support a finding by the jury that such were the scope and purpose of the plan. . . .

In sum, respondents by this and similar evidence offered to establish that the Petroleum Administrative Board knew of the buying programs and acquiesced in them. And respondents by those facts, together with those discussed . . . undertook to show that their objectives under the buying porgrams were in line with those of the federal government under the Code . . .

The court charged the jury that it was a violation of the Sherman Act for a group of individuals or corporations to act together to raise the prices to be charged for the commodity which they manufactured where they controlled a substantial part of the interstate trade and commerce in that commodity. The court stated that where the members of a combination had the power to raise prices and acted together for that purpose, the combination was illegal; and that it was immaterial how reasonable or unreasonable those prices were or to what extent they had been affected by the combination. It further charged that if such illegal combination existed, it did not matter that there may also have been other factors which contributed to the raising of the prices. . . .

In *United States* v. *Trenton Potteries Co.* . . . this Court sustained a conviction under the Sherman Act where the jury was charged that an agreement on the part of the members of a combination, controlling a substantial part of an industry, upon the prices which the members are to charge for their commodity is in itself an unreasonable restraint of trade without regard to the reasonableness of the prices or the good intentions of the combining units. . . . This Court pointed out that the so-called "rule of reason" announced in *Standard Oil co.* v. *United States* . . . and in *United States* v. *American Tobacco Co.* . . . had not affected this view of the illegality of price-fixing agreements. . . .

But respondents claim that other decisions of this Court afford them adequate defenses to the indictment. Among those on which they place reliance are *Appalachian Coals, Inc.* v. *United States* . . .

Thus in reality the only essential thing in common between the instant case and the *Appalachian Coals* case is the presence in each of so-called demoralizing or injurious practices. The methods of dealing with them were quite divergent. In the instant case there were buying programs of distress gasoline which had as their direct purpose and aim the raising and maintenance of spot market prices and of prices to jobbers and consumers in the Mid-Western area, by the elimination of distress gasoline as a market factor. . . . the plan in the *Appalachian Coals* case was not designed to operate *vis-à-vis* the general consuming market and to fix the prices on that market. Furthermore, the effect, if any, of that plan on prices was not only wholly incidental but also highly conjectural. . . .

Thus for over forty years this Court has consistently and without deviation adhered to the principle that price-fixing agreements are unlawful *per se* under the Sherman Act and that no showing of so-called competitive abuses or evils which those agreements were designed to eliminate or alleviate may be interposed as a defense. . . .

Respondents seek to distinguish the *Trenton Potteries* case from the instant one. . . .

But we do not deem those distinctions material.

In the first place, there was abundant evidence that the combination had the purpose to raise prices. And likewise, there was ample evidence that the buying programs at least contributed to the price rise and the stability of the spot markets, and to increases in the price of gasoline sold in the Mid-Western area during the indictment period. . . .

Secondly, the fact that sales on the spot markets were still governed by some competition is of no consequence. For it is indisputable that that competition was restricted through the removal by respondents of a part of the supply which but for the buying programs would have been a factor in determining the going prices on those markets. But the vice of the conspiracy was not merely the restriction of supply of gasoline by removal of a surplus. As we have said, this was a well organized program. The timing and strategic placement of the buying orders for distress gasoline played an important and significant role. Buying orders were carefully placed so as to remove the distress gasoline from weak hands. Purchases were timed. Sellers were assigned to the buyers so that regular outlets for distress gasoline would be available. The whole scheme was carefully planned and executed to the end that distress gasoline would not overhang the markets and depress them at any time. . . .

The elimination of so-called competitive evils is no legal justification for such buying programs. . . . Ruinous competition, financial disaster, evils of price cutting and the like appear throughout our history as ostensible justifications for price-fixing. If the so-called competitive abuses were to be appraised here, the reasonableness of prices would necessarily become an issue in every price-fixing case. In that event the Sherman Act would soon be emasculated . . .

The reasonableness of prices has no constancy due to the dynamic quality of business facts underlying price structures. Those who fixed reasonable prices today would perpetuate unreasonable prices tomorrow, since those prices would not be subject to continuous administrative supervision and readjustment in light of changed conditions. Those who controlled the prices would control or effectively dominate the market. And those who were in that strategic position would have it in their power to destroy or drastically impair the competitive system. But the thrust of the rule is deeper and reaches more than monopoly power. Any combination which tampers with price structures is engaged in an unlawful activity. Even though the members of the price-fixing group were in no position to control the market, to the extent that they raised, lowered, or stabilized prices they would be directly interfering with the free play of market forces. The Act places all such schemes beyond the pale and protects that vital part of our economy against any degree of interference. . . . Whatever may be its peculiar problems and characteristics, the Sherman Act, so far as price-fixing agreements are concerned, establishes one uniform rule applicable to all industries alike. . . .

Nor is it important that the prices paid by the combination were not fixed in the sense that they were uniform and inflexible. Price-fixing as used in the *Trenton Potteries* case has no such limited meaning. An agreement to pay or charge rigid, uniform prices would be an illegal agreement under the Sherman Act. But so would agreements to raise or lower prices whatever machinery for price-fixing was used. That price-fixing includes more than the mere establishment of uniform prices is clearly evident from the *Trenton Potteries* case itself . . . Hence, prices are fixed within the meaning of the *Trenton Potteries* case if the range within which purchases or sales will be made is agreed upon, if the prices paid or charged are to be at a certain level or on ascending or descending scales, if they are to be uniform, or if by various formulae they are related to the market prices. They are fixed because they are agreed upon. And the fact that, as here, they are fixed at the fair going market price is immaterial. . . .

Under the Sherman Act a combination formed for the purpose and with the effect of raising, depressing, fixing, pegging, or stabilizing the price of a commodity in interstate or foreign commerce is illegal *per se*. . . . Price-fixing agreements may have utility to members of the group though the power possessed or exerted falls far short of domination and control. Monopoly power . . . is not the only power which the Act strikes down, as we have said. Proof that a combination was formed for the purpose of fixing prices and that it caused them to be fixed or contributed to that result is proof of the completion of a price-fixing conspiracy under §1 of the Act. The indictment in this case charged that this combination had that purpose and effect. And there was abundant evidence to support it. Hence the existence of power on the part of members of the combination to fix prices was but a conclusion from the finding that the buying programs caused or contributed to the rise and stability of prices.

. . . Admittedly no approval of the buying programs was obtained under the National Industrial Recovery Act prior to its termination on June 16, 1935, [§2 (c)] which would give immunity to respondents from prosecution under the Sherman Act. Though employees of the government may have known of those programs and winked at them or tacitly approved them, no immunity would have thereby been obtained. For Congress had specified the precise manner and method of securing immunity. None other would suffice. Otherwise national policy on such grave and important issues as this would be determined not by Congress nor by those to whom Congress had delegated authority but by virtual volunteers. The method adopted by Congress for alleviating the penalties of the Sherman Act through approval by designated public representatives would be supplanted by a foreign system. But even had approval been obtained for the buying programs, that approval would not have survived the expiration in June 1935 of the Act which was the source of that approval. . . .

The judgment of the Circuit Court of Appeals is reversed and that of the District Court affirmed.

Reversed.

The CHIEF JUSTICE and MR. JUSTICE MURPHY did not participate in the consideration or decision of this case.

MR. JUSTICE ROBERTS, dissenting. . . .

On June 22, 1960, the biggest criminal case in the history of the Sherman Act was filed. Twenty-nine corporations and forty-five of their executives were charged with conspiring to fix prices, rig bids, and divide markets on electrical equipment sales estimated at $1.75 billion annually. The major companies involved—General Electric, Westinghouse, Allis-Chalmers, Federal Pacific, I-T-E Circuit Breaker Co.—understandably did not want a trial that would reveal to the public the details and extent of the conspiracy in full. The corporations and individuals were able to avoid trial by working out pleas of guilty and *nolo contendere* with the Justice Department that were accepted by the court. Seven executives received prison sentences, and twenty-three others were given suspended jail sentences and put on five-year probations. Individual and corporate fines imposed amounted to approximately $2 million.

Judge J. Cullen Ganey viewed the conspiracy as ". . . a shocking indictment of a vast section of our economy, for what is really at stake here is the survival of the kind of economy under which this country has grown great, the free-enterprise system." And although executives in the top echelons of the corporations were not charged, the judge said that we would have to be most naive to believe that such a vast and long-standing conspiracy was not known to them.[3]

Some businessmen had apparently come to believe that agreements to fix prices, rig bids, and divide markets was a "way of life" in our business world. The electrical conspiracy cases should lay to rest any such misconceptions about the legal constraints of our free-enterprise system.

[3] Richard Austin Smith, "The Incredible Electrical Conspiracy," in *The Regulated Businessman*, ed. *John A. Larson* (New York: Holt, Rinehart and Winston, Inc., 1966), pp. 108–31. For a comprehensive report see Clarence C. Walton and Frederick W. Cleveland, Jr., *Corporations on Trial: The Electric Cases* (Belmont, Calif.: Wadsworth Publishing Co., Inc., 1964).

7

Trade Association Activities

Trade associations are formed by business firms and enterprises engaged in the same line of commerce. Their primary purpose is to collect and disseminate market information to members of the industry. With current and accurate information, it is argued, members are far better informed on business and economic conditions. Thus the imperfections of the market are lessened through the greater knowledge on the part of the industry members, making for more effective competition. Trade associations have existed for a long time, even predating the trust movement in the form of pooling arrangements and gentlemen's agreements. On several occasions they have served as the American counterpart of the European cartel.

Trade associations have also served other functions for their members. At different times they have acted as spokesman for the industry before legislative bodies, served as an industry employment bureau, acted as collective bargaining agent with industry unions, conducted market surveys and industrial research, published trade journals, and participated in other such cooperative functions.

In general, the activities of trade associations have promoted healthy competition within their industry. But, despite the overall record for good works, some associations have at times functioned in a manner the courts view as antithetical to our free enterprise system. Many of the price-fixing cases in the previous chapter involved the activities of a trade association. These cases raise numerous questions relating to what are the legitimate, and what are the improper, functions of an association.

Although an overwhelming majority of associations have never been questioned with regard to price-fixing agreements or other dubious activities, it is well established that a trade association may greatly facilitate concerted action designed to manipulate prices, production, or market shares. The courts are faced with the difficult task of distinguishing between those activities which promote anticompetitive behavior and those which do not. Sometimes it is not so much a matter of *what* the association does as *how* it was done. The association should never report to its members in a manner which, either expressly or by implication, tells the members what business decisions are expected.

Prohibited Activities

The Supreme Court decided two important trade association cases in the early 1920s. One involved the American Hardwood Manufacturers' Association, formed in 1918 with a membership of approximately four hundred. The members of the association accounted for one-third of the total market output. The association operated an "open competition plan" whereby all the members exchanged full and minute details of their business. Information exchanged included stocks on hand, production, shipments, prices, names of purchasers, etc. The statistics gathered through this plan were attributed to individual firms and then distributed among the members. Frequent meetings and discussions were held concerning future market conditions. An expert agent hired by the association made strong suggestions about *future* production and pricing policies.

The Supreme Court ruled that this elaborate plan for collecting and disseminating statistical data went much further than merely supplying members with information to make them more knowledgeable about the market. The Court felt that every effort was made, short of an outright agreement, to suppress competition by disclosing full details on production and prices. Alert members were expected to follow the lead of the most "intelligent competitors." The Court believed that genuine competitors would not make such detailed information available to their rivals. Nor would they submit their books to a discretionary audit and inspection by their rivals. The plan did not represent "the conduct of competitors but is so clearly that of men united in an agreement, . . . to act together and pursue a common purpose under a common guide . . . To pronounce such abnormal conduct . . . a 'new form of competition' and not an old form of combination in restraint of trade, . . . would be for this court to confess itself blinded by words . . ." The plan was considered no more than a skillfully devised gentlemen's agreement to evade the law.

AMERICAN COLUMN & LUMBER CO. et al. v. UNITED STATES

257 U.S. 377 (1921)

Mr. Justice Clarke delivered the opinion of the court.[1]

The unincorporated "American Hardwood Manufacturers' Association" was formed in December, 1918, by the consolidation of two similar associations, from one of which it took over a department of activity

---

[1] All the footnotes and most of the citations from the opinions of the Court have been omitted from the cases in this chapter.

designated the "Open Competition Plan," and hereinafter referred to as the "Plan."

Participation in the "Plan" was optional with the members of the Association, but, at the time this suit was commenced, of its 400 members, 365, operating 465 mills, were members of the "Plan." The importance and strength of the Association are shown by the admission in the joint answer that while the defendants operated only five per cent. of the number of mills engaged in hardwood manufacture in the country, they produced one-third of the total production of the United States. . . .

The bill alleged, in substance, that the "Plan" constituted a combination and conspiracy to restrain interstate commerce in hardwood lumber by restricting competition and maintaining and increasing prices, in violation of the Anti-Trust Act of 1890, . . .

The activities which we shall see were comprehended within the "Open Competition Plan," (which is sometimes called "The New Competition"), have come to be widely adopted in our country, and, as this is the first time their legality has been before this court for decision, some detail of statement with respect to them is necessary. . . .

The record shows that the "Plan" was evolved by a committee, which, in recommending its adoption, said:

"The purpose of this plan is to disseminate among members accurate knowledge of production and market conditions so that each member may gauge the market intelligently instead of guessing at it; to make competition open and above board instead of secret and concealed; to substitute, in estimating market conditions, frank and full statements of our competitors for the frequently misleading and colored statements of the buyer."
. . .

Coming now to the fully worked out paper plan as adopted.

It required each member to make six reports to the Secretary, viz.:

1. A *daily* report of all sales actually made, with the name and address of the purchaser, the kind, grade and quality of lumber sold . . .
2. A *daily* shipping report . . .
3. A *monthly* production report . . .
4. A *monthly* stock report . . .
5. Price-lists . . .
6. Inspection reports . . .

All of these reports by members are subject to complete audit by representatives of the association. Any member who fails to report *shall not receive the reports* of the secretary, and failure to report for twelve days in six months shall cause the member failing to be dropped from membership.

Plainly it would be very difficult to devise a more minute disclosure of everything connected with one's business than is here provided for by this "Plan" . . .

This extensive interchange of reports, supplemented as it was by monthly meetings at which an opportunity was afforded for discussion "of all subjects of interest to the members," very certainly constituted an organization through which agreements, actual or implied, could readily be arrived at and maintained, if the members desired to make them. . . .

The "Plan" on paper provided only for reports of past transactions and much is made of this in the record and in argument—that reporting to one another past transactions cannot fix prices for the future. But each of these three questions plainly invited an estimate and discussion of future market conditions by each member, and a coördination of them by an expert analyst could readily evolve an attractive basis for cooperative, even if unexpressed, "harmony" with respect to future prices. . . .

This elaborate plan for the interchange of reports does not simply supply to each member the amount of stock held, the sales made and the prices received, by every other member of the group, thereby furnishing the data for judging the market, on the basis of supply and demand and current prices. It goes much farther. It not only furnishes such information, with respect to stock, sales and prices, but also reports, giving the views of each member as to "market conditions for the next few months"; what the production of each will be for the next "two months"; frequent analyses of the reports by an expert, with, we shall see, significant suggestions as to both future prices and production; and opportunities for future meetings for the interchange of views, which the record shows were very important. It is plain that the only element lacking in this scheme to make it a familiar type of the competition suppressing organization is a definite agreement as to production and prices. . . .

. . . The sanctions of the plan obviously are, financial interest, intimate personal contact, and business honor, all operating under the restraint of exposure of what would be deemed bad faith and of trade punishment by powerful rivals.

The principles of law by which we must judge of the legality of the scheme of doing business thus provided for, as it was worked out in practice, are clearly settled by the Anti-Trust statute and the decisions of this court interpreting it. . . .

With this rule of law and the details of the "Plan" in mind, we come to consider what the record shows as to the purpose of this combination and as to its effect upon interstate commerce.

We have seen that the "Plan" provided for the selection of a man to have charge of the gathering and dissemination of the data, which were to be contained in the various reports, and that the defendant F. R. Gadd was selected for this purpose, with the title of "Manager of Statistics." Mr.

Gadd was a man of large experience in the lumber business, competent and aggressive, and the record makes it clear that he was in complete and responsible charge of all the activities of this "Open Competition Plan." He compiled the summaries of daily, weekly and monthly reports, and wrote the monthly market letter and the market comment in the weekly sales reports, which were distributed to the members. Some disposition appears in the argument, but not in the evidence, to suggest that Gadd exceeded his authority at times, but no objection appears to have been taken to any of his conduct, and the "Secretary-Manager" says in his affidavit that his office adjoins that of Gadd and that "he [Gadd] and the affiant have frequent conferences and discussions relating to their work, and that the affiant is familiar with the activities and methods of the Open Competition Plan."

It has been repeatedly held by this court that the purpose of the statute is to maintain free competition in interstate commerce and that any concerted action by any combination of men or corporations to cause, or which in fact does cause, direct and undue restraint of competition in such commerce falls within the condemnation of the act and is unlawful. . . .

It is plain that as the "Plan" was the "clearing house" of the members, "for information on prices, trade statistics, and practices," so Gadd was the "clearing house" of the "Plan," and that what he said and did, acquiesced in by the members, as it was, must be accepted as the authoritative expression of the combination. . . .

Much more of like purport appears in the minutes of the meetings throughout the year, but this is sufficient to convincingly show that one of the prime purposes of the meetings, held in every part of the lumber district, and of the various reports, was to induce members to cooperate in restricting production, thereby keeping the supply low and the prices high, and that whenever there was any suggestion of running the mills to an extent which would bring up the supply to a point which might affect prices, the advice against operations which might lead to such result was put in the strongest possible terms. The coöperation is palpable and avowed, its purpose is clear, and we shall see that it was completely realized.

Next, the record shows clearly that the members of the combination were not satisfied to secure, each for himself, the price which might be obtainable even as the result of coöperative restriction of production, but that throughout the year they assiduously cultivated, through the letters of Gadd, speaking for them all, and through the discussions at the meetings, the general conviction that higher and higher prices were obtainable and a disposition on the part of all to demand them. The intention to create such a common purpose is too clear to be doubted . . .

Such close coöperation, between many persons, firms, and corporations controlling a large volume of interstate commerce, as is provided for in this "Plan," is plainly in theory, as it proved to be in fact, inconsistent with that free and unrestricted trade which the statute contemplates shall be maintained . . .

To call the activities of the defendants, as they are proved in this record, an "Open Competition Plan" of action is plainly a misleading misnomer.

Genuine competitors do not make daily, weekly and monthly reports of the minutest details of their business to their rivals, as the defendants did; they do not contract, as was done here, to submit their books to the discretionary audit and their stocks to the discretionary inspection of their rivals for the purpose of successfully competing with them; and they do not submit the details of their business to the analysis of an expert, jointly employed, and obtain from him a "harmonized" estimate of the market as it is and as, in his specially and confidentially informed judgment, it promises to be. This is not the conduct of competitors but is so clearly that of men united in an agreement, express or implied, to act together and pursue a common purpose under a common guide that, if it did not stand confessed a combination to restrict production and increase prices in interstate commerce and as, therefore, a direct restraint upon that commerce, as we have seen that it is, that conclusion must inevitably have been inferred from the facts which were proved. To pronounce such abnormal conduct on the part of 365 natural competitors, controlling one-third of the trade of the country in an article of prime necessity, a "new form of competition" and not an old form of combination in restraint of trade, as it so plainly is, would be for this court to confess itself blinded by words and forms to realities which men in general very plainly see and understand and condemn, as an old evil in a new dress and with a new name.

The "Plan" is, essentially, simply an expansion of the gentlemen's agreement of former days, skilfully devised to evade the law. To call it open competition because the meetings were nominally open to the public, or because some voluminous reports were transmitted to the Department of Justice, or because no specific agreement to restrict trade or fix prices is proved, cannot conceal the fact that the fundamental purpose of the "Plan" was to procure "harmonious" individual action among a large number of naturally competing dealers with respect to the volume of production and prices, without having any specific agreement with respect to them, and to rely for maintenance of concerted action in both respects, not upon fines and forfeitures as in earlier days, but upon what experience has shown to be the more potent and dependable restraints, of business honor and social penalties,—cautiously reinforced by many and elaborate reports, which would promptly expose to his associates any disposition in any member to deviate from the tacit understanding that all were to act together under the subtle direction of a single interpreter of their common purposes, as evidenced in the minute reports of what they had done and in their expressed purposes as to what they intended to do. . . .

Convinced, as we are, that the purpose and effect of the activities of the "Open Competition Plan," here under discussion, were to restrict competition and thereby restrain interstate commerce in the manufacture and sale of hardwood lumber by concerted action in curtailing production and in increasing prices, we agree with the District Court that it constituted a combination and conspiracy in restraint of interstate commerce within the meaning of the Anti-Trust Act of 1890 (26 Stat. 209) and the decree of that court must be

Affirmed.

MR. JUSTICE HOLMES, dissenting.

. . . I should have supposed that the Sherman Act did not set itself against knowledge . . . I should have thought that the ideal of commerce was an intelligent interchange made with full knowledge of the facts as a basis for a forecast of the future on both sides. A combination to get and distribute such knowledge, notwithstanding its tendency to equalize, not necessarily to raise, prices, is very far from a combination in unreasonable restraint of trade. It is true that it is a combination of sellers only, but the knowledge acquired is not secret, it is public, and the buyers, I think I may assume, are not less active in their efforts to know the facts. A combination in unreasonable restraint of trade imports an attempt to override normal market conditions. An attempt to conform to them seems to me the most reasonable thing in the world. I see nothing in the conduct of the appellants that binds the members even by merely social sanctions to anything that would not be practised, if we could imagine it, by an allwise socialistic government acting for the benefit of the community as a whole. The parties to the combination are free to do as they will. . . .

MR. JUSTICE BRANDEIS dissenting, with whom MR. JUSTICE McKENNA concurs.

The *American Linseed Oil* case, decided two years later, represented an almost identical situation to the *Hardwood* case. It was also based on an "open competition plan" and included even more stringent provisions for noncompliance. The association was formed in 1918 by twelve firms manufacturing, selling, and distributing linseed oil, cake, and meal. The stated purpose of the organization was to reveal to the agency intimate details of all business transactions with others and for each firm to subject itself to autocratic powers vested in the agency: to pay large fees to the agency and make pecuniary deposits which would be forfeitable upon infractions of the rules; to furnish schedules of prices and terms of sale and adhere to them or notify the agency immediately of any departure therefrom; to attend monthly meetings; and to comply with all reasonable requirements of the agency.

The Supreme Court could only conclude that the purpose of this plan was to restrain trade and suppress competition among the members. The Court summarized its position by stating: "With intimate knowledge of the affairs of other producers . . . but proclaiming themselves to be competitors, the subscribers went forth to deal with widely separated and unorganized customers necessarily ignorant of the true conditions. Obviously they were not *bona fide* competitors; their claim in that regard is at war with common experience . . ."

UNITED STATES v. AMERICAN LINSEED OIL COMPANY et al.

262 U.S. 371 (1923)

MR. JUSTICE McREYNOLDS delivered the opinion of the Court.

By an original bill filed June 30, 1920, the United States charged that appellees—defendants below—were parties to a combination in restraint of interstate trade and commerce forbidden by the Sherman Act, and asked that they be enjoined from continuing therein. The court below held the combination lawful and dismissed the bill. . . .

The defendants are twelve corporations, commonly referred to as "crushers," with principal places of business in six different States, which manufacture, sell and distribute linseed oil, cake and meal; and Julian Armstrong, who operates at Chicago under the name, Armstrong Bureau of Related Industries. This Bureau conducts a so-called "exchange" through which one subscribing manufacturer may obtain detailed information concerning the affairs of others doing like business. The defendant "crushers" constitute one of the groups who contract for this service. They manufacture and distribute throughout the Union a very large part of the linseed products consumed therein and prior to the challenged combination were active, unrestrained competitors. Some time in September or October, 1918, each of them entered into an identical written "Subscription Agreement" with the Armstrong Bureau, and a year thereafter signed another, not essentially different. The latter is summarized and quoted from below.

After stating that "the matter contained herein is for the exclusive and confidential use of the subscriber," the agreement recites that it and other "crushers" of flaxseed desire promptly and economically to secure from and through the Bureau the following things, "which will promote better and more safe, sane, and stable conditions in the linseed oil, cake, and meal industry and increase its service to the commonwealth": Comprehensive data as to market, trade and manufacturing conditions in the linseed oil industry; economies in manufacture and sale by frank exchange of accurate information; the latest authentic information concerning the credit of buyers; a broader market for cake and meal; establishment of uniform cost accounting systems; fair and just freight tariffs and classifications; definite standardization of the products of the industry; economies in the development of foreign markets and increase of sales therein; stabilization of the flaxseed market so far as lawful; shipment of cake and meal to the consumer from the nearest point of production. . . .

When an adequate number of subscriptions had been obtained (September, 1918) the organization began vigorously to function according to letter and spirit of the agreement. It will suffice to state a few of the steps taken.

The United States were divided into eight zones for price quoting; and it was stipulated that each member should quote a basic price for zone number one and should add thereto one, two, four, six, seven, eight and eleven cents, respectively, for the others. At subscribers' meetings regularly held "matters pertaining to the industry" were discussed; members were "put on the carpet" and subjected to searching inquiry concerning their transactions. A meeting held October 29, 1919, adopted the following rule: "In order to provide that the daily market information as relayed by the bureau shall at all times contain the fullest measure of news value, it is agreed that hereafter no council member shall dispatch changes in his prices as last filed with the bureau to more than one buyer without instantly thereafter telegraphing such full and complete information to the bureau as, and in the form, required by the service contract." Another meeting "resolved that it now be recorded that the recommended terms of this council for the sale of oil be 1% discount for cash settlement in 10 days, or 30 days net trade acceptance from date of shipment, and in order that a specific list of the terms of sale of all the council members may now be compiled and distributed, it is further resolved that all council members shall send to the bureau, not later than January 27th, a full explanation of the terms of sale as quoted by them to their trade."

The Bureau displayed great industry in making inquiries, collecting information, investigating the smallest derelictions and giving immediate advice to subscribers. Hundreds of so-called "market letters," relating to divers transactions, were sent to subscribers. A sale of two barrels of oil below schedule was deemed worthy of special attention. Also from time to time it gave counsel concerning "unfair merchandising" and the necessity for establishing sound policy by constructive coöperation. . . .

The obvious policy, indeed the declared purpose, of the arrangement was to submerge the competition theretofore existing among the subscribers and substitute "intelligent competition," or "open competition"; to eliminate "unintelligent selfishness" and establish "100 per cent confidence"—all to the end that the members might "stand out from the crowd as substantial co-workers under modern co-operative business methods."

In *American Column & Lumber Co.* v. *United States*, . . . we considered a combination of manufacturers got up to effectuate this new conception of confidence and competition and held it within the inhibition of the Sherman Act because of inevitable tendency to destroy real competition, as long understood, and thereby restrain trade. . . .

The Sherman Act was intended to secure equality of opportunity and to protect the public against evils commonly incident to monopolies and those abnormal contracts and combinations which tend directly to suppress the conflict for advantage called competition—the play of the contending forces ordinarily engendered by an honest desire for gain. . . .

Certain it is that the defendants are associated in a new form of combination and are resorting to methods which are not normal. If, looking at the entire contract by which they are bound together, in the light of what has been done under it the Court can see that its necessary tendency is to suppress competition in trade between the States, the combination must be declared unlawful. That such is its tendency, we think, must be affirmed. . . .

With intimate knowledge of the affairs of other producers and obligated as stated, but proclaiming themselves competitors, the subscribers went forth to deal with widely separated and unorganized customers necessarily ignorant of the true conditions. Obviously they were not *bona fide* competitors; their claim in that regard is at war with common experience and hardly compatible with fair dealing. . . .

The challenged plan is unlawful and an injunction should go against it as prayed by the original bill. The cause will be remanded to the court below with instructions to issue such an injunction and promptly to take any further action necessary to carry this opinion into effect.

Reversed.

Permissible Activities

The next two cases reveal the emergence of a Rule of Reason being applied to trade association activities. In both the *Maple Flooring* and *Cement Manufacturers* cases the associations were allowed to continue the activities challenged by the government. It is difficult to reconcile the opinions in the *Hardwood* and *Linseed Oil* cases with these next two because many of the activities were common to all four associations. In fact, Justices Taft, Sanford, and McReynolds dissented from the majority opinion on the ground that the four cases should be treated alike because the evidence was substantially the same. It does appear, however, that in the *Maple Flooring* and *Cement Manufacturers* cases, the associations had modified their activities somewhat to eliminate the more objectionable features condemned by the Supreme Court in the earlier cases.

The *Maple Flooring* case involved an association of twenty-two manufacturers accounting for 70 per cent of the industry production. The association required periodic reports and distributed to all members statistics on sales, prices, average cost of all dimensions and grades of flooring, inventories, new orders, and unfilled orders. Before the Court decisions of 1921 and 1923, the association was identifying the statistics by individual firms in addition to distributing a quarterly computation of average costs and a uniform common freight rate book for use in determining delivered prices. After 1923 the association ceased to identify individual firms and gave wider dissemination of the data to others, including the government and customers. It was careful not to discuss prices at meetings, nor did it make any suggestions as to *future* production and pricing policies.

The government argued there was no substantial difference between the present case and previous ones. Uniform prices were bound to emerge through the use of average cost data and the standardized freight rate book. The necessary conclusion should be that trade had been restrained.

The Court agreed that there was a detailed reporting system which could affect prices and production. The majority of the Court, however, did not believe that businesses that unite in gathering and disseminating information from members of their group are engaged in unlawful conspiracy "merely because the ultimate result of their efforts may be to stabilize prices and limit production through a better understanding of economic laws and a more general ability to conform to them, . . ."

The three dissenting Justices were not quite so convinced of the benign effects of such activities. Justice McReynolds stated that he felt the reporting system was a carefully developed plan to cut down normal competition.

MAPLE FLOORING MANUFACTURERS ASSN. et al.
v. UNITED STATES

268 U.S. 563 (1925)

MR. JUSTICE STONE delivered the opinion of the Court. . . .

The defendants are the Maple Flooring Manufacturers Association, an unincorporated "trade association"; twenty-two corporate defendants, members of the Association, engaged in the business of selling and shipping maple, beech and birch flooring in interstate commerce, . . . the several individual representatives of the corporate members of the Association; and George W. Keehn, Secretary of the Association. Of the corporate defendants, approximately one-half own timber lands and saw mills and are producers of the rough lumber from which they manufacture finished flooring, sold and shipped in interstate commerce. The other defendants purchase rough flooring lumber in the open market and manufacture it into finished flooring which is sold and shipped in interstate commerce. . . . Estimates submitted in behalf of the Government indicate that in the year 1922 the defendants produced 70% of the total production of these types of flooring, the percentage having been gradually diminished during the five years preceding, the average for the five years being 74.2%. It is also in evidence that aside from non-member manufacturers who reported to the Government, there are numerous other non-member manufacturers of such flooring in the United States and Canada. The defendants own only a small proportion of the total stand, in the United States, of maple, beech and birch timber from which the various types of flooring produced and sold by defendants are manufactured. . . .

. . . The activities, however, of the present Association of which the Government complains may be summarized as follows:

(1) The computation and distribution among the members of the association of the average cost to association members of all dimensions and grades of flooring.

(2) The compilation and distribution among members of a booklet

showing freight rates on flooring from Cadillac, Michigan, to between five and six thousand points of shipment in the United States.

(3) The gathering of statistics which at frequent intervals are supplied by each member of the Association to the secretary of the Association giving complete information as to the quantity and kind of flooring sold and prices received by the reporting members, and the amount of stock on hand, which information is summarized by the Secretary and transmitted to members without, however, revealing the identity of the members in connection with any specific information thus transmitted.

(4) Meetings at which the representatives of members congregate and discuss the industry and exchange views as to its problems.

Before considering these phases of the activities of the Association, it should be pointed out that it is neither alleged nor proved that there was any agreement among the members of the Association either affecting production, fixing prices or for price maintenance. Both by the articles of association and in actual practice, members have been left free to sell their product at any price they choose and to conduct their business as they please. Although the bill alleges that the activities of the defendants hereinbefore referred to resulted in the maintenance of practical uniformity of net delivered prices as between the several corporate defendants, the evidence fails to establish such uniformity and it was not seriously urged before this Court that any substantial uniformity in price had in fact resulted from the activities of the Association, although it was conceded by defendants that the dissemination of information as to cost of the product and as to production and prices would tend to bring about uniformity in prices through the operation of economic law. . . .

The contention of the Government is that there is a combination among the defendants, which is admitted; that the effect of the activities of the defendants carried on under the plan of the Association must necessarily be to bring about a concerted effort on the part of members of the Association to maintain prices at levels having a close relation to the average cost of flooring reported to members and that consequently there is a necessary and inevitable restraint of interstate commerce and that therefore the plan of the Association itself is a violation of §1 of the Sherman Act which should be enjoined regardless of its actual operation and effect so far as price maintenance is concerned. . . .

Having outlined the substantial issues in the case, it will now be convenient to examine more in detail the several activities of the defendants of which the Government complains.

COMPUTATION AND DISTRIBUTION, AMONG THE MEMBERS, OF INFORMATION AS TO THE AVERAGE COST OF THEIR PRODUCT   There are three principal elements which enter into the computation of the cost of finished flooring.

They are the cost of raw material, manufacturing cost and the percentage of waste in converting rough lumber into flooring. The information as to the cost of rough lumber was procured by the Secretary from reports of actual sales of lumber by members in the open market. . . . Manufacturing costs were ascertained by questionaires sent out to members by which members were requested to give information as to labor costs, cost of warehousing, insurance and taxes, interest at 6% on the value of the plant, selling expense, including commissions and cost of advertising, and depreciation of plant. From the total thus ascertained there was deducted the net profit from wood and other by-products. The net total cost thus ascertained of all members reporting was then averaged.

The percentage of waste in converting the rough lumber into flooring was ascertained by test runs made by selected members of the Association under the direction of the Secretary of the Association, in the course of which a given amount of rough lumber was converted into flooring of different sizes and the actual waste in the process ascertained and stated in terms of percentage. By combining the three elements of cost thus arrived at, the total cost per thousand feet of the aggregate of the different types and grades of flooring produced from a given amount of rough lumber was estimated. . . .

THE COMPILATION AND DISTRIBUTION AMONG MEMBERS OF INFORMATION AS TO FREIGHT RATES Through the agency of the Secretary of the Association a booklet was compiled and distributed to members of the Association showing freight rates from Cadillac, Michigan, to numerous points throughout the United States to which the finished flooring is shipped by members of the Association. It appears from the evidence to have been the usual practice in the maple flooring trade, to quote flooring at a delivered price and that purchasers of flooring usually will not buy on any other basis. The evidence, however, is undisputed that the defendants quote and sell on a f.o.b. mill basis whenever a purchaser so requests. . . .

It cannot, we think, be questioned that data as to the average cost of flooring circulated among the members of the Association when combined with a calculated freight rate . . . could be made the basis for fixing prices or for an agreement for price maintenance . . . But, as we have already said, the record is barren of evidence that the published list of costs and the freight-rate book have been so used by the present Association. . . .

THE GATHERING AND DISTRIBUTING AMONG MEMBERS OF TRADE STATISTICS . . . The Association promptly reported back to the members statistics compiled from the reports of members including the identifying numbers of the mills making the reports, and information as to quantities, grades, prices, freight rates, etc., with respect to each sale. The names of purchasers were not reported and from and after July 19, 1923, the identifying number of the mill making the report was omitted. All reports of sales and prices dealt exclusively with past and closed transactions. The statistics gathered by the defendant Association are given wide publicity. They are published in trade journals which are read by from 90 to 95% of the persons who purchase the products of Association members. They are sent to the Department of Commerce which publishes a monthly survey of current business. They are forwarded to the Federal Reserve and other banks and are available to anyone at any time desiring to use them. . . .

Association Meetings

. . . Trade conditions generally, as reflected by the statistical information disseminated among members, were discussed; the market prices of rough maple flooring were also discussed, as were also manufacturing and market conditions. . . . [And] following the decision in *United States* v. *American Linseed Oil Co.,* . . . there was no discussion of prices in meetings. There was no occasion to discuss past prices, as those were fully detailed in the statistical reports, and the Association was advised by counsel that future prices were not a proper subject of discussion. . . .

We think it might be urged, on the basis of this record, that the defendants, by their course of conduct, instead of evidencing the purpose of persistent violators of law, had steadily indicated a purpose to keep within the boundaries of legality as rapidly as those boundaries were marked out by the decisions of courts interpreting the Sherman Act. . . . The record is barren of evidence tending to establish that there is any agreement or purpose or intention on the part of defendants to produce any effect upon commerce other than which would necessarily flow from the activities of the present Association, and in our view the Government must stand or fall upon its ability to bring the facts of the present case within the rule as laid down in *American Column Co.* v. *United States.*

. . . It is not contended that there was the compulsion of any agreement fixing prices, restraining production or competition or otherwise restraining interstate commerce. In our view, therefore, the sole question presented by this record for our consideration is whether the combination of the defendants in their existing Association, as actually conducted by them, has a *necessary* tendency to cause direct and undue restraint of competition in commerce falling within the condemnation of the Act. . . .

It is the consensus of opinion of economists and of many of the most important agencies of Government that the public interest is served by the gathering and dissemination, in the widest possible manner, of information with respect to the production and distribution, cost and prices in actual sales, of market commodities, because the making available of such information tends to stabilize trade and industry, to produce fairer price levels and to avoid the waste which inevitably attends the unintelligent conduct of economic enterprise. Free competition means a free and open market among both buyers and sellers for the sale and distribution of commodities. Competition does not become less free merely because the conduct of commercial operations becomes more intelligent through the free distribution of knowledge of all the essential factors entering into the commercial transaction. . . .

It was not the purpose or the intent of the Sherman Anti-Trust Law to inhibit the intelligent conduct of business operations, nor do we conceive that its purpose was to suppress such influences as might affect the operations of interstate commerce through the application to them of the individual intelligence of those engaged in commerce, enlightened by accurate information as to the essential elements of the economics of a trade or business, however gathered or disseminated. Persons who unite in gathering and disseminating information in trade journals and statistical reports on industry; who gather and publish statistics as to the amount of production of commodities in interstate commerce, and who report market prices, are not engaged in unlawful conspiracies in restraint of trade merely because the ultimate result of their efforts may be to stabilize prices or limit production through a better understanding of economic laws and a more general ability to conform to them, for the simple reason that the Sherman Law neither repeals economic laws nor prohibits the gathering and dissemination of information. . . .

Viewed in this light, can it be said in the present case, that the character of the information gathered by the defendants, or the use which is being made of it, leads to any necessary inference that the defendants either have made or will make any different or other use of it than would normally be made if like statistics were published in a trade journal or were published by the Department of Commerce, to which all the gathered statistics are made available? The cost of production, prompt information as to the cost of transportation, are legitimate subjects of enquiry and knowledge in any industry. . . .

We realize that such information, gathered and disseminated among the members of a trade or business, may be the basis of agreement or concerted action to lessen production arbitrarily or to raise prices beyond the levels of production and price which would prevail if no such agreement or concerted action ensued and those engaged in commerce were left free to base individual initiative on full information of the essential elements of their business.

. . . But in the absence of proof of such agreement or concerted action having been actually reached or actually attempted, under the present plan of operation of defendants we can find no basis in the gathering and dissemination of such information by them or in their activities under their present organization for the inference that such concerted action will necessarily result within the rule laid down in those cases. . . .

The decree of the District Court is reversed.

MR. CHIEF JUSTICE TAFT and MR. JUSTICE SANFORD dissent . . .

The separate opinion of MR. JUSTICE MCREYNOLDS.

[This case discloses] carefully developed plans to cut down normal competition in interstate trade and commerce. Long impelled by this purpose, appellants have adopted various expedients through which they evidently hoped to defeat the policy of the law without subjecting themselves to punishment.

They are parties to definite and unusual combinations and agreements, whereby each is obligated to reveal to confederates the intimate details of his business and is restricted in his freedom of action. It seems to me that ordinary knowledge of human nature and of the impelling force of greed ought to permit no serious doubt concerning the ultimate outcome of the arrangements. We may confidently expect the destruction of that kind of competition long relied upon by the public for establishment of fair prices, and to preserve which the Anti-Trust Act was passed. . . .

The *Cement Manufacturers* case was decided on the same day as the preceding one. The facts in the *Cement* case were essentially the same as those in *Maple Flooring*. An association consisting of nineteen manufacturers of cement had been formed to collect and disseminate among the members an elaborate set of monthly data on pricing, sales, promotion, and other similar information.

As the Supreme Court rendered decisions involving trade associations, the cement association would modify its practices to conform with the Court's rulings. By the time the *Cement* case was brought to court, the association was no longer identifying the data with the reporting firm, nor was it making policy announcements concerning future production and prices.

Once more the Supreme Court ruled that gathering and reporting information through a cooperative endeavor was not to be condemned as an unlawful restraint of trade even though it might be assumed that the ultimate result would be to bring about uniformity in price. The Court was impressed by the testimony of a number of distinguished economists supporting the thesis that in the case of a standardized product sold at wholesale to fully informed buyers, the inevitable result of free and open competition is a uniform price. But a uniform price will also result when firms are engaged in concerted action.

CEMENT MANUFACTURERS PROTECTIVE ASSOCIATION et al. v. UNITED STATES

268 U.S. 588 (1925)

MR. JUSTICE STONE delivered the opinion of the Court.

This is an appeal from a final decree of the District Court for the Southern District of New York granting a perpetual injunction in a proceeding brought by the United States under . . . the Sherman Act . . .

The Association was organized in January, 1916. Its purposes, as described by the constitution, were the "collection and dissemination of such accurate information as may serve to protect each manufacturer against misrepresentation, deception and imposition, and enable him to conduct his business exactly as he pleases in every respect, and particularly free from misdirection by false or insufficient information . . ."

Cement is a thoroughly standardized product. It is manufactured from limestone and shale which are crushed to extreme fineness, then subjected to high temperatures, which process produces a fused mass which when cooled is known as clinker. The clinker is then ground into the finished product which is then ready for transportation and use. Clinker is not subject to deterioration, but the ground clinker or cement deteriorates rapidly on exposure to moisture and cannot be kept in storage except for a limited period of time. . . .

The activities of defendants on which the Government bases its case for an injunction may summarily be stated as follows: The Government charges that the defendants, through the activities of the Association, control prices and production of cement within the territorial area served by the several defendants in the following manner:

(1) By the use of "specific job contracts" for future delivery of cement, accompanied by a system of reports and trade espionage having as its objective the restriction of deliveries of cement under those contracts.

(2) By compiling and distributing, among the members, freight-rate

books which give the rate of freight from arbitrary basing points to numerous points of delivery within the territorial area served by the several defendants;

(3) By exchange of information concerning credits;

(4) By activities of the Association at its meetings.

The Government asserts that uniformity of prices and limitation of production are necessary results of these activities of the defendants. It does not, however, charge any agreement or understanding between the defendants placing limitations on either prices or production. The evidence does not establish that prices were excessive or unreasonable . . .

The specific job contract is a form of contract in common use by manufacturers of cement whereby cement is sold for future delivery for use in a specific piece of construction which is described in the contract. [This type of contract was customary long before the existence of the association.]

The Association freight-rate book took the place of previous separate publications by individual manufacturers, with a consequent saving of money and increase of accuracy and a more thorough and continuous checking of rates. The basing points from which freight rates were calculated were not selected by the Association, but were the same as those appearing in prior books published by individuals before the publication of the Association freight-rate book. . . .

The use of basing points for the purpose of computing freight rates appears not to have been the result of any collective activity on the part of defendants or cement manufacturers generally, nor were they arbitrarily selected. Their use is rather the natural result of the development of the business within certain defined geographical areas. . . .

Each member of the Association, in addition to the reports on specific job contracts already referred to, sends to the Association a monthly statement of its production of clinker and ground cement, shipments and stock on hand for the past month and for the corresponding periods of the previous year. These were compiled and distributed to members without any change or comment. In addition, semi-monthly statements of shipments were also received and likewise distributed. Each member of the Association was thus given full information as to the available supply of cement and by whom it was held. . . .

From these various activities of the defendants, the Government deduces a purpose to control the price of cement, which it is charged was to be accomplished by the control of the supply of cement on the market and by intimate association of the defendants in the exchange of information and a ready means of quoting a delivered price at any point. . . . The two essential elements in the conspiracy to restrain commerce charged therefore are (a) the gathering and reporting of information which would enable individual members of the Association to avoid making deliveries of cement on specific job contracts which by the terms of the contracts they are not bound to deliver, and (b) the gathering of information as to production, price of cement sold on specific job contracts and transportation costs. . . .

That a combination existed for the purpose of gathering and distributing these two classes of information is not denied. . . .

. . . But for reasons stated more at length in our opinion in *Maple Flooring Association* v. *United States, supra,* we cannot regard the procuring and dissemination of information which tends to prevent the procuring of fraudulent contracts or to prevent the fraudulent securing of deliveries of merchandise on the pretense that the seller is bound to deliver it by his contract, as an unlawful restraint of trade even though such information be gathered and disseminated by those who are engaged in the trade or business principally concerned.

Nor, for the reasons stated, can we regard the gathering and reporting of information, through the co-operation of the defendants in this case, with reference to production, price of cement in actual closed specific job contracts and of transportation costs from chief points of production in the cement trade, as an unlawful restraint of commerce; even though it be assumed that the result of the gathering and reporting of such information tends to bring about uniformity in price.

Agreements or understanding among competitors for the maintenance of uniform prices are of coruse unlawful and may be enjoined, but the Government does not rely on any agreement or understanding for price maintenance. It relies rather upon the necessary leveling effect upon prices of knowledge disseminated among sellers as to some of the important factors which enter into price. . . .

. . . [S]uch activities are not in themselves unlawful restraints upon commerce and are not prohibited by the Sherman Act.

The judgment of the District Court is reversed.

The CHIEF JUSTICE and MR. JUSTICE SANFORD, and MR. JUSTICE MC-REYNOLDS in a separate opinion, dissented . . .

Limits on Restrictive Practices

The Supreme Court was not called upon to review a trade association program again until the *Sugar Institute* case of 1936. Like the *Hardwood* and *Linseed* cases, the decision went against the Institute because the Court believed the concerted activities of the members went far beyond the mere correction of injurious practices and promoting more perfect competitive conditions. The Institute's actions caused an unreasonable restraint of trade that could not be justified by pointing to the evils that had characterized the industry or the "laudable purpose" of removing them.

Fifteen companies, which refined nearly all of the imported raw cane sugar in this country and supplied 70 to 80 per cent of the refined sugar consumed, formed The Sugar Institute in 1927, a trade association ostensibly for the purpose of doing away with unfair merchandising practices by adopting an "open price plan." The primary aim was to curtail the granting of secret concessions and rebates to customers, a practice that had grown up over the years. The members agreed that all discriminations among customers should be abolished and that, to that end, each company should publicly announce in advance its prices, terms, and conditions of sale and then adhere strictly to them until they were publicly changed. Several supplementary restrictions were agreed upon relating to the employment of brokers and warehousemen, transportation, consignment points, long-term contracts, quantity discounts, and the withholding of statistical information.

Chief Justice Hughes, in writing the seven-member unanimous opinion, believed that the agreement and supporting requirements went considerably beyond eliminating abusive trade practices and did impose an unreasonable restraint. His opinion pointed out that the real vice of the plan was not found solely in the advanced announcement of prices and terms, or in the relaying of such announcements, but in the elaborate steps taken to secure undeviating compliance with the announced prices and terms, whereby opportunities for variation in the course of competition were cut off.

Maintenance of competition among the refiners was a matter of public concern. Since refined sugar is a highly standardized product, the existing competition must necessarily relate to prices, terms, and conditions of sale. The strong tendency toward uniformity of price resulting from the standardized product made it even more important that any existing opportunities for fair competition should not be obstructed.

The Court outlawed a large number of restrictive practices of the Institute, although it would not order its dissolution. The decision must have been effective, however, because the Institute was disbanded a short time afterward.

SUGAR INSTITUTE, INC. et al. v. UNITED STATES

297 U.S. 553 (1936)

MR. CHIEF JUSTICE HUGHES delivered the opinion of the Court.

This suit was brought to dissolve The Sugar Institute, Inc., a trade association, and to restrain the sugar refining companies which composed it, and the individual defendants, from engaging in an alleged conspiracy in restraint of interstate and foreign commerce in violation of the Sherman Anti-Trust Act. . . . Final decree was entered, which, while it did not dissolve the Institute, permanently enjoined the defendants from engaging directly or indirectly in forty-five stated activities.

. . . We shall attempt to deal only with the salient and controlling points of the controversy. These involve (1) the special characteristics of the sugar industry and the practices which obtained before the organization of The Sugar Institute, (2) the purposes for which the Institute was founded, (3) the agreement and practices of the members of the Institute, and (4) the application of the Anti-Trust Act and the provisions of the decree.

FIRST.—THE SUGAR INDUSTRY AND PRACTICES PRIOR TO THE FORMATION OF THE SUGAR INSTITUTE . . . [The lower court found that] "price, not brand, was always the vital consideration." And in the other sales, "one refiner could not ordinarily, by virtue of preference for his brand, obtain a higher price except insofar as another refiner might be giving a lower price by secret concessions."

. . . The declining profits for the year 1927 were attributable at least in large part, the court found, to causes other than the secret concession system, such as the "slimness campaign," over-production and dumping.

But whatever question there may be as to particulars, the evidence and findings leave no doubt that the industry was in a demoralized state which called for remedial measures. . . .

SECOND.—THE PURPOSES FOR WHICH THE INSTITUTE WAS FOUNDED . . . Defendants urge that the abolition of the vicious and discriminatory system of secret concessions, through the adoption of the principle of open prices publicly announced, without discrimination, was their dominant purpose in forming the Institute, and that other purposes were the supplying of accurate trade statistics, the elimination of wasteful practices, the creation of a credit bureau, and the institution of an advertising campaign. . . .

[But the lower court found the dominant purpose to be] ". . . to create and maintain a uniform price structure, thereby eliminating and suppressing price competition among themselves and other competitors; to maintain relatively high prices for refined, as compared with contemporary prices of raw sugar; to improve their own financial position by limiting and suppressing numerous contract terms and conditions; and to make as certain as possible that no secret concessions should be granted. In their efforts to accomplish these purposes, defendants have ignored the interests of distributors and consumers of sugar." . . .

THIRD.—THE AGREEMENT AND PRACTICES OF THE MEMBERS OF THE INSTITUTE . . . The findings of restraints of trade rest upon the basic agreement of the refiners to sell only upon prices and terms openly announced, and upon certain supplementary restrictions.

1. *The "basic agreement."*—The "Code of Ethics" provided as follows:

"All discriminations between customers should be abolished. To that end, sugar should be sold only upon open prices and terms publicly announced." . . .

The distinctive feature of the "basic agreement" was not the advance announcement of prices, or a concert to maintain any particular basis price for any period, but a requirement of adherence, without deviation, to the prices and terms publicly announced. . . .

It was because of the range and effect of this restriction, and the consequent deprivation of opportunity to make special arrangements, that the court found that the agreement and the course of action under it constituted an unreasonable restraint of trade. . . .

FOURTH.—THE APPLICATION OF THE ANTI-TRUST ACT AND THE PROVISIONS OF THE DECREE   The restrictions imposed by the Sherman Act are not mechanical or artificial. . . . Designed to frustrate unreasonable restraints, they do not prevent the adoption of reasonable means to protect interstate commerce from destructive or injurious practices and to promote competition upon a sound basis. Voluntary action to end abuses and to foster fair competitive opportunities in the public interest may be more effective than legal processes. And coöperative endeavor may appropriately have wider objectives than merely the removal of evils which are infractions of positive law. Nor does the fact that the correction of abuses may tend to stabilize a business, or to produce fairer price levels, require that abuses should go uncorrected or that an effort to correct them should for that reason alone be stamped as an unreasonable restraint of trade. Accordingly we have held that a coöperative enterprise otherwise free from objection, which carries with it no monopolistic menace, is not to be condemned as an undue restraint merely because it may effect a change in market conditions where the change would be in mitigation of recognized evils and would not impair, but rather foster, fair competitive opportunities. . . .

The freedom of concerted action to improve conditions has an obvious limitation. The end does not justify illegal means. The endeavor to put a stop to illicit practices must not itself become illicit. As the statute draws the line at unreasonable restraints, a coöperative endeavor which transgresses that line cannot justify itself by pointing to evils afflicting the industry or to a laudable purpose to remove them. . . . while the collection and dissemination of trade statistics are in themselves permissible and may be a useful adjunct of fair commerce, a combination to gather and supply information as a part of a plan to impose unwarrantable restrictions, as, for example, to curtail production and raise prices, has been condemned. . . .

. . . Questions of reasonableness are necessarily questions of relation and degree. In the instant case, a fact of outstanding importance is the relative position of defendants in the sugar industry. We have noted that the fifteen refiners, represented in the Institute, refine practically all the imported raw sugar processed in this country. They supply from 70 to 80 per cent of the sugar consumed. . . . Another outstanding fact is that defendants' product is a thoroughly standardized commodity. In their competition, price, rather than brand, is generally the vital consideration. The question of unreasonable restraint of competition thus relates in the main to competition in prices, terms and conditions of sales. The fact that, because sugar is a standardized commodity, there is a strong tendency to uniformity of price, makes it the more important that such opportunities as may exist for fair competition should not be impaired. . . .

. . . The unreasonable restraints which defendants imposed lay not in advance announcements, but in the steps taken to secure adherence, without deviation, to prices and terms thus announced. It was that concerted undertaking which cut off opportunities for variation in the course of competition however fair and appropriate they might be. . . .

THE DECREE The court below did not dissolve the Institute. The practices which had been found to constitute unreasonable restraints were comprehensively enjoined. The injunction restrains defendants "individually and collectively, in connection with the sale, marketing, shipment, transportation, storage, distribution or delivery of refined sugar," from engaging with one another or with any competitor through any *"program"* in any of the activities separately described. . . .

Paragraphs one and two of the specifications enjoin the carrying out of the open price plan so far as it seeks to compel uniform terms, regardless of circumstances, and an adherence to prices, terms, etc. announced in advance.

Following the provisions for injunction, the decree properly provides that jurisdiction is retained for the purpose of "enforcing, enlarging or modifying" its terms. It is further provided that the injunction is without prejudice to application by any party for modification in order to permit the adoption of any "program" that may be permissible under "the National Industrial Recovery Act" of June 16, 1933, or the "Emergency Farm Relief Act" of May 12, 1933, or "any other present or future statutes of the United States." This subdivision of the decree should be modified so as to refer simply to "any applicable Act of Congress."

The decree is modified in the particulars above stated and, as thus modified, is affirmed.

Modified and affirmed.

MR. JUSTICE SUTHERLAND and MR. JUSTICE STONE took no part in the consideration and decision of this cause.

Use of Trade Statistics

The most recent case of any significance concerning trade association activities is a 1949 court of appeals decision involving the Tag Mfrs. Institute. The Federal Trade Commission, after a protracted hearing involving approximately twenty-five hundred pages of testimony and fifteen hundred exhibits, issued a cease-and-desist order enjoining certain practices of the Institute. Upon appeal, the Court reversed the order of the FTC basing its decision largely on the *Maple Flooring* precedent. The FTC did not appeal to the Supreme Court.

The Tag Mfrs. Institute was organized in 1933 and consisted of thirty-one member firms that manufactured and sold 95 per cent of the tag products. Certain standardized tags were made and stocked, but four-fifths of the tag business on a made-to-order basis. Under a plan administered by the executive director of the Institute, the members reported their tag specifications, prices, terms, and conditions of sale or contracts to sell tags. The director compiled and circulated the data among the members, to public agencies, and the same information was usually available to customers. The members did not have to adhere to reported prices, but deviations from list prices had to be reported daily, with failure to report punishable by fine.

The Commission believed the Institute was fixing and maintaining prices, thereby restraining trade and lessening competition. The court of appeals reversed the Commission on the grounds that the Institute's activities fell within the *Maple Flooring* precedent. The pricing reports were not secret, they were confined to past transactions, no suggestions were made as to future prices, and strict adherence to reported prices was not required.

TAG MFRS. INSTITUTE et al. v. FEDERAL TRADE COMMISSION

174 F. 2d 452 (1949)

MAGRUDER, Chief Judge.

Petitioners in this case ask us . . . to review and set aside or modify a cease and desist order of the Federal Trade Commission . . .

[The FTC charged] that beginning more than three years prior to May 2, 1941, and continuing to that date, petitioners "have entered into and carried out an understanding, agreement, combination, and conspiracy to restrict, restrain, suppress and eliminate price competition in the sale and distribution of said tag products" in interstate commerce; that pursuant to said agreement, petitioners "have fixed and maintained, and still fix and maintain, uniform prices, terms and conditions of sale for said tag products"; that the acts and practices of petitioners "have a dangerous tendency to and have actually hindered and prevented price competition" in the sale of tags in interstate commerce, have placed in petitioners the power to control and enhance prices on said products, have unreasonably restrained such commerce "and constitute unfair methods of competition in commerce within the intent and meaning of the Federal Trade Commission Act."

The manufacturing petitioners sell and distribute approximately 95 per cent of the tag products purchased and used in the United States, with 55 per cent of the business of the industry shared by the four largest manufacturers.

Certain standardized tags are made in advance of sale and sold out of stock, such as plain unprinted stock shipping tags. However, over 80 per cent of the business is in made-to-order tags, the varieties of which are almost unlimited . . . The much greater part of the products of the industry, particularly of made-to-order tags, is sold direct to consumers, but there is a considerable volume of sales to distributors and others for resale. To some extent, tag manufacturers buy from other manufacturers, for resale, types of tags which they do not themselves manufacture. Orders for tags generally small in dollar value, averaging between $20 to $40, and a thousand or more orders for tags are placed with manufacturers each business day.

In such an industry, it would evidently not be practicable for a manufacturer to give a price on each order, based upon an individual cost estimate of that order. Hence, early in the history of the industry, manufacturers began to issue price lists to their salesmen, distributors and customers. The simple stock tags were customarily listed at stated prices for the finished product. . . .

The issuance of price lists by tag manufacturers had become established as a general practice in the industry prior to the formation of the Institute and prior to the execution of the various Tag Industry Agreements . . .

The Institute was organized in 1933, and has operated continuously since that time. All the manufacturing petitioners have become members of the Institute. . . .

While the National Industrial Recovery Act, 48 Stat. 195, was in effect, a Code of Fair Competition for the Tag Industry was promulgated February 1, 1934. . . . Petitioners concede that these price-fixing provisions of the Code would have been illegal except for the exemption from the anti-trust laws contained in the National Industrial Recovery Act.

After the National Industrial Recovery Act was invalidated . . . members of the industry adopted a succession of four Tag Industry Agreements, so-called, in 1935, 1936, 1937 and 1940. . . .

. . . [A]greements were concerned chiefly with the reporting and dissemination of industry statistics.

. . . The Commission found that the prices of each of the subscribing manufacturers as contained in the Compilation "constituted both the current and future prices" of said manufacturers. Petitioners, on the other hand, say that the Compilation "is a book of reference with respect to past market conditions only." . . . the Tag Industry Agreement specifically recognizes that the manufacturers are free to make off-list sales; and in practice all of the subscribing manufacturers have freely done so. Therefore the Commission is inaccurate in its finding that, when a price list is filed with Baxter, the prices so listed become and remain the prices for tag products of the Subscriber so filing until revised by notice to Baxter and the filing with him of a revised price list. . . .

On the other hand, it is obvious that the Compilation in the hands of the Subscribers is more than an object of academic historical interest and is designed for a practical business purpose. Manufacturers do not change their price lists every day. A price list may remain in effect for weeks, often for months, without change. . . .

. . . The evidence does not, however, warrant the Commission's finding that the effect of the operation of the Tag Industry Agreements "has resulted in a substantial uniformity of prices for tags and tag products among the respondent members." In the first place, this implies that the instances of departure from uniformity are insignificant and unsubstantial —which certainly cannot be said. In the second place, there is no evidence that such uniformity as has existed as a result of the operation of the Tag Industry Agreements . . .

In support of its conclusion, the Commission refers to the provisions in the Tag Industry Agreements designed to insure compliance with the reporting commitments of the Subscribers. Baxter was given access to the books and records of the Subscribers in the investigation of complaints of violations and in routine periodic checkups. The Commission found that Baxter "caused periodic checks to be made of the books and records of the various respondent members by a representative of his office to determine if they were adhering to the published prices and reporting all deviations therefrom." As phrased, this finding contains an ambiguous overtone which seems to imply that there was an agreement to adhere to list prices, and that Baxter examined the books to see if this agreement was being fulfilled. As previously indicated, there was no such agreement. . . .

There has been some tendency to look askance at reporting agreements between competitors, where the information exchanged is reserved exclusively to themselves and withheld from buyers or the public generally. Presumably this is because such secrecy more readily suggests the inference that the agreement is inspired by some unlawful purpose and precludes the argument that the information thus secretly exchanged serves a function similar to that of market information made available through the activities of commodity exchanges, trade journals, etc. . . .

We have come to the conclusion that the reporting agreements herein, and the practices of petitioners thereunder, are lawful under the controlling authorities. In the sense indicated earlier in this opinion, the issuance of a price list may be said to be an "announcement of future prices." The nature of price lists has not changed under the Tag Industry Agreements from what it has historically been in the industry. The price list is subject to change without notice, and may be freely revised at any time. Even while a particular price list is extant, the manufacturer is free to make sales at off-list prices. This has always been so (except under the NRA Code), and still remains so under the Tag Industry Agreement. . . . Once a price list has been issued to the trade it necessarily becomes pretty much public property. There is certainly nothing secret about it. It would be no great feat for a manufacturer to obtain copies of his competitors' price lists. The Tag Industry Agreement merely facilitates the assembling of such data. As to the obligation of Subscribers to report off-list sales and to furnish copies of all invoices, that is no more than the reporting of past transactions. The Commission has endeavored to show that the agreement was something more than this, that it was a price-fixing agreement having the purpose and actual effect of restraining and prevent price competition. We believe that such findings are unsupported by the evidence or by any reasonable inferences to be drawn therefrom. . . .

A judgment will be entered setting aside the order of the Commission.

PART TWO

Interference with Distribution Channels

8

Price Discrimination

Price discrimination refers to the charging of different prices to different buyers for essentially the identical goods or commodities. Wilcox defines it more completely when he says: "Discrimination occurs most clearly when the same goods, of the same quality, are sold in the same quantity, at the same time, under the same conditions, and on the same terms, to different buyers at different prices."[1] Of course, price discrimination refers to more than just price variations—it can occur when services attendant to the goods vary, or when discounts allowed are arbitrary and do not reflect savings in costs, or when quality differs.

The original Section 2 of the Clayton Act was the principal statute concerned with discriminatory pricing. The Act declared it illegal to discriminate in price between different purchasers of commodities. The Act permitted price discrimination when there were differences in grade, quality, or quantity; when due allowance reflected the cost of selling or transportation; or when the lower prices were offered in "good faith" to meet competition.[2]

Price discrimination problems are often classified as geographical or personal discrimination. When Section 2 of the Clayton Act was passed, it was principally intended to combat the predatory geographical device of "cut-throat" competition—the practice of selling goods below rivals' costs in communities where there was competition. Prices were raised to an even higher level after the competitors were driven out of business. But outside of delivered pricing systems—which can be called forms of geographical price discrimination—there have seldom been any problems in this area within recent times. Probably the availability of almost instantaneous and widespread market information prevents unjustified geographical discrimination.

Whereas the 1914 version of Section 2 was aimed primarily at geographical price discrimination, the 1936 Robinson-Patman amendment to Section 2 was concerned more with personal discrimination by a seller to customers who are themselves competitors. The Robinson-Patman amendment was aimed at eliminating unwarranted price concessions to large-scale buyers in the form of (1) broker's commissions, (2) promotional and advertising allowances, and (3) quantity discounts. The price discrimination prohibition is conditonal because it applies only when competition "may" be injured. The statute forbids

---

[1] Clair Wilcox, *Public Policies Toward Business*, 3d ed. (Homewood, Ill.: Richard D. Irwin, Inc., 1966), p. 202.

[2] See Section 2, Clayton Act, in the Appendix.

discrimination in price "where the effect of such discrimination may be substantially to lessen competition or tend to create a monopoly in any line of commerce . . ." Therefore, not all price discrimination is to be condemned.

Price Discrimination under Original Section 2

In an early case the Federal Trade Commission was unsuccessful in attacking price discrimination by a seller to competing buyers. The Mennen Company refused to grant wholesale discounts to a retail druggist cooperative. The Federal Trade Commission declared this illegal price discrimination. The circuit court of appeals, certiorari denied by the Supreme Court,[3] reversed the FTC order, primarily on the ground that competition between the Mennen Company and *other manufacturers* was not lessened by the Mennen Company's policy. The Clayton Act, according to this narrow interpretation of "any line of commerce," prohibited price discrimination only if the seller's competitors were injured—ignoring any injury to competition among the seller's customers.

This narrow interpretation stood for only six years, being reversed, not in any government action, but in a private suit between Van Camp Company and American Can Company. George Van Camp & Sons Company accused the American Can Company of unlawful price discrimination in the sale of tin cans and in the rental of sealing machines. George Van Camp & Sons claimed that American Can sold its tin cans to its competitor, the Van Camp Packing Company, at 20 per cent below the price it sold to George Van Camp & Sons. Another claim was that American Can leased its sealing machines at a fixed rental to George Van Camp & Sons, but furnished them free of charge to the Van Camp Packing Company.

The George Van Camp & Sons Company contended that "any line of commerce" included lines other than the one engaged in by the discriminator, arguing for a broad interpretation. American Can, relying on the *Mennen* case, argued for the narrow interpretation. The line of commerce is the tin can business, not the canned goods business, they insisted; the competition referred to in Section 2 is that between the discriminator and his competitors.

The Supreme Court rejected both the argument of American Can and the decision in the *Mennen* case. The Court held that the phrase, "any line of commerce," is comprehensive and that a violation occurs "by a discrimination in prices exacted by the seller from different purchasers of similar goods . . ."

---

[3] *Mennen Co.* v. *FTC*, 288 Fed. 774 (1923); certiorari denied, 262 U.S. 759 (1923).

GEORGE VAN CAMP & SONS COMPANY v. AMERICAN CAN COMPANY et al.

278 U.S. 245 (1929)

MR. JUSTICE SUTHERLAND delivered the opinion of the Court.[4]

This suit was brought in the Federal District Court for the District of Indiana to enjoin violations of §2 of the Clayton Act, . . . From a decree dismissing the bill for want of equity, an appeal was taken to the court below. Under §239 of the Judicial Code as amended . . . , that court has certified the following questions concerning which instructions are desired for the proper disposition of the cause:

"Question 1. Does section 2 of the 'Clayton Act' . . . have application to cases of price discrimination, the effect of which may be to substantially lessen competition, or tend to create a monopoly, not in the line of commerce wherein the discriminator is engaged, but in the line of commerce in which the vendee of the discriminator is engaged?

"Question 2. Where one who makes an article and sells it, interstate, to persons engaged, interstate, in a line of commerce different from that of the maker, discriminates in price between such buyers (said discrimination not being made on account of differences in the grade, quality or quantity of the commodity sold, nor being made as only due allowance for the difference in the cost of selling or transportation, nor being made in good faith to meet competition) and the effect of such discrimination may be to substantially lessen competition or tend to create a monopoly in the line of commerce wherein the buyers are engaged, does the maker and seller of the article, making such price discrimination, transgress section 2 of the 'Clayton Act' . . . ?"

The relevant facts upon which the questions are based are set forth as follows:

"The bill charges that appellant, George Van Camp & Sons Company, is engaged, interstate, in the business of packing and selling food products in tin cans, and that appellee Van Camp Packing Company is engaged in the same business, and is a competitor of appellant; and that appellee American Can Company manufactures, in very great quantities,

---

[4] All the footnotes and most of the citations from the opinions of the Court have been omitted from the cases in this chapter.

and sells, interstate, to food packers, tin cans used in the food packing industry, and owns the monopoly for certain machines which are necessary for sealing the cans of its manufacture, and that it sells such cans in large quantities to appellant and to appellee Van Camp Packing Company, and leases to them its machines for sealing these cans;

"That the American Can Company is unlawfully discriminating between different purchases of its commodities, in that the price at which it offered and offers and sold and sells its said cans to appellee Van Camp Packing Company is 20% below its publicly announced standard prices and the prices at which it contracted to sell and did and does sell its cans of the same kind to appellant, George Van Camp & Sons Company; that the American Can Company furnishes food packers, including appellant, its machines necessary for sealing its said cans at a fixed rental, and furnishes the same machines to the Van Camp Packing Company free of charge; that the American Can Company paid and pays the Van Camp Packing Company large sums of money by way of bonus, discounts, and reductions from the price of cans fixed in contracts between them, none of such bonus, discounts, or reductions being allowed or paid to appellant; and that these discriminations were and are not made on account of differences in grade, quality, or quantity of the commodity sold, nor of the machines leased, nor on account of any difference in the cost of selling or transportation, nor made in good faith to meet competition;

"That the effect of such discrimination is to substantially lessen competition, and tends to create a monopoly in the line of interstate commerce, in which the appellant, George Van Camp & Sons Company, and the appellee Van Camp Packing Company are both engaged, namely, the packing and selling of food products in tin cans. . . ."

Section 2, . . . provides that it shall be unlawful for any person engaged in commerce, in the course of such commerce, to discriminate in price between different purchasers . . . where the effect of such discrimination may be to substantially lessen competition or tend to create a monopoly in any line of commerce. . . .

These facts bring the case within the terms of the statute, unless the words "in any line of commerce" are to be given a narrower meaning than a literal reading of them conveys. The phrase is comprehensive and means that if the forbidden effect or tendency is produced in *one* out of *all* the various lines of commerce, the words "in *any* line of commerce" literally are satisfied. The contention is that the words must be confined to the particular line of commerce in which the discriminator is engaged, and that they do not include a different line of commerce in which purchasers from the discriminator are engaged in competition with one another. . . . The words being clear, they are decisive. There is nothing to construe. To search elsewhere for a meaning either beyond or short of that which they disclose is to invite the danger, in the one case, of converting what was meant to be open and precise, into a concealed trap for the unsuspecting, or, in the other, of relieving from the grasp of the statute some whom the legislature definitely meant to include. . . .

. . . The fundamental policy of the legislation is that, in respect of persons engaged in the same line of interstate commerce, competition is desirable and that whatever substantially lessens it or tends to create a monopoly in such line of commerce is an evil. Offence against this policy, by a discrimination in prices exacted by the seller from different purchasers of similar goods, is no less clear when it produces the evil in respect of the line of commerce in which they are engaged than when it produces the evil in respect of the line of commerce in which the seller is engaged. In either case, a restraint is put upon "the freedom of competition in the channels of interstate trade which it has been the purpose of all the anti-trust acts to maintain." . . .

We have not failed carefully to consider *Mennen Co.* v. *Federal Trade Comm'n,* . . . cited as contrary to the conclusion we have reached. The decision in that case was based upon the premise that the statute was ambiguous and required the aid of committee reports, etc., to determine its meaning, a premise which we have rejected as unsound.

Both questions submitted are answered in the affirmative.

Question No. 1, Yes.
Question No. 2, Yes.

The last important decision under the original Section 2 of the Clayton Act was the *Goodyear Tire & Rubber Company* case. The Federal Trade Commission issued its order to cease and desist shortly before Section 2 was amended by the Robinson-Patman Act. The case did not reach final decision until 1939, due to legal sparring on the technical question of whether the issue was now moot because of the Robinson-Patman amendment.

Goodyear had contracted with Sears, Roebuck & Company to supply them with their tire requirements at cost plus 6 per cent profit. The FTC found that Goodyear realized on its sales to Sears a "net profit of $7,715,794.56, and on its sales of equal volume to service-station dealers a net profit of $20,425,-807.21. The difference of $12,710,012.65 in net profit it found to be the aggregate net price discrimination . . ." The Commission claimed that quantity discounts must be reasonably related to the cost savings, which in this case bore no relation to the discounts given Sears.

The pertinent provision of the statute reads: "That nothing herein contained shall prevent discrimination in price between purchasers of commodities on account of differences in the grade, quality, or quantity of the commodity sold, or [this "or" is the key word in the Court's interpretation] that makes only due allowance for the difference in the cost of selling or transportation . . ." The appellate court ruled against the FTC, stating that the proviso of "due allowances for differences in the cost" did not limit the proviso exempting quantity discounts. Therefore, any difference in quantity justified any difference in price. This interpretation, in effect, would have permitted just about any price discrimination.

GOODYEAR TIRE & RUBBER CO. v. FEDERAL TRADE COMMISSION

101 F. 2d 620 (1939)

SIMONS, Circuit Judge. . . .

The case is here for the second time. . . .

As indicated in our former opinion, the controversy involves principally an interpretation given by the Commission to §2 of the Clayton Act. That section declares it to be unlawful to discriminate in price between purchasers of commodities where the effect of such discrimination may be to substantially lessen competition or tend to create a monopoly in any line of commerce, subject to the proviso: "That nothing herein contained shall prevent discrimination in price between purchasers of commodities on account of differences in the grade, quality, or quantity of the commodity sold, or that makes only due allowance for difference in the cost of selling or transportation, or discrimination in price in the same or different communities made in good faith to meet competition." The petitioner contends that a discrimination in price is permitted if based upon the quantity of the commodity sold, without respect to whether it makes only due allowance for difference in cost of selling or transportation. The Commission contends that while the proviso permits discrimination on account of differences in quantity, such discrimination is not permitted unless reasonably related to and approximately no more than the difference in cost, and that a price discrimination is contrary to §2 unless it can be shown that it represents and fairly approximates lower costs.

Prior to 1926 the large mail order house of Sears, Roebuck & Company, with retail stores in many cities of the United States, bought its tires from one or more small manufacturers. Though doing a much larger general business than its principal competitor, Montgomery, Ward & Company, its tire business failed to keep pace with that of the latter. It set about to improve this condition by changing the personnel of its tire

department and inaugurating a vigorous advertising campaign, and sought
Goodyear as a source of tire supply. Its first contract with Goodyear in
1926 covered its requirements for a period of three years. The price was
cost of manufacture plus a profit of 6%, later adjusted in some instances to
6½%. Sears was to do its own advertising and to sell the tires under trade-
names of its own. In May, 1928, a second contract was concluded covering
requirements to December 31, 1932, but terminable on that date by a year
of advance notice. In the summer of 1931, Sears, signifying its intention to
terminate, a new arrangement was made by which a ten year contract was
entered into upon Goodyear paying to Sears a consideration in cash and
common stock amounting to $1,250,000. Like preceding arrangements, the
contract called for a price of cost plus profit.

Under its several contracts with Sears, Goodyear manufactured and
sold to Sears during the eight-year period, 1926–1933, more than 19,000,000
tires, for which Sears paid to it a gross sum of $129,252,984, and a net
sum of $116,359,367. The Commission made an exhaustive study of the
cost of tires sold by Goodyear under the Sears contracts and that of tires
sold to its independent dealers upon a similar volume of business. It found
that based upon the profit and loss statement of Goodyear adjusted as the
result of such study, Goodyear realized on its sales to Sears during the
entire period a total net profit of $7,715,794.56, and on its sales of equal
volume to service-station dealers a net profit of $20,425,807.21. The
difference of $12,710,012.65 in net profit it found to be the aggregate net
price discrimination not accounted for by differences in cost of transportation and selling according to the respondent's own calculations and based
upon the method which it itself suggested. It concluded that this price
discrimination in favor of Sears against independent service-station dealers
was not justified by differences in cost of transportation or selling. Conceding that quantity discounts are exempt because they involve some economic utility that should be preserved, the Commission asserts that the
quantity exception does not permit price discrimination without limit or
restraint, that while a difference in quantity of the commodity sold must
be given reasonable weight in determining whether the discriminatory
price is warranted, yet in arriving at a price on account of quantity it is
necessary that the difference in price be reasonably related to the difference
in cost, though remote and unsubstantial differences in cost may be
disregarded.

The petitioner, conceding that price discrimination on account of
quantity does not mean discrimination without limit, denies that such
discrimination must be based on difference in cost or be reasonably related
to such difference. It points to the value to Goodyear of the Sears
requirements in removing hazard and insuring stability, the avoidance of
profit fluctuation inevitable in its other business, and the casting upon
Sears of the risk which Goodyear normally bore of raw material price

decline and credit losses. It asserts that these advantages, over and above mere savings in costs, are substantial and real, even though they may not readily be measured in terms of dollars, and that the statute by its language permits a discrimination that will measure economic advantage of quantity sales beyond mere savings in cost.

The Commission dismissed from its consideration all intangible economic advantages of quantity sales over and above savings in cost as being too speculative and remote to justify price discrimination. . . .

Primary consideration must necessarily be given to the meaning of §2 of the Clayton Act. It will be observed that by the proviso, nothing contained in the section is to prevent discrimination in price between purchasers of commodities (1) "on account of differences in the grade, quality, or quantity of the commodity sold," or (2) "that makes only due allowance for difference in the cost of selling or transportation," or (3) "discrimination in price in the same or different communities made in good faith to meet competition." With the third exception of the proviso we are not concerned, and as to the meaning of the second exception there is no dispute. It is conceded that there may be a discrimination in price based upon quantity, but the Commission would read the second exception as a limitation or qualification of the first. We see no warrant for such construction and the structure of the proviso as well as the history of the section repel it.

The three exceptions of the proviso would seem to be mutually exclusive. If the second qualifies and limits the first, the word "quantity" in the first exception appears to be redundant. . . .

. . . The Clayton Act was passed in 1914, but until the present investigation began the Commission never assumed it had the power to prohibit price discrimination on account of quantity when unrelated to differences in cost. . . .

We defer to the rule that when the meaning of an Act of Congress is plain on its face there is no occasion to resort to the reports of Congressional Committees concerning it, . . . and it seems to be clear that §2 of the Clayton Act permits discrimination in price on account of quantity without relation to savings in cost, and that the distinguishing phraseology employed in the two exceptions must not be ignored. . . .

It is urged that the finding that excess discrimination was not on account of quantity is supported by evidentiary facts, including the fact that prices did not vary according to the varying volume of the Sears business, that there was no quantity commitment in the Sears' contracts, and that the discrimination was proportionally greater than that allowed dealers in view of the economic principle that at some point saturation must be reached beyond which no increase in quantity would justify an increase in discount. These evidentiary circumstances do not of themselves, however, sustain an ultimate finding that the differential was not on account of quantity. The lack of a definite commitment when the contract was for Sears' entire requirements, less minor checking orders, the failure of the price to rise and fall concurrently with the rise and fall of quantity shipments, and the lack of relation between the discount to Sears and the gradations of discount to independent dealers, are all inherent in the nature of a cost-plus agreement of such unusual volume as was expected to and did result from the Sears business, for the evidence discloses that it was from thirteen to thirty-six times the volume of that of Goodyear's largest independent customer.

All this aside, however, it seems perfectly clear that the findings and conclusions of the Commission that the discrimination in price was not on account of quantity, were all based upon the Commission's interpretation of the law. . . . Section 17 of the Commission's findings dealing with the present question is a composite of evidentiary facts, reasoning and conclusion. Without denying that there are economic advantages in dealing with a large customer on the basis of hazard, the stabilizing of production and profit and other factors not translated into dollar and cents advantage, it is determined without pretense of appraising such advantages that they are too speculative, intangible and remote to justify a price discrimination. It is further determined that the discrimination was not a quantity discount as customarily understood in the trade, because the Commission, weighing the testimony of expert economists pro and con, concluded that quantity discounts not justified on approximate savings are in that field considered as a form of price cutting, and so condemned by the law. The conclusion is inescapable that any discrimination in price exceeding by more than a negligible amount a due allowance for differences in cost must have brought about the same result. The Commission found no standard in the law by which a discrimination on account of quantity unrelated to savings in cost is to be judged. . . . Once a discrimination is found unrelated to savings in cost, it is ipso facto to be condemned. So is there not only a misconstruction of the law, but a refusal to recognize a standard of judgment not based on such misconstruction and so impossibility of its application to the facts, if rightly construed. . . .

. . . We conclude that the Commission had no power to command discontinuance of price differentials reasonably based on quantity, and there is no finding which properly construed determines that those here involved are not so based, since no standard for the making of such finding is recognized.

The order of the respondent is set aside.

HAMILTON, Circuit Judge (dissenting). . . .

Price Discrimination under Amended Section 2

The leading case involving price discrimination based on quantity discounts under Section 2 of the Clayton Act, as modified by the Robinson-Patman amendment, is the *Morton Salt* case. Morton Salt Company had a cumulative "standard" quantity discount system available to all customers. But only five large grocery chains (American Stores, National Tea, Kroger, Safeway, and A & P) could buy in sufficient quantities to take advantage of Morton's maximum discount. In fact, these five companies were able to sell Morton's salt at retail cheaper than wholesale purchasers could sell to retail stores.

The Federal Trade Commission concluded that Morton's discounts were not based on actual savings in cost and therefore had discriminated in price between different purchasers of like grade and quality. Morton Salt's basic defense was that its standard quantity discounts which are "available to all on equal terms . . . are not discriminatory within the meaning of the Robinson-Patman Act." The Supreme Court rejected the contention, stating: "Theoretically, these discounts are equally available to all, but functionally they are not." Another defense of Morton Salt was that its discounts, if discriminatory, did not injure competition. The Court agreed with the FTC's findings that the competitive opportunity of certain merchants was injured. In upholding the Commission's order to cease and desist, the Court said that the law does not require that competition was in fact harmed, "But only that there is a reasonable possibility that [price discriminations] 'may' have such an effect."

In a dissenting opinion, Justice Jackson, while concurring with the Court's decision, disagreed that the law prohibits discounts if there is a reasonable possibility of injury to competition. He said the law requires that the record "show a reasonable *probability*" of injury. His interpretation would have required a greater degree of proof of injury to competition before a discriminatory price would be declared unlawful.

FEDERAL TRADE COMMISSION v. MORTON SALT CO.

334 U.S. 37 (1948)

MR. JUSTICE BLACK delivered the opinion of the Court.

The Federal Trade Commission, after a hearing, found that the respondent, which manufactures and sells table salt in interstate commerce, had discriminated in price between different purchasers of like grades and qualities, and concluded that such discriminations were in violation of §2 of the Clayton Act, . . . , as amended by the Robinson-Patman Act, . . . It accordingly issued a cease and desist order. . . . Upon petition of the respondent the Circuit Court of Appeals, with one judge dissenting, set aside the Commission's findings and order, . . .

Respondent manufactures several different brands of table salt and sells them directly to (1) wholesalers or jobbers, who in turn resell to the retail trade, and (2) large retailers, including chain store retailers. Respondent sells its finest brand of table salt, known as Blue Label, on what it terms a standard quantity discount system available to all customers. Under this system the purchasers pay a delivered price and the cost to both wholesale and retail purchasers of this brand differs according to the quantities bought. These prices are as follows, after making allowance for rebates and discounts:

	Per case
Less-than-carload purchases	$1.60
Carload purchases	1.50
5,000-case purchases in any consecutive 12 months	1.40
50,000-case purchases in any consecutive 12 months	1.35

Only five companies have ever bought sufficient quantities of respondent's salt to obtain the $1.35 per case price. These companies could buy in such quantities because they operate large chains of retail stores in various parts of the country. As a result of this low price these five companies have been able to sell Blue Label salt at retail cheaper than wholesale purchasers from respondent could reasonably sell the same brand of salt to independently operated retail stores, many of whom competed with the local outlets of the five chain stores.

Respondent's table salts, other than Blue Label, are also sold under a quantity discount system differing slightly from that used in selling Blue Label. Sales of these other brands in less-than-carload lots are made at list price plus freight from plant to destination. Carload purchasers are granted approximately a 5 per cent discount; approximately a 10 per cent discount is granted to purchasers who buy as much as $50,000 worth of all brands of salt in any consecutive twelve-month period. Respondent's quantity discounts on Blue Label and on other table salts were enjoyed by certain wholesalers and retailers who competed with other wholesalers and retailers to whom these discounts were refused. . . .

FIRST Respondent's basic contention, which it argues this case hinges upon, is that its "standard quantity discounts, available to all on equal terms, as contrasted, for example, to hidden or special rebates, allowances, prices or discounts, are not discriminatory within the meaning of the Robinson-Patman Act." Theoretically, these discounts are equally available to all, but functionally they are not. For as the record indicates (if reference to it on this point were necessary) no single independent retail grocery store, and probably no single wholesaler, bought as many as 50,000 cases or as much as $50,000 worth of table salt in one year. Furthermore, the record shows that, while certain purchasers were enjoying one or more of respondent's standard quantity discounts, some of their competitors made purchases in such small quantities that they could not qualify for any of respondent's discounts, even those based on carload shipments. The legislative history of the Robinson-Patman Act makes it abundantly clear that Congress considered it to be an evil that a large buyer could secure a competitive advantage over a small buyer solely because of the large buyer's quantity purchasing ability. The Robinson-Patman Act was passed to deprive a large buyer of such advantages except to the extent that a lower price could be justified by reason of a seller's diminished costs due to quantity manufacture, delivery or sale, or by reason of the seller's good faith effort to meet a competitor's equally low price.

Section 2 of the original Clayton Act had included a proviso that nothing contained in it should prevent "discrimination in price . . . on account of differences in the grade, quality, or quantity of the commodity sold, or that makes only due allowance for difference in the cost of selling or transportation. . . ." That section has been construed as permitting quantity discounts, such as those here, without regard to the amount of the seller's actual savings in cost attributable to quantity sales or quantity deliveries. *Goodyear Tire & Rubber Co.* v. *Federal Trade Comm'n,* . . . The House Committee Report on the Robinson-Patman Act considered that the Clayton Act's proviso allowing quantity discounts so weakened §2 "as to render it inadequate, if not almost a nullity." The Committee considered the present Robinson-Patman amendment to §2 "of great importance." Its purpose was to limit "the use of quality price differentials to the sphere of actual cost differences. . . ." And it was in furtherance of this avowed purpose—to protect competition from all price differentials except those based in full on cost savings—that §2 (a) of the amendment provided "That nothing herein contained shall prevent differentials which make only due allowance for differences in the cost of manufacture, sale, or delivery resulting from the differing methods or quantities in which such commodities are to such purchasers sold or delivered." . . .

SECOND The Government interprets the opinion of the Circuit Court of Appeals as having held that in order to establish "discrimination in price" under the Act the burden rested on the Commission to prove that respondent's quantity discount differentials were not justified by its cost savings. Respondent does not so understand the Court of Appeals decision, and furthermore admits that no such burden rests on the Commission. We agree that it does not. First, the general rule of statutory construction that the burden of proving justification or exemption under a special exception to the prohibitions of a statute generally rests on one who claims its benefits, requires that respondent undertake this proof under the proviso of §2 (a). Secondly, §2 (b) of the Act specifically imposes the burden of showing justification upon one who is shown to have discriminated in prices. . . .

THIRD   It is argued that the findings fail to show that respondent's discriminatory discounts had in fact caused injury to competition. There are specific findings that such injuries had resulted from respondent's discounts, although the statute does not require the Commission to find that injury has actually resulted. The statute requires no more than that the effect of the prohibited price discriminations "may be substantially to lessen competition . . . or to injure, destroy, or prevent competition." After a careful consideration of this provision of the Robinson-Patman Act, we have said that "the statute does not require that the discriminations must in fact have harmed competition, but only that there is a reasonable possibility that they 'may' have such an effect." *Corn Products Co.* v. *Federal Trade Comm'n,* . . .

FOURTH   It is urged that the evidence is inadequate to support the Commission's findings of injury to competition. As we have pointed out, however, the Commission is authorized by the Act to bar discriminatory prices upon the "reasonable possibility" that different prices for like goods to competing purchasers may have the defined effect on competition. That respondent's quantity discounts did result in price differentials between competing purchasers sufficient in amount to influence their resale prices of salt was shown by evidence. This showing in itself is adequate to support the Commission's appropriate findings that the effect of such price discriminations "may be substantially to lessen competition . . . and to injure, destroy, and prevent competition." . . .

It is also argued that respondent's less-than-carload sales are very small in comparison with the total volume of its business and for that reason we should reject the Commission's finding that the effect of the carload discrimination may substantially lessen competition and may injure competition between purchasers who are granted and those who are denied this discriminatory discount. To support this argument, reference is made to the fact that salt is a small item in most wholesale and retail businesses and in consumers' budgets. For several reasons we cannot accept this contention.

There are many articles in a grocery store that, considered separately, are comparatively small parts of a merchant's stock. Congress intended to protect a merchant from competitive injury attributable to discriminatory prices on any or all goods sold in interstate commerce, whether the particular goods constituted a major or minor portion of his stock. Since a grocery store consists of many comparatively small articles, there is no possible way effectively to protect a grocer from discriminatory prices except by applying the prohibitions of the Act to each individual article in the store.

Furthermore, in enacting the Robinson-Patman Act, Congress was especially concerned with protecting small businesses which were unable to buy in quantities, such as the merchants here who purchased in less-than-carload lots. To this end it undertook to strengthen this very phase of the old Clayton Act. . . .

The judgment of the Circuit Court of Appeals is reversed and the proceedings are remanded to that court to be disposed of in conformity with this opinion.

Reversed.

MR. JUSTICE JACKSON, with whom MR. JUSTICE FRANKFURTER joins, dissenting in part.

While I agree with much of the Court's opinion, I cannot accept its most significant feature, which is a new interpretation of the Robinson-Patman Act that will sanction prohibition of any discounts if "there is a reasonable *possibility* that they 'may' have" the effect to wit: to lessen, injure, destroy or prevent competition. [Emphasis supplied.] I think the law as written by the Congress and as always interpreted by this Court requires that the record show a reasonable *probability* of that effect. The difference, as every lawyer knows, is not unimportant and in many cases would be decisive.

The law rarely authorizes judgments on proof of mere possibilities. . . .

The Court uses overtones of hostility to all quantity discounts, which I do not find in the Act, but they are translated into a rule which is fatal to any discount the Commission sees fit to attack. . . .

Injury to Competition

Section 2 of the Clayton Act, as amended by the Robinson-Patman Act, declares it unlawful to discriminate in price "where the effect of such discrimination may be substantially to lessen competition . . . or to injure, destroy, or prevent competition . . ." Therefore, price discrimination is not unlawful unless there is an *injury to competition*. Actual injury is not required; the statute requires only that the effect of the discrimination "may" be substantially to lessen competition. In the *Morton Salt* case, reported above, the Supreme Court interpreted that key phrase to require only that there be a reasonable possibility that injury to competition will result.

In 1967 the Supreme Court decided the *Utah Pie* case involving the issue of injury to competition. Utah Pie Company in 1958 had 66.5 per cent of the frozen dessert pie market in the Salt Lake City area. It was a relatively small company, selling only in Utah and surrounding states. Utah Pie's major competitors were three large companies—Pet, Carnation, and Continental Baking. A price war ensued driving Utah's market share down to 45.5 per cent and its price of frozen pies down from $4.15 to $2.75 per dozen; Pet's went from $4.92 to $3.46; Carnation's dropped from $4.82 to $3.46; and Continental's prices declined from more than $5.00 to a low of $2.85 per dozen. The market share of the three large companies increased. Utah Pie brought a suit for treble damages against the companies, charging a conspiracy under the Sherman Act and a violation of Section 2 of the Clayton Act.

The Supreme Court, in finding for Utah Pie, indicated that a reasonable possibility of injury to competition can exist even though the volume of sales is increasing and some competitors continue to make a profit. The Court said: "We believe that the Act reaches price discrimination that erodes competition as much as it does price competition that is intended to have immediate destructive impact."

In a dissenting opinion, Justice Stewart stated that Utah Pie had a quasi-monopolistic share of the market. He said that "if we assume that the price discrimination proven against [Pet, Carnation, and Continental] had any effect on competition, that effect must have been beneficent."

UTAH PIE COMPANY v. CONTINENTAL BAKING CO. et al.

386 U.S. 685 (1967)

MR. JUSTICE WHITE delivered the opinion of the Court.

This suit for treble damages and injunction . . . was brought by petitioner, Utah Pie Company, against respondents, Continental Baking Company, Carnation Company and Pet Milk Company. The complaint charged a conspiracy under §§1 and 2 of the Sherman Act, . . . and violations by each respondent of §2(a) of the Clayton Act as amended by the Robinson-Patman Act, . . . The jury found for respondents on the conspiracy charge and for petitioner on the price discrimination charge. Judgment was entered for petitioner for damages and attorneys' fees and respondents appealed on several grounds. The Court of Appeals reversed, addressing itself to the single issue of whether the evidence against each of the respondents was sufficient to support a finding of probable injury to competition within the meaning of §2(a) and holding that it was not. . . . We granted certiorari. . . . We reverse.

The product involved is frozen dessert pies—apple, cherry, boysenberry, peach, pumpkin, and mince. The period covered by the suit comprised the years 1958, 1959, and 1960 and the first eight months of 1961. Petitioner is a Utah corporation which for 30 years has been baking pies in its plant in Salt Lake City and selling them in Utah and surrounding States. It entered the frozen pie business in late 1957. It was immediately successful with its new line and built a new plant in Salt Lake City in 1958. The frozen pie market was a rapidly expanding one: 57,060 dozen frozen pies were sold in the Salt Lake City market in 1958, 111,729 dozen in 1959, 184,569 dozen in 1960, and 266,908 dozen in 1961. Utah's share of this market in those years was 66.5%, 34.3%, 45.5%, and 45.3% respectively, its sales volume steadily increasing over the four years. Its financial position also improved. Petitioner is not, however, a large company. At the time of the trial, petitioner operated with only 18 employees, nine of whom were members of the Rigby family, which controlled the business. Its net worth increased from $31,651.98 on October 31, 1957, to $68,802.13 on October 31, 1961. . . .

Each of the respondents is a large company and each of them is a major factor in the frozen pie market in one or more of the regions of the country. Each entered the Salt Lake City frozen pie market before petitioner began freezing dessert pies. None of them had a plant in Utah. . . . The Salt Lake City market was supplied by respondents chiefly from their California operations. They sold primarily on a delivered price basis. . . .

We deal first with petitioner's case against the Pet Milk Company. . . . Pet's initial emphasis was on quality, but in the face of competition from regional and local companies and in an expanding market where price proved to be a crucial factor, Pet was forced to take steps to reduce the price of its pies to the ultimate consumer. . . .

First, Pet successfully concluded an arrangement with Safeway, which is one of the three largest customers for frozen pies in the Salt Lake market, whereby it would sell frozen pies to Safeway under the latter's own "Belair" label at a price significantly lower than it was selling its comparable "Pet-Ritz" brand in the same Salt Lake market and elsewhere. . . .

Second, it introduced a 20-ounce economy pie under the "Swiss Miss" label and began selling the new pie in the Salt Lake market in August 1960 at prices ranging from $3.25 to $3.30 for the remainder of the period. This pie was at times sold at a lower price in the Salt Lake City market than it was sold in other markets.

Third, Pet became more competitive with respect to the prices for its "Pet-Ritz" proprietary label. For 18 of the relevant 44 months its offering price for Pet-Ritz pies was $4 per dozen or lower, and $3.70 or lower for six of these months. According to the Court of Appeals, in seven of the 44 months Pet's prices in Salt Lake were lower than prices charged in the California markets. This was true although selling in Salt Lake involved a 30- to 35-cent freight cost.

The Court of Appeals first concluded that Pet's price differential on sales to Safeway must be put aside in considering injury to competition because in its view of the evidence the differential had been completely cost justified and because Utah would not in any event have been able to enjoy the Safeway custom. Second, it concluded that the remaining discriminations on "Pet-Ritz" and "Swiss Miss" pies were an insufficient predicate on which the jury could have found a reasonably possible injury either to Utah Pie as a competitive force or to competition generally.

We disagree with the Court of Appeals in several respects. First, there was evidence from which the jury could have found considerably more price discrimination by Pet with respect to "Pet-Ritz" and "Swiss Miss" pies than was considered by the Court of Appeals. In addition to the seven months during which Pet's prices in Salt Lake were lower than prices in the California markets, there was evidence from which the jury could reasonably have found that in 10 additional months the Salt Lake City prices for "Pet-Ritz" pies were discriminatory as compared with sales in western markets other than California. Likewise, with respect to "Swiss Miss" pies, there was evidence in the record from which the jury could have found that in five of the 13 months during which the "Swiss Miss" pies were sold prior to the filing of this suit, prices in Salt Lake City were lower than those charged by Pet in either California or some other western market.

Second, with respect to Pet's Safeway business, the burden of proving cost justification was on Pet and, in our view, reasonable men could have found that Pet's lower priced, "Bel-air" sales to Safeway were not cost justified in their entirety. . . .

With respect to whether Utah would have enjoyed Safeway's business absent the Pet contract with Safeway, it seems clear that whatever the fact is in this regard, it is not determinative of the impact of that contract on competitors other than Utah and on competition generally. There were other companies seeking the Safeway business, including Continental and Carnation, whose pies may have been excluded from the Safeway shelves by what the jury could have found to be discriminatory sales to Safeway. . . .

Third, the Court of Appeals almost entirely ignored other evidence which provides material support for the jury's conclusion that Pet's behavior satisfied the statutory test regarding competitive injury. This evidence bore on the issue of Pet's predatory intent to injure Utah Pie. As an initial matter, the jury could have concluded that Pet's discriminatory pricing was aimed at Utah Pie; Pet's own management, as early as 1959, identified Utah Pie as an "unfavorable factor," one which "d[u]g holes in our operation" and posed a constant "check" on Pet's performance in the Salt Lake City market. Moreover, Pet candidly admitted that during the period when it was establishing its relationship with Safeway, it sent into Utah Pie's plant an industrial spy to seek information that would be of use to Pet in convincing Safeway that Utah Pie was not worthy of its custom. Pet denied that it ever in fact used what it had learned against Utah Pie in competing with Safeway's business. . . .

Petitioner's case against Continental is not complicated. Continental was a substantial factor in the market in 1957. But its sales of frozen 22-ounce dessert pies, sold under the "Morton" brand, amounted to only 1.3% of the market in 1958, 2.9% in 1959, and 1.8% in 1960. Its problems were primarily that of cost and in turn that of price, the controlling factor in the market. In late 1960 it worked out a co-packing arrangement in California by which fruit would be processed directly from the trees into the finished pie without large intermediate packing, storing, and shipping expenses. Having improved its position, it attempted to increase its share of the Salt Lake City market by utilizing a local broker and offering short-term price concessions in varying amounts. Its efforts for seven months were not spectacularly successful. Then in June 1961, it took the steps which are the heart of petitioner's complaint against it. Effective for the last two weeks of June it offered its 22-ounce frozen apple pies in the Utah area at $2.85 per dozen. It was then selling the same pies at substantially higher prices in other markets. The Salt Lake City price was less than its direct cost plus an allocation for overhead. Utah's going price at the time for its 24-ounce "Frost 'N' Flame" apple pie sold to Associated Grocers was $3.10 per dozen, and for its "Utah" brand $3.40 per dozen. . . . Utah's response was immediate. It reduced its price on all of its apple pies to $2.75 per dozen. . . . Continental's total sales of frozen pies increased from 3,350 dozen in 1960 to 18,800 dozen in 1961. Its market share increased from 1.8% in 1960 to 8.3% in 1961. The Court of Appeals concluded that Continental's conduct had had only minimal effect, that it had not injured or weakened Utah Pie as a competitor, that it had not substantially lessened competition and that there was no reasonable possibility that it would do so in the future.

We again differ with the Court of Appeals. Its opinion that Utah was not damaged as a competitive force apparently rested on the fact that Utah's sales volume continued to climb in 1961 and on the court's own factual conclusion that Utah was not deprived of any pie business which it otherwise might have had. But this retrospective assessment fails to note that Continental's discriminatory below-cost price caused Utah Pie to reduce its price to $2.75. The jury was entitled to consider the potential impact of Continental's price reduction absent any responsive price cut by Utah Pie. Price was a major factor in the Salt Lake City market. . . . It could also reasonably conclude that a competitor who is forced to reduce his price to a new all-time low in a market of declining prices will in time feel the financial pinch and will be a less effective competitive force. . . .

. . . We think there was sufficient evidence from which the jury could find a violation of §2(a) by Continental.

The Carnation Company entered the frozen dessert pie business in 1955 through the acquisition of "Mrs. Lee's Pies" which was then engaged in manufacturing and selling frozen pies in Utah and elsewhere under the "Simple Simon" label. Carnation also quickly found the market extremely sensitive to price. Carnation decided, however, not to enter an economy product in the market, and during the period covered by this suit it offered only its quality "Simple Simon" brand. Its primary method of meeting competition in its markets was to offer a variety of discounts and other reductions, and the technique was not unsuccessful. In 1958, for example, Carnation enjoyed 10.3% of the Salt Lake City market, and although its volume of pies sold in that market increased nearly 100% in the next year, its percentage of the market temporarily slipped to 8.6%. However, 1960 was a turnaround year for Carnation in the Salt Lake City market; it more than doubled its volume of sales over the preceding year and thereby gained 12.1% of the market. And while the price structure in the market deteriorated rapidly in 1961 Carnation's position remained important. . . .

. . . We cannot say that the evidence precluded the jury from finding it reasonably possible that Carnation's conduct would injure competition.

Section 2(a) does not forbid price competition which will probably injure or lessen competition by eliminating competitors, discouraging entry into the market or enhancing the market shares of the dominant sellers. But Congress has established some ground rules for the game. Sellers may not sell like goods to different purchasers at different prices if the result may be to injure competition in either the sellers or the buyers market unless such discriminations are justified as permitted by the Act. This case concerns the sellers market. In this context, the Court of Appeals placed heavy emphasis on the fact that Utah Pie constantly increased its sales volume and continued to make a profit. But we disagree with its apparent view that there is no reasonably possible injury to competition as long as the volume of sales in a particular market is expanding and at least some of the competitors in the market continue to operate at a profit. Nor do we think that the Act only comes into play to regulate the conduct of price discriminators when their discriminatory prices consistently undercut other competitors. It is true that many of the primary line cases that have reached the courts have involved blatant predatory price discriminations employed with the hope of immediate destruction of a particular competitor. On the question of injury to competition such cases present courts with no difficulty, for such pricing is clearly within the heart of the proscription of the Act. . . . We believe that the Act reaches price discrimination that erodes competition as much as it does price discrimination that is intended to have immediate destructive impact. In this case, the evidence shows a drastically declining price structure which the jury could rationally attribute to continued or sporadic price discrimination. The jury was entitled to conclude that "the effect of such discrimination," by each of these respondents, "may be substantially to lessen competition . . . or to injure, destroy, or prevent competition with any person who either grants or knowingly receives the benefit of such discrimination. . . ." The statutory test is one that necessarily looks forward on the basis of proven conduct in the past. Proper application of that standard here requires reversal of the judgment of the Court of Appeals. . . .

It is so ordered.

THE CHIEF JUSTICE took no part in the decision of this case.

MR. JUSTICE STEWART, with whom MR. JUSTICE HARLAN joins, dissenting.

I would affirm the judgment, agreeing substantially with the reasoning of the Court of Appeals as expressed in the thorough and conscientious opinion of Judge Phillips.

There is only one issue in this case in its present posture: Whether the respondents engaged in price discrimination "where the effect of such discrimination may be substantially to lessen competition or tend to create a monopoly in any line of commerce, or to injure, destroy, or prevent competition with any person who either grants or knowingly receives the benefit of such discrimination. . . ." Phrased more simply, did the respondents' actions have the anticompetitive effect required by the statute as an element of a cause of action?

The Court's own description of the Salt Lake City frozen pie market from 1958 through 1961, shows that the answer to that question must be no. In 1958 Utah Pie had a quasi-monopolistic 66.5% of the market. In 1961—after the alleged predations of the respondents—Utah Pie still had a commanding 45.3%, Pet had 29.4%, and the remainder of the market was divided almost equally between Continental, Carnation, and other, small local bakers. Unless we disregard the lessons so laboriously learned in scores of Sherman and Clayton Act cases, the 1961 situation has to be considered more competitive than that of 1958. Thus, if we assume that the price discrimination proven against the respondents had any effect on competition, that effect must have been beneficent.

That the Court has fallen into the error of reading the Robinson-Patman Act as protecting competitors, instead of competition, can be seen from its unsuccessful attempt to distinguish cases relied upon by the respondents. Those cases are said to be inapposite because they involved "no general decline in price structure," and no "lasting impact upon prices." But lower prices are the hallmark of intensified competition.

The Court of Appeals squarely identified the fallacy which the Court today embraces:

> . . . a contention that Utah Pie was entitled to hold the extraordinary market share percentage of 66.5, attained in 1958, falls of its own dead weight. To approve such a contention would be to hold that Utah Pie was entitled to maintain a position which approached, if it did not in fact amount to a monopoly, and could not exist in the face of proper and healthy competition. . . .

I cannot hold that Utah Pie's monopolistic position was protected by the federal antitrust laws from effective price competition, and I therefore respectfully dissent.

"Good Faith" Defense

The original Section 2 of the Clayton Act provided that "nothing herein contained shall prevent . . . discrimination in price . . . made in good faith to meet competition . . . ." Robinson-Patman amended this part so that it now reads: "Nothing herein contained shall prevent a seller rebutting the prima facie case thus made by showing that his lower price . . . was made in good faith to meet an equally low price of a competitor. . . ." The wording of the statute makes it clear that the "good faith" claim can be used only to defend one's market share by *meeting* a competitor's price. "Good faith" does not sanction aggressive price discrimination used to increase the market share and thereby inflict injury on competition. The "good faith" defense is a complete one, regardless of injury to competition, if the required conditions are satisfied.

Standard Oil of Indiana successfully asserted the "good faith" defense against the charge of illegal price discrimination. Standard Oil sold gasoline to four large "jobbers" in Detroit at 1.5 cents per gallon less than its tank-wagon prices to service station customers. The price differential apparently could not be justified as a cost-saving quantity discount. Standard Oil presented evidence that its price to the jobbers was made in order to retain them as customers and in good faith to meet the equally low price of a competitor. The Federal Trade Commission found against Standard Oil and issued a cease-and-desist order. In finding in favor of Standard Oil, the Supreme Court, speaking through Justice Burton, said that the "heart of our national economic policy long has been faith in the value of competition. . . . Congress did not seek by the Robinson-Patman Act . . . so radically to curtail it that a seller would have no . . . right of self-defense against a price raid by a competitor." After being remanded to the FTC for further findings, the case was finally concluded in 1958.[5]

STANDARD OIL CO. v. FEDERAL TRADE COMMISSION

340 U.S. 231 (1951)

MR. JUSTICE BURTON delivered the opinion of the Court.

In this case the Federal Trade Commission challenged the right of the Standard Oil Company, under the Robinson-Patman Act, to sell gasoline to four comparatively large "jobber" customers in Detroit at a less price per gallon than it sold like gasoline to many comparatively small service station customers in the same area. The company's defenses were that (1) the sales involved were not in interstate commerce and (2) its lower price to the jobbers was justified because made to retain them as customers and in good faith to meet an equally low price of a competitor. The Commission, with one member dissenting, ordered the company to cease and desist from making such a price differential. . . . The Court of Appeals slightly modified the order and required its enforcement as modified. . . . We granted certiorari on petition of the company because the case presents an important issue under the Robinson-Patman Act which has not been settled by this Court. . . .

FACTS

. . . Since the effective date of the Robinson-Patman Act, June 19, 1936, petitioner has sold its Red Crown gasoline to its "jobber" customers at its tank-car prices. Those prices have been 1½¢ per gallon less than its

[5] FTC v. Standard Oil Co., 355 U.S. 396.

tank-wagon prices to service station customers for identical gasoline in the same area. In practice, the service stations have resold the gasoline at the prevailing retail service station prices. Each of petitioner's so-called "jobber" customers has been free to resell its gasoline at retail or wholesale. Each, at some time, has resold some of it at retail. One now sells it only at retail. The others now resell it largely at wholesale. As to resale prices, two of the "jobbers" have resold their gasoline only at the prevailing wholesale or retail rates. The other two, however, have reflected, in varying degrees, petitioner's reductions in the cost of the gasoline to them by reducing their resale prices of that gasoline below the prevailing rates. The effect of these reductions has thus reached competing retail service stations in part through retail stations operated by the "jobbers" and in part through retail stations which purchased gasoline from the "jobbers" at less than the prevailing tank-wagon prices. The Commission found that such reduced resale prices "have resulted in injuring, destroying, and preventing competition between said favored dealers and retail dealers in respondent's [petitioner's] gasoline and other major brands of gasoline. . . ." The distinctive characteristics of these "jobbers" are that each (1) maintains sufficient bulk storage to take delivery of gasoline in tank-car quantities (of 8,000 to 12,000 gallons) rather than in tank-wagon quantities (of 700 to 800 gallons) as is customary for service stations; (2) owns and operates tank wagons and other facilities for delivery of gasoline to service stations; (3) has an established business sufficient to insure purchases of from one to two million gallons a year; and (4) has adequate credit responsibility. While the cost of petitioner's sales and deliveries of gasoline to each of these four "jobbers" is no doubt less, per gallon, than the cost of its sales and deliveries of like gasoline to its service station customers in the same area, there is no finding that such difference accounts for the entire reduction in price made by petitioner to these "jobbers," and we proceed on the assumption that it does not entirely account for that difference.

Petitioner placed its reliance upon evidence offered to show that its lower price to each jobber was made in order to retain that jobber as a customer and in good faith to meet an equally low price offered by one or more competitors. . . .

The Sales Were Made in Interstate Commerce

In order for the sales here involved to come under the Clayton Act, as amended by the Robinson-Patman Act, they must have been made in interstate commerce. The Commission and the court below agree that the sales were so made. . . .

Facts determining this were found by the Commission as follows:

Petitioner is an Indiana corporation, whose principal office is in Chicago. Its gasoline is obtained from fields in Kansas, Oklahoma, Texas and Wyoming. Its refining plant is at Whiting, Indiana. It distributes its products in 14 middle western states, including Michigan. . . . Gasoline delivered to customers in Detroit, upon individual orders for it, is taken from the gasoline at the terminal in interstate commerce en route for delivery in that area. Such sales are well within the jurisdictional requirements of the Act. . . .

There Should Be a Finding as to Whether or Not Petitioner's Price Reduction Was Made in Good Faith to Meet a Lawful Equally Low Price of a Competitor

Petitioner presented evidence tending to prove that its tank-car price was made to each "jobber" in order to retain that "jobber" as a customer and in good faith to meet a lawful and equally low price of a competitor. Petitioner sought to show that it succeeded in retaining these customers, although the tank-car price which it offered them merely approached or matched, and did not undercut, the lower prices offered them by several competitors of petitioner. The trial examiner made findings on the point but the Commission declined to do so, saying:

> Based on the record in this case the Commission . . . does not attempt to find the facts regarding those matters because, even though the lower prices in question may have been made by respondent in good faith to meet the lower prices of competitors, this does not constitute a defense in the face of affirmative proof that the effect of the discrimination was to injure, destroy and prevent competition with the retail stations operated by the said named dealers and with stations operated by their retailer-customers. . . .

There is no doubt that under the Clayton Act, before its amendment by the Robinson-Patman Act, this evidence would have been material and, if accepted, would have established a complete defense to the charge of unlawful discrimination. . . .

The question before us, therefore, is whether the amendments made by the Robinson-Patman Act deprived those facts of their previously recognized effectiveness as a defense. . . .

This right of a seller, under §2(b), to meet in good faith an equally low price of a competitor has been considered here before. . . . There would have been no occasion thus to review it under the theory now contended for by the Commission. While this Court did not sustain the seller's defense in either case, it did unquestionably recognize the relevance of the evidence in support of that defense. . . .

In addition, there has been widespread understanding that, under the Robinson-Patman Act, it is a complete defense to a charge of price discrimination for the seller to show that its price differential has been made in good faith to meet a lawful and equally low price of a competitor. . . . We see no reason to depart now from that interpretation. . . .

The heart of our national economic policy long has been faith in the value of competition. In the Sherman and Clayton Acts, as well as in the Robinson-Patman Act, "Congress was dealing with competition, which it sought to protect, and monopoly, which it sought to prevent." . . . Congress did not seek by the Robinson-Patman Act either to abolish competition or so radically to curtail it that a seller would have no substantial right of self-defense against a price raid by a competitor. For example, if a large customer requests his seller to meet a temptingly lower price offered to him by one of his seller's competitors, the seller may well find it essential, as a matter of business survival, to meet that price rather than to lose the customer. It might be that this customer is the seller's only available market for the major portion of the seller's product, and that the loss of this customer would result in forcing a much higher unit cost and higher sales price upon the seller's other customers. There is nothing to show a congressional purpose, in such a situation, to compel the seller to choose only between ruinously cutting its prices to all its customers to match the price offered to one, or refusing to meet the competition and then ruinously raising its prices to its remaining customers to cover increased unit costs. There is, on the other hand, plain language and established practice which permits a seller, through §2(b), to retain a customer by realistically meeting in good faith the price offered to that customer, without necessarily changing the seller's price to its other customers. . . .

. . . On the other hand, the proviso is readily understandable as simply continuing in effect a defense which is equally absolute, but more limited in scope than that which existed under §2 of the original Clayton Act.

The judgment of the Court of Appeals, accordingly, is reversed and the case is remanded to that court with instructions to remand it to the Federal Trade Commission to make findings in conformity with this opinion.

It is so ordered.

Mr. Justice Minton took no part in the consideration or decision of this case.

MR. JUSTICE REED, dissenting. . . .

THE CHIEF JUSTICE and MR. JUSTICE BLACK join in this dissent.

The "good faith" defense was again asserted in the *Sun Oil* case decided in 1963. McLean was a lessee and operator of a Sunoco gas station in Jacksonville, Florida. Super Test, a cut-rate gasoline company, opened a station across the street from McLean. Super Test sporadically reduced its price below the "normal" two-cent differential between its price and that of the major brands. McLean's sales suffered substantially. Sun Oil, to help McLean meet the competition of Super Test, lowered its price to him, but did not lower its price to the other thirty-seven Sunoco stations in the Jacksonville area.

After a hearing, the Federal Trade Commission decided that the defense of "good faith to meet an equally low price of a competitor" was unavailable to Sun Oil under the circumstances. The court of appeals reversed the Commission. In reversing the court of appeals, the Supreme Court said that the "phrase 'equally low price of a competitor' would seem to refer to the price of a competitor of the seller who grants, and not of the buyer who receives, the discriminatory price cut." But Sun Oil contended that McLean, with his limited resources, could not survive in a gasoline price war. Relying on the Act's general purpose of protecting the small businessman, Sun Oil argued that the statutory policy supported its price cutting aid to McLean. The Court replied that to allow a supplier to aid his retailer against another retailer would "convert the normal competitive struggle between retailers into an unequal contest between one retailer and the combination of another retailer and his supplier [and] is hardly an element of reasonable and fair competition."

FEDERAL TRADE COMMISSION v. SUN OIL CO.

371 U.S. 505 (1963)

MR. JUSTICE GOLDBERG delivered the opinion of the Court.

This case grows out of a gasoline "price war" in Jacksonville, Florida. The question presented is whether a refiner-supplier of gasoline charged with the granting of a price discrimination in violation of §2(a) of the Clayton Act, as amended by the Robinson-Patman Act, has available to it, under §2(b) of the Act, the defense that the discriminatory lower price was given "in good faith to meet an equally low price of a competitor," when the gasoline refiner-supplier shows that it gave the discriminatory price to only one of a number of its independently owned retail station customers in a particular region in order to enable that station to meet price reductions of a competing service station owned and operated by a retail chain selling a different brand of gasoline.

The Federal Trade Commission held the §2(b) defense to be unavailable under such circumstances. . . . The Court of Appeals for the Fifth Circuit reversed, . . . and this Court granted certiorari, . . . to review this difficult and important question concerning the scope and application of the §2(b) defense.

The relevant facts are not seriously disputed.

Respondent, Sun Oil Company ("Sun"), is a New Jersey corporation and a major integrated refiner and distributor of petroleum products, including gasoline. At the time of the alleged violation here in issue, Sun marketed in 18 States a single grade of gasoline sold under the trade name "Sunoco." Sun does not ordinarily sell directly to the motorist, but usually distributes its gasoline and other related products to the consuming public through retail service station operators who lease their stations from it.

In 1955, Gilbert McLean was the lessee and operator of a Sunoco gas station located on the corner of 19th and Pearl Streets in Jacksonville, Florida. He was one of Sun's 38 retail dealers in the Jacksonville area, . . .

Commencing operation of the station in February 1955, McLean bought gasoline from Sun at 24.1 cents per gallon and resold it at 28.9 cents per gallon to the motoring public; the other Sun dealers in Jacksonville purchased from Sun at the same price and obtained the same 4.8-cent-per-gallon margin of gross profit.

In June 1955, about four months after McLean began business, the Super Test Oil Company, which operated about 65 retail service stations, opened a Super Test station diagonally across the street from McLean and began selling its "regular" grade of gasoline at 26.9 cents per gallon. It appears that this was Super Test's first and only station in Jacksonville. The record does not disclose that Super Test was anything more than a retail dealer; nor does it indicate the source from which Super Test obtained its gasoline.

The two-cent-per-gallon difference in price between McLean and Super Test represented the "normal" price differential then prevailing in the area between "major" and "non-major" brands of gasoline. This "normal" differential represents the price spread which can obtain between the two types of gasoline without major competitive repercussions. Thus, McLean was apparently not adversely affected to any substantial degree by this first-posted price of Super Test.

Thereafter, however, Super Test sporadically reduced its price at its Jacksonville station, usually on weekends. Some of the price cuts were advertised in the local newspaper and all were posted on curbside signs. For example, on August 27, 1955, the Super Test station reduced its price to 21.9 cents a gallon and on the following day to 20.9 cents per gallon. While these lower prices were normally short-lived, at least one was maintained for a week. On the occasion of each price reduction by the Super Test station, McLean's sales of Sunoco declined substantially.

When Super Test began lowering its price below the normal two-cent differential, McLean, who was maintaining his price of 28.9 cents per gallon, from time to time protested to Sun and sought relief in the form of a price concession from it. For about four months, Sun took no action, but in December 1955, after further periodic price reductions by Super Test and a complaint by McLean that he would be forced out of business absent help from Sun, Sun told McLean that it would come to his aid in the event of further price cuts. When, on December 27, 1955, Super Test dropped its price for "regular" gasoline to 24.9 cents per gallon, McLean told Sun that he would have to post a price of 25.9 cents in order to meet the competition. On the same day, Sun gave McLean a price allowance or discount of 1.7 cents per gallon. . . . In lowering his price to within one cent of Super Test's, McLean absorbed 1.3 cents and Sun 1.7 cents of the per gallon price reduction. No corresponding price reduction was given by Sun to any of its other dealers in the area. . . .

. . . At about the same time, a general price war developed in the Jacksonville area and several other suppliers made price reductions. Sun then dropped its price equally to all of its dealers in the area. . . .

During the period between the December 27, 1955, price reduction by McLean and the February 1956 date on which Sun extended its discount to all of its area dealers, a number of Sun dealers located at distances varying from less than a mile (about 11 blocks) to about three and one-half miles from McLean's station suffered substantial declines in sales of Sunoco gasoline. Some of these Sun dealers who testified below said that they saw former customers of theirs buying gas from McLean and two declared that their customers had told them that they switched to McLean because of his lower price. Some of these dealers complained to Sun about the favored treatment accorded McLean and, prior to the February general price reductions, unsuccessfully sought compensating discounts from Sun for themselves. . . .

In September 1956 the Federal Trade Commission filed a complaint against Sun charging it with illegal price discrimination in violation of §2(a) of the Clayton Act, as amended, and with entry into a price-fixing agreement with McLean in violation of §5 of the Federal Trade Commission Act. . . . The Commission also found that there had been actual competitive injury to the nonfavored Sun dealers by virtue of Sun's discriminatory December 27 price allowance to McLean and rejected Sun's asserted defense under §2(b) of the Clayton Act because Sun was not meeting its own competition, that is a price cut by another wholesale seller . . .

Considering Super Test to be an integrated supplier-retailer of gasoline, the Court of Appeals reversed, reasoning: first, that McLean was but a "conduit" for the marketing of Sun's products and therefore Sun, as a practical matter, was really competing with Super Test for sales of its gasoline; . . .

The only issue thus before the Court is whether Sun is here entitled to avail itself of the §2(b) defense that its December 27 "lower price" to McLean was extended "in good faith to meet an equally low price of a competitor."

As indicated, the Court of Appeals assumed, . . . that Super Test was an integrated supplier-retailer of gasoline. The record does not support this conclusion, however, and therefore, as the case comes to us, availability of the §2(b) defense to Sun is determined on the assumption that Super Test was engaged solely in retail operations; . . .

Section 2(b) of the Act contains a proviso permitting a seller to rebut a *prima facie* case of discrimination in violation of §2(a) by "showing that his lower price or the furnishing of services or facilities to any purchaser or purchasers was made in good faith to meet an equally low price of a competitor, or the services or facilities furnished by a competitor." This proviso is usually referred to as the "good faith meeting competition" defense. The seller has the burden of bringing himself within the exculpating provision of §2(b), which has been interpreted to afford an absolute defense to a charge of violating §2(a), notwithstanding the existence of the statutorily prohibited anticompetitive effect, *Standard Oil Co.* v. *Federal Trade Comm'n*, . . .

Reading the words to have "their normal and customary meaning," *Schwegmann Bros.* v. *Calvert Corp.*, . . . the §2(b) phrase "equally low price of a competitor" would seem to refer to the price of a competitor of the seller who grants, and not of the buyer who receives, the discriminatory price cut. (In this case, this would mean a competitor of Sun, the refiner-supplier, and not a competitor of McLean, the retail dealer.) Were something more intended by Congress, we would have expected a more explicit recitation . . .

The fact that §2(b) permits a seller to meet the competitor's "equally low" price is similarly suggestive of an interpretation which limits application of the proviso to situations in which the seller's reduction in price is made in response to a price cut by its own competitor rather than by a competitor of its customer. Linguistically and practically, it makes but little sense to talk, for example, of a wholesaler's meeting of the "equally low" price of one of his purchaser's retail competitors. The reduced retail price of the purchaser's competitor will almost invariably be higher than the supplier's wholesale price; even in those instances in which this is not so, it cannot seriously be suggested that under §2(b) the wholesaler is entitled to reduce discriminatorily his wholesale price to the lower retail level. Such a result is not only economically unrealistic, but strains normal language use. . . .

Recognizing the incongruity of such an interpretation, and having no need to go quite so far, respondent argues merely that as a wholesaler it is protected under §2(b) when it lowers its own price sufficiently to allow its retail dealer, in turn, to reduce his retail price to meet a competitive retail offer. But this too extends the statute beyond its immediately apparent meaning; . . .

Relying on the general purpose of the Act to protect the small independent businessman, respondent Sun argues that the statutory policy supports its price-cutting action, even though discriminatory, because that action was designed to protect and preserve a small independent businessman, McLean. It is asserted that the limited resources available to McLean bar his survival in a gasoline price war of any duration. McLean's small margin of profit, his relative inability to lower his retail price because a direct function of the price he pays his supplier, here Sun, and other factors make his continued independent existence in a present-day price war wholly dependent upon receipt of aid—in the form of a price reduction—from his supplier. Whatever their accuracy, these assertions ignore the other station operators—the nearby Sun dealers competing with McLean—who were also vitally interested in the particular competitive struggle to which Sun was moved to respond by making price concessions only to McLean. These dealers were hurt, it was found below, by Sun's discriminatory price to McLean and this finding is not challenged here by Sun. . . .

. . . It is the very operators of the other Sun stations which compete with McLean who are the direct objects of protection under the Robinson-Patman Act. The basic purpose of the Act was to insure that such purchasers from a single supplier, Sun, would not be injured by that supplier's discriminatory practices. . . .

Similarly, the mere fact that McLean was a small retailer does not make the good faith defense applicable. While, as noted, the immediate and generating cause of the Robinson-Patman amendments may have been a congressional reaction to what were believed to be predatory uses of mass purchasing power by chain stores, neither the scope nor the intent of the statute was limited to that precise situation or set of circumstances. Congress sought generally to obviate price discrimination practices threatening independent merchants and businessmen, presumably from whatever source. . . .

Limiting invocation of the §2(b) defense to those situations in which the discriminatory price cut is made in response to a lower price of the seller's own competitor comports, we think, not only with the objectives of the Robinson-Patman Act but with the general antitrust policy of preserving the benefits of competition.

To allow a supplier to intervene and grant discriminatory price concessions designed to enable its customer to meet the lower price of a retail competitor who is unaided by his supplier would discourage rather than promote competition. So long as the price cutter does not receive a price "break" from his own supplier, his lawful reductions in price are presumably a function of his own superior merit and efficiency. To permit a competitor's supplier to bring his often superior economic power to bear narrowly and discriminatorily to deprive the otherwise resourceful retailer of the very fruits of his efficiency and convert the normal competitive struggle between retailers into an unequal contest between one retailer and the combination of another retailer and his supplier is hardly an element of reasonable and fair competition. We see no justification for such a result in §2(b). . . .

We see no reason to permit Sun discriminatorily to pit its greater strength at the supplier level against Super Test, which, so far as appears from the record, is able to sell its gasoline at a lower price simply because it is a more efficient merchandiser, particularly when Super Test's challenge as an "independent" may be the only meaningful source of price competition offered the "major" oil companies, of which Sun is one. . . .

Thus, consistent with overall antitrust policy and the language and very purposes of the Robinson-Patman amendments, we conclude that §2 (b) of the Act contemplates that the lower price which may be met by one who would discriminate must be the lower price of his own competitor; since there is in this record no evidence of any such price having been set, or offered to anyone, by any competitor of Sun, within the meaning of §2 (b), Sun's claim to the benefit of the good-faith meeting of competition defense must fail. Accordingly, the judgment of the Court of Appeals is

Reversed.

9

Delivered Pricing Systems

Another type of business practice that resulted in price discrimination was the use of basing points to quote delivered prices. The *delivered pricing method* is essentially one in which all the firms in an industry will only sell to their customers at a delivered price, a price that includes the f.o.b. mill price plus an additional charge for transporting the goods to the customer's place of business. Delivered pricing deprives buyers of any locational advantages, tending to make them locate near the basing point site.

Before the court decisions curtailing the use of this pricing method, it was impossible to purchase goods in certain industries on any basis other than delivered price, even if a customer were to provide his own transportation to haul away the goods from the producer's doorstep. In order to have an effective delivered pricing system, it was imperative that all firms in the industry adhere to the practice by refusing to quote prices on any other basis, and all firms had to recognize the same basing point from which transportation charges were calculated. Some industries followed single basing-point systems while others used multiple basing-point systems.

Ever since the end of World War I, when the economic effects first came to be recognized, the Federal Trade Commission had engaged in an almost continuous battle to outlaw delivered pricing systems, arguing that they involved price discrimination and were an unfair method of competition. The Commission was unsuccessful in most of its endeavors until the end of World War II when the Supreme Court finally moved to strike down delivered pricing. As a result of the decisions, the Commission was subjected to a great deal of criticism for its relentless efforts. Subsequently, several attempts were made in Congress to pass legislation that would have legalized delivered pricing. The efforts were never successful, although the veto of President Truman was required to prevent one bill from becoming law.[1]

Single Basing-Point Delivered Pricing

The *single basing-point pricing system* first gained notoriety in the steel industry—the so-called "Pittsburgh-plus" delivered price. At the turn of the century, United States Steel Corporation devised the plan of having all its mills

[1] Clair Wilcox, *Public Policies Toward Business*, 3d ed. (Homewood Ill.: Richard D. Irwin, Inc., 1966), pp. 248–49.

charge the base price at Pittsburgh plus transportation cost to the buyer's location. This delivered price was charged regardless of the actual origin of the shipment. The smaller industry members soon followed the same practice.

In 1921 the Federal Trade Commission issued a complaint against U.S. Steel, charging that this pricing method injured competition among the buyers of steel. The FTC ordered U.S. Steel to cease using the Pittsburgh-plus pricing system. U.S. Steel made a halfhearted gesture of compliance. Today the corporation uses, in effect, nonsystematic, multiple basing-point pricing.[2]

Despite the fact that delivered pricing had been practiced since before the turn of the century, the first cases to reach the Supreme Court did not come until 1945. The first one involved a single basing-point system used by the Corn Products Refining Company, a large manufacturer of glucose used extensively in candymaking.

Corn Products operated two plants, one in Chicago and the other in Kansas City. The firm was using the Chicago plant as a basing point in computing its delivered prices. This meant that candymakers in the Kansas City area had to pay the base price for glucose plus a delivery charge from Chicago to Kansas City even though shipments were made from the Kansas City plant. The FTC argued that this involved price discrimination, and the increased prices paid by the candymakers in the Kansas City area made it extremely difficult for them to compete with candymakers in the Chicago area which did not have to pay for phantom freight. Furthermore, several candymakers were induced to relocate near Chicago because of the lower price charged there for glucose.

Corn Products attempted to justify its delivered pricing system by pointing out that there was no discrimination between buyers at the *same points of delivery*. The Supreme Court rejected this plea since there is nothing in the wording of the statute that pertains to locality. Next, it was argued that delivered pricing was well known before enactment of the Robinson-Patman Act and that Congress could have outlawed the practice if it had so desired. Since there are no statements to the contrary, the intent of Congress must have been to sanction the practice. The Court would not accept this argument either. Finally, the Court observed that the law requires only *reasonable probability* that the effect of price discrimination will have an adverse effect on competition; it does not require that injury to competition has in fact occurred. Thus the first time the Supreme Court had the opportunity, it condemned single basing-point delivered pricing as a violation of the Robinson-Patman Act. And the basis for violation was discrimination in *net return* among customers, not a difference in *delivered price at the same location*.

[2] Vernon A. Mund, *Government and Business*, 4th ed. (New York: Harper & Row, 1965), pp. 244–45.

CORN PRODUCTS REFINING CO. et al. v. FEDERAL TRADE COMMISSION

324 U.S. 726 (1945)

MR. CHIEF JUSTICE STONE delivered the opinion of the Court.[3]

Petitioners, a parent corporation and its sales subsidiary, use a basing point system of pricing in their sales of glucose. They sell only at delivered prices, computed by adding to a base price at Chicago the published freight tariff from Chicago to the several points of delivery, even though deliveries are in fact made from their factory at Kansas City as well as from their Chicago factory. Consequently there is included in the delivered price on shipments from Kansas City an amount of "freight" which usually does not correspond to freight actually paid by petitioners.

The Federal Trade Commission instituted this proceeding under §11 of the Clayton Act, . . . charging that petitioners' use of this single basing point system resulted in discriminations in price between different purchasers of the glucose, and violated §2(a) of the Act, as amended by §1 of the Robinson-Patman Act, . . . The complaint also charged petitioners with other discriminations in prices, or in services rendered to favored customers, which will presently be stated in detail, all in violation of §2(a) or §2(e) of the Clayton Act, as amended. . . .

We granted certiorari, . . . because the questions involved are of importance in the administration of the Clayton Act in view of the widespread use of basing point price systems. The principal questions for decision are whether, when shipments are made from Kansas City, petitioners' basing point system results in discriminations in price between different purchasers of glucose, within the meaning of §2(a); and, if so, whether there is support in the evidence for the finding of the Commission that these discriminations have the effect on competition defined by that section. Further questions are raised as to whether the other discriminations charged violate §2(a) and §2(e).

The evidence as to petitioners' basing point system for the sale of glucose was stipulated. The Commission found from the evidence that petitioners have two plants for the manufacture of glucose or corn syrup,

[3] All the footnotes and most of the citations from the opinions of the Court have been omitted from the cases in this chapter.

one at Argo, Illinois, within the Chicago switching district, and the other at Kansas City, Missouri. . . .

Much of petitioners' glucose is sold to candy manufacturers, who are in competition with each other in the sale of their candy. Glucose is the principal ingredient in many varieties of low-priced candies, which are sold on narrow margins of profit. Customers for such candies may be diverted from one manufacturer to another by a difference in price of a small fraction of a cent per pound.

The Commission found that the higher prices paid for glucose purchased from petitioners by candy manufacturers located in cities other than Chicago, result in varying degree in higher costs of producing the candies. The degree in each instance varies with the difference in the delivered price of the glucose, and the proportion of glucose in the particular candy. Manufacturers who pay unearned or phantom freight under petitioners' basing point system necessarily pay relatively higher costs for their raw material than do those manufacturers whose location with relation to the basing point is such that they are able to purchase at the base price plus only the freight actually paid. The Commission found that the payment of these increased prices imposed by the basing point system "may . . . diminish" the manufacturers' ability to compete with those buyers at lower prices.

The Commission concluded from these facts that petitioners' basing point system resulted in discriminations in price among purchasers of glucose, and that the discriminations result in substantial harm to competition among such purchasers. Petitioners challenge each conclusion.

FIRST. . . . Petitioners' pricing system results inevitably in systematic price discriminations, since the prices they receive upon deliveries from Kansas City bear relation to factors other than actual costs of production or delivery. . . .

In either event, on shipments from Kansas City, the delivered price to the purchaser depends not only on the base price plus the actual freight from Kansas City, but also upon the difference between the actual freight paid and the freight rate from Chicago which is included in the delivered price. This difference also results in varying net prices to petitioners at their factory at Kansas City, according to the destination of the glucose. The factory net varies according as petitioners collect phantom freight or absorb freight, and in each case in the amount of this freight differential. The price discriminations resulting from this systematic inclusion of the freight differential in computing the delivered price are not specifically permitted by the statute. Hence they are unlawful, unless, as petitioners argue, there is an implicit exception to the statute for such a basing point system.

Petitioners point out that there is no discrimination under their basing point system between buyers at the same points of delivery, and urge that the prohibition of §2(a) is directed only at price discriminations between buyers at the same delivery points. There is nothing in the words of the statute to support such a distinction, since the statute is not couched in terms of locality. And its purpose to prevent injuries to competition through price discriminations would preclude any such distinction, not required by its language. The purchasers of glucose from petitioners are found to be in competition with each other, even though they are in different localities. The injury to the competition of purchasers in different localities is no less harmful than if they were in the same city.

We find nothing in the legislative history of the Clayton or Robinson-Patman Acts to support the suggested distinction. . . .

Petitioners further contend that basing point systems were well known prior to the enactment of the Robinson-Patman Act and were considered by Congress to be legal. From this petitioners conclude that they remained legal in the absence of a clear command to the contrary. . . . But we think that the premise falls, and with it the conclusion, whatever it might be if the premise were valid.

In support of the legality of basing point systems, petitioners rely on *Maple Flooring Assn.* v. *United States,* . . . and *Cement Manufacturers Assn.* v. *United States,* . . . But these were suits to restrain violations of the Sherman Act, and did not involve the prohibition of the Clayton Act upon discriminations in price. The only question for decision in those cases was whether there was a concerted price-fixing scheme among competing sellers, accomplished in part by their adoption of a uniform basing point system; in fact, no prohibited concert of action was found.

In any event, the basing point systems involved in those cases were quite unlike that used by petitioners. In the *Maple Flooring* case, *supra,* the single basing point was so close to most of the points of production as to result in but trivial freight variances; and the defendants in that case were willing to sell on a f.o.b. mill basis, whenever the purchaser so requested. In the *Cement* case, *supra,* the defendants used a multiple basing point system, with a basing point at or near each point of production. Under this system, any manufacturer, in order to compete in the territory closer freightwise to another, would absorb freight, by adjusting his mill price to make his delivered price as low as that of his competitors. Under this system the delivered price for any locality was determined by the nearest basing point. . . .

Finally, petitioners argue that Congress, by the rejection of a provision of the Robinson-Patman Bill, which would have in effect prohibited all basing point systems, has indicated its intention to sanction all such systems.

Such a drastic change in existing pricing systems as would have been effected by the proposed amendment engendered opposition, which finally led to the withdrawal of the provision by the House Committee on the Judiciary. . . . We think this legislative history indicates only that Congress was unwilling to require f.o.b. factory pricing, and thus to make all uniform delivered price systems and all basing point systems illegal per se. On the contrary we think that it left the legality of such systems to be determined accordingly as they might be within the reach of §2(a), as enacted, and its more restricted prohibitions of discriminations in delivered prices.

We conclude that the discriminations involved in petitioners' pricing system are within the prohibition of the Act. We pass to the question whether these discriminations had the prescribed effect on competition.

SECOND. . . . It is to be observed that §2(a) does not require a finding that the discriminations in price have in fact had an adverse effect on competition. The statute is designed to reach such discriminations "in their incipiency," before the harm to competition is effected. It is enough that they "may" have the prescribed effect. . . .

Since petitioners' basing point system results in a Chicago delivered price which is always lower than any other, including that at Kansas City, a natural effect of the system is the creation of a favored price zone for the purchasers of glucose in Chicago and vicinity, which does not extend to other points of manufacture and shipment of glucose. Since the cost of glucose, a principal ingredient of low-priced candy, is less at Chicago, candy manufacturers there are in a better position to compete for business, and manufacturers of candy located near other factories producing glucose, distant from the basing point, as Kansas City, are in a less favorable position. The consequence is, as found by the Commission, that several manufacturers of candy, who were formerly located in Kansas City or other cities served from petitioners' Kansas City plant, have moved their factories to Chicago.

Further, we have seen that prices in cities to which shipments are made from Kansas City, are frequently discriminatory, since the prices in such cities usually vary according to factors, phantom freight or freight absorption, which are unrelated to any proper element of actual cost. And these systematic differentials are frequently appreciable in amount. The Commission's findings that glucose is a principal ingredient of low priced candy and that differences of small fractions of a cent in the sales price of such candy are enough to divert business from one manufacturer to another, readily admit of the Commission's inference that there is a reasonable probability that the effect of the discriminations may be substantially to lessen competition. . . .

The several violations of §§2(a) and 2(e) of the Clayton Act, found by the Commission, sustained by the court below, and brought here for review, fall within the prohibitions of the Act. The Commission's conclusions are amply supported by its findings and the evidence, and the judgment is

Affirmed.

MR. JUSTICE ROBERTS took no part in the consideration or decision of this case.

MR. JUSTICE JACKSON concurs in the result.

Multiple Basing-Point Delivered Pricing

A 1948 Supreme Court decision, condemning a *multiple basing-point system,* received considerably more attention than previous ones. The system was being used by the Cement Institute, an unincorporated trade association consisting of seventy-four manufacturers of cement.

The case was an important one for several reasons. It was a massive case, involving a large number of firms and producing thousands of pages of testimony and exhibits. The decision firmly established that multiple basing-point delivered pricing was discriminatory just as a single basing-point plan. The Federal Trade Commission also charged the Institute members were engaged in an unfair method of competition, a violation of Section 5 of the Federal Trade Commission Act, when they acted in concert to implement their multiple basing-point system. The ultimate result of such a system was that customers always faced identical prices and terms of sale of cement at any given destination. Furthermore, the FTC charged that such a system was in violation of the Robinson-Patman Act since it did involve price discrimination.

The Institute believed that its actions were not in violation of either the Federal Trade Commission Act or the Robinson-Patman Act. The argument was that their activities would not be considered as a restraint of trade under Section 1 of the Sherman Act; therefore, they could hardly be considered an "unfair method of competition" under Section 5. Justice Black, writing for the six-member majority, ruled otherwise, holding that individual or concerted actions that might fall short of a Sherman Act conviction may still constitute an unfair method of competition. The Court found ample evidence to support the Commission's contention that numerous activities had been carried on in order to make the multiple basing-point system effective and eliminate competition in quality, price, and terms of sale. Among the collective methods used "were boycotts; discharge of uncooperative employees; organized opposition to the erection of new cement plants; selling cement in a recalcitrant price cutter's sales territory at a price so low that the recalcitrant was forced to adhere to the established basing-point prices; discouraging the shipment of cement by truck or barge; . . ." The Court declared these activities did constitute an unfair method of competition.

The price discrimination charge was considered next. Here the Court relied upon its two recent decisions in Corn Products and A. E. Staley. The Court made explicit reference to these cases and said that "a pricing system involving both phantom freight and freight absorption violates Section 2(a) . . ." If the system is one in which prices are computed for products actually shipped from one plant on the "fiction" that they are shipped from another, it will be condemned by the Court.

FEDERAL TRADE COMMISSION v. CEMENT INSTITUTE et al.

333 U.S. 683 (1948)

MR. JUSTICE BLACK delivered the opinion of the Court.

We granted certiorari to review the decree of the Circuit Court of Appeals which, with one judge dissenting, vacated and set aside a cease and desist order issued by the Federal Trade Commission against the respondents. . . . Those respondents are: The Cement Institute, an unincorporated trade association composed of 74 corporations which manufacture, sell and distribute cement; the 74 corporate members of the Institute; and 21 individuals who are associated with the Institute. . . .

The proceedings were begun by a Commission complaint of two counts. The first charged that certain alleged conduct set out at length constituted an unfair method of competition in violation of §5 of the Federal Trade Commission Act. . . . The core of the charge was that the respondents had restrained and hindered competition in the sale and distribution of cement by means of a combination among themselves made effective through mutual understanding or agreement to employ a multiple basing point system of pricing. It was alleged that this system resulted in the quotation of identical terms of sale and identical prices for cement by the respondents at any given point in the United States. This system had worked so successfully, it was further charged, that for many years prior to the filing of the complaint, all cement buyers throughout the nation, with rare exceptions, had been unable to purchase cement for delivery in any given locality from any one of the respondents at a lower price or on more favorable terms than from any of the other respondents.

The second count of the complaint, resting chiefly on the same allegations of fact set out in Count I, charged that the multiple basing point system of sales resulted in systematic price discriminations between the customers of each respondent. These discriminations were made, it was alleged, with the purpose of destroying competition in price between the various respondents in violation of §2 of the Clayton Act, . . . as amended by the Robinson-Patman Act, . . .

Resting upon its findings, the Commission ordered that respondents cease and desist from "carrying out any planned common course of action, understanding, agreement, combination, or conspiracy" to do a number of things, . . . all of which things, the Commission argues, had to be restrained in order effectively to restore individual freedom of action among the separate units in the cement industry. . . .

. . . Assuming, without deciding, that the conduct charged in each count constitutes a violation of the Sherman Act, we hold that the Commission does have jurisdiction to conclude that such conduct may also be an unfair method of competition and hence constitute a violation of §5 of the Federal Trade Commission Act.

As early as 1920 this Court considered it an "unfair method of competition" to engage in practices "against public policy because of their dangerous tendency unduly to hinder competition or create monopoly." . . . Thus it appears that soon after its creation the Commission began to interpret the prohibitions of §5 as including those restraints of trade which also were outlawed by the Sherman Act, and that this Court has consistently approved that interpretation of the Act.

Despite this long and consistent administrative and judicial construction of §5, we are urged to hold that these prior interpretations were wrong and that the term "unfair methods of competition" should not be construed as embracing any conduct within the ambit of the Sherman Act. . . .

. . . We can conceive of no greater obstacle this Court could create to the fulfillment of these congressional purposes than to inject into every Trade Commission proceeding brought under §5 and into every Sherman Act suit brought by the Justice Department a possible jurisdictional question.

We adhere to our former rulings. The Commission has jurisdiction to declare that conduct tending to restrain trade is an unfair method of competition even though the selfsame conduct may also violate the Sherman Act. . . .

We find nothing to justify a holding that the filing of a Sherman Act suit by the Attorney General requires the termination of these Federal Trade Commission proceedings. In the first place, although all conduct violative of the Sherman Act may likewise come within the unfair trade practice prohibitions of the Trade Commission Act, the converse is not necessarily true. It has long been recognized that there are many unfair methods of competition that do not assume the proportions of Sherman Act violations. . . .

. . . One other challenge to the Commission's jurisdiction is specially raised by Northwestern Portland and Superior Portland. The Commission found that "Northwestern Portland makes no sales or shipments outside the State of Washington," and that "Superior Portland, with few exceptions, makes sales and shipments outside the State of Washington only to Alaska." These two respondents contend that, since they did not engage in interstate commerce and since §5 of the Trade Commission Act applies only to unfair methods of competition in interstate commerce, the Commission was without jurisdiction to enter an order against them under Count I of the complaint. . . .

We cannot sustain this contention. The charge against these respondents was not that they, apart from the other respondents, had engaged in unfair methods of competition and price discriminations simply by making intrastate sales. Instead, the charge was, as supported by the Commission's findings, that these respondents in combination with others agreed to maintain a delivered price system in order to eliminate price competition in the sale of cement in interstate commerce. . . .

. . . The Commission would be rendered helpless to stop unfair methods of competition in the form of interstate combinations and conspiracies if its jurisdiction could be defeated on a mere showing that each conspirator had carefully confined his illegal activities within the borders of a single state. . . .

FINDINGS AND EVIDENCE   It is strongly urged that the Commission failed to find, as charged in both counts of the complaint, that the respondents had by combination, agreements, or understandings among themselves utilized the multiple basing point delivered price system as a restraint to accomplish uniform prices and terms of sale. A subsidiary contention is that assuming the Commission did so find, there is no substantial evidence to support such a finding. We think that adequate findings of combination were made and that the findings have support in the evidence.

The Commission's findings of fact set out at great length and with painstaking detail numerous concerted activities carried on in order to make the multiple basing point system work in such way that competition in quality, price and terms of sale of cement would be nonexistent, and that uniform prices, job contracts, discounts, and terms of sale would be continuously maintained. The Commission found that many of these activities were carried on by the Cement Institute, the industry's unincorporated trade association, and that in other instances the activities were under the immediate control of groups of respondents. Among the collective methods used to accomplish these purposes, according to the findings, were boycotts; discharge of uncooperative employees; organized opposition to the erection of new cement plants; selling cement in a recalcitrant price cutter's sales territory at a price so low that the recalcitrant was forced to adhere to the established basing point prices; discouraging the shipment of cement by truck or barge; and preparing and distributing freight rate books which provided respondents with similar figures to use as actual or "phantom" freight factors, thus guaranteeing that their delivered prices (base prices plus freight factors) would be identical on all sales whether made to individual purchasers under open bids or to governmental agencies under sealed bids. . . .

Thus we have a complaint which charged collective action by respondents designed to maintain a sales technique that restrained competition, detailed findings of collective activities by groups of respondents to achieve that end, then a general finding that respondents maintained the combination, and finally an order prohibiting the continuance of the combination. It seems impossible to conceive that anyone reading these findings in their entirety could doubt that the Commission found that respondents collectively maintained a multiple basing point delivered price system for the purpose of suppressing competition in cement sales. The findings are sufficient. The contention that they are not is without substance. . . .

. . . In this case, which involves the evidence and findings of the Federal Trade Commission, we likewise see no reason for upsetting the essential findings of the Commission. Neither do we find it necessary to refer to all the voluminous testimony in this record which tends to support the Commission's findings. . . .

UNFAIR METHODS OF COMPETITION We sustain the Commission's holding that concerted maintenance of the basing point delivered price system is an unfair method of competition prohibited by the Federal Trade Commission Act. . . .

We cannot say that the Commission is wrong in concluding that the delivered-price system as here used provides an effective instrument which, if left free for use of the respondents, would result in complete destruction of competition and the establishment of monopoly in the cement industry. . . . We uphold the Commission's conclusion that the basing point delivered price system employed by respondents is an unfair trade practice which the Trade Commission may suppress.

THE PRICE DISCRIMINATION CHARGE IN COUNT TWO   The Commission found that respondents' combination to use the multiple basing point delivered price system had effected systematic price discrimination in violation of §2 of the Clayton Act as amended by the Robinson-Patman Act. . . .

The Commission held that the varying mill nets received by respondents on sales between customers in different localities constituted a "discrimination in price between different purchasers" within the prohibition of §2(a), and that the effect of this discrimination was the substantial lessening of competition between respondents. . . .

The respondents contend that the differences in their net returns from sales in different localities which result from use of the multiple basing point delivered price system are not price discriminations within the meaning of §2(a). If held that these net return differences are price discriminations prohibited by §2(a), they contend that the discriminations were justified under §2(b) because "made in good faith to meet an equally low price of a competitor." . . .

Section 2(b) permits a single company to sell one customer at a lower price than it sells to another if the price is "made in good faith to meet an equally low price of a competitor." But this does not mean that §2(b) permits a seller to use a sales system which constantly results in his getting more money for like goods from some customers than he does from others. We held to the contrary in the *Staley* case. . . .

We hold that the Commission properly concluded that respondents' pricing system results in price discriminations. Its finding that the discriminations substantially lessened competition between respondents and that they were not made in good faith to meet a competitor's price are supported by evidence. Accordingly, the Commission was justified in issuing a cease and desist order against a continuation of the unlawful discriminatory pricing system.

THE ORDER   There are several objections to the Commission's cease and desist order. We consider the objections, having in mind that the language of its prohibitions should be clear and precise in order that they may be understood by those against whom they are directed.

In the present proceeding the Commission has exhibited the familiarity with the competitive problems before it which Congress originally anticipated the Commission would achieve from its experience. The order it has prepared is we think clear and comprehensive. At the same time the prohibitions in the order forbid no activities except those which if continued would directly aid in perpetuating the same old unlawful practices.

Most of the objections to the order appear to rest on the premise that its terms will bar an individual cement producer from selling cement at delivered prices such that its net return from one customer will be less than from another, even if the particular sale be made in good faith to meet the lower price of a competitor. The Commission disclaims that the order can possibly be so understood. Nor do we so understand it. As we read the order, all of its separate prohibiting paragraphs and subparagraphs, which need not here be set out, are modified and limited by a preamble. This preamble directs that all of the respondents "do forthwith cease and desist from entering into, continuing, cooperating in, or carrying out any planned common course of action, understanding, agreement, combination, or conspiracy between and among any two or more of said respondents, or between any one or more of said respondents and others not parties hereto, to do or perform any of the following things. . . ." Then follow the prohibitory sentences. It is thus apparent that the order by its terms is directed solely at concerted, not individual activity on the part of the respondents.

The Commission's order should not have been set aside by the Circuit Court of Appeals. Its judgment is reversed and the cause is remanded to that court with directions to enforce the order.

It is so ordered.

MR. JUSTICE DOUGLAS and MR. JUSTICE JACKSON took no part in the consideration or decision of these cases.

MR. JUSTICE BURTON, dissenting. . . .

Zone Delivered Pricing

Delivered pricing can also be achieved by the use of zones. Under the zone delivered system, the country is divided into regions with the same price charged all buyers within that region. The zone price consists of a base price plus the average freight to all points within the zone. In any given zone, this results in a buyer living nearest the seller paying the same price as the buyer living farthest away. One pays for "phantom freight"; the other has part of his freight absorbed by the seller.

In 1957 the Supreme Court rendered a decision involving zone delivered pricing in the National Lead Co. case. At meetings begun in 1933, the industry had agreed to sell lead pigments "on the basis of flat delivered prices to customers within designated zones . . ." The zones were highly artificial, sometimes leading to bizarre results whereby a purchaser near a plant paid more than another much farther away.

The Federal Trade Commission found that National Lead, together with the other members of the industry, used the zone system to "match exactly their offer to sell lead pigments . . . thereby eliminating competition between and among themselves." The Commission issued its order prohibiting the industry from carrying out any planned common course of action, agreement, or conspiracy to use a zone delivered system. The order also directed the members to cease using, as individuals, a zone delivered system.

National Lead contended that the second part of the order, in effect, bans the noncollusive, individual use of zone pricing which is a lawful sales method. Thus, they argued, the order was beyond the power of the Commission. The Supreme Court upheld the FTC, saying that the order did not prohibit independent delivering zone pricing *per se*, but that "decrees often [justifiably] suppress a lawful device when it is used to carry out an unlawful purpose."

FEDERAL TRADE COMMISSION v. NATIONAL LEAD CO. *et al.*

352 U.S. 419 (1957)

MR. JUSTICE CLARK delivered the opinion of the Court.

The sole question involved in this proceeding under §5 of the Federal Trade Commission Act concerns the power of the Commission in framing an order pursuant to its finding that respondents had conspired to adopt and use a zone delivered pricing system in their sale of lead pigments. In its general cease and desist order prohibiting concert of action among respondents in the further use of such system, the Commission inserted a provision directing each respondent individually to cease and desist from adopting the same or a similar system of pricing for the purpose or with the effect of "matching" the prices of competitors. The respondents assert that this is beyond the power of the Commission, and the Court of Appeals agreed, . . . We restore the stricken provision of the Commission order, permitting it to stand with the interpretations placed upon it in this opinion. . . .

. . . The findings material here are as follows: . . .

Beginning in July 1933, the industry held a series of meetings in Chicago for the ostensible purpose of drafting a code of fair competition to govern it under the National Industrial Recovery Act. These meetings resulted in an understanding and agreement among those attending, including respondents, to sell lead pigments "on the basis of flat delivered prices to customers within designated zones, with uniform differentials applicable as between such zones. . . ." . . . Four zoning systems were established covering the various lead pigments. As an example, the system for white lead in oil and "keg" products consisted of 12 geographical zones, one known as a par zone. The remaining zones in this system were known as premium zones, the price in each being determined by adding a set premium to the par zone price. . . . The zones were highly artificial and zone boundaries led to bizarre results at times, with purchasers located near the plants of respondents being charged higher prices than those located at a distance from the plants. The industry, including respondents, not only agreed to sell at the same zone delivered prices in identical geographical zones but also adopted uniform discounts, terms of sale, and differentials with respect to certain of their products. . . .

The Commission entered an order prohibiting respondents from entering into or carrying out an "planned common course of action," agreement, or conspiracy to sell at prices determined pursuant to a "zone delivered price system," or any other system resulting in identical prices at the points of sale. The order also included a provision, to which respondents strenuously object, directing each of them to cease and desist from

> quoting or selling lead pigments at prices calculated or determined in whole or in part pursuant to or in accordance with a zone delivered price system for the purpose or with the effect of systematically matching the delivered price quotations or the delivered prices of other sellers of lead pigments and thereby preventing purchasers from finding any advantage in price in dealing with one or more sellers as against another. . . .

The Commission, in an accompanying opinion, stated that in all cases where it found violations of the law, "it is the Commission's duty to determine to the best of its ability the remedy necessary to suppress such activity and to take every precaution to preclude its revival." . . . In this case, the opinion pointed out, the respondents cooperatively revised the pricing practices in the industry by establishing a "uniform zone pricing system." Detailed discussions were carried on which resulted not only in an agreement, but "maps showing the boundaries of the zones to be observed . . . were distributed" by the individual respondents. . . . Each respondent has "since that time . . . followed the pricing system and adhered to the zone boundaries so discussed and shown on these maps." . . . Commission in its opinion further noted that charges were included against each respondent as to its individual use of and adherence to the zone system of selling " 'for the purpose and with the effect of enabling the respondents to match exactly their offers to sell lead pigments to any prospective purchaser at any destination, thereby eliminating competition between and among themselves.' . . . It was the adherence by each of them to this system of pricing that made the combination work. . . . Unless and until each of the respondents is prohibited from so adhering to the system and from so using the zones, the evils springing from the combination, one of which is to eliminate price competition, may well continue indefinitely. Unless the respondents, representing practically the entire economic power in the industry, are deprived of the device which made their combination effective, an order merely prohibiting the combination may well be a useless gesture." . . . In its view, the Commission added, the "prohibition is necessary, not because it is unlawful in all circumstances for an individual seller, acting independently, to sell its products on a delivered price basis in specified territories, but to make the order fully effective against the trade restraining conspiracy in which each of the respondents [defendants] participated." . . .

At the beginning we must understand the limits of the contested portion of the order. *First,* it is temporary. Though its life expectancy is not definite, it is clear that the Commission was creating a breathing spell during which independent pricing might be established without the hangover of the long-existing pattern of collusion. *Second,* the order is directed solely at the use of a zone delivered pricing system and no other. This system is a pricing method based on geographic divisions or zones, the boundaries of which are entirely drawn by the seller. His delivered price is the same throughout a particular geographic zone so drawn up by him. Customarily the delivered price is different between zones, though as here, widely separated zones, geographically, might have the same delivered price. It is well to mention here that while this Court has passed upon the validity of basing point systems of sales, *Corn Products Refining Co.* v. *Federal Trade Commission,* . . . it has not decided the validity of the zone pricing plan used here. *Third,* zone delivered pricing *per se* is not banned by the order. . . .

. . . And so, delivered zone pricing violates the order only when two conditions are present: (1) identical prices with competitors (2) resulting from zone delivered pricing. Considering these conditions with the mechanics of the zone plan, we see that the only way prices can be systematically identical is for the zones of competitors to be so drawn as to be in whole or in part identical and for zone prices to be the same in those zones which coincide or overlap. . . .

It is the contention of respondents that the contested paragraph of the order effectively bans the noncollusive, individual use of zone pricing, a lawful, competitive sales method, and is therefore beyond the authority of the Commission. . . .

We pass on to respondents' major contention questioning the power of the Commission. As the Court has said many times before, the Commission may exercise only the powers granted it by the Act. *Federal Trade Commission* v. *Western Meat Co.*, 272 U.S. 554, 559 (1926). The relevant sections empower the Commission to prevent the use of unfair methods of competition and authorize it, after finding an unfair method present, to enter an order requiring the offender "to cease and desist" from using such unfair method.

The Court has held that the Commission is clothed with wide discretion in determining the type of order that is necessary to bring an end to the unfair practices found to exist. . . .

. . . Does the remedy selected have a "reasonable relation to the unlawful practices found to exist"? We believe that it does. First, the simplicity of operation of the plan lends itself to unlawful manipulation; second, it had been used in the industry for almost a quarter of a century; and, third, its originator and chief beneficiary had been previously adjudged a violator of the antitrust laws. . . .

The respondents were found to have plainly disregarded the law. . . . Respondents made no appeal here from some of the findings as to their guilt. Having lost the battle on the facts, they hope to win the war on the type of decree. They fight for the right to continue to use individually the very same weapon with which they carried on their unlawful enterprise. The Commission concluded that this must not be permitted. It was "not obliged to assume, contrary to common experience, that a violator of the antitrust laws will relinquish the fruits of his violation more completely than [it] requires. . . ." . . . Although the zone plan might be used for some lawful purposes, decrees often suppress a lawful device when it is used to carry out an unlawful purpose. . . . In such instances the Court is obliged not only to suppress the unlawful practice but to take such reasonable action as is calculated to preclude the revival of the illegal practices. . . . We therefore conclude that, under the circumstances here, the Commission was justified in its determination that it was necessary to include some restraint in its order against the individual corporations in order to prevent a continuance of the unfair competitive practices found to exist. . . . We shall now examine the restraint imposed. . . .

. . . It is our conclusion that the order was not intended to and does not prohibit or interfere with independent delivered zone pricing *per se*. Nor does it prohibit the practice of the absorption of actual freight as such in order to foster competition. Furthermore, as we have said, there is read into the order the provision of §2(b) of the Clayton Act as to the right of a seller in good faith to meet the lower price of a competitor. This is not to say that a seller may plead this section in defense of the use of an entire pricing system. The section is designed to protect competitors in individual transactions. . . .

Reversed.

Inferred Conspiracy from Delivered Pricing

A second decision in 1948 involving delivered pricing was handed down by an appellate court. The verdict in the *Cement Institute* case rested on evidence showing an agreement did exist among the firms participating in the system. In the *Triangle Conduit & Cable* case, with essentially the same pricing system as the cement companies, the Court took the position that no direct proof of an agreement or conspiracy was necessary to find a violation of Section 5 of the Federal Trade Commission Act. Conscious parallelism of action—the concurrent use of a delivered pricing system by individual firms with the knowledge that other firms were also adhering to it and with the result that price competition was eliminated—was considered sufficient evidence for upholding the Federal Trade Commission's position.

Judge Kerner did not say that delivered pricing would be a *per se* violation when used as an individual pricing tactic in order to meet competition in good faith. He did point out that its use as part of an overall industry pricing tactic would be held unlawful. This decision was sustained when the case was appealed to the Supreme Court, which divided 4–4 in 1949.[4]

TRIANGLE CONDUIT & CABLE CO. INC., et al. v. FEDERAL TRADE COMMISSION

168 F. (2d) 175 (1948)

KERNER, Circuit Judge.

Petitioners, fourteen corporate manufacturers of rigid steel conduit, and five representatives of these corporations ask us to review and set aside a cease and desist order of the Federal Trade Commission, upon a complaint in two counts, charging that petitioners collectively have violated §5 of the Federal Trade Commission Act, . . .

In substance the first count alleged the existence and continuance of a conspiracy for the purpose and with the effect of substantially restricting and suppressing actual and potential competition in the distribution and sale of rigid steel conduit in commerce, effectuated by the adoption and use of a basing point method of quoting prices for rigid steel conduit. The

---

[4] *Clayton Mark & Co. v. FTC*, 336 U.S. 956.

second count did not rest upon an agreement or combination. It charged that each corporate petitioner and others violated §5 of the Federal Trade Commission Act "through their concurrent use of a formula method of making delivered price quotations with the knowledge that each did likewise, with the result that price competition between and among them was unreasonably restrained." It alleged that nearby customers were deprived of price advantages which they would have naturally enjoyed by reason of their proximity to points of production, and that such course of action created in said conduit sellers a monopolistic control over price in the sale and distribution of rigid steel conduit.

Rigid steel conduit is a steel pipe, used primarily in the roughing-in stage of building contstruction where electrical wiring is necessary in order to furnish a continuous channel or container for the wiring. It is made from standard steel pipe and is produced in two types differing only in the nature of the coating applied to it. It is a standard commodity. . . .

In addition to freight rate bulletins, another aid in computing delivered prices was the use of delivery charge tables, which were designed to simplify the procedure of figuring the delivered prices, and each petitioner refrained from publishing price quotations f. o. b. point of production or shipment, but used the practice and method of quoting price sheets, which it termed "Price Cards," in which it designated base prices f. o. b. Pittsburgh, Pa, and f. o. b. Chicago, Ill. . . .

It also appears that instead of petitioner conduit sellers using an absolute Pittsburgh plus system for all designations in their price quotations, they collectively discussed and considered the matter of maintaining and utilizing Chicago as a basing point, . . . Accordingly, at the time of the hearings each of the petitioner conduit sellers quoted delivered prices for conduit based on Chicago as well as on Pittsburgh as basing points and sold at that base price.

There was testimony that the system thus used was an effective means of matching bids and price quotations, and that the quotations made by each conduit seller irrespective of whether it had a manufacturing plant located at or near Pittsburgh or Chicago, enabled them to match their price quotations. . . .

The findings upon which the order of the Commission is based are lengthy and of a comprehensive nature. . . . Essentially the findings are, that there was collective consideration of pricing policies on the part of representatives of petitioners in 1930 and collective considerations by such representatives of those matters through November, 1939; that by petitioners' adherence to their formula or system of pricing, their matching of bids under seal and the matching of their delivered price quotations was made effective, and a combination and conspiracy was maintained by petitioners to deprive purchasers of conduit of the benefits of competition in price, to maintain artificial and monopolistic methods and prices in the sale and distribution of conduit, to prepare and maintain common rate factors or freight adders used and useful in determining and establishing price quotations and prices for conduit, to classify customers of conduit and determine the treatment to be accorded them, to establish and maintain uniform discounts, terms and conditions of sale, to determine and control the use of warehouses in the distribution of conduit, to prepare, adopt, and use for the purpose of aiding in price maintenance and control, uniform contracts for distributors and for contractors buying for specific projects, and to enforce the terms of such contracts through investigations and reports thereon, to support and maintain their price structure through the conduct of investigations of sales and offers to sell, and the circulation of reports thereon; and that the acts and practices performed thereunder and in connection therewith, hindered, lessened and suppressed competition among sellers in the sale and distribution of conduit in interstate commerce.

. . . Upon these findings of fact the Commission concluded that these acts and practices constituted unfair methods of competition in commerce within the meaning of §5 of the Act, and directed petitioners, other than General Electric Supply Corporation and Spang Chalfant, to cease and desist from entering into, continuing in, or carrying out any planned common course of action, understanding, agreement, combination, or conspiracy between any two or more of petitioners, or between any one or more of petitioners and others not parties hereto, to do or perform any of the things specifically set forth in the order. . . .

Petitioners also stress the point that the use of the basing point method of pricing does not have any adverse effect on competition and is not oppressive. . . .

The argument is that there is no direct evidence of any conspiracy; that if the Commission made such a finding, it is based upon a series of inferences; and that the general use of the basing point method of pricing and the uniformity of price does not justify an inference of conspiracy. We think there was direct proof of the conspiracy, but whether there was or was not, in determining if such a finding is supported, it is not necessary that there be direct proof of an agreement. Such an agreement may be shown by circumstantial evidence. . . .

In this case there was evidence showing collective action to eliminate the Evanston basing point, and collective activities in promoting the general use of the formula presently to be noted. The record clearly establishes the fact that conduit manufacturers controlling 93% of the industry use a system under which they quote only delivered prices, which are determined in accordance with a formula consisting of a base price at Pittsburgh or Chicago plus rail freight, depending upon which basing point price controls at any particular destination or in any particular section of the United States; that as a result of using that formula the conduit producers were enabled to match their delivered price quotations, and purchasers everywhere were unable to find price advantages anywhere; and that purchasers at or near a place of production could not buy more cheaply from their nearby producer than from producers located at greater distances, and producers located at great distances from any given purchaser quoted as low a delivered price as that quoted by the nearest producer. . . .

. . . Our study of this record and of the applicable law has convinced us that the Commission was justified in drawing the inference that the petitioners acted in concert in a price-fixing conspiracy.

We now turn to consider petitioners' contention that the individual use of the basing point method, with knowledge that other sellers use it, does not constitute an unfair method of competition. . . .

Briefly, the argument is that individual freight absorption is not illegal per se, and that the Commission's order is a denial of the right to meet competition. More specifically, petitioners say that conduit is a homogeneous product; that no buyer will pay more for the product of one seller than he will for that of another; that the buyer is not interested in the seller's cost of transportation or in any other factor of the seller's cost; that effective competition requires that traders have large freedom of action when conducting their own affairs; that in any particular market, the seller must adjust his own price to meet the market price or retire from that market altogether; that it has always been the custom of merchants to send their goods to distant markets to be sold at the prices there prevailing; that there is no lessening of competition, or injury to competitors, when a seller absorbs freight traffic to meet lawful competition; and that it is for the court to decide as a matter of law what constitutes an unfair method of competition under §5 of the Act. . . .

On the other hand, the Commission contends that unfair methods of competition include not only methods that involve deception, bad faith, and fraud, but methods that involve oppression or such as are against public policy because of their dangerous tendency unduly to hinder competition or create monopoly.

As already noted, each conduit seller knows that each of the other sellers is using the basing point formula; each knows that by using it he will be able to quote identical delivered prices and thus present a condition of matched prices under which purchasers are isolated and deprived of choice among sellers so far as price advantage is concerned. . . .

In this situation, and indeed all parties to these proceedings agree, the legal question presented is identical with the one the Supreme Court considered in the Federal Trade Commission v. Cement Institute . . .

In the light of that opinion, we cannot say that the Commission was wrong in concluding that the individual use of the basing point method as here used does constitute an unfair method of competition.

In their briefs and upon oral argument, petitioners have raised additional points. These, too, have been examined and considered by the Supreme Court in the Federal Trade Commission v. Cement Institute case, supra, and were found lacking in merit. Hence they need not be discussed by us.

The Commission's order is affirmed and an enforcement decree will be entered. It is so ordered.

"Good Faith" Defense

In another decision handed down the same day as the Corn Products decision, the Supreme Court rejected the "good faith" defense of the A. E. Staley Manufacturing Co. The circumstances of the latter case were almost identical to those of the first one. A. E. Staley was also engaged in manufacturing glucose in two different locations—Decatur, Illinois, and Chicago. It had adopted a single basing-point delivered pricing plan similar to that of Corn Products and other manufacturers of glucose. Customers in the Decatur area had to pay the normal price plus freight charges from Chicago even though the product was shipped from the Decatur plant. The majority opinion, written by Chief Justice Stone in both cases, followed the same rule applied in the Corn Products case: the delivered pricing system did involve illegal price discrimination.

The defendant sought to justify its pricing method by pointing out that it was only acting in good faith to meet the equally low price of a competitor—namely, the Corn Products Refining Company. The Court would not accept this argument because the evidence showed that Staley had never attempted to set up a pricing policy of its own independent of what other firms were doing. Staley had systematically adopted the delivered pricing system of Corn Products and established artificially high prices that took advantage of the competitor's higher costs of delivery. This policy could hardly be considered an action undertaken in good faith to meet a competitor's low price.

FEDERAL TRADE COMMISSION v. A. E. STALEY MANUFACTURING CO. et al.

324 U.S. 746 (1945)

MR. CHIEF JUSTICE STONE delivered the opinion of the Court.

Respondents, a parent company and its sales subsidiary, are engaged in the manufacture and sale of glucose or corn syrup in competition with others, including the Corn Products Refining Company, whose methods of marketing and pricing its products are described in our opinion in *Corn Products Refining Co. v. Federal Trade Commission*, . . . Respondents, in selling their glucose, have adopted a basing point delivered price system comparable to that of the Corn Products Refining Company. Respondents sell their product, manufactured at Decatur, Illinois, at delivered prices based on Chicago, Illinois, the price in each case being the Chicago price plus freight from Chicago to point of delivery.

In this proceeding, . . . Federal Trade Commission charged that respondents' pricing system resulted in price discriminations between different purchasers of glucose in violation of §2 (a) of the Clayton Act, as amended by the Robinson-Patman Act, . . .

The principal question for decision is whether respondents, who adopted the discriminatory price system of their competitors, including the Corn Products Refining Company, have sustained the burden of justifying their price system under §2 (b) of the Clayton Act, as amended, by showing that their prices were made "in good faith" to meet the equally low prices of competitors. . . .

The Commission found that at all relevant times respondents have sold glucose, shipped to purchasers from their plant at Decatur, Illinois, on a delivered price basis, the lowest price quoted being for delivery to Chicago purchasers. Respondents' Chicago price is not only a delivered price at that place. It is also a basing point price upon which all other delivered prices, including the price at Decatur, are computed by adding to the base price, freight from Chicago to the point of delivery. The Decatur price, as well as the delivered price at all points at which the freight from Decatur is less than the freight from Chicago, includes an item of un-earned or "phantom" freight, ranging in amount, in instances mentioned by the Commission, from 1 cent per hundred pounds at St. Joseph, Missouri, to 18 cents at Decatur. . . .

The Commission found that this inclusion of unearned freight or absorption of freight in calculating the delivered prices operated to discriminate against purchasers at all points where the freight rate from Decatur was less than that from Chicago and in favor of purchasers at points where the freight rate from Decatur was greater than that from Chicago. It also made findings comparable to those made in the *Corn Products Refining Company* case that the effect of these discriminations between purchasers, who are candy and syrup manufacturers competing with each other, was to diminish competition between them. . . .

These findings, and the conclusion of the Commission that the price discriminations involved are prohibited by §2 (a), are challenged here. But, for the reasons we have given in our opinion in the *Corn Products Refining Company* case, the challenge must fail. The sole question we find it necessary to discuss here is whether respondents have succeeded in justifying the discriminations by an adequate showing that the discriminations were made "in good faith" to meet equally low prices of competitors.

We consider first, respondents' asserted justification of the discriminations involved in its basing point pricing system. As we hold in the *Corn Products Refining Company* case with respect to a like system, price discriminations are necessarily involved where the price basing point is distant from the point of production. This is because, as in respondents' case, the delivered prices upon shipments from Decatur usually include an item of unearned or phantom freight or require the absorption of freight with the consequent variations in the seller's net factory prices. Since such freight differentials bear no relation to the actual cost of delivery, they are systematic discriminations prohibited by §2 (a), whenever they have the defined effect upon competition. . . .

Section 2 (b) of the Clayton Act provides:

> Upon proof being made, at any hearing on a complaint under this section, that there has been discrimination in price . . . , the burden of rebutting the prima-facie case thus made by showing justification shall be upon the person charged with a violation of this section, and unless justification shall be affirmatively shown, the Commission is authorized to issue an order terminating the discrimination: *Provided, however,* That nothing herein contained shall prevent a seller rebutting the prima-facie case thus made by showing that his lower price . . . was made in good faith to meet an equally low price of a competitor . . .

It will be noted that the defense that the price discriminations were made in order to meet competition, is under the statute a matter of "rebutting" the Commission's "prima-facie case." Prior to the Robinson-Patman amendments, §2 of the Clayton Act provided that nothing contained in it "shall prevent" discriminations in price "made in good faith to meet competition." The change in language of this exception was for the purpose of making the defense a matter of evidence in each case, raising a question of fact as to whether the competition justified the discrimination. . . .

But respondents argue that they have sustained their burden of proof, as prescribed by §2 (b), by showing that they have adopted and followed the basing point system of their competitors. In the *Corn Products Refining Company* case we hold that this price system of respondents' competitor in part involves unlawful price discriminations, to the extent that freight differentials enter into the computation of price, as a result of the selection as a basing point of a place distant from the point of production and shipment. Thus it is the contention that a seller may justify a basing point delivered price system, which is otherwise outlawed by §2, because other competitors are in part violating the law by maintaining a like system. If respondents' argument is sound, it would seem to follow that even if the competitor's pricing system were wholly in violation of §2 of the Clayton Act, respondents could adopt and follow it with impunity.

This startling conclusion is admissible only upon the assumption that the statute permits a seller to maintain an otherwise unlawful system of discriminatory prices, merely because he had adopted it in its entirety, as a means of securing the benefits of a like unlawful system maintained by his competitors. . . .

The statutory test is whether respondents, by their basing point system, adopted a "lower price . . . in good faith to meet an equally low price of a competitor." This test presupposes that the person charged with violating the Act would, by his normal, non-discriminatory pricing methods, have reached a price so high that he could reduce it in order to meet the competitor's equally low price. On the contrary, respondents have used their pricing system to adopt the delivery prices of their Chicago competitors, by charging their own customers upon shipments from Decatur the Chicago base price plus their competitors' costs of delivery from Chicago. Even though respondents, at many delivery points, enjoyed freight advantages over their competitors, they did not avail of the opportunity to charge lower delivered prices. Instead they maintained their own prices at the level of their competitors' high prices, based upon the competitors' higher costs of delivery, by including phantom freight in their own delivered prices.

Respondents have never attempted to establish their own non-discriminatory price system, and then reduced their price when necessary to meet competition. Instead they have slavishly followed in the first instance a pricing policy which, in their case, resulted in systematic discriminations, by charging their customers upon shipments from Decatur, the Chicago base price plus their competitors' actual costs of delivery from Chicago. . . .

The Commission's conclusion seems inescapable that respondents' discriminations, such as those between purchasers in Chicago and Decatur, were established not to meet equally low Chicago prices of competitors there, but in order to establish elsewhere the artificially high prices whose discriminatory effect permeates respondents' entire pricing system. The systematic adoption of a competitor's prices by including unearned freight in respondents' delivery price or, what amounts to the same thing, the maintenance of a discriminatory and artificially high f. o. b. factory price in order to take advantage of the correspondingly high prices of a competitor, based on its higher costs of delivery, is not sufficient to justify the discrimination, for respondent fails to show, as the statute requires, the establishment of a "lower price" made in good faith to meet the equally low price of a competitor. . . .

We cannot say that a seller acts in good faith when it chooses to adopt such a clearly discriminatory pricing system, at least where it has never attempted to set up a non-discriminatory system, giving to purchasers, who have the natural advantage of proximity to its plant, the price advantages which they are entitled to expect over purchasers at a distance. . . .

. . . In the present case, the Commission's finding that respondents' price discriminations were not made to meet a "lower" price and consequently were not in good faith, is amply supported by the record, and we think the Court of Appeals erred in setting aside this portion of the Commission's order to cease and desist. . . .

The Commission's order will be sustained. The judgment below will be reversed, and the cause remanded with instructions to enforce the Commission's order.

So ordered.

MR. JUSTICE ROBERTS took no part in the consideration or decision of this case.

MR. JUSTICE JACKSON concurs in the result.

10

Tying Contracts and Exclusive Dealing Arrangements

Tying contracts and exclusive dealing arrangements are two more business practices that have been used to restrain the forces of competition and used in some manner to extend monopolistic positions. These practices have been employed for a number of years and as a general rule have received favorable sanction from the courts in the early cases litigated under the Sherman Act. Because of the lenient position taken by the courts, Section 3 of the Clayton Act was passed for the purpose of outlawing such devices when their effect would tend to lessen competition, a much lighter burden of proof than under the Sherman Act. Section 3 states:

> That it shall be unlawful for any person engaged in commerce, in the course of such commerce, to lease or make a sale or contract for sale of goods, wares, merchandise, machinery, supplies, or other commodities, whether patented or unpatented, for use, consumption, or resale within the United States or any Territory thereof or the District of Columbia or any insular possession or other place under the jurisdiction of the United States, or fix a price charged therefor, or discount from, or rebate upon, such price, on the condition, agreement, or understanding that the lessee or purchaser thereof shall not use or deal in the goods, wares, merchandise, machinery, supplies, or other commodity of a competitor or competitors of the lessor or seller, where the effect of such lease, sale, or contract for sale or such condition, agreement, or understanding may be to substantially lessen competition or tend to create a monopoly in any line of commerce.

As the name suggests, *tying contracts* arise when the seller of a product requires that the purchaser must also buy another product in order to acquire the first. The purchaser is then forced to accept the second, which he may or may not want, in order to receive the first. The harm resulting from these agreements has usually taken the form of denying market access to competing producers and enlarging the market position of a product in which the producer already enjoys a dominant position. A common practice has been for the holder of a valid patent to tie other products or services to his legal monopoly in order to enhance his market position. Other instances may occur in which the seller has substantial market power and forces the purchase of other of his products in which his market power is not so great. Such tactics have consistently been condemned by the courts, and it appears from the *Northern Pacific* case that tying contracts will be considered *per se* violations in the future when certain conditions are met.

Exclusive dealing contracts may or may not have beneficial economic effects. To the extent that exclusive dealing is used to foreclose markets to competitors or expand a substantial market share, the courts take a dim view of the activity. Especially vulnerable is the contract that requires a customer to handle only the merchandise of the seller and exclude the products of competitors. A further consideration in these instances is the share of the market involved. When it is deemed "substantial," exclusive dealing arrangements will be struck down.

Tying Contracts

The first tying contract case to be decided by the Supreme Court under Section 3 was an outgrowth of the government's earlier unsuccessful bid to break up the United Shoe Machinery Company. In the 1918 case, presented in Chapter 1, the government charged United Shoe's previous mergers and leasing system violated Sections 1 and 2 of the Sherman Act. But the Court at that time did not yield to the government's plea to dissolve the company. Since the suit had been initiated in 1911 and the Clayton Act was subsequently passed, the second time around in 1922 the government attacked only United Shoe's leasing system under Section 3. United Shoe claimed that it had already been cleared by the 1918 decision, but the Supreme Court ruled differently. The second case did not involve the "same cause of action." The first case sought dissolution; the second, to enjoin the use of specified restrictions in leases on patented machinery.

Because of a number of restrictive clauses in the leases that would tend to lessen competition, the Court ruled that United Shoe was violating Section 3. Among the condemned restrictions were: (1) requiring supplies for United's machines to be purchased exclusively from it; (2) requiring additional machinery to be obtained from the lessor; (3) prohibiting the use of United's machines on shoes when certain basic operations had been performed by other than the lessor's machinery; (4) restricting insole operations exclusively to United's patented machine; and (5) granting United the right to cancel all leases for the breach of one lease. The Court pointed out that tying contracts may be justified, if essential for protecting royalty revenues and for assuring the machine's protection through proper use and care. At any rate, United's leasing agreements went beyond that necessary to insure protection of its equipment and patent.

UNITED SHOE MACHINERY CORPORATION et al. v.
UNITED STATES

258 U.S. 451 (1922)

MR. JUSTICE DAY delivered the opinon of the court.[1]

This suit was brought by the United States against the defendants, United Shoe Machinery Company (of Maine), United Shoe Machinery Corporation, United Shoe Machinery Company (of New Jersey), and the officers and directors of these corporations, under the provisions of the Clayton Act . . . to enjoin them from making leases containing certain clauses, terms and conditions alleged to be violative of the act. . . .

Section 3 of the Clayton Act, so far as pertinent, makes it unlawful for persons engaged in interstate commerce in the course of such commerce to lease machinery, supplies or other commodities, whether patented or unpatented, for use, consumption or resale within the United States, or to fix a price therefor, or to discount from, or rebate upon, such price upon the condition, agreement or understanding that the lessee thereof shall not use or deal in the machinery, supplies or other commodities of the competitor or competitors of the lessor, where the effect of such lease, agreement or understanding may be to substantially lessen competition or tend to create a monopoly. . . .

Our own examination of the testimony gives little occasion to modify the findings of fact made by the District Court. The record discloses that the United Shoe Machinery Corporation, hereinafter called the United Company, controlled a very large portion of the business of supplying shoe machinery of the classes involved in this case. The court below found that it controlled more than 95% of such business in the United States. Whether this finding is precisely correct it is immaterial to inquire. It is evident from this record that the United Company occupies a dominant position in the production of such machinery and makes and supplies throughout the United States a very large percentage of such machinery used by manufacturers. . . .

. . . The machines of the United Company are protected by patents granted prior to the passage of the Clayton Act, and the validity of none of them is called in question here. . . .

---

[1] All the footnotes and most of the citations from the opinions of the Court have been omitted from the cases in this chapter.

Turning to the decree, it will be found that the court enjoined the use of (1) the restricted use clause, which provides that the leased machinery shall not, nor shall any part thereof, be used upon shoes, etc., or portions, thereof, upon which certain other operations have not been performed on other machines of the defendants; (2) the exclusive use clause, which provides that if the lessee fails to use exclusively machinery of certain kinds made by the lessor, the lessor shall have the right to cancel the right to use all such machinery so leased; (3) the supplies clause, which provides that the lessee shall purchase supplies exclusively from the lessor; (4) the patent in-sole clause, which provides that the lessee shall only use machinery leased on shoes which have had certain other operations performed upon them by the defendants' machines; (5) the additional machinery clause, which provides that the lessee shall take all additional machinery for certain kinds of work from the lessor or lose his right to retain the machines which he has already leased; (6) the factory output clause, which requires the payment of a royalty on shoes operated upon by machines made by competitors; (7)the discriminatory royalty clause, providing lower royalty for lessees who agree not to use certain machinery on shoes lasted on machines other than those leased from the lessor. The defendant's restrictive form of leases embraces the right of the lessor to cancel a lease for the breach of a provision in such lease, or in any other lease or license agreement between the lessor and the lessee. . . .

While the clauses enjoined do not contain specific agreements not to use the machinery of a competitor of the lessor, the practical effect of these drastic provisions is to prevent such use. We can entertain no doubt that such provisions as were enjoined are embraced in the broad terms of the Clayton Act which cover all conditions, agreements or understandings of this nature. That such restrictive and tying agreements must necessarily lessen competition and tend to monopoly is, we believe, equally apparent. When it is considered that the United Company occupies a dominating position in supplying shoe machinery of the classes involved, these covenants signed by the lessee and binding upon him effectually prevent him from acquiring the machinery of a competitor of the lessor except at the risk of forfeiting the right to use the machines furnished by the United Company which may be absolutely essential to the prosecution and success of his business.

This system of "tying" restrictions is quite as effective as express covenants could be and practically compels the use of the machinery of the lessor except upon risks which manufacturers will not willingly incur. . . .

It is contended that the decree in favor of the defendants affirmed in the former suit of the Government under the Sherman Act, . . . between the same parties, is res judicata of the issues in the present case. . . .

In other words, to determine the effect of a former judgment pleaded as an estoppel, two questions must be answered: (1) Was the former judgment rendered on the same cause of action? (2) If not, was some matter litigated in the former suit determinative of the matter in controversy in the second suit? To answer these questions we must look to the pleadings making the issues, and examine the record to determine the questions essential to the decision of the former controversy.

The Sherman Act suit had for its object the dissolution of the United Company, which had been formed by the union of other shoe machinery companies. It also attacked and sought to enjoin the use of the restrictive and tying clauses contained in the leases as being in themselves contracts in violation of the Sherman Act. . . .

That the leases were attacked under the former bill as violative of the Sherman Act is true, but they were sustained as valid and binding agreements within the rights of holders of patents. The Clayton Act specifically applies to goods, wares, machinery, etc., whether "*patented or unpatented.*" This provision was inserted in the Clayton Act with the express purpose of preventing rights granted by letters patent from securing immunity from the inhibitions of the act. The determination of the questions now raised under the Clayton Act was not essential to the former decision. The defendants in their argument seize upon isolated passages in the opinion of the court in the former case, and contend that they are decisive here. But the effect of the former judgment as an estoppel is not to be thus determined. . . .

The issue whether the restrictive clauses were valid in view of the provision of the Clayton Act concerning machinery patented or unpatented was not and could not have been involved or decided in the former suit. It is true that the court speaks of the excellence and efficiency of the United Company's machinery as a sufficient inducement for its installation by the lessees, and, we may add that there is much testimony in the record tending to show that it was the excellence of the United Company's machinery and the efficiency of its service which induced lessees to acquire its machinery, but these considerations are apart from the pertinent issues which here confront us. No matter how good the machines of the United Company may be, or how efficient its service, it is not at liberty to lease its machines upon conditions prohibited by a valid law of the United States. Congress has undertaken to deny the protection of patent rights to such covenants as come within the terms of the Clayton Act, and if the statute is constitutional, the sole duty of the court is to enforce it in accordance with its terms.

It is contended that the act is an unconstitutional limitation upon the rights secured to a patentee under the laws of the United States, and that it takes away from the patentees without due process of law property secured to them by the grant of the patent. . . .

. . . Undoubtedly the patentee has the right to grant the use of the rights or privileges conferred by his patent to others by making licenses and agreements with them which are not in themselves unlawful, but the right to make regulation in the public interest under the police power of the States or in the exertion of the authority of Congress over matters within its constitutional power is controlled by general principles of law, and the patent right confers no privilege to make contracts in themselves illegal, and certainly not to make those directly violative of valid statutes of the United States. . . .

Other matters are urged, but we have noticed those deemed necessary to a decision of the case. We find no error in the decree of the court below, and the same is

Affirmed.

MR. JUSTICE MCKENNA dissents.

MR. JUSTICE BRANDEIS took no part in the consideration or decision of this case.

The next Supreme Court decision to consider the implications of tying contracts came in the 1936 *International Business Machines* case. IBM was the leading producer of business machines, and all its machines were being produced under valid patents. The equipment was leased to customers, and the agreement required lessees to operate the machines only with supplies purchased from IBM, thereby precluding the use of tabulating cards of competitors. IBM contended that the arrangement was legal because it possessed patents on both the machines and the cards. Nevertheless, Section 3 is applicable whether the items are patented or unpatented.

The Court observed that IBM enjoyed a dominant market position and that other cards were suitable for use with the machines. The ultimate result of the tying contract was to extend further the already dominant market position of the firm. IBM claimed that the use of cards with certain specifications was necessary to insure proper functioning of the machines and protection of the company's good will. The unanimous Court opinion pointed out that IBM was not prevented from proclaiming the virtue of its own cards, and nothing prevented the insertion in lease agreements of the requirement that cards of certain quality and specifications be used with the machines. These measures would protect the good will of the firm without suppressing competition, as the tying contracts did.

INTERNATIONAL BUSINESS MACHINES CORP. v. UNITED STATES

298 U.S. 131 (1936)

MR. JUSTICE STONE delivered the opinion of the Court.

This is an appeal, . . . from so much of a decree of a District Court for Southern New York as enjoins the appellant from leasing its tabulating and other machines upon the condition that the lessees shall use with such machines only tabulating cards manufactured by appellant, as a violation of §3 of the Clayton Act, . . .

Appellant's machines and those of Remington Rand, Inc., are now the only ones on the market which perform certain mechanical tabulations and computations, without any intervening manual operation, by the use in them of cards upon which are recorded data which are the subject of tabulation or computation. Appellant manufactures three types of machines, known as punching machines, sorters and tabulators. . . .

To insure satisfactory performance by appellant's machines it is necessary that the cards used in them conform to precise specifications as to size and thickness, and that they be free from defects due to slime or carbon spots, which cause unintended electrical contacts and consequent inaccurate results. The cards manufactured by appellant are electrically tested for such defects.

Appellant leases its machines for a specified rental and period, upon condition that the lease shall terminate in case any cards not manufactured by the lessor are used in the leased machine. . . .

Appellant insists that the condition of its leases is not within the prohibition of the Clayton Act, and it has assigned as error the conclusion of the district court that the condition tends to create monopoly. But its principal contentions are that its leases are lawful because the protection secured by the condition does not extend beyond the monopoly which it has acquired by patents on the cards and on the machines in which they are used, . . .

The conclusion of the trial court that appellant's leases infringe the monopoly provisions of the section does not want for support in the record. The agreed use of the "tying clause" by appellant and its only competitors, and the agreement by each of them to restrict its competition in the sale of cards to the lessees of the others, have operated to prevent competition and to create a monopoly in the production and sale of tabu-

lating cards suitable for appellant's machines, as the district court found.
. . . These facts, and others, which we do not stop to enumerate, can
leave no doubt that the effect of the condition in appellant's leases "may
be to substantially lessen competition," and that it tends to create monopoly, and has in fact been an important and effective step in the creation
of monopoly.

On the trial appellant offered to prove its ownership of patents
which, it asserts, give it a monopoly of the right to manufacture, use and
vend the cards, separately, and in combination with its sorting and tabulating machines, of which, it insists, they are a part. It argues that the
condition of its leases is lawful because it does not enlarge the monopoly
secured by the patents, and that the trial court erred in refusing to
consider appellant's patent monopoly as a defense to the suit.

Appellant's patents appear to extent only to the cards when perforated, and to have no application to those which the lessees purchase
before they are punched. The contention is thus reduced to the dubious
claim that the sale of the un-punched cards is a contributory infringement
of the patents covering the use of perforated cards separately and in
combination with the machines. . . .

But we do not place our decision on this narrow ground. We rest it
rather on the language of §3 of the Clayton Act which expressly makes
tying clauses unlawful, whether the machine leased is "patented or unpatented." The section does not purport to curtail the patent monopoly of
the lessor or to restrict its protection by suit for infringement. But it does
in terms deny to the lessor of a patented, as well as of an unpatented
machine, the benefit of any condition or agreement that the lessee shall
not use the supplies of a competitor. The only purpose or effect of the
tying clause, so far as it could be effectively applied to patented articles, is
either to prevent the use, by a lessee, of the product of a competitor of the
lessor, . . .

Despite the plain language of §3, making unlawful the tying clause
when it tends to create a monopoly, appellant insists that it does not forbid
tying clauses whose purpose and effect are to protect the good will of the
lessor in the leased machines, even though monopoly ensues. . . . It is
essential to the successful performance of the leased machines that the
cards used in them conform, with relatively minute tolerances, to specifications as to size, thickiness and freedom from defects which would affect
adversely the electrical circuits indispensable to the proper operation of the
machines. . . . There is no contention that others than appellant cannot
meet these requirements. It affirmatively appears, by stipulation, that
others are capable of manufacturing cards suitable for use in appellant's
machines, and that paper required for that purpose may be obtained from
the manufacturers who supply appellant. . . .

Appellant is not prevented from proclaiming the virtues of its own cards or warning against the danger of using, in its machines, cards which do not conform to the necessary specifications, or even from making its leases conditional upon the use of cards which conform to them. For aught that appears such measures would protect its good will, without the creation of monopoly or resort to the suppression of competition.

The Clayton Act names no exception to its prohibition of monopolistic tying clauses. . . . We can perceive no tenable basis for an exception in favor of a condition whose substantial benefit to the lessor is the elimination of business competition and the creation of monopoly, rather than the protection of its good will, and where it does not appear that the latter can not be achieved by methods which do not tend to monopoly and are not otherwise unlawful.

Affirmed.

MR. JUSTICE ROBERTS took no part in the consideration or decision of this case.

In a 6–3 decision in 1947, the Supreme Court went even further in condemning tying contracts. It held that such contracts, like price-fixing agreements, are *per se* violations of both Section 1 of the Sherman Act and Section 3 of the Clayton Act when they foreclose competitors from any substantial market. The International Salt Company was the largest producer of industrial salt and possessed patents on two salt-dispensing machines. A large number of leases for the machines had been negotiated whereby lessees were required to purchase all salt products to be used in the machines from the lessor. The Court ruled that agreements of this nature tended to create a monopoly and that it does not matter if the tendency is a creeping one or one that "proceeds at full gallop." The direction of the movement is to be condemned before reaching its goal.

International Salt sought to justify its contracts by alleging that the requirements were necessary to assure proper performance of the machines. The Court referred to the *IBM* case and reaffirmed that a lessor may impose reasonable restrictions to minimize maintenance and assure satisfactory performance. Several competitors were known to produce salt of acceptable quality. The firm also pointed out that the tying clause was not insisted upon in every agreement. The Court believed its use was general enough to prohibit further continuation. Finally, International Salt protested that the contracts were not unreasonable because lessees were given the benefits of price reductions in the lessor's products. If competitors were underselling the lessor, machine users always had the option of buying at the lower price. The Court felt that this served only to maintain International's market position by meeting a competitor's price. The volume of business ($500,000 in previous years) was not "insignificant," and the contracts were held to be in violation of both the Sherman Act and the Clayton Act.

INTERNATIONAL SALT CO., INC. v. UNITED STATES

332 U.S. 392 (1947)

MR. JUSTICE JACKSON delivered the opinion of the Court.

The Government brought this civil action to enjoin the International Salt Company, appellant here, from carrying out provisions of the leases of its patented machines to the effect that lessees would use therein only International's salt products. The restriction is alleged to violate §1 of the Sherman Act, and §3 of the Clayton Act. Upon appellant's answer and admissions of fact, the Government moved for summary judgment . . . upon the ground that no issue as to a material fact was presented and that, on the admissions, judgment followed as matter of law. . . . Judgment was granted and appeal was taken directly to this Court.

It was established by pleadings or admissions that the International Salt Company is engaged in interstate commerce in salt, of which it is the country's largest producer for industrial uses. It also owns patents on two machines for utilization of salt products. One, the "Lixator," dissolves rock salt into a brine used in various industrial processes. The other, the "Saltomat," injects salt, in tablet form, into canned products during the canning process. The principal distribution of each of these machines is under leases which, among other things, require the lessees to purchase from appellant all unpatented salt and salt tablets consumed in the leased machines. . . .

The appellant's patents confer a limited monopoly of the invention they reward. . . . But the patents confer no right to restrain use of, or trade in, unpatented salt. By contracting to close this market for salt against competition, International has engaged in a restraint of trade for which its patents afford no immunity from the antitrust laws. . . .

Appellant contends, however, that summary judgment was unauthorized because it precluded trial of alleged issues of fact as to whether the restraint was unreasonable within the Sherman Act or substantially lessened competition or tended to create a monopoly in salt within the

Clayton Act. We think the admitted facts left no genuine issue. Not only is price-fixing unreasonable, *per se*, *United States* v. *Socony-Vacuum Oil Co.*, . . . *United States* v. *Trenton Potteries Co.*, . . . but also it is unreasonable, *per se*, to foreclose competitors from any substantial market. . . . The volume of business affected by these contracts cannot be said to be insignificant or insubstantial and the tendency of the arrangement to accomplishment of monopoly seems obvious. Under the law, agreements are forbidden which "tend to create a monopoly," and it is immaterial that the tendency is a creeping one rather than one that proceeds at full gallop; nor does the law await arrival at the goal before condemning the direction of the movement. . . .

. . . The appellant had at all times a priority on the business at equal prices. A competitor would have to undercut appellant's price to have any hope of capturing the market, while appellant could hold that market by merely meeting competition. We do not think this concession relieves the contract of being a restraint of trade, . . .

Appellant also urges that since under the leases it remained under an obligation to repair and maintain the machines, it was reasonable to confine their use to its own salt because its high quality assured satisfactory functioning and low maintenance cost. . . .

Of course, a lessor may impose on a lessee reasonable restrictions designed in good faith to minimize maintenance burdens and to assure satisfactory operation. . . . But it is not pleaded, nor is it argued, that the machine is allergic to salt of equal quality produced by anyone except International. If others cannot produce salt equal to reasonable specifications for machine use, it is one thing; but it is admitted that, at times, at least, competitors do offer such a product. They are, however, shut out of the market by a provision that limits it, not in terms of quality, but in terms of a particular vendor. Rules for use of leased machinery must not be disguised restraints of free competition, though they may set reasonable standards which all suppliers must meet. . . .

Appellant urges other objections to the summary judgment. The tying clause has not been insisted upon in all leases, nor has it always been enforced when it was included. But these facts do not justify the general use of the restriction which has been admitted here. . . .

. . . The fact is established that the appellant already has wedged itself into this salt market by methods forbidden by law. The District Court is not obliged to assume, contrary to common experience, that a violator of the antitrust laws will relinquish the fruits of his violation more completely than the court requires him to do. And advantages already in hand may be held by methods more subtle and informed, and more difficult to prove, than those which, in the first place, win a market. When the purpose to restrain trade appears from a clear violation of law, it is not necessary that all of the untraveled roads to that end be left open and that only the worn one be closed. The usual ways to the prohibited goal may be blocked against the proven transgressor and the burden put upon him to bring any proper claims for relief to the court's attention. . . .

. . . In an equity suit, the end to be served is not punishment of past transgression, nor is it merely to end specific illegal practices. A public interest served by such civil suits is that they effectively pry open to competition a market that has been closed by defendants' illegal restraints. If this decree accomplishes less than that, the Government has won a lawsuit and lost a cause. . . .

. . . We leave the appellant to proper application to the court below and deny the relief here, upon the present state of the record, without prejudice.

Judgment affirmed.

Mr. Justice Frankfurter, whom Mr. Justice Reed and Mr. Justice Burton join, dissenting in part. . . .

The next tying contract case is somewhat peculiar because it was brought as a Sherman Act case rather than under Section 3 of the Clayton Act. The reasoning of the Justice Department is unclear as to why a Sherman Act violation was selected. The government probably thought advertising space was not a "commodity" within the meaning of Section 3. The burden of proof would have been less under the Clayton Act and precedents had already been well established under Section 3.

The Times-Picayune Publishing Company owned and published a morning and evening newspaper in New Orleans. Its sole competitor in the daily newspaper field was an independent evening newspaper. Classified and general display advertisers in the company's publications were forced to purchase combined insertions in both the morning and evening papers, not in either separately. The government challenged the use of the "unit" contracts as unreasonable restraints of trade in violation of Section 1 of the Sherman Act and as an attempt to monopolize trade in violation of Section 2. By a 5–4 decision handed down in 1953, the Supreme Court ruled against the government.

Justice Clark attempted to bring together the relevant parts of previous tying contract cases in the majority opinion. A tying arrangement violates Section 1 of the Sherman Act when two conditions are met: (1) the seller holds a monopoly position in the market for the "tying" product, *and* (2) a substantial volume of commerce in the "tied" product is restrained. A substantial lessening of competition can be inferred, necessary to satisfy the narrower Section 3 standard, when *either* of the two above conditions are met.

The Court did not believe that the Times-Picayune morning newspaper's share of the total general and classified advertising linage in all three editions, some 40 per cent in recent years, was sufficient to give the "tying" product a dominant position. Thus the first condition for a Sherman Act violation was not met, so there was no necessity of inquiring into the volume of commerce that would be restrained by the "tied" product. Leverage did not exist in one market to exclude sellers from a second.

The next question to consider was whether the case fell under the general prohibition of the Sherman Act against unreasonable restraints of trade. The factual data in the case did not demonstrate to the Court that the unit contracts had unduly handicapped the other existing newspaper. The adoption of the plan was motivated by legitimate business aims. As a matter of fact, the competing publisher had used unit contracts in the past when it was publishing both a morning and evening edition. Since there was no proof of restraint of trade or of a monopoly position, the government had to show a specific intent to monopolize. Such an intent was not established by the record in the case.

TIMES-PICAYUNE PUBLISHING CO. et al. v. UNITED STATES

345 U.S. 594 (1953)

MR. JUSTICE CLARK delivered the opinion of the Court.

At issue is the legality under the Sherman Act of the Times-Picayune Publishing Company's contracts for the sale of newspaper classified and general display advertising space. The Company in New Orleans owns and publishes the morning Times-Picayune and the evening States. Buyers of space for general display and classified advertising in its publications may purchase only combined insertions appearing in both the morning and evening papers, and not in either separately. The United States filed a civil suit under the Sherman Act, challenging these "unit" or "forced combination" contracts as unreasonable restraints of interstate trade, banned by §1, and as tools in an attempt to monopolize a segment of interstate commerce, in violation of §2. After intensive trial of the facts, the District Court found violations of both sections of the law and entered a decree enjoining the Publishing Company's use of these unit contracts and related arrangements for the marketing of advertising space. . . .

Testimony in a voluminous record retraces a history of over twenty-five years. Prior to 1933, four daily newspapers served New Orleans. The Item Company, Ltd., published the Morning Tribune and the evening Item. The morning Times-Picayune was published by its present owners, and the Daily States Publishing Company, Ltd., an independent organization, distributed the evening States. In 1933, the Times Picayune Publishing Company purchased the name, good will, circulation, and advertising contracts of the States, and continued to publish it evenings. The Morning Tribune of the Item Co., Ltd., suspended publication in 1941. Today the Times-Picayune, Item, and States remain the sole significant newspaper media for the dissemination of news and advertising to the residents of New Orleans.

The Times-Picayune Publishing Company distributes the leading newspaper in the area, the Times-Picayune. . . . Although both publications adhere to a single general editorial policy, distinct features and format differentiate the morning Times-Picayune from the evening States. 1950 data reveal a daily average circulation of 188,402 for the Times-Picayune, 114,660 for the Item, and 105,235 for the States. The Times-Picayune thus sold nearly as many copies as the circulation of the Item and States together.

Each of these New Orleans publications sells advertising in various forms. Three principal classes of advertising space are sold: classified, general, and local display. . . . since 1950 general and classified advertisers cannot buy space in either the Times-Picayune or the States alone, but must insert identical copy in both or none. Against that practice the Government levels its attack grounded on §§1 and 2 of the Sherman Act. . . .

. . . The District Court enjoined the Times-Picayune Publishing Company from (A) selling advertising space in any newspaper published by it "upon the condition, expressed or implied, that the purchaser of such space will contract for or purchase advertising space in any other newspaper published by it"; (B) refusing to sell advertising space separately in each newspaper which it publishes; (C) using its "dominant position" in the morning field "to sell any newspaper advertising at rates lower than those approximating either (1) the cost of producing and selling such advertising or (2) comparable newspaper advertising rates in New Orleans." Hence these appeals. . . .

Tying arrangements, we may readily agree, flout the Sherman Act's policy that competition rule the marts of trade. Basic to the faith that a free economy best promotes the public weal is that goods must stand the cold test of competition; that the public, acting through the market's impersonal judgment, shall allocate the Nation's resources and thus direct the course its economic development will take. . . . By conditioning his sale of one commodity on the purchase of another, a seller coerces the abdication of buyers' independent judgment as to the "tied" product's merits and insulates it from the competitive stresses of the open market. But any intrinsic superiority of the "tied" product would convince freely choosing buyers to select it over others, anyway. . . . Conversely, the effect on competing sellers attempting to rival the "tied" product is drastic: to the extent the enforcer of the tying arrangement enjoys market control, other existing or potential sellers are foreclosed from offering up their goods to a free competitive judgment; they are effectively excluded from the marketplace. . . .

. . . From the "tying" cases a perceptible pattern of illegality emerges: When the seller enjoys a monopolistic position in the market for the "tying" product, *or* if a substantial volume of commerce in the "tied" product is restrained, a tying arrangement violates the narrower standards expressed in §3 of the Clayton Act because from either factor the requisite potential lessening of competition is inferred. And because for even a lawful monopolist it is "unreasonable, *per se*, to foreclose competitors from any substantial market," a tying arrangement is banned by §1 of the Sherman Act whenever *both* conditions are met. . . .

In this case, the rule of *International Salt* can apply only if both its ingredients are met. The Government at the outset elected to proceed not under the Clayton but the Sherman Act. . . .

Once granted that the volume of commerce affected was not "insignificant or insubstantial," the Times-Picayune's market position becomes critical to the case. The District Court found that the Times-Picayune occupied a dominant position" in New Orleans; the sole morning daily in the area, it led its competitors in circulation, number of pages and advertising linage. But every newspaper is a dual trader in separate though interdependent markets; it sells the paper's news and advertising content to its readers; in effect that readership is in turn sold to the buyers of advertising space. This case concerns solely one of these markets. The Publishing Company stands accused not of tying sales to its readers but only to buyers of general and classified space in its papers. For this reason, dominance in the advertising market, not in readership, must be decisive in gauging the legality of the Company's unit plan. . . .

The "market," as most concepts in law or economics, cannot be measured by metes and bounds. Nor does the substance of Sherman Act violations typically depend on so flexible a guide. Section 2 outlaws monopolization of any "appreciable part" of interstate commerce, and by §1 unreasonable restraints are banned irrespective of the amount of commerce involved. . . . But the essence of illegality in tying agreements is the wielding of monopolistic leverage; a seller exploits his dominant position in one market to expand his empire into the next. Solely for testing the strength of that lever, the whole and not part of a relevant market must be assigned controlling weight. . . .

We do not think that the Times-Picayune occupied a "dominant" position in the newspaper advertising market in New Orleans. Unlike other "tying" cases where patents or copyrights supplied the requisite market control, any equivalent market "dominance" in this case must rest on comparative marketing data. . . .

. . . [T]he Times-Picayune's sales of both general and classified linage over the years hovered around 40%. . . . If each of the New Orleans publications shared equally in the total volume of linage, the Times-Picayune would have sold 33⅓%; in the absence of patent or copyright control, the small existing increment in the circumstances here disclosed cannot confer that market "dominance" which, in conjunction with a "not insubstantial" volume of trade in the "tied" product, would result in a Sherman Act offense under the rule of *International Salt.* . . .

. . . Although advertising space in the Times-Picayune, as the sole morning daily, was doubtless essential to blanket coverage of the local newspaper readership, nothing in the record suggests that advertisers viewed the city's newspaper readers, morning or evening, as other than fungible customer potential. We must assume, therefore, that the readership "bought" by advertisers in the Times-Picayune was the selfsame "product" sold by the States and, for that matter, the Item.

. . . The common core of the adjudicated unlawful tying arrangements is the forced purchase of a second distinct commodity with the desired purchase of a dominant "tying" product, resulting in economic harm to competition in the "tied" market. Here, however, two newspapers under single ownership at the same place, time, and terms sell indistinguishable products to advertisers; no dominant "tying" product exists (in fact, since space in neither the Times-Picayune nor the States can be bought alone, one may be viewed as "tying" as the other); no leverage in one market excludes sellers in the second, because for present purposes the products are identical and the market the same. . . . In short, neither the rationale nor the doctrines evolved by the "tying" cases can dispose of the Publishing Company's arrangements challenged here.

The Publishing Company's advertising contracts must thus be tested under the Sherman Act's general prohibition on unreasonable restraints of trade. . . .

The record's factual data, in sum, do not demonstrate that the Publishing Company's advertising contracts unduly handicapped its extant competitor, the Item. In the early years when four-cornered newspaper competition for classified linage prevailed in New Orleans, the ascendancy of the Publishing Company's papers over their morning-evening competitor soon became manifest. With unit plan pitted on even terms against unit plan, over the years the local market pattern steadily evolved from the Times-Picayune Company's rise and the Item Company's decline. . . .

. . . And the case has not met the *per se* criteria of Sherman Act §1 from which proscribed effect automatically must be inferred. . . . Under the broad general policy directed by §1 against unreasonable trade restraints, guilt cannot rest on speculation; the Government here has proved neither actual unlawful effects nor facts which radiate a potential for future harm.

While even otherwise reasonable trade arrangements must fall if conceived to achieve forbidden ends, legitimate business aims predominantly motivated the Publishing Company's adoption of the unit plan. Because the antitrust laws strike equally at nascent and accomplished restraints of trade, monopolistic designs as well as results are reached by the prohibitions of the Sherman Act. . . .

Consequently, no Sherman Act violation has occurred unless the Publishing Company's refusal to sell advertising space except *en bloc*, viewed alone, constitutes a violation of the Act. Refusals to sell, without more, do not violate the law. . . .

We conclude, therefore, that this record does not establish the charged violations of §1 and §2 of the Sherman Act. We do not determine that unit advertising arrangements are lawful in other circumstances or in other proceedings. Our decision adjudicates solely that this record cannot substantiate the Government's view of this case. Accordingly, the District Court's judgment must be

Reversed.

MR. JUSTICE BURTON, with whom MR. JUSTICE BLACK, MR. JUSTICE DOUGLAS, and MR. JUSTICE MINTON join, dissenting.

The majority opinion seeks to avoid the effect of *United States* v. *Griffith*, 334 U.S. 100, and of *International Salt Co.* v. *United States*, . . . by taking the position that the Times-Picayune does not enjoy a "dominant position" in the general newspaper advertising market of New Orleans, including all three papers, as a single market. The complaint, however, is not and need not be dependent upon the relation of the Times-Picayune to that entire market.

The complaint is that the Times-Picayune enjoys a distinct, conceded and complete monopoly of access to the morning newspaper readers in the New Orleans area and that it uses that monopoly to restrain unreasonably the competition between its evening newspaper, the New Orleans States, and the independent New Orleans Item, in the competitive field of evening newspaper advertising. Insistence by the Times-Picayune upon acceptance of its compulsory combination advertising contracts makes payment for, and publication of, classified and general advertising in its own evening paper an inescapable part of the price of access to the all-important columns of the single morning paper. I agree with the District Court that such conduct violates the Sherman Act under the circumstances here presented. . . .

The most recent Supreme Court decision involving tying contracts was handed down in the 1958 *Northern Pacific Railway* case. As in the *Times-Picayune* case, the government brought charges under the Sherman Act rather than the Clayton Act. This time, however, the Justice Department was successful in securing a conviction. It appears from this decision that tying contracts, like price fixing and market sharing, will be considered *per se* violations of the Sherman Act when there is sufficient economic power to impose an appreciable restraint on competition in the market for the tied product *and* a "not insubstantial" amount of commerce is involved.

Several million acres of land had originally been granted to the Northern Pacific Railroad to facilitate construction of its line. In disposing of the land, the railroad incorporated in its deeds and leases "preferential routing" agreements compelling the users of the land to ship over the railroad's lines all commodities produced or manufactured on the land, provided that its rates (and in some instances its services) were equal to those of competing carriers. No patent was involved in these tying arrangements, nor was there any contention of a monopolistic position for the tying product.

The majority of the Court believed the facts were indisputable that Northern Pacific did possess "substantial economic power" due to its extensive landholdings. This power was used as leverage to induce large numbers of land possessors to give the railroad preference over its competitors. Furthermore, there was no doubt that a "not insubstantial" amount of commerce was affected by the restrictive provisions. The essential elements for treating the tying arrangements as unreasonable *per se* were established and nothing was offered by the railroad in defense to alter that conclusion.

Justice Harlan's dissenting opinion had two important criticisms of the majority position. First, he did not believe that the "essential prerequisites" for a finding of unreasonable *per se* had been established in the lower court. According to the *International Salt* and *Times-Picayune* cases, such a finding requires that the defendant possess a "dominant position" in the market for the tying product, and now the majority has equated this with "sufficient economic power." Second, he believed the use of a summary judgment by the lower court was inappropriate since it produced no facts to support a finding of economic power. Therefore, he believed the case should have been returned to the lower court for a trial on the question of market dominance.

NORTHERN PACIFIC RAILWAY CO. et al. v. UNITED STATES

356 U.S. 1 (1958)

MR. JUSTICE BLACK delivered the opinion of the Court.

In 1864 and 1870 Congress granted the predecessor of the Northern Pacific Railway Company approximately forty million acres of land in several Northwestern States and Territories to facilitate its construction of a railroad line from Lake Superior to Puget Sound. In general terms, this grant consisted of every alternate section of land in a belt 20 miles wide on each side of the track through States and 40 miles wide through Territories. . . . By 1949 the Railroad had sold about 37,000,000 acres of its holdings, but had reserved mineral rights in 6,500,000 of those acres. Most of the unsold land was leased for one purpose or another. In a large number of its sales contracts and most of its lease agreements the Railroad had inserted "preferential routing" clauses which compelled the grantee or lessee to ship over its lines all commodities produced or manufactured on the land, provided that its rates (and in some instances its service) were equal to those of competing carriers. . . .

In 1949 the Government filed suit under §4 of the Sherman Act seeking a declaration that the defendant's "preferential routing" agreements were unlawful as unreasonable restraints of trade under §1 of that Act. . . .

The Sherman Act was designed to be a comprehensive charter of economic liberty aimed at preserving free and unfettered competition as the rule of trade. . . .

. . . [T]here are certain agreements or practices which because of their pernicious effect on competition and lack of any redeeming virtue are conclusively presumed to be unreasonable and therefore illegal without elaborate inquiry as to the precise harm they have caused or the business excuse for their use. . . .

For our purposes a tying arrangement may be defined as an agreement by a party to sell one product but only on the condition that the buyer also purchases a different (or tied) product, or at least agrees that he will not purchase that product from any other supplier. Where such conditions are successfully exacted competition on the merits with respect to the tied product is inevitably curbed. . . . They are unreasonable in and of themselves whenever a party has sufficient economic power with respect to the tying product to appreciably restrain free competition in the market for the tied product and a "not insubstantial" amount of interstate commerce is affected. . . .

In this case we believe the district judge was clearly correct in entering summary judgment declaring the defendant's "preferential routing" clauses unlawful restraints of trade. We wholly agree that the undisputed facts established beyond any genuine question that the defendant possessed substantial economic power by virtue of its extensive landholdings which it used as leverage to induce large numbers of purchasers and lessees to give it preference, to the exclusion of its competitors, in carrying goods or produce from the land transferred to them. Nor can there be any real doubt that a "not insubstantial" amount of interstate commerce was and is affected by these restrictive provisions. . . .

As pointed out before, the defendant was initially granted large acreages by Congress in the several Northwestern States through which its lines now run. . . . In disposing of its holdings the defendant entered into contracts of sale or lease covering at least several million acres of land which included "preferential routing" clauses. The very existence of this host of tying arrangements is itself compelling evidence of the defendant's great power, at least where, as here, no other explanation has been offered for the existence of these restraints. . . . In short, we are convinced that the essential prerequisites for treating the defendant's tying arrangements as unreasonable "*per se*" were conclusively established below and that the defendant has offered to prove nothing there or here which would alter this conclusion. . . .

The defendant attempts to evade the force of *International Salt* on the ground that the tying product there was patented while here it is not. But we do not believe this distinction has, or should have, any significance. In arriving at its decision in *International Salt* the Court placed no reliance on the fact that a patent was involved nor did it give the slightest intimation that the outcome would have been any different if that had not been the case. If anything, the Court held the challenged tying arrangements unlawful *despite* the fact that the tying item was patented, not because of it. . . . Nor have subsequent cases confined the rule of *per se* unreasonableness laid down in *International Salt* to situations involving patents. . . .

While there is some language in the *Times-Picayune* opinion which speaks of "monopoly power" or "dominance" over the tying product as a necessary precondition for application of the rule of *per se* unreasonableness to tying arrangements, we do not construe this general language as requiring anything more than sufficient economic power to impose an appreciable restraint on free competition in the tied product (assuming all the time, of course, that a "not insubstantial" amount of interstate commerce is affected). . . .

The defendant contends that its "preferential routing" clauses are subject to so many exceptions and have been adminstered so leniently that they do not significantly restrain competition. It points out that these clauses permit the vendee or lessee to ship by competing carrier if its rates are lower (or in some instances if its service is better) than the defendant's. Of course if these restrictive provisions are merely harmless sieves with no tendency to restrain competition, as the defendant's argument seems to imply, it is hard to understand why it has expended so much effort in obtaining them in vast numbers and upholding their validity, or how they are of any benefit to anyone, even the defendant. But however that may be, the essential fact remains that these agreements are binding obligations held over the heads of vendees which deny defendant's competitors access to the fenced-off market on the same terms as the defendant. All of this is only aggravated, of course, here in the regulated transportation industry where there is frequently no real rate competition at all and such effective competition as actually thrives takes other forms.

Affirmed.

MR. JUSTICE CLARK took no part in the consideration or decision of this case.

MR. JUSTICE HARLAN, whom MR. JUSTICE FRANKFURTER and MR. JUSTICE WHITTAKER join, dissenting.

The Court affirms summary judgment for the Government by concluding that "the essential prerequisites for treating the defendant's tying arrangements as unreasonable *'per se'* were conclusively established below. . . ." In my view, these prerequisites were not established, and this case should be remanded to the District Court for a trial on the issue whether appellants' landholdings gave them that amount of control over the relevant market for land necessary under this Court's past decisions to make the challenged tying clauses violative *per se* of the Sherman Act. . . .

. . . *Times-Picayune Publishing Co.* v. *United States*, . . . has made it clear beyond dispute that both *proof* of dominance in the market for the tying product *and* a showing that an appreciable volume of business in the tied product is restrained are essential conditions to judicial condemnation of a tying clause as a *per se* violation of the Sherman Act. . . . It is not, as the Court intimates at one point in its opinion, that under the Sherman Act the tying clause is illegal *per se;* the *per se* illegality results from its use by virtue of a vendor's dominance over the tying interest to foreclose competitors from a substantial market in the tied interest.

My primary difficulty with the Court's affirmance of the judgment below is that the District Court made no finding that the appellants had a "dominant position" or, as this Court now puts it, "sufficient economic power," in the relevant land market. . . .

The reliance on *International Salt* with the new scope the Court now gives it is puzzling in light of the Court's express recognition that a finding of sufficient economic power over land to restrict competition in freight services is an essential element here. The Court heightens this paradox by its effort to satisfy this requirement with the assertion that "undisputed facts" conclusively established the existence of this power. . . .

I do not understand the Court to excuse findings as to control by adopting the Government's argument that this case should be brought within *International Salt* by analogy of the ownership of land to that of a patent, so that the particular tract of land involved in each purchase or lease itself constitutes the relevant market. . . .

. . . As already indicated, I should think that a showing of "sufficient economic power" in cases of this kind could be based upon a variety of factors, such as significant percentage control of the relevant market, desirability of the product to the purchaser, use of tying clauses which would be likely to result in economic detriment to vendees or lessees, and such uniqueness of the tying product as to suggest comparison with a monopoly by patent. But I venture to predict that the language of the Court, taken in conjunction with its approval of the summary disposition of this case, will leave courts and lawyers in confusion as to what the proper standards now are for judging tying clauses under the Sherman Act.

The Court's action in affirming the judgment below sanctions what I deem to be a serious abuse of the summary judgment procedures. . . . A record barren of facts adequate to support either a finding of economic power over a relevant land market or a finding that the land involved is so unique as to constitute in itself the relevant market is remedied by this Court's reliance upon "common sense" and judicial notice of appellants' commanding position. But these are poor substitutes for the proof to which the Government should be put. I would remand to the District Court for a trial and findings on the issue of "dominance."

Exclusive Dealing Arrangements

When compared to tying contracts, the water is murkier with regard to the lawfulness of *exclusive dealing arrangements*. Exclusive dealing also comes under the provisions of Section 3 of the Clayton Act. Unlike two of the tying cases brought under the Sherman Act, all of the leading ones in this area have been decided under the Clayton Act provision. The cases presented in this section show that the courts have condemned exclusive dealing arrangements when the firm promulgating the contracts has had considerable market power so that potential competitors are excluded from a sizable segment of the market.

The first exclusive dealing arrangement receiving a Supreme Court interpretation was the 1922 *Standard Fashion* case. Standard Fashion, a maker of dress patterns and controlling two-fifths of the pattern agencies in the country, contracted with Magrane-Houston Company, a retailer, to sell exclusively the patterns of Standard Fashion for a two-year period. The contract specifically required the purchaser not to deal in goods of the seller's competitors. The contract provided certain incentives for the retailer to handle only the products of Standard Fashion. Among these were a 50 per cent discount from retail prices, returning discarded patterns, and other beneficial considerations. Before expiration of the contract, the retailer discontinued the exclusive sale of Standard Fashion patterns and started selling those of a competitor. Standard Fashion brought suit to enforce the contract, arguing that it was one of agency or joint venture, and not one of sale.

In a unanimous opinion, the Supreme Court ruled against Standard Fashion and held that the contract was clearly one of sale and not one of agency since the retailer acquired full title. The Court noted that Section 3 was intended to prevent contracts such as this one where there was a *probability* for lessening of competition. The exclusive dealing contract of Standard Fashion was one that would probably lessen competition. The primary test for illegality was the market control of the pattern maker. The economic effect of such contracts by a firm controlling two-fifths of the market would be to insure a virtual monopoly in most small communities as well as a commanding position in many large cities.

STANDARD FASHION COMPANY v. MAGRANE-HOUSTON COMPANY

258 U.S. 346 (1922)

MR. JUSTICE DAY delivered the opinion of the court.

Petitioner brought suit in the United States District Court for the District of Massachusetts to restrain the respondent from violating a certain contract concerning the sale of patterns for garments worn by women and children, called Standard Patterns. The bill was dismissed by the District Court and its decree was affirmed by the Circuit Court of Appeals. . . .

Petitioner is a New York corporation engaged in the manufacture and distribution of patterns. Respondent conducted a retail dry goods business at the corner of Washington Street and Temple Place in the City of Boston. On November 25, 1914, the parties entered into a contract by which the petitioner granted to the respondent an agency for the sale of Standard Patterns at respondent's store, for a term of two years from the date of the contract, and from term to term thereafter until the agreement should be terminated as thereinafter provided. Petitioner agreed to sell to respondent Standard Patterns at a discount of 50% from retail prices, with advertising matter and publications upon terms stated; and to allow respondent to return discarded patterns semiannually between January 15th and February 15th, and July 15th and August 15th, in exchange at nine-tenths cost for other patterns to be shipped from time to time thereafter. The contract provided that patterns returned for exchange must have been purchased from the petitioner and must be delivered in good order to the general office of the seller in New York. Respondent agreed to purchase a substantial number of standard fashion sheets, to purchase and keep on hand at all times, except during the period of exchange, $1,000 value in Standard Patterns at net invoice prices, and to pay petitioner for the pattern stock to be selected by it on terms of payment which are stated. Respondent agreed not to assign or transfer the agency, or to remove it from its original location without the written consent of the petitioner, and not to sell or permit to be sold on its premises during the term of the contract any other make of patterns, and not to sell Standard Patterns except at label prices. Respondent agreed to permit petitioner to take account of pattern stock whenever it desired, to pay proper attention to the sale of Standard Patterns, to conserve the best interests of the agency at all times, and to reorder promptly as patterns were sold. Either party desiring to terminte the agreement was required to give the other party three months' notice in writing, within thirty days after the expiration of any contract period, the agency to continue during such three months. Upon expiration of such notice respondent agreed to promptly return to petitioner all Standard Patterns, and petitioner agreed to credit respondent for the same on receipt in good order at three-fourths cost. Neglect to return the pattern stock within two weeks after the expiration of the three months' notice to relieve the petitioner from all obligation to redeem the same. It was further stipulated that in the event the business property of the respondent, or a substantial part thereof, should be disposed of by respondent for business other than that of dry goods or as a general department store, the respondent should have the privilege of terminating the contract by giving the petitioner due notice of such change. Two weeks after the change in the premises had been made the respondent might deliver its stock of Standard Patterns to the petitioner for repurchase under the repurchase clause of the contract. . . .

The principal question in the case and the one upon which the writ of certiorari was granted involves the construction of §3 of the Clayton Act, . . . That section, so far as pertinent here, provides:

"It shall be unlawful . . . to lease or make a sale or contract for sale of goods, . . . or fix a price charged therefor, or discount from, or rebate upon, such price, on the condition, agreement or understanding that the lessee or purchaser thereof shall not use or deal in the goods . . . of a competitor or competitors of the lessor or seller, where the effect of such lease, sale, or contract for sale or such condition, agreement or understanding may be to substantially lessen competition or tend to create a monopoly in any line of commerce."

The contract contains an agreement that the respondent shall not sell or permit to be sold on its premises during the term of the contract any other make of patterns. It is shown that on or about July 1, 1917, the respondent discontinued the sale of the petitioner's patterns and placed on sale in its store patterns of a rival company known as the McCall Company.

It is insisted by the petitioner that the contract is not one of sale, but is one of agency or joint venture, but an analysis of the contract shows that a sale was in fact intended and made. It is provided that patterns returned for exchange must have been purchased from the petitioner. Respondent agreed to purchase a certain number of patterns. Upon expiration of the notice of termination the respondent agreed to promptly return all Standard Patterns bought under the contract. In the event of the disposition of the business property of the respondent at Washington Street and Temple Place, the respondent might deliver its stock of Standard Patterns to the petitioner for repurchase under the repurchase clause of the contract.

Full title and dominion passed to the buyer. While this contract is denominated one of agency, it is perfectly apparent that it is one of sale. . . .

. . . The real question is: Does the contract of sale come within the third section of the Clayton Act because the covenant not to sell the patterns of others "may be to substantially lessen competition or tend to create a monopoly." . . .

The Clayton Act sought to reach the agreements embraced within its sphere in their incipiency, and in the section under consideration to determine their legality by specific tests of its own which declared illegal contracts of sale made upon the agreement or understanding that the purchaser shall not deal in the goods of a competitor or competitors of the seller, which may "substantially lessen competition or tend to create a monopoly." . . .

Section 3 condemns sales or agreements where the effect of such sale or contract of sale "may" be to substantially lessen competition or tend to create monopoly. It thus deals with consequences to follow the making of the restrictive covenant limiting the right of the purchaser to deal in the goods of the seller only. But we do not think that the purpose in using the word "may" was to prohibit the mere possibility of the consequences described. It was intended to prevent such agreements as would under the circumstances disclosed probably lessen competition, or create an actual tendency to monopoly. That it was not intended to reach every remote lessening of competition is shown in the requirement that such lessening must be substantial.

Both courts below found that the contract interpreted in the light of the circumstances surrounding the making of it was within the provisions of the Clayton Act as one which substantially lessened competition and tended to create monopoly. These courts put special stress upon the fact found that, of 52,000 so-called pattern agencies in the entire country, the petitioner, or a holding company controlling it and two other pattern companies, approximately controlled two-fifths of such agencies. . . .

We agree with these conclusions, and have no doubt that the contract, properly interpreted, with its restrictive covenant, brings it fairly within the section of the Clayton Act under consideration.

Affirmed.

The *Sinclair Refining Company* case, decided in 1923, combines aspects of tying contracts and exclusive dealing arrangements. Most observers, however, include it in the exclusive dealing category. In a number of proceedings against more than thirty refiners and wholesalers of gasoline, the Federal Trade Commission ordered the abandonment of the practice of leasing underground tanks and pumps at nominal fees with the stipulation that the equipment must be used exclusively with gasoline supplied by the lessor. There was no attempt on the part of Sinclair to limit the right of its lessees to deal in the products of rivals. The only requirement was to prohibit the use of rival products from being used with the equipment leased from the supplier. The lessee was still free to sell the products of another.

Small, independent refiners contended that the cost of financing and installing equipment in order to obtain market outlets for their brand erected a competitive barrier and foreclosed a substantial part of the market to them. The Court did not feel that the contracts violated Section 3 since retailers could handle more than one brand if they chose to do so. Furthermore, the FTC could not interfere with ordinary business methods and restrict competition with arbitrary standards. There was no evidence of fraud, misrepresentation, or bad faith. Consequently, the charge of unfair competition in violation of Section 5 of the Federal Trade Commission Act was not sustained.

FEDERAL TRADE COMMISSION v. SINCLAIR REFINING COMPANY

261 U.S. 463 (1923)

MR. JUSTICE MCREYNOLDS delivered the opinion of the Court.

In separate proceedings against thirty or more refiners and wholesalers, the Federal Trade Commission condemned and ordered them to abandon the practice of leasing underground tanks with pumps to retail dealers at nominal prices and upon condition that the equipment should be used only with gasoline supplied by the lessor. . . .

July 18, 1919, the Commission issued a complaint charging that respondent, Sinclair Refining Company, was purchasing and selling refined oil and gasoline and leasing and loaning storage tanks and pumps as part of interstate commerce in competition with numerous other concerns similarly engaged; and that it was violating both the Federal Trade Commission Act . . . and the Clayton Act, . . .

The particular facts relied on to show violation of the Federal Trade Commission Act are thus alleged—

"Paragraph Three. That respondent in the conduct of its business, as aforesaid, with the effect of stifling and suppressing competition in the sale of the aforesaid products and in the sale, leasing, or loaning of the aforesaid devices and other equipments for storing and handling the same, and with the effect of injuring competitors who sell such products and devices, has within the four years last past sold, leased, or loaned and now sells, leases, or loans the said devices and their equipment for prices or considerations which do not represent reasonable returns on the investments in such devices and their equipments; that many such sales, leases, or loans of the aforesaid devices are made at prices below the cost of producing and vending the same; that many of such contracts for the lease or loan of such devices and their equipments provide or are entered into with the understanding that the lessee or borrower shall not place in such devices, or use in connection with such devices and their equipments, any refined oil or gasoline of a competitor; . . ."

Respondent's written contract does not undertake to limit the lessee's right to use or deal in the goods of a competitor of the lessor, but leaves him free to follow his own judgment. It is not properly described by the complaint and is not within the letter of the Clayton Act. But counsel for the Commission insist that inasmuch as lessees generally—except garage men in the larger places—will not encumber themselves with more than one equipment, the practical effect of the restrictive covenant is to confine most dealers to the products of their lessors; and we are asked to hold that, read in the light of these facts, the contract falls within the condemnation of the statute. . . .

In the *Standard Fashion Co. Case* the purchaser expressly agreed not to sell or permit sale of any other make of patterns on its premises. It had a retail store in Boston and sales elsewhere were not within contemplation of the parties. This Court construed the contract as embodying an undertaking not to sell other patterns. . . .

There is no covenant in the present contract which obligates the lessee not to sell the goods of another; and its language cannot be so construed. Neither the findings nor the evidence show circumstances similar to those surrounding the "tying" covenants of the Shoe Machinery Company. Many competitors seek to sell excellent brands of gasoline and no one of them is essential to the retail business. The lessee is free to buy wherever he chooses; he may freely accept and use as many pumps as he wishes and may discontinue any or all of them. He may carry on business as his judgment dictates and his means permit, save only that he cannot use the lessor's equipment for dispensing another's brand. By investing a comparatively small sum, he can buy an outfit and use it without hindrance. He can have respondent's gasoline, with the pump or without the pump, and many competitors seek to supply his needs. . . .

Is the challenged practice an unfair method of competition within the meaning of §5 of the Federal Trade Commission Act? Reviewing the circumstances, four circuit courts of appeals have answered, no. And we can find no sufficient reason for a contrary conclusion. Certainly the practice is not opposed to good morals because characterized by deception, bad faith, fraud or oppression. . . .

The powers of the Commission are limited by the statutes. It has no general authority to compel competitors to a common level, to interfere with ordinary business methods or to prescribe arbitrary standards for those engaged in the conflict for advantage called competition. The great purpose of both statutes was to advance the public interest by securing fair opportunity for the play of the contending forces ordinarily engendered by an honest desire for gain. And to this end it is essential that those who adventure their time, skill and capital should have large freedom of action in the conduct of their own affairs.

The suggestion that the assailed practice is unfair because of its effect upon the sale of pumps by their makers is sterile and requires no serious discussion.

The judgments below must be

Affirmed.

Before 1949, all cases of exclusive dealing involved a firm which possessed a dominant market position. The *Standard Oil of California* case was the first in which the maker of such contracts did not enjoy a dominant position. Standard Oil sold 23 per cent of the gasoline in seven western states. It entered into exclusive dealing contracts with about six thousand independent dealers, selling less than 7 per cent of the gasoline in the area. The dealers agreed to purchase exclusively from the company all their requirements for one or more products, including gasoline and other petroleum products as well as tires, tubes, and accessories. There was widespread adoption of similar requirements contracts by competitors of Standard Oil; this practice had been common for many years.

Justice Frankfurter delivered the 5–4 majority opinion and stated that a violation of Section 3 is sustained by showing that a "substantial portion of commerce is affected" by exclusive dealing contracts. Admittedly, these contracts covered "a substantial number of outlets and a substantial amount of products, . . ." But does 7 per cent of the gasoline sold in a seven-state regional market comprise a "substantial portion"? The conclusion of the Court was affirmative. The contract of Standard Oil did create the kind of "potential clog on competition" that Section 3 was designed to remove.

Justice Douglas dissented on the grounds that the alternatives to exclusive dealing contracts were even worse. He pointed out that the independent dealers would likely be "swallowed up" by major oil companies, and "clerks responsible to a superior in a distant place take the place of resident proprietors . . ." The result would be greater concentration of industry into fewer and fewer hands. The exclusive dealing contracts "at least keeps the independents alive."

Justice Jackson dissented on the grounds that no evidence was introduced to show a substantial lessening of competition. The Court, he felt, was upsetting business practices of long standing and widespread adoption without an adequate basis.

STANDARD OIL COMPANY OF CALIFORNIA et al. v. UNITED STATES

337 U.S. 293 (1949)

Mr. Justice Frankfurter delivered the opinion of the Court.

This is an appeal to review a decree enjoining the Standard Oil Company of California and its wholly-owned subsidiary, Standard Stations,

Inc., from enforcing or entering into exclusive supply contracts with any independent dealer in petroleum products and automobile accessories. . . .

The Standard Oil Company of California, a Delaware corporation, owns petroleum-producing resources and refining plants in California and sells petroleum products in what has been termed in these proceedings the "Western area"—Arizona, California, Idaho, Nevada, Oregon, Utah and Washington. It sells through its own service stations, to the operators of independent service stations, and to industrial users. It is the largest seller of gasoline in the area. In 1946 its combined sales amounted to 23% of the total taxable gallonage sold there in that year: sales by company-owned service stations constituted 6.8% of the total, sales under exclusive dealing contracts with independent service stations, 6.7% of the total; the remainder were sales to industrial users. . . .

Exclusive supply contracts with Standard had been entered into, as of March 12, 1947, by the operators of 5,937 independent stations, or 16% of the retail gasoline outlets in the Western area, . . . Some outlets are covered by more than one contract so that in all about 8,000 exclusive supply contracts are here in issue. These are of several types, but a feature common to each is the dealer's undertaking to purchase from Standard all his requirements of one or more products. Two types, covering 2,777 outlets, bind the dealer to purchase of Standard all his requirements of gasoline and other petroleum products as well as tires, tubes, and batteries. The remaining written agreements, 4,368 in number, bind the dealer to purchase of Standard all his requirements of petroleum products only. . . .

Since §3 of the Clayton Act was directed to prohibiting specific practices even though not covered by the broad terms of the Sherman Act, it is appropriate to consider first whether the enjoined contracts fall within the prohibition of the narrower Act. . . .

The District Court held that the requirement of showing an actual or potential lessening of competition or a tendency to establish monopoly was adequately met by proof that the contracts covered "a substantial number of outlets and a substantial amount of products, whether considered comparatively or not." . . . Given such quantitative substantiality, the substantial lessening of competition—so the court reasoned—is an automatic result, for the very existence of such contracts denies dealers opportunity to deal in the products of competing suppliers and excludes suppliers from access to the outlets controlled by those dealers. . . . The court likewise deemed it unnecessary to make findings, on the basis of evidence that was admitted, whether the number of Standard's competitors had increased or decreased since the inauguration of the requirements-contract system, whether the number of their dealers had increased or decreased, and as to other matters which would have shed light on the comparative status of Standard and its competitors before and after the adoption of that system. . . .

The issue before us, therefore, is whether the requirement of showing that the effect of the agreements "may be to substantially lessen competition" may be met simply by proof that a substantial portion of commerce is affected or whether it must also be demonstrated that competitive activity has actually diminished or probably will diminish. . . .

. . . Standard's share of the retail market for gasoline, even including sales through company-owned stations, is hardly large enough to conclude as a matter of law that it occupies a dominant position, nor did the trial court so find. . . .

Thus, even though the qualifying clause of §3 is appended without distinction of terms equally to the prohibition of tying clauses and of requirements contracts, pertinent considerations support, certainly as a matter of economic reasoning, varying standards as to each for the proof necessary to fulfill the conditions of that clause. If this distinction were accepted, various tests of the economic usefulness or restrictive effect of requirements contracts would become relevant. Among them would be evidence that competition has flourished despite use of the contracts, and under this test much of the evidence tendered by appellant in this case would be important. . . .

Yet serious difficulties would attend the attempt to apply these tests. We may assume, as did the court below, that no improvement of Standard's competitive position has coincided with the period during which the requirements-contract system of distribution has been in effect. We may assume further that the duration of the contracts is not excessive and that Standard does not by itself dominate the market. But Standard was a major competitor when the present system was adopted, and it is possible that its position would have deteriorated but for the adoption of that system. When it is remembered that all the other major suppliers have also been using requirements contracts, and when it is noted that the relative share of the business which fell to each has remained about the same during the period of their use, it would not be farfetched to infer that their effect has been to enable the established suppliers individually to maintain their own standing and at the same time collectively, even though not collusively, to prevent a late arrival from wresting away more than an insignificant portion of the market. If, indeed, this were a result of the system, it would seem unimportant that a short-run by-product of stability may have been greater efficiency and lower costs, for it is the theory of the antitrust laws that the long-run advantage of the community depends upon the removal of restraints upon competition. . . . If in fact it is economically desirable for service stations to confine themselves to the sale of the petroleum products of a single supplier, they will continue to do so though not bound by contract, and if in fact it is important to retail dealers to assure the supply of their requirements by obtaining the commitment of a single supplier to fulfill them, competition for their patronage should enable them to insist upon such an arrangement without binding them to refrain from looking elsewhere.

We conclude, therefore, that the qualifying clause of §3 is satisfied by proof that competition has been foreclosed in a substantial share of the line of commerce affected. It cannot be gainsaid that observance by a dealer of his requirements contract with Standard does effectively foreclose whatever opportunity there might be for competing suppliers to attract his patronage, and it is clear that the affected proportion of retail sales of petroleum products is substantial. In view of the widespread adoption of such contracts by Standard's competitors and the availability of alternative ways of obtaining an assured market, evidence that competitive activity has not actually declined is inconclusive. Standard's use of the contracts creates just such a potential clog on competition as it was the purpose of §3 to remove wherever, were it to become actual, it would impede a substantial amount of competitive activity.

Since the decree below is sustained by our interpretation of §3 of the Clayton Act, we need not go on to consider whether it might also be sustained by §1 of the Sherman Act. . . .

The judgment below is

Affirmed.

MR. JUSTICE DOUGLAS.

The economic theories which the Court has read into the Anti-Trust Laws have favored rather than discouraged monopoly. . . .

The lessons Brandeis taught on the curse of bigness have largely been forgotten in high places. Size is allowed to become a menace to existing and putative competitors. Price control is allowed to escape the influences of the competitive market and to gravitate into the hands of the few. But beyond all that there is the effect on the community when independents are swallowed up by the trusts and entrepreneurs become employees of absentee owners. Then there is a serious loss in citizenship. Local leadership is diluted. He who was a leader in the village becomes dependent on outsiders for his action and policy. Clerks responsible to a superior in a distant place take the place of resident proprietors beholden to no one. These are the prices which the nation pays for the almost ceaseless growth in bigness on the part of industry. . . .

The elimination of these requirements contracts sets the stage for Standard and the other oil companies to build service-station empires of their own. The opinion of the Court does more than set the stage for that development. It is an advisory opinion as well, stating to the oil companies how they can with impunity build their empires. The formula suggested by the Court is either the use of the "agency" device, which in practical effect means control of filling stations by the oil companies . . . or the outright acquisition of them by subsidiary corporations or otherwise. . . .

When the choice is thus given, I dissent from the outlawry of the requirements contract on the present facts. The effect which it has on competition in this field is minor as compared to the damage which will flow from the judicially approved formula for the growth of bigness tendered by the Court as an alternative. Our choice must be made on the basis not of abstractions but of the realities of modern industrial life. . . .

MR. JUSTICE JACKSON, with whom THE CHIEF JUSTICE and MR. JUSTICE BURTON join, dissenting.

I am unable to join the judgment or opinion of the Court for reasons I will state, but shortly.

. . . The number of dealers and the volume of sales covered by the arrangement of course was sufficient to be substantial. That is to say, this arrangement operated on enough commerce to violate the Act, provided its effects were substantially to lessen competition or tend to create a monopoly. But proof of their quantity does not prove that they had this forbidden quality; and the assumption that they did, without proof, seems to me unwarranted. . . .

But if they must decide, the only possible way for the courts to arrive at a fair determination is to hear all relevant evidence from both parties and weigh not only its inherent probabilities of verity but also compare the experience, disinterestedness and credibility of opposing witnesses. This is a tedious process and not too enlightening, but without it a judicial decree is but a guess in the dark. That is all we have here and I do not think it is an adequate basis on which to upset long-standing and widely practiced business arrangements. . . .

. . . I am not convinced that the requirements contract as here used is a device for suppressing competition instead of a device for waging competition. If we look only at its effect in relation to particular retailers who become parties to it, it does restrain their freedom to purchase their requirements elsewhere and prevents other companies from selling to them. Many contracts have the effect of taking a purchaser out of the market for goods he already has bought or contracted to take. . . . It means to me, if I must decide without evidence, that these contracts are an almost necessary means to maintain this all-important competition for consumer business, in which it is admitted competition is keen. . . .

If the courts are to apply the lash of the antitrust laws to the backs of businessmen to make them compete, we cannot in fairness also apply the lash whenever they hit upon a successful method of competing. That, insofar as I am permitted by the record to learn the facts, appears to be the case before us. I would reverse.

Although the *Standard Stations* case seemed to suggest that almost any exclusive dealing contract involving even a small amount of trade or dollar volume would be outlawed, the FTC did not elect to bring charges in subsequent years unless there was some actual injury to competition. This course of action was verified as a prudent one when the Supreme Court decided the *Tampa Electric* case in 1961. The Court recognized that a number of market factors, in addition to the quantitative magnitude of trade, must be considered in a requirements contract.

Tampa Electric Company, a producer of electrical energy in the Tampa, Florida, vicinity, contracted with the Nashville Coal Company to purchase all its coal requirements for a new generating plant over a twenty-year period. Before the first deliveries were made, Nashville Coal advised Tampa that the contract was illegal under the antitrust laws and therefore would not be fulfilled. Tampa then brought suit to require enforcement. Consideration of market factors revealed that there were some seven hundred coal suppliers in the Appalachian territory that could serve as suppliers for Tampa. Furthermore, Tampa's maximum anticipated requirements over the next twenty years would only approximate 1 per cent of the total consumed.

The Court observed that an exclusive dealing contract must have a probable effect of lessening competition before it is illegal. To determine this effect, three considerations are necessary: (1) the line of commerce, (2) the area of effective competition (relevant market area) in which the seller operates, and (3) the competition foreclosed must constitute a substantial share of the relevant market. The Court was convinced that foreclosure of 1 per cent of the total relevant coal market is "conservatively speaking, quite insubstantial." Within the general context of antitrust legislation, requirements contracts may be suspect, but they are not illegal *per se*. Just because a contract involves a substantial amount of dollars is ordinarily of no great consequence. A substantial—not remote—lessening of competition still must be shown in order for a violation to occur. The Tampa contract appeared to confer economic advantages on both buyer and seller. A twenty-year contract is no particular vice when public utilities are involved because it is in the public interest for the supplier to have assurance of a steady supply of fuel.

TAMPA ELECTRIC CO. v. NASHVILLE COAL CO. et al.

365 U.S. 320 (1961)

Mr. Justice Clark delivered the opinion of the Court.

We granted certiorari to review a declaratory judgment holding illegal under §3 of the Clayton Act a requirements contract between the parties providing for the purchase by petitioner of all the coal it would require as boiler fuel at its Gannon Station in Tampa, Florida, over a 20-year period. . . . We cannot agree that the contract suffers the claimed antitrust illegality . . .

THE FACTS

Petitioner Tampa Electric Company is a public utility located in Tampa, Florida. It produces and sells electric energy to a service area, including the city, extending from Tampa Bay eastward 60 miles to the center of the State, and some 30 miles in width. . . . In 1955 Tampa Electric decided to expand its facilities by the construction of an additional generating plant to be comprised ultimately of six generating units, and to be known as the "Francis J. Gannon Station." Although every electrical generating plant in peninsular Florida burned oil at that time, Tampa Electric decided to try coal as boiler fuel in the first two units constructed at the Gannon Station. Accordingly, it contracted with the respondents to furnish the expected coal requirements for the units. The agreement, dated May 23, 1955, embraced Tampa Electric's "total requirements of fuel . . . for the operation of its first two units to be installed at the Gannon Station . . . not less than 225,000 tons of coal per unit per year," for a period of 20 years. . . . Tampa Electric had the further option of reducing, up to 15%, the amount of its coal purchases covered by the contract after giving six months' notice of an intention to use as fuel a by-product of any of its local customers. The minimum price was set at $6.40 per ton delivered, subject to an escalation clause based on labor cost and other factors. . . .

In April 1957, soon before the first coal was actually to be delivered and after Tampa Electric, in order to equip its first two Gannon units for the use of coal, had expended some $3,000,000 more than the cost of constructing oil-burning units, and after respondents had expended approximately $7,500,000 readying themselves to perform the contract, the latter advised petitioner that the contract was illegal under the antitrust laws, would therefore not be performed, and no coal would be delivered. This turn of events required Tampa Electric to look elsewhere for its coal requirements. . . .

The record indicates that the total consumption of coal in peninsular Florida, as of 1958, aside from Gannon Station, was approximately 700,000 tons annually. It further shows that there were some 700 coal suppliers in the producing area where respondents operated, and that Tampa Electric's anticipated maximum requirements at Gannon Station, i.e., 2,250,000 tons annually, would approximate 1% of the total coal of the same type produced and marketed from respondents' producing area. . . . The District Court, however, granted respondents' motion for summary judgment on the sole ground that the undisputed facts, recited above, showed the contract to be a violation of §3 of the Clayton Act. The Court of Appeals agreed. . . .

Decisions of District Court and Court of Appeals

Both courts admitted that the contract "does not expressly contain the 'condition' " that Tampa Electric would not use or deal in the coal of respondents' competitors. Nonetheless, they reasoned, the "total requirements" provision had the same practical effect, for it prevented Tampa Electric for a period of 20 years from buying coal from any other source for use at that station. . . .

In practical application, even though a contract is found to be an exclusive-dealing arrangement, it does not violate the section unless the court believes it probable that performance of the contract will foreclose competition in a substantial share of the line of commerce affected. Following the guidelines of earlier decisions, certain considerations must be taken. *First*, the line of commerce, . . . *Second*, the area of effective competition in the known line of commerce must be charted by careful selection of the market area in which the seller operates, and to which the purchaser can practicably turn for supplies. . . .

Third, and last, the competition foreclosed by the contract must be found to constitute a substantial share of the relevant market. . . .

To determine substantiality in a given case, it is necessary to weigh the probable effect of the contract on the relevant area of effective competition, taking into account the relative strength of the parties, the proportionate volume of commerce involved in relation to the total volume of commerce in the relevant market area, and the probable immediate and future effects which pre-emption of that share of the market might have on effective competition therein. It follows that a mere showing that the contract itself involves a substantial number of dollars is ordinarily of little consequence. . . .

RELEVANT MARKET OF EFFECTIVE COMPETITION

Neither the Court of Appeals nor the District Court considered in detail the question of the relevant market. They do seem, however, to have been satisfied with inquiring only as to competition within "Peninsular Florida." . . . Respondents contend that the coal tonnage covered by the contract must be weighed against either the total consumption of coal in peninsular Florida, or all of Florida, or the Bituminous Coal Act area comprising peninsular Florida and the Georgia "finger," or, at most, all of Florida and Georgia. If the latter area were considered the relevant market, Tampa Electric's proposed requirements would be 18% of the tonnage sold therein. Tampa Electric says that both courts and respondents are in error, because the "700 coal producers who could serve" it, as recognized by the trial court and admitted by respondents, operated in the Appalachian coal area and that its contract requirements were less than 1% of the total marketed production of these producers; that the relevant effective area of competition was the area in which these producers operated, and in which they were willing to compete for the consumer potential.

We are persuaded that on the record in this case, neither peninsular Florida, nor the entire State of Florida, nor Florida and Georgia combined constituted the relevant market of effective competition. We do not believe that the pie will slice so thinly. By far the bulk of the overwhelming tonnage marketed from the same producing area as serves Tampa is sold outside of Georgia and Florida, and the producers were "eager" to sell more coal in those States. While the relevant competitive market is not ordinarily susceptible to a "metes and bounds" definition, cf. *Times-Picayune Pub. Co.* v. *United States*, . . . it is of course the area in which respondents and the other 700 producers effectively compete. . . . it clearly appears that the proportionate volume of the total relevant coal product as to which the challenged contract pre-empted competition, less than 1%, is, conservatively speaking, quite insubstantial. . . .

EFFECT ON COMPETITION IN THE RELEVANT MARKET

It may well be that in the context of antitrust legislation protracted requirements contracts are suspect, but they have not been declared illegal *per se.* Even though a single contract between single traders may fall within the initial broad proscription of the section, it must also suffer the qualifying disability, tendency to work a substantial—not remote—lessening of competition in the relevant competitive market. . . .

The remaining determination, therefore, is whether the pre-emption of competition to the extent of the tonnage involved tends to substantially foreclose competition in the relevant coal market. We think not. . . . There is here neither a seller with a dominant position in the market as in *Standard Fashions, supra;* nor myriad outlets with substantial sales volume, coupled with an industry-wide practice of relying upon exclusive contracts, as in *Standard Oil, supra;* nor a plainly restrictive tying arrangement as in *International Salt, supra.* On the contrary, we seem to have only that type of contract which "may well be of economic advantage to buyers as well as to sellers." . . . The 20-year period of the contract is singled out as the principal vice, but at least in the case of public utilities the assurance of a steady and ample supply of fuel is necessary in the public interest. Otherwise consumers are left unprotected against service failures owing to shutdowns; and increasingly unjustified costs might result in more burdensome rate structures eventually to be reflected in the consumer's bill. . . . In weighing the various factors, we have decided that in the competitive bituminous coal marketing area involved here the contract sued upon does not tend to foreclose a substantial volume of competition. . . .

The judgment is reversed and the case remanded to the District Court for further proceedings not inconsistent with this opinion.

It is so ordered.

Mr. Justice Black and Mr. Justice Douglas are of the opinion that the District Court and the Court of Appeals correctly decided this case and would therefore affirm their judgments.

11

Resale Price Maintenance
and Refusal to Deal

Resale price maintenance is an arrangement between the producer of the goods and the retailer whereby the producer sets a minimum price below which the retailer may not sell to the consumer. Such arrangements are an outgrowth of mass production and the consequent national advertising engaged in by the producer to stimulate demand for his goods. The producer's interest in resale price maintenance is to preserve his good will, the integrity of his trade name, and the "image" or prestige of his product—all of which he has presumably created and enhanced by his national advertising program.

Many producers believe that if retailers are allowed to sell below the established price or to use the goods as a loss leader, consumers may come to believe that the normal price is inflated and overvalued. The producer also may fear that the number of outlets handling his goods will decline because other dealers will not try to compete with the aggressive, price-cutting retailer. The smaller dealers favor resale price maintenance as a device in helping them compete with chain stores and "discount" houses. From the consumer's point of view, it is obvious that resale price maintenance eliminates price competition.

Complaints of refusal to deal are most often associated with attempts to enforce resale prices. Of course, the law permits sellers to choose with whom they will deal. Section 2 of the Clayton Act provides "That nothing herein contained shall prevent persons . . . from selecting their own customers in bona fide transactions and not in restraint of trade. . . ." A refusal to deal is illegal if its purpose is to restrain trade. Sometimes the methods used by a producer to enforce the resale price of his goods may result in restraint of trade. This seems especially true when the producer engages others in a conspiracy or combination to help him enforce his resale price.

Resale Price Maintenance under the Sherman Act

Before the Sherman Act was amended by the Miller-Tydings Act in 1937, the leading case on resale price maintenance was *Dr. Miles Medical Company v. John D. Park & Sons Company.* The Dr. Miles Medical Company manufactured proprietary medicines, prepared by secret formulas but not patented. By contractual agreement, the firm set the price at which wholesalers and retailers sold its medicines. It claimed this was necessary to protect its products from loss of reputation and decreasing demand which resulted when its medicines were sold at "cut-rate" prices. The John D. Park & Sons Company, a drug wholesaler, had obtained a supply of these medicines and had sold them below stipulated prices. Thereupon Dr. Miles Company sued, seeking an injunction to restrain the drug wholesaler.

In ruling against Dr. Miles Medical Company, the Supreme Court said that merely because the goods were proprietary and manufactured under a secret process did not give the company greater rights than if the goods were produced under ordinary conditions. The Court declared that the company's agreements to maintain prices prevented competition among those who traded in its products and were in restraint of trade. It said that the company "having sold its product at prices satisfactory to itself, the public is entitled to whatever advantage may be derived from competition in the subsequent traffic."

DR. MILES MEDICAL COMPANY v. JOHN D. PARK & SONS COMPANY

220 U.S. 373 (1911)

MR. JUSTICE HUGHES, . . . delivered the opinion of the court.[1]

The complainant, a manufacturer of proprietary medicines which are prepared in accordance with secret formulas, presents by its bill a system, carefully devised, by which it seeks to maintain certain prices fixed by it for all the sales of its products both at wholesale and retail. Its purpose is to establish minimum prices at which sales shall be made by its vendees and by all subsequent purchasers who traffic in its remedies. Its plan is thus to govern directly the entire trade in the medicines it manufactures, embracing interstate commerce as well as commerce within the States respectively. To accomplish this result it has adopted two forms of restrictive agreements limiting trade in the articles to those who become parties to one or the other. The one sort of contract known as "*Consignment Contract—Wholesale*," has been made with over four hundred jobbers and wholesale dealers, and the other, described as "*Retail Agency Contract*," with twenty-five thousand retail dealers in the United States.

The defendant is a wholesale drug concern which has refused to enter into the required contract, and is charged with procuring medicines for sale at "cut prices" by inducing those who have made the contracts to

---

[1] All the footnotes and most of the citations from the opinions of the Court have been omitted from the cases in this chapter.

violate the restrictions. The complainant invokes the established doctrine that an actionable wrong is committed by one who maliciously interferes with a contract between two parties and induces one of them to break that contract to the injury of the other . . .

The principal question is as to the validity of the restrictive agreements.

Preliminarily there are opposing contentions as to the construction of the agreements, or at least of that made with jobbers and wholesale dealers. The complainant insists that the "consignment contract" contemplates a true consignment for sale for account of the complainant, and that those who make sales under it are the complainant's agents and not its vendees. The court below did not so construe the agreement and considered it an effort "to disguise the wholesale dealers in the mask of agency upon the theory that in that character one link in the system for the suppression of the 'cut rate' business might be regarded as valid," and that under this agreement "the jobber must be regarded as the general owner and engaged in selling for himself and not as a mere agent of another." . . .

Turning to the agreement itself, we find that it purports to appoint the party with whom it is made one of the complainant's "Wholesale Distributing Agents," . . .

If, however, we consider the "consignment contract" as one which in legal effect provides for consignments of goods to be sold by an agent for his principal's account, . . . this alone would not be sufficient to support the bill.

The bill charges that the defendant has unlawfully and fraudulently procured the proprietary medicines from the complainant's "wholesale and retail agents" in violation of their contracts. But it does not allege that the goods procured by the defendant from "wholesale agents" were goods consigned to the latter for sale. . . .

. . . But if the restrictions of the "consignment contract," as to prices and vendees, are to be deemed to apply to the sale of goods which one wholesale dealer has purchased from another, it is evident that the validity of the restrictions in this aspect must be supported on some other ground than that such sale is made by the wholesale dealer as the agent of the complainant. The case presented by the bill cannot properly be regarded as one for inducing breach of trust by an agent.

The other form of contract, adopted by the complainant, while described as a "retail agency contract," is clearly an agreement looking to sale and not to agency. The so-called "retail agents" are not agents at all, either of the complainant or of its consignees, but are contemplated purchasers who buy to sell again, that is, retail dealers. . . .

The bill asserts complainant's "right to maintain and preserve the aforesaid system and method of contracts and sales adopted and established by it." It is, as we have seen, a system of interlocking restrictions by which the complainant seeks to control not merely the prices at which its agents may sell its products, but the prices for all sales by all dealers at wholesale or retail, whether purchasers or subpurchasers, and thus to fix the amount which the consumer shall pay, eliminating all competition. . . .

That these agreements restrain trade is obvious. That, having been made, as the bill alleges, with "most of the jobbers and wholesale druggists and a majority of the retail druggists of the country" and having for their purpose the control of the entire trade, they relate directly to interstate as well as intrastate trade, and operate to restrain trade or commerce among the several States, is also clear. . . .

But it is insisted that the restrictions are not invalid either at common law or under the act of Congress of July 2, 1890, . . . upon the following grounds, which may be taken to embrace the fundamental contentions for the complainant: (1) That the restrictions are valid because they relate to proprietary medicines manufactured under a secret process; and (2) that, apart from this, a manufacturer is entitled to control the prices on all sales of his own products.

FIRST   The first inquiry is whether there is any distinction, with respect to such restrictions as are here presented, between the case of an article manufactured by the owner of a secret process and that of one produced under ordinary conditions. The complainant urges an analogy to rights secured by letters patent. . . . In the case cited, there were licenses for the manufacture and sale of articles covered by letters patent with stipulations as to the prices at which the licensee should sell. The court said, referring to the act of July 2, 1890 . . . : "But that statute clearly does not refer to that kind of restraint of interstate commerce which may arise from reasonable and legal conditions imposed upon the assignee or licensee of a patent by the owner thereof, restricting the terms upon which the article may be used and the price to be demanded therefor. . . .

The complainant has no statutory grant. . . . Its case lies outside the policy of the patent law, and the extent of the right which that law secures is not here involved or determined. . . .

SECOND   We come, then, to the second question, whether the complainant, irrespective of the secrecy of its process, is entitled to maintain the restrictions by virtue of the fact that they relate to products of its own manufacture.

The basis of the argument appears to be that, as the manufacturer may make and sell, or not, as he chooses, he may affix conditions as to the use of the article or as to the prices at which purchasers may dispose of it. The propriety of the restraint is sought to be derived from the liberty of the producer.

But because a manufacturer is not bound to make or sell, it does not follow that in case of sales actually made he may impose upon purchasers every sort of restriction. . . .

Nor can the manufacturer by rule and notice, in the absence of contract or statutory right, even though the restriction be known to purchasers, fix prices for future sales. It has been held by this court that no such privilege exists under the copyright statutes, although the owner of the copyright has the sole right to vend copies of the copyrighted production. . . . It will hardly be contended, with respect to such a matter, that the manufacturer of an article of commerce, not protected by any statutory grant, is in any better case. . . .

The present case is not analogous to that of a sale of good will, or of an interest in a business, or of the grant of a right to use a process of manufacture. The complainant has not parted with any interest in its business or instrumentalities of production. It has conferred no right by virtue of which purchasers of its products may compete with it. It retains complete control over the business in which it is engaged, manufacturing what it pleases and fixing such prices for its own sales as it may desire. Nor are we dealing with a single transaction, conceivably unrelated to the public interest. The agreements are designed to maintain prices, after the complainant has parted with the title to the articles, and to prevent competition among those who trade in them. . . .

But agreements or combinations between dealers, having for their sole purpose the destruction of competition and the fixing of prices, are injurious to the public interest and void. They are not saved by the advantages which the participants expect to derive from the enhanced price to the consumer. . . .

The complainant's plan falls within the principle which condemns contracts of this class. It, in effect, creates a combination for the prohibited purposes. No distinction can properly be made by reason of the particular character of the commodity in question. It is not entitled to special privilege or immunity. It is an article of commerce and the rules concerning the freedom of trade must be held to apply to it. . . . The complainant having sold its product at prices satisfactory to itself, the public is entitled to whatever advantage may be derived from competition in the subsequent traffic. . . .

Judgment affirmed.

Mr. Justice Lurton took no part in the consideration and decision of this case.

MR. JUSTICE HOLMES, dissenting. . . .

. . . I think that we greatly exaggerate the value and importance to the public of competition in the production or distribution of an article (here it is only distribution), as fixing a fair price. What really fixes that is the competition of conflicting desires. We, none of us, can have as much as we want of all the things that we want. Therefore, we have to choose. As soon as the price of something that we want goes above the point at which we are willing to give up other things to have that, we cease to buy it and buy something else. Of course, I am speaking of things that we can get along without. There may be necessaries that sooner or later must be dealt with like short rations in a shipwreck, but they are not Dr. Miles's medicines. With regard to things like the latter it seems to me that the point of most profitable returns marks the equilibrium of social desires and determines the fair price in the only sense in which I can find meaning in those words.

Although the *Dr. Miles* case declared that resale price maintenance agreements violated the Sherman Act, the manufacturer could still achieve the same result in two ways: by an agency arrangement or by refusing to sell to price cutters. The agency arrangement is one whereby the manufacturer retains the title to the goods, appointing the seller as his representative or agent to sell the goods to consumers. If the agreement is one of genuine agency, the court will uphold it.[2]

In the *Colgate* case, the manufacturer did not resort to agreements to maintain resale prices but rather used various means of persuasion. The company distributed letters, circulars, and lists showing the uniform prices to be charged, urged dealers to adhere to these prices, requested information about dealers who cut prices, and announced that it would not sell to dealers who did not adhere to the announced prices. The United States brought an indictment, charging Colgate with restraint of trade in violation of the Sherman Act. In holding for Colgate, the Supreme Court said that in the absence of an intent to create or maintain a monopoly the Sherman Act "does not restrict the long recognized right of trader or manufacturer . . . freely to exercise his own independent discretion as to parties with whom he will deal."

2 *U.S.* v. *General Electric Co.,* 272 U.S. 476 (1926).

UNITED STATES v. COLGATE & CO.

250 U.S. 300 (1919)

MR. JUSTICE McREYNOLDS delivered the opinion of the court. . . .

We are confronted by an uncertain interpretation of an indictment itself couched in rather vague and general language. Counsel differ radically concerning the meaning of the opinion below and there is much room for the controversy between them.

The indictment runs only against Colgate & Company, a corporation engaged in manufacturing soap and toilet articles and selling them throughout the Union. It makes no reference to monopoly, and proceeds solely upon the theory of an unlawful combination. After setting out defendant's organization, place and character of business and general methods of selling and distributing products through wholesale and retail merchants, it alleges—

"During the aforesaid period of time, within the said eastern district of Virginia and throughout the United States, the defendant knowingly and unlawfully created and engaged in a combination with said wholesale and retail dealers, in the eastern district of Virginia and throughout the United States, for the purpose and with the effect of procuring adherence on the part of such dealers (in reselling such products sold to them as aforesaid) to resale prices fixed by the defendant, and of preventing such dealers from reselling such products at lower prices, thus suppressing competition amongst such wholesale dealers, and amongst such retail dealers, in restraint of the aforesaid trade and commerce among the several States, . . ."

Following this is a summary of things done to carry out the purposes of the combination: Distribution among dealers of letters, telegrams, circulars and lists showing uniform prices to be charged; urging them to adhere to such prices and notices, stating that no sales would be made to those who did not; requests, often complied with, for information concerning dealers who had departed from specified prices; investigation and discovery of those not adhering thereto and placing their names upon "suspended lists"; requests to offending dealers for assurances and promises of future adherence to prices, which were often given; uniform refusals to sell to any who failed to give the same; sales to those who did; similar assurances and promises required of, and given by, other dealers followed by sales to them; unrestricted sales to dealers with established accounts who had observed specified prices, etc. . . .

Our problem is to ascertain, as accurately as may be, what interpretation the trial court placed upon the indictment—not to interpret it ourselves; and then to determine whether, so construed, it fairly charges violation of the Sherman Act. Counsel for the Government maintain, in effect, that, as so interpreted, the indictment adequately charges an unlawful combination (within the doctrine of *Dr. Miles Medical Co.* v. *Park & Sons Co.,* . . . resulting from restrictive agreements between defendant and sundry dealers whereby the latter obligated themselves not to resell except at agreed prices; . . . On the other hand, defendant maintains that looking at the whole opinion it plainly construes the indictment as alleging only recognition of the manufacturer's undoubted right to specify resale prices and refuse to deal with anyone who failed to maintain the same.

Considering all said in the opinion (notwithstanding some serious doubts) we are unable to accept the construction placed upon it by the Government. We cannot, *e.g.,* wholly disregard the statement that "The retailer, after buying, could, if he chose, give away his purchase, or sell it at any price he saw fit, or not sell it at all; his course in these respects being affected only by the fact that he might by his action incur the displeasure of the manufacturer, who could refuse to make further sales to him, as he had the undoubted right to do." And we must conclude that, as interpreted below, the indictment does not charge Colgate & Company with selling its products to dealers under agreements which obligated the latter not to resell except at prices fixed by the company.

The position of the defendant is more nearly in accord with the whole opinion and must be accepted. And as counsel for the Government were careful to state on the argument that this conclusion would require affirmation of the judgment below, an extended discussion of the principles involved is unnecessary.

The purpose of the Sherman Act is to prohibit monopolies, contracts and combinations which probably would unduly interfere with the free exercise of their rights by those engaged, or who wish to engage, in trade and commerce—in a word to preserve the right of freedom to trade. In the absence of any purpose to create or maintain a monopoly, the act does not restrict the long recognized right of trader or manufacturer engaged in an entirely private business, freely to exercise his own independent discretion as to parties with whom he will deal. And, of course, he may announce in advance the circumstances under which he will refuse to sell. . . .

The judgment of the District Court must be

Affirmed.

State Fair Trade Laws

California was the first state to enact a *fair trade law,* which was soon copied by other states. The typical fair trade act declared that contracts setting resale prices were not to be deemed in violation of any law of that state. It also contained a *nonsigner clause* which provided that retailers who had not signed such agreements were nevertheless bound by them, provided they had knowledge that such agreements existed.

The Supreme Court upheld the validity of the fair trade laws in the *Old Dearborn* case, decided in 1936. In upholding the Illinois Fair Trade Act, the Court emphasized the importance of the manufacturer's trademark and good will. The Court said that although the retailers own the commodity, "they do not own the mark or the good will that the mark symbolizes. And good will is property in a very real sense, injury to which, . . . is a proper subject for legislation." Therefore, a fair trade law was a proper method for protecting the trademark and good will of the manufacturer.

OLD DEARBORN DISTRIBUTING CO. v. SEAGRAM-DISTILLERS CORP.

299 U.S. 183 (1936)

MR. JUSTICE SUTHERLAND delivered the opinion of the Court.

These appeals bring here for decision the question of the constitutional validity of §§1 and 2 of the Fair Trade Act of Illinois . . . providing as follows:

> Section 1. No contract relating to the sale or resale of a commodity which bears, or the label or content of which bears, the trade mark, brand or name of the producer or owner of such commodity and which is in fair and open competition with commodities of the same general class produced by others shall be deemed in violation of any law of the State of Illinois by reason of any of the following provisions which may be contained in such contract:
>
> (1) That the buyer will not resell such commodity except at the price stipulated by the vendor. . . .
>
> Section 2. Wilfully and knowingly advertising, offering for sale or selling any commodity at less than the price stipulated in any contract entered into pursuant to the provisions of section 1 of this Act, whether the person so advertising, offering for sale or sell-

ing is or is not a party to such contract, is unfair competition and is actionable at the suit of any person damaged thereby. . . .

Appellee is a dealer in alcoholic beverages at wholesale. It buys the products here in question from the producers. The whiskies bear labels and trade-marks, and are in fair and open competition with commodities of the same general class produced by others. Appellant is a corporation operating four retail liquor stores in Chicago, and selling at both wholesale and retail. Appellee's sales in Chicago are made to wholesale distributors. It has not sold any of the whiskies in controversy to appellant, but has sold other liquors. Contracts in pursuance of the Fair Trade Act have been executed between appellee and certain distributors, and numerous Illinois retailers. . . . Appellant sold the products in question at cut prices—that is to say, at prices below those stipulated—and continued to do so after appellee's demand that it cease such practice. . . .

. . . It is plain enough, however, that appellant had knowledge of the original contractual restrictions and that they constituted conditions upon which sales thereafter were to be made.

. . . Where a manufacturer puts out an article of general production identified by a special trade-mark or brand, the result of an agreement fixing the subsequent sales price affects competition between the identified articles alone, leaving competition between articles so identified by a given manufacturer and all other articles of like kind to have full play. . . .

FIRST   In respect of the due process of law clause, it is contended that the statute is a price-fixing law, which has the effect of denying to the owner of property the right to determine for himself the price at which he will sell. . . .

Section 1 affirms the validity of contracts of sale or resale of commodities identified by the trade-mark, brand or name of the producer or owner, which are in fair and open competition with commodities of the same general class produced by others . . . It is clear that this section does not attempt to fix prices, nor does it delegate such power to private persons. It *permits* the designated private persons to contract with respect thereto. It contains no element of compulsion but simply legalizes their acts, leaving them free to enter into the authorized contract or not as they may see fit. . . .

The challenge is directed against §2, which provides that wilfully and knowingly advertising, offering for sale or selling any commodity at less than the price stipulated in any contract made under §1, whether the person doing so is or is not a party to the contract, shall constitute unfair competition, giving rise to a right of action in favor of anyone damaged thereby.

It is first to be observed that §2 reaches not the *mere* advertising, offering for sale or selling at less than the stipulated price, but the doing of any of these things *wilfully* and *knowingly*. . . .

. . . The essence of the statutory violation then consists not in the bare disposition of the commodity, but in a forbidden use of the trade-mark, brand or name in accomplishing such disposition. The primary aim of the law is to protect the property—namely, the good will—of the producer, which he still owns. The price restriction is adopted as an appropriate means to that perfectly legitimate end, and not as an end in itself. . . .

. . . Appellants own the commodity; they do not own the mark or the good will that the mark symbolizes. And good will is property in a very real sense, injury to which, like injury to any other species of property, is a proper subject for legislation. Good will is a valuable contributing aid to business—sometimes the most valuable contributing asset of the producer or distributor of commodities. And distinctive trade-marks, labels and brands, are legitimate aids to the creation or enlargement of such good will. . . . There is nothing in the act to preclude the purchaser from removing the mark or brand from the commodity—thus separating the physical property, which he owns, from the good will, which is the property of another—and then selling the commodity at his own price, provided he can do so without utilizing the good will of the latter as an aid to that end.

. . . Enough appears already in this opinion to show the essential difference between trade-marked goods and others not so identified. . . .

But it is unnecessary to pursue the subject further; for, since the sole purpose of the present law is to afford a legitimate remedy for an injury to the good will which results from the use of trade-marks, brands or names, it is obvious that its provisions would be wholly inapplicable to goods which are unmarked.

Decrees affirmed.

The Miller-Tydings Amendment

The state resale price maintenance laws—the fair trade acts—whose validity were upheld in the *Old Dearborn* case, applied only to *intrastate* transactions. Independent retailer associations, with the National Association of Retail Druggists in the forefront, were able to persuade Congress to enact a similar law to apply to interstate commerce. In 1937 Congress enacted the Miller-Tydings amendment to the Sherman Act. This Act exempted resale price maintenance agreements from the federal antitrust laws when the goods, moving in *interstate* commerce, were sold in states having fair trade laws.

The heart of the fair trade laws is the nonsigner clause. It would be unduly burdensome for the manufacturer to make a specific contract with every retailer. Therefore, the nonsigner clause is vital to the effectiveness of the resale price laws.

In a case decided in 1951, Schwegmann Brothers challenged the validity of the nonsigner clause when applied to interstate trade. The Supreme Court agreed with Schwegmann Brothers, declaring that the nonsigner clause was in violation of the Sherman Act when applied to commodities in interstate commerce. The Court said that fixing minimum prices, as any other type of price fixing, is illegal *per se*, unless specifically exempt from the law. Then Justice Douglas, delivering the Court's opinion, pointed out that the Miller-Tydings Act exempts only "contracts or agreements" and that the nonsigner provision is omitted from the federal law. He said that distributors and retailers can agree to fix a minimum price with impunity when state law permits. But, Justice Douglas added, "When they seek, however, to impose price fixing on persons who have not contracted or agreed to the scheme, the situation is vastly different. That is not price fixing by contract or agreement; that is price fixing by compulsion."

SCHWEGMANN BROTHERS et al. v. CALVERT DISTILLERS CORP.

341 U.S. 384 (1951)

MR. JUSTICE DOUGLAS delivered the opinion of the Court.

Respondents, Maryland and Delaware corporations, are distributors of gin and whiskey. They sell their products to wholesalers in Louisiana, who in turn sell to retailers. Respondents have a price-fixing scheme whereby they try to maintain uniform retail prices for their products. They endeavor to make retailers sign price-fixing contracts under which the buyers promise to sell at not less than the prices stated in respondents' schedules. They have indeed succeeded in getting over one hundred Louisiana retailers to sign these agreements. Petitioner, a retailer in New Orleans, refused to agree to the price-fixing scheme and sold respondents' products at a cut-rate price. Respondents thereupon brought this suit . . .

It is clear from our decisions under the Sherman Act . . . that this interstate marketing arrangement would be illegal, that it would be enjoined, that it would draw civil and criminal penalties, and that no court would enforce it. Fixing minimum prices, like other types of price fixing, is illegal *per se*. . . . The fact that a state authorizes the price fixing does not, of course, give immunity to the scheme, absent approval by Congress.

Respondents, however, seek to find legality for this marketing arrangement in the Miller-Tydings Act enacted in 1937 as an amendment to §1 of the Sherman Act. . . . That amendment provides in material part that "nothing herein contained shall render illegal, *contracts or agreements* prescribing minimum prices for the resale" of specified commodities when "*contracts or agreements of that description* are lawful as applied to intrastate transactions" under local law. (Italics added.)

Louisiana has such a law. . . . It permits a "contract" for the sale or resale of a commodity to provide that the buyer will not resell "except at the price stipulated by the vendor." The Louisiana statute goes further. It not only allows a distributor and retailer to make a "contract" fixing the resale price; but once there is a price-fixing "contract," known to a seller, with any retailer in the state, it also condemns as unfair competition a sale at less than the price stipulated even though the seller is not a party to the "contract." In other words, the Louisiana statute enforces price fixing not only against parties to a "contract" but also against nonsigners. . . . And the argument is that the Miller-Tydings Act permits the same range of price fixing.

The argument is phrased as follows: the present action is outlawed by the Sherman Act—the Miller-Tydings Act apart—only if it is a contract, combination, or conspiracy in restraint of trade. But if a contract or agreement is the vice, then by the terms of the Miller-Tydings Act that contract or agreement is immunized, provided it is immunized by state law. . . .

The argument at first blush has appeal. But we think it offends the statutory scheme.

We note to begin with that there are critical differences between Louisiana's law and the Miller-Tydings Act. The latter exempts only "contracts or agreements prescribing minimum prices for the resale." . . . The omission of the nonsigner provision from the federal law is fatal to respondents' position unless we are to perform a distinct legislative function by reading into the Act a provision that was meticulously omitted from it.

A refusal to read the nonsigner provision into the Miller-Tydings Act makes sense if we are to take the words of the statute in their normal and customary meaning. The Act sanctions only "contracts or agreements." If a distributor and one or more retailers want to agree, combine, or conspire to fix a minimum price, they can do so if state law permits. Their contract, combination, or conspiracy—hitherto illegal—is made lawful. They can fix minimum prices pursuant to their contract or agreement with impunity.

When they seek, however, to impose price fixing on persons who have not contracted or agreed to the scheme, the situation is vastly different. That is not price fixing by contract or agreement; that is price fixing by compulsion. . . .

It should be noted in this connection that the Miller-Tydings Act expressly continues the prohibitions of the Sherman Act against "horizontal" price fixing by those in competition with each other at the same functional level. Therefore, when a state compels retailers to follow a parallel price policy, it demands private conduct which the Sherman Act forbids. . . .

. . . Had Congress desired to eliminate the consensual element from the arrangement and to permit blanketing a state with resale price fixing if only one retailer wanted it, we feel that different measures would have been adopted—either a nonsigner provision would have been included or resale price fixing would have been authorized without more. Certainly the words used connote a voluntary scheme. Contracts or agreements convey the idea of a cooperative arrangement, not a program whereby recalcitrants are dragged in by the heels and compelled to submit to price fixing. . . .

It should be remembered that it was the state laws that the federal law was designed to accommodate. Federal regulation was to give way to state regulation. When state regulation provided for resale price maintenance by both those who contracted and those who did not, and the federal regulation was relaxed only as respects "contracts or agreements," the inference is strong that Congress left the noncontracting group to be governed by preexisting law. . . .

Reversed.

MR. JUSTICE JACKSON, whom MR. JUSTICE MINTON joins, concurring.

MR. JUSTICE FRANKFURTER, whom MR. JUSTICE BLACK and MR. JUSTICE BURTON join, dissenting. . . .

The McGuire Amendment

The *Schwegmann* decision was a serious setback to resale price maintenance because, as previously noted, the nonsigner provision contains the real teeth of these laws. Congress was subjected to much pressure to amend the law and legalize the nonsigner clause in interstate commerce. Accordingly, one year after the *Schwegmann* decision, in 1952, Congress amended Section 5 of the Federal Trade Commission Act with the McGuire Act. This Act reversed the

Schwegmann case and exempted the nonsigner clause from the antitrust laws. Almost immediately thereafter, the Schwegmann Brothers firm was back in court contending that both the state and federal nonsigner provisions were unconstitutional.[3] Schwegmann lost in the lower courts and the Supreme Court refused to review the case. But, as so often seems the case, no sooner is a law enacted than a new loophole is discovered. This was the case in *General Electric Company* v. *Masters Mail Order Company*. To avoid the New York fair trade law, Masters established operations in Washington, D.C., which had no such law. It then proceeded to advertise and solicit mail orders from New York. General Electric sued to enjoin Masters from selling its products in New York. Although Masters had entered into no resale price agreement, General Electric claimed that Masters was bound by the nonsigner provision since General Electric had entered into such contracts with dealers in New York. In interpreting the McGuire Act, the court of appeals noted, that although the Act made exceptions to the long-standing policy against restraints of trade, "we are 'bound to construe them strictly, since resale price maintenance is a privilege restrictive of a free economy.' " The appellate court concluded that the sales occurred in Washington, D.C., and therefore the New York fair trade law did not apply. The Supreme Court refused to review the case.[4]

GENERAL ELECTRIC COMPANY v. MASTERS MAIL ORDER COMPANY OF WASHINGTON, D.C., INC.

244 F. 2d 681 (1957)

CLARK, Chief Judge.

This is an appeal from a decision, . . . enjoining a mail order discount house in the District of Columbia from advertising, offering for sale, or selling plaintiff-manufacturer's products in New York below New York "fair trade" prices. The action was brought under the New York Fair Trade (Feld-Crawford) Act, . . .

Since the passage of the McGuire Act, . . . the plaintiff, General Electric Company, has entered into numerous fair trade agreements with retailers in New York and other states and has systematically given notice of the agreements and the uniform minimum resale prices in effect to the 175,000 known retailers of its products. It has vigorously enforced the

---

[3] *Schwegmann Brothers* v. *Eli Lilly & Co.*, 205 F. (2d) 788 (1953).
[4] 335 U.S. 824 (1957).

agreements, by lawsuits when necessary. The defendant is a retail store in the District of Columbia which sells General Electric appliances both over the counter and by mail order. Two-thirds of its sales are over the counter. It is a wholly owned subsidiary of Masters, Inc., a New York retail corporation and has been controlled and closely supervised by the parent corporation at all relevant times. . . .

Our first question is whether the Feld-Crawford Act, so applied, conflicts with the Sherman Antitrust Law's ban on enforcement of resale price maintenance agreements as to goods moving in interstate commerce. . . . Although the McGuire Act carves some exceptions to this long-standing national policy against restraints on trade, we are "bound to construe them strictly, since resale price maintenance is a privilege restrictive of a free economy." . . .

Subsections (a) (2) and (3) of §2 of the McGuire Act, . . . restricts the exception for resale maintenance contracts to contracts governing resales in jurisdictions that have adopted "fair trade" as a policy. A contract made in a fair trade state, but governing a resale in a non-fair trade state, would be illegal by the terms of the subsection. . . . Therefore no enforcement action lies unless the resales in question occur in a fair trade state. . . .

Plaintiff protests that our reading of the statute will allow the District of Columbia to impose its policies on economic activities in New York. But the opposite construction will simply allow New York to dominate the economic activities of the District of Columbia (and other like free trade areas). Since Congress has left the regulation of this part of interstate commerce to the option of the individual states, it is inevitable that when a single transaction affects states with conflicting policies one state or the other must see its policies slighted. We have no clearer guide in choosing the dominant state than the language of the statute itself. . . . From all that appears Congress was concerned with the place where resales occurred, . . .

. . . The critical question is still the place of resale, and no enforcement action may be brought for advertising or offering goods for sale below fair trade prices unless the ad or offer contemplated resales in a fair trade jurisdiction. . . . Hence an enforcement action under the New York statute is valid only if the resales occurred in New York.

. . . In my view the place where title passed is critical.

The intent of the parties governs the passage of title between them, although statutes and case law provide guides for ascertaining such intent. Here the predominant interest of both the seller and buyers was to take advantage of the absence of resale price maintenance legislation in the District of Columbia. The defendant's history and operations testify to its concern, and its various pieces of advertising brought home the same desire to New York consumers. For example, one of its order blanks announced "discounts on all the 'fair-traded' brands of merchandise that are being sold only at list price in 45 states." Since the parties had the power to determine for themselves where title would pass, they indubitably selected the District of Columbia, where their agreements would be enforceable, rather than New York, where they would not. . . .

My brother WATERMAN criticizes use of the concept of title in determining the place of "resale" and suggests that we look instead to the situs of the retailer. The title approach seems required by the congressional language and the case law; in reality it adds precision to the statutory term by drawing upon precedents from the law of sales . . .

. . . In accordance with these views the order of injunction must be reversed and the action must be dismissed on the merits.

WATERMAN, Circuit Judge, concurring. . . .

LUMBARD, Circuit Judge, dissenting. . . .

We must not forget that Congress has twice indicated—the second time despite strong opposition—that the states are to be allowed to prevent price-competition among those selling branded products in the home market. . . . This was to avoid damage to the good will of the manufacturer in the eyes of local consumers and to protect local small businessmen against the price-cutting powers of the large firms. . . . The defendant's activities have frustrated and will continue to frustrate both purposes in the New York market unless they are enjoined.

Enforcing Resale Prices by Refusal to Deal

In states having no fair trade law, the manufacturer may control the resale price of his goods by refusal to deal with price cutters. In the *Colgate* case, discussed previously, the Supreme Court had said that the antitrust law "does not restrict the long recognized right of a trader or manufacturer . . . freely to exercise his own independent discretion as to parties with whom he will deal." Section 2 of the Clayton Act emphasizes that it must be a "bona fide transaction and not in restraint of trade." Therefore, it is obvious that the right to refuse to deal is not without limit.

The leading case marking off the limits of the right to choose one's customers is the *Parke, Davis & Co.* case. Parke, Davis instituted a program of refusing to sell in order to enforce maintenance of resale prices. The wholesalers were told that Parke, Davis would refuse to sell to them if they did not adhere to the announced prices, and also that Parke, Davis would refuse to sell to them if they sold to retailers who engaged in price cutting. Parke, Davis also told the retailers that they would not be able to buy from the company or the wholesalers unless they observed the resale prices. The Justice Department charged that Parke, Davis, by "entwining the wholesalers and retailers" in a program to promote its resale prices, had gone "beyond mere customer selection and had created combinations or conspiracies" in violation of the Sherman Act. The Supreme Court agreed with the government's position, saying that Parke, Davis had exceeded the limits of the *Colgate* case because it had not merely announced its policy and then refused to deal with those who disregarded it. The Court found that Parke, Davis had used the refusal to deal with wholesalers to get their help in denying products to retailers who failed to abide by the resale prices. The Court said, "In thus involving the wholesalers to stop the flow of Parke, Davis products to retailers, thereby inducing retailers' adherence to its suggested retail price, Parke, Davis created a combination with the retailers and the wholesalers to maintain retail prices and violated the Sherman Act."

UNITED STATES v. PARKE, DAVIS & CO.

362 U.S. 29 (1960)

MR. JUSTICE BRENNAN delivered the opinion of the Court.

The Government sought an injunction under §4 of the Sherman Act against the appellee, Parke, Davis & Company, on a complaint alleging that Parke, Davis conspired and combined, in violation of §§1 and 3 of the Act, with retail and wholesale druggists in Washington, D.C., and Richmond, Virginia, to maintain the wholesale and retail prices of Parke, Davis pharmaceutical products. The violation was alleged to have occurred during the summer of 1956 when there was no Fair Trade Law in the District of Columbia or the State of Virginia. . . .

Parke, Davis makes some 600 pharmaceutical products which it markets nationally through drug wholesalers and drug retailers. The retailers buy these products from the drug wholesalers or make large quantity purchases directly from Parke, Davis. Sometime before 1956 Parke, Davis announced a resale price maintenance policy in its wholesalers' and retailers' catalogues. The wholesalers' catalogue contained a Net Price Selling Schedule listing suggested minimum resale prices on Parke, Davis products sold by wholesalers to retailers. The catalogue stated that it was Parke, Davis' continuing policy to deal only with drug wholesalers who observed that schedule and who sold only to drug retailers authorized by law to fill prescriptions. Parke, Davis, when selling directly to retailers, quoted the same prices listed in the wholesalers' Net Price Selling Schedule but granted retailers discounts for volume purchases. Wholesalers were not authorized to grant similar discounts. The retailers' catalogue contained a schedule of minimum retail prices applicable in States with Fair Trade Laws and stated that this schedule was suggested for use also in States not having such laws. . . .

There are some 260 drugstores in Washington, D.C., and some 100 in Richmond, Virginia. Many of the stores are units of Peoples Drug Stores, a large retail drug chain. There are five drug wholesalers handling Parke, Davis products in the locality who do business with the drug retailers. The wholesalers observed the resale prices suggested by Parke, Davis. However, during the spring and early summer of 1956 drug retailers in the two cities advertised and sold several Parke, Davis vitamin products at prices substantially below the suggested minimum retail prices; in some instances the prices apparently reflected the volume discounts on direct purchases from Parke, Davis since the products were sold below the prices listed in the wholesalers' Net Price Selling Schedule. . . . Thereafter in July the branch manager put into effect a program for promoting observance of the suggested minimum retail prices by the retailers involved. The program contemplated the participation of the five drug wholesalers. In order to insure that retailers who did not comply would be cut off from sources of supply, representatives of Parke, Davis visited the wholesalers and told them, in effect, that not only would Parke, Davis refuse to sell to wholesalers who did not adhere to the policy announced in its catalogue, but also that it would refuse to sell to wholesalers who sold Parke, Davis products to retailers who did not observe the suggested minimum retail prices. Each wholesaler was interviewed individually but each was informed that his competitors were also being apprised of this. The wholesalers without exception indicated a willingness to go along.

Representatives called contemporaneously upon the retailers involved, individually, and told each that if he did not observe the suggested minimum retail prices, Parke, Davis would refuse to deal with him, and that furthermore he would be unable to purchase any Parke, Davis products from the wholesalers. Each of the retailers was also told that his competitors were being similarly informed.

Several retailers refused to give any assurances of compliance and continued after these July interviews to advertise and sell Parke, Davis products at prices below the suggested minimum retail prices. Their names were furnished by Parke, Davis to the wholesalers. Thereafter Parke, Davis refused to fill direct orders from such retailers and the wholesalers likewise refused to fill their orders. . . .

The District Court held that the Government's proofs did not establish a violation of the Sherman Act because "the actions of [Parke, Davis] were properly unilateral and sanctioned by law under the doctrine laid down in the case of United States v. Colgate & Co. . . .

The Government concedes for the purposes of this case that under the *Colgate* doctrine a manufacturer, having announced a price maintenance policy, may bring about adherence to it by refusing to deal with customers who do not observe that policy. The Government contends, however; that subsequent decisions of this Court compel the holding that what Parke, Davis did here by entwining the wholesalers and retailers in a program to promote general compliance with its price maintenance policy went beyond mere customer selection and created combinations or conspiracies to enforce resale price maintenance in violation of §§1 and 3 of the Sherman Act. . . .

The program upon which Parke, Davis embarked to promote general compliance with its suggested resale prices plainly exceeded the limitations of the *Colgate* doctrine . . . Parke, Davis did not content itself with announcing its policy regarding retail prices and following this with a simple refusal to have business relations with any retailers who disregarded that policy. Instead Parke, Davis used the refusal to deal with the wholesalers in order to elicit their willingness to deny Parke, Davis products to retailers and thereby help gain the retailers' adherence to its suggested minimum retail prices. The retailers who disregarded the price policy were promptly cut off when Parke, Davis supplied the wholesalers with their names. . . . In thus involving the wholesalers to stop the flow of Parke, Davis products to the retailers, thereby inducing retailers' adherence to its suggested retail prices, Parke, Davis created a combination with the retailers and the wholesalers to maintain retail prices and violated the Sherman Act. . . .

. . . It was only by actively bringing about substantial unanimity among the competitors that Parke, Davis was able to gain adherence to its policy. It must be admitted that a seller's announcement that he will not deal with customers who do not observe his policy may tend to engender confidence in each customer that if he complies his competitors will also. But if a manufacturer is unwilling to rely on individual self-interest to bring about general voluntary acquiescence which has the collateral effect of eliminating price competition, and takes affirmative action to achieve uniform adherence by inducing each customer to adhere to avoid such price competition, the customers' acquiescence is not then a matter of individual free choice prompted alone by the desirability of the product. . . .

The judgment is reversed and the case remanded to the District Court with directions to enter an appropriate judgment enjoining Parke,

Davis from further violations of the Sherman Act unless the company elects to submit evidence in defense and refutes the Government's right to injunctive relief established by the present record.

It is so ordered.

Mr. Justice Stewart, concurring. . . .

Mr. Justice Harlan, whom Mr. Justice Frankfurter and Mr. Justice Whittaker join, dissenting. . . .

Other Instances of Refusal to Deal

Most often, the improper use of the limited right of refusal to deal involves attempts at maintaining resale prices. Another illegal use aims at eliminating competition. This may involve individual action or concerted effort. Reported below are examples of each.

In the *Lorain Journal* case a newspaper was accused of attempting to monopolize interstate commerce. From 1933 to 1948 the newspaper had a monopoly in the distribution of news and advertising in Lorain, a city in Ohio of about fifty-two thousand population. In 1948 a radio station was granted a license to operate in the area whereupon the newspaper refused to accept advertisements from merchants advertising on the radio station. Since the newspaper reached 99 per cent of the families in Lorain, advertising in it was virtually indispensable for merchants selling in that area. The United States charged the newspaper with attempting to monopolize in violation of the Sherman Act. In a decision holding against the newspaper, the Supreme Court said that the result of its conduct was not only to strengthen its monopoly in the field of advertising in the Lorain area, "but more significantly tended to destroy and eliminate [the radio station] altogether."

LORAIN JOURNAL CO. et al. v. UNITED STATES

342 U.S. 143 (1951)

Mr. Justice Burton delivered the opinion of the Court.

The principal question here is whether a newspaper publisher's conduct constituted an attempt to monopolize interstate commerce, justifying the injunction issued against it under §§2 and 4 of the Sherman

Antitrust Act. For the reasons hereafter stated, we hold that the injunction was justified. . . .

The appellant corporation, here called the publisher, has published the Journal in the City of Lorain since before 1932. In that year it, with others, purchased the Times-Herald which was the only competing daily paper published in that city. Later, without success, it sought a license to establish and operate a radio broadcasting station in Lorain. . . .

The court below describes the position of the Journal, since 1933, as "a commanding and an overpowering one. It has a daily circulation in Lorain of over 13,000 copies and it reaches ninety-nine per cent of the families in the city." . . . Lorain is an industrial city on Lake Erie with a population of about 52,000 occupying 11,325 dwelling units. The Sunday News, appearing only on Sundays, is the only other newspaper published there. . . .

From 1933 to 1948 the publisher enjoyed a substantial monopoly in Lorain of the mass dissemination of news and advertising, both of a local and national character. However, in 1948 the Elyria-Lorain Broadcasting Company, a corporation independent of the publisher, was licensed by the Federal Communications Commission to establish and operate in Elyria, Ohio, eight miles south of Lorain, a radio station whose call letters, WEOL, stand for Elyria, Oberlin and Lorain. Since then it has operated its principal studio in Elyria and a branch studio in Lorain. Lorain has about twice the population of Elyria and is by far the largest community in the station's immediate area. Oberlin is much smaller than Elyria and eight miles south of it.

While the station is not affiliated with a national network it disseminates both intrastate and interstate news and advertising. . . .

The court below found that appellants knew that a substantial number of Journal advertisers wished to use the facilities of the radio station as well. For some of them it found that advertising in the Journal was essential for the promotion of their sales in Lorain County. It found that at all times since WEOL commenced broadcasting, appellants had executed a plan conceived to eliminate the threat of competition from the station. Under this plan the publisher refused to accept local advertisements in the Journal from any Lorain County advertiser who advertised or who appellants believed to be about to advertise over WEOL. The court found expressly that the purpose and intent of this procedure was to destroy the broadcasting company.

The court characterized all this as "bold, relentless, and predatory commercial behavior." . . . To carry out appellants' plan, the publisher monitored WEOL programs to determine the identity of the station's local Lorain advertisers. Those using the station's facilities had their contracts with the publisher terminated and were able to renew them only after ceasing to advertise through WEOL. The program was effective.

Numerous Lorain County merchants testified that, as a result of the publisher's policy, they either ceased or abandoned their plans to advertise over WEOL. . . .

1. *The conduct complained of was an attempt to monopolize interstate commerce.* It consisted of the publisher's practice of refusing to accept local Lorain advertising from parties using WEOL for local advertising. Because of the Journal's complete daily newspaper monopoly of local advertising in Lorain and its practically indispensable coverage of 99% of the Lorain families, this practice forced numerous advertisers to refrain from using WEOL for local advertising. That result not only reduced the number of customers available to WEOL in the field of local Lorain advertising and strengthened the Journal's monopoly in that field, but more significantly tended to destroy and eliminate WEOL altogether.

2. *The publisher's attempt to regain its monopoly of interstate commerce by forcing advertisers to boycott a competing radio station violated §2.* The findings and opinion of the trial court describe the conduct of the publisher upon which the Government relies. The surrounding circumstances are important. The most illuminating of these is the substantial monopoly which was enjoyed in Lorain by the publisher from 1933 to 1948, together with a 99% coverage of Lorain families. Those factors made the Journal an indispensable medium of advertising for many Lorain concerns. Accordingly, its publisher's refusals to print Lorain advertising for those using WEOL for like advertising often amounted to an effective prohibition of the use of WEOL for that purpose.

WEOL's greatest potential source of income was local Lorain advertising. Loss of that was a major threat to its existence. The court below found unequivocally that appellants' conduct amounted to an attempt by the publisher to destroy WEOL and, at the same time, to regain the publisher's pre-1948 substantial monopoly over the mass dissemination of all news and advertising.

The publisher claims a right as a private business concern to select its customers and to refuse to accept advertisements from whomever it pleases. We do not dispute that general right. "But the word 'right' is one of the most deceptive of pitfalls; it is so easy to slip from a qualified meaning in the premise to an unqualified one in the conclusion. Most rights are qualified." *American Bank & Trust Co.* v. *Federal Bank,* 256 U.S. 350, 358. The right claimed by the publisher is neither absolute nor exempt from regulation. Its exercise as a purposeful means of monopolizing interstate commerce is prohibited by the Sherman Act. The operator of the radio station, equally with the publisher of the newspaper, is entitled to the protection of that Act. "*In the absence of any purpose to create or maintain a monopoly,* the act does not restrict the long recognized right of trader or manufacturer engaged in an entirely private business, freely to exercise his own independent discretion as to parties with whom he will deal." (Emphasis supplied.) *United States* v. *Colgate & Co.* . . .

3. *The injunction does not violate any guaranteed freedom of the press.* The publisher suggests that the injunction amounts to a prior restraint upon what it may publish. We find in it no restriction upon any guaranteed freedom of the press. The injunction applies to a publisher what the law applies to others. The publisher may not accept or deny advertisements in an "attempt to monopolize . . . any part of the trade or commerce among the several States. . . ."

The judgment accordingly is

Affirmed.

The *General Motors* case involved the concerted action of many in bringing about an illegal refusal to deal. "Discount houses" in the late 1950s began selling new cars at allegedly bargain prices in the Los Angeles area. Their source of cars was franchised dealers. Members of three associations of Chevrolet dealers complained to General Motors and sought its help in preventing a dozen or so dealers from selling Chevrolets to the discount houses. As a result, General Motors personnel contacted every dealer in the area and obtained promises not to deal with the discounters, and the three associations policed these agreements. The government charged General Motors and the Chevrolet dealers' associations with a conspiracy to restrain trade in violation of the Sherman Act. In a decision in favor of the government, the Supreme Court stated that "Neither individual dealers nor the associations acted independently or separately." It found that they had collaborated among themselves and with General Motors to prevent dealings with the discounters. The Court, in describing the conduct of General Motors and the dealers, said, "We have here a classic conspiracy in restraint of trade: joint, collaborative action by dealers . . . and General Motors to eliminate a class of competitors . . ."

UNITED STATES v. GENERAL MOTORS CORP. et al.

384 U.S. 127 (1966)

MR. JUSTICE FORTAS delivered the opinion of the Court.

This is a civil action brought by the United States to enjoin the appellees from participating in an alleged conspiracy to restrain trade in violation of §1 of the Sherman Act. The United States District Court for the Southern District of California concluded that the proof failed to establish the alleged violation, and entered judgment for the defendants. . . . We reverse.

The appellees are the General Motors Corporation, which manufactures, among other things, the Chevrolet line of cars and trucks, and three associations of Chevrolet dealers in and around Los Angeles, California. All of the Chevrolet dealers in the area belong to one or more of the appellee associations. . . .

Beginning in the late 1950's, "discount houses" engaged in retailing consumer goods in the Los Angeles area and "referral services" began offering to sell new cars to the public at allegedly bargain prices. Their sources of supply were the franchised dealers. By 1960 a number of individual Chevrolet dealers, without authorization from General Motors, had developed working relationships with these establishments. . . .

. . . By 1960 these methods for retailing new cars had reached considerable dimensions. Of the 100,000 new Chevrolets sold in the Los Angeles area in that year, some 2,000 represented discount house or referral sales. One Chevrolet dealer attributed as much as 25% of its annual sales to participation in these arrangements, while another accounted for between 400 and 525 referral sales in a single year.

Approximately a dozen of the 85 Chevrolet dealers in the Los Angeles area were furnishing cars to discounters in 1960. As the volume of these sales grew, the nonparticipating Chevrolet dealers located near one or more of the discount outlets began to feel the pinch. Dealers lost sales because potential customers received, or thought they would receive, a more attractive deal from a discounter who obtained its Chevrolets from a distant dealer. The discounters vigorously advertised Chevrolets for sale, with alluring statements as to price savings. The discounters also advertised that all Chevrolet dealers were obligated to honor the new-car warranty and to provide the free services contemplated therein; and General Motors does indeed require Chevrolet dealers to service Chevrolet cars, wherever purchased, pursuant to the new-car warranty and service agreement. Accordingly, nonparticipating dealers were increasingly called upon to service, without compensation, Chevrolets purchased through discounters. . . .

On June 28, 1960, at a regular meeting of the appellee Losor Chevrolet Dealers Association, member dealers discussed the problem and resolved to bring it to the attention of the Chevrolet Division's Los Angeles zone manager, Robert O'Connor. . . . When no help was forthcoming, Owen Keown, a director of Losor, took matters into his own hands. First, he spoke to Warren Biggs and Wilbur Newman, Chevrolet dealers who were then doing a substantial business with discounters. According to Keown's testimony, Newman told him that he would continue the practice "until . . . told not to by" Chevrolet, and that "when the Chevrolet Motor Division told him not to do it, he knew that they wouldn't let some other dealer carry on with it."

Keown then reported the foregoing events at the association's annual meeting in Honolulu on November 10, 1960. The member dealers present agreed immediately to flood General Motors and the Chevrolet Division with letters and telegrams asking for help. Salesmen, too, were to write.

Hundreds of letters and wires descended upon Detroit—with telling effect. Within a week Chevrolet's O'Connor was directed to furnish his superiors in Detroit with "a detailed report of the discount house operations . . . as well as what action we in the Zone are taking to curb such sales." . . .

. . . We have here a classic conspiracy in restraint of trade: joint, collaborative action by dealers, the appellee associations, and General Motors to eliminate a class of competitors by terminating business dealings between them and a minority of Chevrolet dealers and to deprive franchised dealers of their freedom to deal through discounters if they so choose. . . .

These findings by the trial judge compel the conclusion that a conspiracy to restrain trade was proved. The error of the trial court lies in its failure to apply the correct and established standard for ascertaining the existence of a combination or conspiracy under §1 of the Sherman Act. . . . The trial court attempted to justify its conclusion on the following reasoning: That each defendant and alleged co-conspirator acted to promote its own self-interest . . .

These factors do not justify the result reached. It is of no consequence, for purposes of determining whether there has been a combination or conspiracy under §1 of the Sherman Act, that each party acted in its own lawful interest. . . . And although we regard as clearly erroneous and irreconcilable with its other findings the trial court's conclusory "finding" that there had been no "agreement" among the defendants and their alleged co-conspirators, it has long been settled that explicit agreement is not a necessary part of a Sherman Act conspiracy—certainly not where, as here, joint and collaborative action was pervasive in the initiation, execution, and fulfillment of the plan. . . .

Neither individual dealers nor the associations acted independently or separately. The dealers collaborated, through the associations and otherwise, among themselves and with General Motors, both to enlist the aid of General Motors and to enforce dealers' promises to forsake the discounters. The associations explicitly entered into a joint venture to assist General Motors in policing the dealers' promises, and their joint proffer of aid was accepted and utilized by General Motors.

Nor did General Motors confine its activities to the contractual boundaries of its relationships with individual dealers. As the trial court found . . . General Motors at no time announced that it would terminate the franchise of any dealer which furnished cars to the discounters. The evidence indicates that it had no intention of acting in this unilateral fashion. On the contrary, overriding corporate policy with respect to proper dealer relations dissuaded General Motors from engaging in this sort of wholly unilateral conduct, the validity of which under the antitrust laws was assumed, without being decided, in *Parke, Davis, supra.*

There can be no doubt that the effect of the combination or conspiracy here was to restrain trade and commerce within the meaning of the Sherman Act. Elimination, by joint collaborative action, of discounters from access to the market is a *per se* violation of the Act.

The principle of these cases is that where businessmen concert their actions in order to deprive others of access to merchandise which the latter wish to sell to the public, we need not inquire into the economic motivation underlying their conduct. . . .

We note, moreover, that inherent in the success of the combination in this case was a substantial restraint upon price competition—a goal unlawful *per se* when sought to be effected by combination or conspiracy. . . .

There is in the record ample evidence that one of the purposes behind the concerted effort to eliminate sales of new Chevrolet cars by discounters was to protect franchised dealers from real or apparent price competition. The discounters advertised price savings. . . . Some purchasers found and others believed that discount prices were lower than those available through the franchised dealers. . . . Certainly, complaints about price competition were prominent in the letters and telegrams with which the individual dealers and salesmen bombarded General Motors in November 1960. . . .

Accordingly, we reverse and remand to the United States District Court for the Southern District of California in order that it may fashion appropriate equitable relief. . . .

It is so ordered.

Mr. Justice Harlan, concurring in the result. . . .

12

Fraud and Deceptive Practices

One of the basic faiths of our free enterprise system is that the public interest will be best served and protected through competition. Most often the public interest—in the economic sense—is equated with the consumer interest. In most instances the consumer interest will be safeguarded by maintaining competition. But there are other times when this is not so. There are some practices which, while they do not necessarily suppress competition or create a monopoly, do injure the consumer. This occurs when the dishonest and unethical seller markets adulterated goods or misrepresents their worth or capabilities. Competitors who use fraudulent and deceptive practices injure the public interest in two ways. First, the consumer is injured because he paid for something he did not get. He received goods which were not as they should have been because of the misrepresentation. Second, the ethical competitor is injured because his dishonest rival gained an unearned advantage in attracting customers.

The principal statute which protects the public interest against fraud and deceptive practices is the Federal Trade Commission Act. As originally enacted in 1914, Section 5 of the Act provided "that unfair methods of competition in commerce are hereby declared unlawful." In an early case this prohibition was interpreted as protecting only the competitors of the dishonest seller, not the customers. Subsequently, in 1938, the Act was amended to read, "Unfair methods of competition in commerce, and unfair or deceptive acts or practices in commerce, are hereby declared unlawful." The amendment also gave the Commission the express authority to proceed against false advertising.

Early Attempts to Protect
Against Fraud and Deceptive Practices

Before the passage of the Federal Trade Commission Act, one of the earliest attempts to protect the public from fraud and deception was the Pure Food and Drugs Act of 1906. Patent medicines and canned foods pointed up the need for public protection in this area. With mass use of canned goods, the public could no longer ascertain the ingredients or the quality of the food they were purchasing. And, of course, the public has never been able to evaluate the merit of medicines. Many early patent medicine companies seemed to have had an incurable affliction—which their own nostrums apparently could not cure—and that was the propensity to make extravagant "cure-all" claims for their wares. The Pure Food and Drugs Act attempted to furnish the needed protection by prohibiting adulteration and misbranding of food and drugs.

One of the first cases under the Pure Food and Drugs Act was that of *United States* v. *Johnson,* decided in 1911. Johnson was indicted for the interstate shipment of medicine bearing labels which stated that the contents were effective in curing cancer. The labels read, in part, "This is an effective tonic . . . It enters the circulation at once, utterly destroying and removing impurities from the blood and entire system . . . and when taken in connection with the Mild Combination Treatment gives splendid results in the treatment of cancer and other malignant diseases . . ." The district court quashed the indictment and the United States appealed. The issue on appeal was whether the medicines were misbranded within the meaning of the Pure Food and Drugs Act. The Supreme Court, speaking through Justice Holmes, was of the opinion that the statutory prohibition against statements "which shall be false or misleading in any particular . . ." was not aimed "at all possible false statements, but only at such as determine the identity of the article, . . ." Excluded from the prohibition of the law were statements concerning "an estimate or prophecy concerning their effect." The Court pointed out that Congress had left the determination of whether an article is misbranded to the Bureau of Chemistry of the Department of Agriculture. The Court concluded that such determination by the Bureau of Chemistry was "most natural if the question concerns ingredients and kind, but hardly so as to medical effects."

Three Justices dissented. They felt that the Court gave undue importance to the wording of the law and had overlooked the intent of Congress. Had Congress intended to apply the law only to misstatements of identity, it could have easily and clearly said so. The dissenters believed that the offense of misbranding had occurred if "the so-called remedy was absolutely worthless and hence the label demonstrably false; . . ."

UNITED STATES v. JOHNSON

221 U.S. 488 (1911)

MR. JUSTICE HOLMES delivered the opinion of the court.[1]

This is an indictment for delivering for shipment from Missouri to Washington, D.C., packages and bottles of medicine bearing labels that stated or implied that the contents were effective in curing cancer, the

---

[1] The citations and footnotes from the opinions of the Court have been, with a few exceptions, omitted from the cases in this chapter.

defendant well knowing that such representations were false. On motion of the defendant the District Judge quashed the indictment . . . , and the United States brought this writ of error . . .

The question is whether the articles were misbranded within the meaning of §2 of the Food and Drugs Act of June 30, 1906, . . . making the delivery of misbranded drugs for shipment to any other State or Territory or the District of Columbia a punishable offense. By §5 the term drug includes any substance or mixture intended to be used for the cure, mitigation or prevention of disease. By §8, . . . the term misbranded "shall apply to all drugs, or articles of food, . . . the package or label of which shall bear any statement, design, or device regarding such article, or the ingredients or substances contained therein which shall be false or misleading in any particular, and to any food or drug product which is falsely branded as to the State, Territory, or country in which it is manufactured or produced. . . . An article shall also be deemed to be misbranded: In case of drugs: First. If it be an imitation of or offered for sale under the name of another article. Second. [In case of a substitution of contents,] or if the package fail to bear a statement on the label of the quantity or proportion of any alcohol, morphine, opium, cocaine, heroin, alpha or beta eucaine, chloroform, cannabis indica, chloral hydrate, or acetanilide, or any derivative or preparation of any such substances contained therein."

It is a postulate, as the case comes before us, that in a certain sense the statement on the label was false, or, at least, misleading. What we have to decide is whether such misleading statements are aimed at and hit by the words of the act. It seems to us that the words used convey to an ear trained to the usages of English speech a different aim; and although the meaning of a sentence is to be felt rather than to be proved, generally and here the impression may be strengthened by argument, as we shall try to show. . . .

. . . But we are of opinion that the phrase is aimed not at all possible false statements, but only at such as determine the identity of the article, possibly including its strength, quality and purity, dealt with in §7. In support of our interpretation the first thing to be noticed is the second branch of the sentence: 'Or the ingredients or substances contained therein.' One may say with some confidence that in idiomatic English this half, at least, is confined to identity, and means a false statement as to what the ingredients are. Logically it might mean more, but idiomatically it does not. But if the false statement referred to is a misstatement of identity as applied to a part of its objects, idiom and logic unite in giving it the same limit when applied to the other branch, the article, whether simple or one that the ingredients compose. Again, it is to be noticed that the cases of misbranding, specifically mentioned and following the general words that we have construed, are all cases analogous to the statement of identity and not at all to inflated or false commendation of wares. The first is a false statement as to the country where the article is manufactured or produced; a matter quite unnecessary to specify if the preceding words had a universal scope, yet added as not being within them. The next case is that of imitation and taking the name of another article, of which the same may be said, and so of the next, a substitution of contents. The last is breach of an affirmative requirement to disclose the proportion of alcohol and certain other noxious ingredients in the package—again a matter of plain past history concerning the nature and amount of the poisons employed, not an estimate or prophecy concerning their effect. In further confirmation, it should be noticed that although the indictment alleges a wilful fraud, the shipment is punished by the statute if the article is misbranded, and that the article may be misbranded without any conscious fraud at all. It was natural enough to throw this risk on shippers with regard to the identity of their wares, but a very different and unlikely step to make them answerable for mistaken praise. It should be noticed still further that by §4 the determination whether an article is misbranded is left to the Bureau of Chemistry of the Department of Agriculture, which is most natural if the question concerns ingredients and kind, but hardly so as to medical effects.

To avoid misunderstanding we should add that, for the purposes of this case, at least, we assume that a label might be of such a nature as to import a statement concerning identity, within the statute, although in form only a commendation of the supposed drug. . . . But such a statement as to contents, undescribed and unknown, is shown to be false only in its commendatory and prophetic aspect, and as such is not within the act.

In view of what we have said by way of simple interpretation we think it unnecessary to go into considerations of wider scope. We shall say nothing as to the limits of constitutional power, and but a word as to what Congress was likely to attempt. It was much more likely to regulate commerce in food and drugs with reference to plain matter of fact, so that food and drugs should be what they professed to be, when the kind was stated, than to distort the uses of its constitutional power to establishing criteria in regions where opinions are far apart. . . . As we have said above, the reference of the question of misbranding to the Bureau of Chemistry for determination confirms what would have been our expectation and what is our understanding of the words immediately in point.

Judgment affirmed.

MR. JUSTICE HUGHES, with whom MR. JUSTICE HARLAN and MR. JUSTICE DAY concurred, dissenting: . . .

The articles were labeled respectively "Cancerine tablets," "Antiseptic tablets," "Blood purifier," "Special No. 4," "Cancerine No. 17," and "Cancerine No. 1,"—the whole constituting what was termed in substance "Dr. Johnson's Mild Combination Treatment for Cancer." There were several counts in the indictment with respect to the different articles. The labels contained the words "Guaranteed under the Pure Food and Drugs Act, June 30, 1906;" and some of the further statements were as follows:

"Blood Purifier. This is an effective tonic and alterative. It enters the circulation at once, utterly destroying and removing impurities from the blood and entire system. Acts on the bowels, kidneys, and skin, eliminating poisons from the system, and when taken in connection with the Mild Combination Treatment gives splendid results in the treatment of cancer and other malignant diseases. I always advise that the Blood Purifier be continued some little time after the cancer has been killed and removed and the sore healed.

"Special No. 4. . . . It has a strong stimulative and absorptive power; will remove swelling, arrest development, restore circulation, and remove pain. Is indicated in all cases of malignancy where there is a tendency of the disease to spread, and where there is considerable hardness surrounding the sore. Applied thoroughly to a lump or to an enlarged gland will cause it to soften, become smaller, and be absorbed.

"Cancerine No. 1. . . . Tendency is to convert the sore from an unhealthy to a healthy condition and promote healing. Also that it destroys and removes dead and unhealthy tissue."

In each case the indictment alleged that the article was "wholly worthless," as the defendant well knew. . . .

Section 8 provides:

"SEC. 8. That the term 'misbranded,' as used herein, shall apply to all drugs, or articles of food, or articles which enter into the composition of food, the package or label of which shall bear any statement, design, or device regarding such article, or the ingredients or substances contained therein which shall be false or misleading in any particular, and to any food or drug product which is falsely branded as to the State, Territory, or country in which it is manufactured or produced." . . .

. . . And the offense of misbranding is committed if the package or label of such an article bears any statement regarding it "which shall be false or misleading in any particular."

But it is said that these words refer only to false statements which fix the identity of the article. . . .

I fail to find a sufficient warrant for this limitation, and on the contrary, it seems to me to be opposed to the intent of Congress and to deprive the act of a very salutary effect. . . .

It is strongly stated that the clause in §8,—"or the ingredients or substances contained therein,"—has reference to identity and that this controls the interpretation of the entire provision. This, in my judgment, is to ascribe an altogether undue weight to the wording of the clause and to overlook the context. . . . If Congress had intended to restrict the offense to misstatements as to identity, it could easily have said so. . . .

I entirely agree that in any case brought under the act for misbranding,—by a false or misleading statement as to curative properties of an article,—it would be the duty of the court to direct an acquittal when it appeared that the statement concerned a matter of opinion. Conviction would stand only where it had been shown that, apart from any question of opinion, the so-called remedy was absolutely worthless and hence the label demonstrably false; but in such case it seems to me to be fully authorized by the statute.

Accordingly, I reach the conclusion that the court below erred in the construction that it gave the statute, and hence in quashing the indictment, and that the judgment should be reversed.

Fraud and Deceptive Practices under Original Section 5, FTC Act

It became apparent that the public needed better protection against fraud and deceptive practices. It was also felt that preventing "unfair" competition through the use of fraud would also help prevent monopolization. In response to this public concern, Congress enacted the Federal Trade Commission Act in 1914. Its main provision was Section 5, stating "That unfair methods of competition in commerce are hereby declared unlawful." The Act created an independent agency, removed from "political" control, whose chief function was to investigate and prosecute violations under the FTC and Clayton Acts. It was believed that an independent agency, composed of impartial economic and legal experts, could act more quickly and effectively in preventing and halting unfair practices which would tend to create a monopoly or restrain trade. Experience had already shown that the judicial process was rather slow and cumbersome.

In the first FTC case of significance to reach the Supreme Court, the Commission's order against a misleading representation was upheld.[2] The Winsted Hosiery Company sold underwear, socks, and other knit goods made only partly of wool, but labeled them "natural merino," "natural wool," "Australian Wool," and other similar names implying that the goods were all wool. The Supreme Court found that "The labels were false and calculated to deceive, and did in fact deceive, a substantial portion of the purchasing public. . . . [T]he practice constitutes an unfair method of competition as against those manufacturers of all wool knit underwear and as against those

[2] *FTC v. Winsted Hosiery Co.*, 258 U.S. 483 (1922).

manufacturers of mixed wool and cotton underwear who brand their product truthfully."

The lack of consumer protection, in the absence of injury to a competitor as contained in the Supreme Court's decision in the *Winsted Hosiery* case, was not fully apparent until the *Raladam* case. The Raladam Co. was selling an "obesity cure" which, it claimed, was the result of scientific research, was safe and effective, and could be used without "danger of harmful results to health." The Supreme Court agreed with the Federal Trade Commission that "Findings, supported by evidence, warrant the conclusion that the preparation is one which cannot be used generally with safety to physical health except under medical direction and advice." But the Court ruled against the cease-and-desist order, holding that the Commission had no jurisdiction in this case. The Court found that there was no evidence or finding "of prejudice or injury to any competitor." For the Commission to have authority to proceed against "unfair methods of competition," there must be competitors who are injured. Apparently other "anti-obesity" producers were using similarly deceptive advertisements and were not "injured" by Raladam's methods.

Speaking for the Court, Justice Sutherland said: "It is obvious that the word 'competition' imports the existence of present or potential competitors, and the unfair methods must be such as injuriously affect or tend thus to affect the business of these competitors . . ."

FEDERAL TRADE COMMISSION v. *RALADAM CO.*

283 U.S. 643 (1931)

MR. JUSTICE SUTHERLAND delivered the opinion of the court.

Under §5 of the Federal Trade Commission Act, . . . the Commission issued its complaint charging the respondent with using unfair methods of competition in interstate commerce.

Respondent manufactures a preparation for internal use, denominated an "obesity cure." The complaint charges that this preparation is sold by respondent in and throughout the several States, generally to wholesalers who resell to retailer dealers, and these, in turn, to consumers; that it is offered for sale and sold in competition with other persons who are engaged "in offering for sale, and selling, printed professional advice, books of information and instruction, and other methods and means and certain remedies and appliances for dissolving or otherwise removing excess flesh of the human body"; that respondent advertises . . . that the preparation is the result of scientific research, knowledge and accuracy, that it is safe and effective and may be used without discomfort, inconvenience or danger of harmful results to health. Among the ingredients is "desiccated thyroid," which, it is alleged, cannot be prescribed to act with reasonable uniformity on the bodies of all users, or without impairing the health of a substantial portion of them, etc., or with safety, without previous consultation with, and continuing observation and advice of, a competent medical adviser. The complaint further avers that many persons are seeking obesity remedies, and respondent's advertisements are calculated to mislead and deceive the purchasing public into the belief that the preparation is safe, effective, dependable, and without danger of harmful results. By way of conclusion, it is said that "the acts and practices of the respondent are all to the prejudice of the public and of competitors of respondent, . . . and constitute unfair methods of competition." . . .

. . . The Commission found against respondent and issued a cease and desist order. The findings in general follow the language of the complaint. There was no finding of prejudice or injury to any competitor, but the conclusion was drawn from the findings of fact that the practice of respondent was to the prejudice of the public and respondent's competitors, and constituted an unfair method of competition.

The court of appeals reviewed the action of the Commission upon respondent's petition, and reversed the order. . . .

In substance the Commission ordered the respondent to cease and desist from representing that its preparation is a scientific method for treating obesity, is the result of scientific research, or that the formula is a scientific formula; and from representing its preparation as a remedy for obesity, unless accompanied by the statement that it cannot be taken safely except under medical advice and direction. Findings, supported by evidence, warrant the conclusion that the preparation is one which cannot be used generally with safety to physical health except under medical direction and advice. If the necessity of protecting the public against dangerously misleading advertisements of a remedy sold in interstate commerce were all that is necessary to give the Commission jurisdiction, the order could not successfully be assailed. But this is not all.

By the plain words of the act, the power of the Commission to take steps looking to the issue of an order to desist depends upon the existence of three distinct prerequisites: (1) that the methods complained of are *unfair*; (2) that they are methods of *competition* in commerce; and (3) that a proceeding by the Commission to prevent the use of the methods appears to be in the *interest of the public*. We assume the existence of the first and third of these requisites; and pass at once to the consideration of the second. . . .

. . . The object of the Trade Commission Act was to stop in their incipiency those methods of competition which fall within the meaning of the word "unfair." . . . In a case arising under the Trade Commission Act, the fundamental questions are, whether the methods complained of are "unfair," and whether, as in cases under the Sherman Act, they tend to the substantial injury of the public by restricting competition in interstate trade and "the common liberty to engage therein." The paramount aim of the act is the protection of the public from the evils likely to result from the destruction of competition or the restriction of it in a substantial degree, and this presupposes the existence of some substantial competition to be affected, since the public is not concerned in the maintenance of competition which itself is without real substance. . . .

It is obvious that the word "competition" imports the existence of present or potential competitors, and the unfair methods must be such as injuriously affect or tend thus to affect the business of these competitors— that is to say, the trader whose methods are assailed as unfair must have present or potential rivals in trade whose business will be, or is likely to be, lessened or otherwise injured. It is that condition of affairs which the Commission is given power to correct, and it is against that condition of affairs, and not some other, that the Commission is authorized to protect the public. . . .

The foregoing view of the powers of the Commission under the Act finds confirmation, if that be needed, in the committee reports . . . It was urged that the best way to stop monopoly at the threshold was to prevent unfair competition; that the unfair competition sought to be reached was that which must ultimately result in the extinction of rivals and the establishment of monopoly; that by the words "unfair methods" was meant those resorted to for the purpose of destroying competition or of eliminating a competitor or of introducing monopoly—such as tend unfairly to destroy or injure the business of a competitor; . . .

Findings of the Commission justify the conclusion that the advertisements naturally would tend to increase the business of respondent; but there is neither finding nor evidence from which the conclusion legitimately can be drawn that these advertisements substantially injured or tended thus to injure the business of any competitor or of competitors generally, whether legitimate or not. None of the supposed competitors appeared or was called upon to show what, if any, effect the misleading advertisements had, or were likely to have, upon his business. . . . It is impossible to say whether, as a result of respondent's advertisements, any business was diverted, or was likely to be diverted, from others engaged in like trade, or whether competitors, identified or unidentified, were injured in their business, or were likely to be injured, or, indeed, whether any other anti-obesity remedies were sold or offered for sale in competition, or were of such a character as naturally to come into any real competition, with respondent's preparation in the interstate market. All this was left without proof and remains, at best, a matter of conjecture. . . .

A proceeding under §5 is not one instituted before the Commission by one party against another. It is instituted by the Commission itself, and is authorized whenever the Commission has reason to believe that unfair methods of competition in commerce are being used, and that a proceeding by it in respect thereof would be to the interest of the public. . . . But one of the facts necessary to support jurisdiction to make the final order to cease and desist, is the existence of competition; and the Commission cannot, by assuming the existence of competition, if in fact there be none, give itself jurisdiction to make such an order. If, as a result of the inquiry, it turn out that the preliminary assumption of competition is without foundation, jurisdiction to make that order necessarily fails, and the proceeding must be dismissed by the Commission. . . .

The decree of the court below is

Affirmed.

Fraud and Deceptive Practices under Amended FTC Act

The *Raladam* decision left the Federal Trade Commission powerless to protect consumers from fraud or deception. Consumer protection was an incidental result only if accompanied by a finding of injury to competitors. Certainly, the logic of the Court was hard to assail, but the public interest would seem better served by a broader interpretation. But, in any event, the law was modified by Congress in favor of the consumer. The Wheeler-Lea Act amended the FTC Act and closed this loophole by declaring unlawful "deceptive acts or practices in commerce." The amendment also gave the FTC power to attack false advertising. The FTC could now proceed to protect the consumer, whether or not there was injury to competitors.

In the *Sewell* case, the Commission charged that the advertisements used by the company in promoting its shoe insert were false and misleading and constituted a deceptive act and practice. The company claimed in its ads that use of its shoe insert would give better poise and balance and possessed therapeutic value for aching feet. The advertisement also claimed that the shoe insert had a special effect on the cuboid bone and that it was a scientific device. The Commission found the advertisement false and misleading because of the broad and unequivocal claims, such as "now everyone can enjoy better posture, poise and balance," and "especially designed to help you enjoy increased foot health and comfort." The claims made in the company's ads assured everyone, without qualification, that use of the shoe insert would bring better health, posture, and balance.

The court of appeals did not agree with the Commission's cease-and-desist order except to the extent that it forbade claims of special effect on the cuboid bone or that the insert was a scientific device. The appellate court felt that the other claims of Sewell "are within the legitimate field of 'puffing' of the ad man." The essence of the claims was simply that a "better fitting shoe should result in better foot balance, some relief from aches and pains . . . better foot health and better comfort."

In a dissenting opinion, Judge Pope, quoting the Supreme Court, said: " 'The findings of the Commission as to facts, if supported by testimony, shall be conclusive.' " He stated that the medical testimony accepted by the Commission showed that "generally speaking people with foot trouble must be prescribed for individually . . ." Since the Commission's finding of unfair and deceptive advertising was supported by reasonable evidence, he believed that the Commission's order should be upheld.

Upon appeal, the Supreme Court reversed the court of appeals, merely saying, "The case is remanded with direction to affirm and enforce the order of the Federal Trade Commission."[3]

SEWELL v. FEDERAL TRADE COMMISSION

240 F. 2d 228 (1956)

CHAMBERS, Circuit Judge.

Sewell, petitioner here, and respondent before the Federal Trade Commission, has successfully built in and from Santa Ana, California, a large business in the manufacture and sale of an article which we can call a shoe insert. Its basic name is Cuboids. This is a derivation from the cuboid bone in the arch of the human foot. Various names are used in marketing like "Cuboid balancer" or "Doggies." A ready market for the device is found among the legion of Americans who complain about their feet.

The insert is ordinarily sold in department stores in metropolitan centers where representatives on the payroll of Sewell sell the product, usually for the account of Sewell, rather than the department store. Those who sell it have had some training in fitting shoes and selling corrective devices. Some sales are made by mail order after a customer has filled out a questionnaire which is intended to elicit his complaints. Some sales are

[3] *FTC v. Sewell*, 353 U.S. 969 (1957).

made by stores that do not have a Sewell representative on the premises. . . .

The attack initiated by the Federal Trade Commission is on Sewell's advertising. We assume that Sewell would readily admit that his advertising has been a big factor in building his business: that the product has not entirely sold itself.

Some of the lines of Sewell's advertising which were the subject of the Commission's complaint were as follows:

Cuboids help to balance your body weight . . .

Now everyone can enjoy better posture, poise and balance with . . . , Cuboids.

Especially designed to help you enjoy increased foot health and comfort. . . .

Cuboid foot balancers make housework less tiring. . . .

The feet are the body's foundation. Cuboids balance this foundation and provide the basis for correct posture. . . .

After peripatetic hearings in various parts of the United States, the examiner filed a report which proscribed not only the foregoing claims, but which recommended that Sewell be forbidden to use advertising matter which he had discontinued four years previously. The Commission followed the examiner on the advertising set forth above shown to be in current use but refused to whip the dead horse of Sewell's discontinued advertising.[4] Now, Sewell seeks review here.

Before the examiner, medical men, orthopaedic specialists, testified for Sewell's claims and against them. Sewell showed that medical doctors, presumably reputable, in great numbers regularly prescribe his device. He had much testimony that people are regularly pleased with the device. He showed that only three per cent of all purchasers take advantage of their "satisfaction guaranteed or your money back" offer.

But be the foregoing as it may, the Commission entered an order forbidding:

1. Disseminating or causing to be disseminated by means of the United States mails, or by any means in commerce, . . . any advertisement which represents directly or by implication:

---

[4] . . . Had the examiner eliminated these claims at the outset from consideration of his inquiry, the hearings could have been materially shortened.

Tactically the trial of these more or less specific claims easily permitted the Commission's experts to condemn Sewell's devices more stridently and to overlook the real issue of: Do the supports frequently give relief to those who complain of their feet?

(a) That the wearing of respondents' device will assist in balancing the feet or body.

(b) That respondents' device possesses therapeutic value for aching or painful feet. . . .

This court is satisfied that the Commission must be affirmed insofar as advertising claims assert that the device has a special effect on the cuboid bone of the foot or is a "scientific" device. That is a highly technical matter upon which experts testified both ways. There the Commission could take its choice. . . .

On the other hand, we are not disposed to issue our mandate to cease and desist with respect to the general claims in the advertising on the assertions made with reference to "balance," "balancers," "improved health," "poise," "improvement of stance," "elimination of foot fatigue," "better posture," and "better foot action." . . .

We think that the respondent Sewell by his witnesses demonstrated, simply stated, that people wearing shoes that do not fit their feet, for reasons inherent either in the customer's foot or his shoe, do very, very frequently get a better platform to walk on with the addition of Sewell's insert. Why, we cannot say with certainty. The Commission doctors who roundly condemned the device say there is no reason that the device should relieve one's foot ills. We do not think the doctors' opinion and their few case histories of failures of the device overcome the proof of frequent successful use. There is no proof the device ever did any damage. . . .

We believe that if we concede that when often the addition of the device produces a better fitting shoe that every one of Sewell's claims naturally flows, except those based on the assertion of special effect on the cuboid bone or the device being scientific. A better fitting shoe should result in better foot balance, some relief from aches and pains, better poise and balance, better poise, posture and balance, better foot health and better comfort. And even housewife's drudgery ought to be lessened. . . .

We think perhaps there are two basic mistakes in the case and which lead us to believe that the Commission was legally wrong in part and justify our declination to enforce the order in full. First, we believe in the testimony of the experts of the Commission, they have failed to start with the premise that Sewell fitter starts with. That is, that the shoe of the customer prospect for some reason does not fit the foot or the foot does not fit the shoe. Maybe a different shoe would often give the customer balance, relief from aches and pains, give him better posture and poise and stance. But if the customer gets it by a Sewell device, we see no objection to advertising that it does. . . .

Secondly, we think the examiner and the Commission have reduced generality to specificity, when it was not justified. For example, the approach to "balance" seems to have been in the sense of the physicist in the laboratory. We think there is in the vernacular lexicon a meaning for the word which imports a feeling of well being, a feeling "that it fits."

While we must accept the Commission's determination, right or wrong in the abstract, that the claims of special efficacy on the cuboid bone is false science and that it is not a scientific device, we think the other claims of Sewell are within the legitimate field of "puffing" of the ad man. . . .

On this review, the Commission's order is affirmed insofar as it prohibits Sewell from advertising special efficacy on the cuboid bone and on other related bones, and insofar as he advertises the device is "scientific;" otherwise, not.

JAMES ALGER FEE, Circuit Judge, concurring.

In view of the fact that a dissent is to be filed, the following may add clarity to our determination.

The right of the people who buy shoes and have individual ideas in respect to comfort, poise, balance and posture is involved here. It is not a contest between a selfish seller and an administrative body. Insofar as purely scientific and medical claims are concerned, the Commission is fully supported by this Court. . . . Where almost every individual in the nation passes, perhaps once, perhaps many times a year, through the hands of shoe salesmen, balance, poise, posture and comfort are, in essential, the bases of the sales. In regard to these matters, the individual exercises his own ideas. . . .

Even after sale, a multitude of wearers of shoes use devices of various sorts to change the balance, poise and posture of the individual or the fit of the shoe to attain comfort. Ankle supports, arch supports, metatarsal pads, rubber sponge, inner soles, corn and bunion pads are added. Shoes are stretched and heels are heightened or raised in part. Outer soles are added. Half soles are placed. Each of these operations may well affect balance, posture and poise of the individual. The wearer ordinarily uses devices for comfort and to give him relief from some real or fancied discomfort. . . . Here the Commission holds that the distributor may not even suggest in advertising that the articles which he makes for the specific purpose of affecting balance, poise and posture to advantage may accomplish it to the satisfaction of the wearer. . . .

. . . The opinions of the experts, adduced by the agency, contain highly esoteric discussions of the balance of the foot and theories of various schools of scientific thought. The question before the agency was not one for expert opinion. The lay testimony alone was substantial on this issue. . . . The question is not one for the exercise of expertise or even for appraisal of expert opinion, but of common sense. . . .

This advertising was not as a matter of law deceptive. It is true, some of it is rather warm in expression. But it is no more expressive than the claims made for the colors and comfort of modern automobiles. If all such claims so expressed were deceptive, practically all modern magazines would cease business.

The courts have exercised the power to overturn decisions of the Commission which were less flagrantly in error than this.

POPE, Circuit Judge.

I dissent. It seems to me clear that the court has assumed a power which it does not have and has meddled in a decision which it is not authorized to make. . . . [t]he Supreme Court described what has happened here in language which could not be more apt if it had been spoken concerning this very case. Said the Supreme Court: " 'The findings of the Commission as to facts, if supported by testimony, shall be conclusive.' . . . The Court of Appeals, though professing adherence to this mandate, honored it, we think, with lip service only. . . . In fact what the court did was to make its own appraisal of the testimony, picking and choosing for itself among uncertain and conflicting inferences. . . ." This is a clear case in which the majority of the court stepping into the shoes of the Commission, have undertaken to say how they would decide it. The clue to their fundamental error is to be found in the last sentence of the opinion's footnote 4 where it is stated that the "real issue" is "Do the supports frequently give relief to those who complain of their feet?" I think it is demonstrable that this was not the issue before the Commission and that it is even less an issue before this court. . . . In the language of the Supreme Court, the conclusions and findings of an administrative body are to be supported if they have "rational basis" and "warrant in the record" . . . By no means can the conclusions of the Commission here be said to be irrational. . . .

The concurring opinion, instead of adding "clarity to our determination," seems to me to travel even more wide of the mark. . . .

Listing all these practices which shoe wearers may try for themselves might furnish a plausible reason why the Commission should not concern itself with as small a matter as cuboids, on the theory that if the public do not try cuboids, they will probably try something else.

But those are considerations not within our competence. The Commission has found the methods of advertising unfair and deceptive, and petitioner's claims that "every one" will be helped by this cure-for-all are false. The finding has a rational basis and warrant in the record. It is not for us "to determine independently what is in the public interest."

In a case decided in 1965, the Federal Trade Commission charged an advertiser and the advertising agency with deceptive practices in the use of a prop in a television commercial. The case involved an ad used by Colgate-Palmolive Co. to show that its shaving cream, Rapid Shave, "could outshave them all." The commercial purported to give the television viewers proof that the shaving cream could soften and shave sandpaper. But what appeared to be sandpaper was a "mock-up" made of plexiglass to which sand had been applied. Rapid Shave was applied to this and immediately thereafter, with one stroke, the razor cut a clean path through it. Actual tests showed that Rapid Shave had to soak real sandpaper for about eighty minutes before it could be shaved as shown in the commercial.

The FTC found that since Rapid Shave could not shave sandpaper in the short time shown in the commercial, the company had misrepresented the product's moisturizing power. The Commission issued its cease-and-desist order. The Supreme Court, with Chief Justice Warren writing the opinion, upheld the Commission. The Court agreed with the Commission's conclusion that an advertiser, even if he himself has conducted the test, "may not convey to television viewers the false impression that they are seeing the test, . . . when they are not because of the undisclosed use of mock-ups." Therefore, the undisclosed use of plexiglass and sand was a "material deceptive practice."

Justice Harlan, in a dissenting opinion, said that if the claim is true, then the technique for portraying it is purely within the advertiser's art. Must what is done in the studio be exactly true? Justice Harlan then mentioned the well-known fact that white colors appear dingy gray on television, but blue looks sparkling white. He then asked whether it would be proper for Colgate to demonstrate the "effectiveness" of a competitor's detergent by washing a white (not blue) sheet with the competitor's product. He was emphasizing his conviction that the proper test is not what goes on in the studio, but rather whether what appears on the screen is an accurate representation.

FEDERAL TRADE COMMISSION v. COLGATE-PALMOLIVE CO. et al.

380 U.S. 374 (1965)

MR. CHIEF JUSTICE WARREN delivered the opinion of the Court.

The basic question before us is whether it is a deceptive trade practice, prohibited by §5 of the Federal Trade Commission Act, to represent falsely that a televised test, experiment, or demonstration provides a viewer with visual proof of a product claim, regardless of whether the product claim is itself true.

The case arises out of an attempt by respondent Colgate-Palmolive Company to prove to the television public that its shaving cream, "Rapid Shave," outshaves them all. Respondent Ted Bates & Company, Inc., an advertising agency, prepared for Colgate three one-minute commercials designed to show that Rapid Shave could soften even the toughness of sandpaper. Each of the commercials contained the same "sandpaper test." The announcer informed the audience that, "To prove RAPID SHAVE's super-moisturizing power, we put it right from the can onto this tough, dry sandpaper. It was apply . . . soak . . . and off in a stroke." While the announcer was speaking, Rapid Shave was applied to a substance that appeared to be sandpaper, and immediately thereafter a razor was shown shaving the substance clean.

The Federal Trade Commission issued a complaint against respondents Colgate and Bates charging that the commercials were false and deceptive. The evidence before the hearing examiner disclosed that sandpaper of the type depicted in the commercials could not be shaved immediately following the application of Rapid Shave, but required a substantial soaking period of approximately 80 minutes. The evidence also showed that the substance resembling sandpaper was in fact a simulated prop, or "mock-up," made of plexiglass to which sand had been applied. However, the examiner found that Rapid Shave could shave sandpaper, even though not in the short time represented by the commercials, and that if real sandpaper had been used in the commercials the inadequacies of television transmission would have made it appear to viewers to be nothing more than plain, colored paper. The examiner dismissed the complaint because neither misrepresentation—concerning the actual moistening time or the identity of the shaved substance—was in his opinion a material one that would mislead the public.

The Commission, in an opinion dated December 29, 1961, reversed the hearing examiner. It found that since Rapid Shave could not shave sandpaper within the time depicted in the commercials, respondents had misrepresented the product's moisturizing power. Moreover, the Commission found that the undisclosed use of a plexiglass substitute for sandpaper was an additional material misrepresentation that was a deceptive act separate and distinct from the misrepresentation concerning Rapid Shave's underlying qualities. Even if the sandpaper could be shaved just as depicted in the commercials, the Commission found that viewers had been misled into believing they had seen it done with their own eyes. As a result of these findings the Commission entered a cease-and-desist order against the respondents.

An appeal was taken to the Court of Appeals for the First Circuit which rendered an opinion on November 20, 1962. That court sustained the Commission's conclusion that respondents had misrepresented the qualities of Rapid Shave, but it would not accept the Commission's order forbidding the future use of undisclosed simulations in television commercials. It set aside the Commission's order and directed that a new order be entered. On May 7, 1963, the Commission, over the protest of respondents, issued a new order narrowing and clarifying its original order to comply with the court's mandate. The Court of Appeals again found unsatisfactory that portion of the order dealing with simulated props and refused to enforce it. . . .

In reviewing the substantive issues in the case, it is well to remember the respective roles of the Commission and the courts in the administration of the Federal Trade Commission Act. When the Commission was created by Congress in 1914, it was directed by §5 to prevent "[u]nfair methods of competition in commerce." Congress amended the Act in 1938 to extend the Commission's jurisdiction to include "unfair or deceptive acts or practices in commerce"—a significant amendment showing Congress' concern for consumers as well as for competitors. . . .

This statutory scheme necessarily gives the Commission an influential role in interpreting §5 and in applying it to the facts of particular cases arising out of unprecedented situations. Moreover, as an administrative agency which deals continually with cases in the area, the Commission is often in a better position than are courts to determine when a practice is "deceptive" within the meaning of the Act. This Court has frequently stated that the Commission's judgment is to be given great weight by reviewing courts. This admonition is especially true with respect to allegedly deceptive advertising since the finding of a §5 violation in this field rests so heavily on inference and pragmatic judgment. . . .

We are not concerned in this case with the clear misrepresentation in the commercials concerning the speed with which Rapid Shave could shave sandpaper, . . . We granted certiorari to consider the Commission's conclusion that even if an advertiser has himself conducted a test, experiment or demonstration which he honestly believes will prove a certain product claim, he may not convey to television viewers the false impression that they are seeing the test, experiment or demonstration for themselves, when they are not because of the undisclosed use of mock-ups.

We accept the Commission's determination that the commercials involved in this case contained three representations to the public: (1) that sandpaper could be shaved by Rapid Shave; (2) that an experiment had been conducted which verified this claim; and (3) that the viewer was seeing this experiment for himself. Respondents admit that the first two representations were made, but deny that the third was. The Commission, however, found to the contrary, and, since this is a matter of fact resting on an inference that could reasonably be drawn from the commercials themselves, the Commission's finding should be sustained. . . . The parties agree that §5 prohibits the intentional misrepresentation of any fact which would constitute a material factor in a purchaser's decision whether to buy. They differ, however, in their conception of what "facts" constitute a "material factor" in a purchaser's decision to buy. Respondents submit, in effect, that the only material facts are those which deal with the substantive qualities of a product. The Commission, on the other hand, submits that the misrepresentation of *any* fact so long as it materially induces a purchaser's decision to buy is a deception prohibited by §5.

The Commission's interpretation of what is a deceptive practice seems more in line with the decided cases than that of respondents. . . . It has long been considered a deceptive practice to state falsely that a product ordinarily sells for an inflated price but that it is being offered at a special reduced price, even if the offered price represents the actual value of the product and the purchaser is receiving his money's worth. . . .

It has also been held a violation of §5 for a seller to misrepresent to the public that he is in a certain line of business, even though the misstatement in no way affects the qualities of the product. . . .

Respondents claim that all these cases are irrelevant to our decision because they involve misrepresentations related to the product itself and not merely to the manner in which an advertising message is communicated. This distinction misses the mark for two reasons. In the first place, the present case is not concerned with a mode of communication, but with a misrepresentation that viewers have objective proof of a seller's product claim over and above the seller's word. Secondly, all of the above cases, like the present case, deal with methods designed to get a consumer to purchase a product, not with whether the product, when purchased, will perform up to expectations. . . .

We agree with the Commission, therefore, that the undisclosed use of plexiglass in the present commercials was a material deceptive practice, independent and separate from the other misrepresentation found. We find unpersuasive respondents' other objections to this conclusion. Respondents claim that it will be impractical to inform the viewing public that it is not seeing an actual test, experiment or demonstration, but we think it inconceivable that the ingenious advertising world will be unable, if it so desires, to conform to the Commission's insistence that the public be not misinformed. If, however, it becomes impossible or impractical to show simulated demonstrations on television in a truthful manner, this indicates that television is not a medium that lends itself to this type of commercial, not that the commercial must survive at all costs. . . .

We turn our attention now to the order issued by the Commission. It has been repeatedly held that the Commission has wide discretion in determining the type of order that is necessary to cope with the unfair practices found, . . . However, this Court has also warned that an order's prohibitions "should be clear and precise in order that they may be understood by those against whom they are directed," . . .

The Court of Appeals has criticized the reference in the Commission's order to "test, experiment or demonstration" as not capable of practical interpretation. It could find no difference between the Rapid Shave commercial and a commercial which extolled the goodness of ice cream while giving viewers a picture of a scoop of mashed potatoes appearing to be ice cream. We do not understand this difficulty. In the ice cream case the mashed potato prop is not being used for additional proof of the product claim, while the purpose of the Rapid Shave commercial is to give the viewer objective proof of the claims made. If in the ice cream hypothetical the focus of the commercial becomes the undisclosed potato prop and the viewer is invited, explicitly or by implication, to see for himself the truth of the claims about the ice cream's rich texture and full color, and perhaps compare it to a "rival product," then the commercial has become similar to the one now before us. Clearly, however, a commercial which depicts happy actors delightedly eating ice cream that is in fact mashed potatoes or drinking a product appearing to be coffee but which is in fact some other substance is not covered by the present order.

The crucial terms of the present order—"test, experiment or demonstration . . . represented . . . as actual proof of a claim"—are as specific as the circumstances will permit. . . . In commercials where the emphasis is on the seller's word, and not on the viewer's own perception, the respondents need not fear that an undisclosed use of props is prohibited by the present order. On the other hand, when the commercial not only makes a claim, but also invites the viewer to rely on his own perception for demonstrative proof of the claim, the respondents will be aware that the use of undisclosed props in strategic places might be a material deception. We believe that respondents will have no difficulty applying the Commission's order to the vast majority of their contemplated future commercials. . . .

Finally, we find no defect in the provision of the order which prohibits respondents from engaging in similar practices with respect to "any product" they advertise. . . . In this case the respondents produced three different commercials which employed the same deceptive practice. This we believe gave the Commission a sufficient basis for believing that the respondents would be inclined to use similar commercials with respect to the other products they advertise. We think it reasonable for the Commission to frame its order broadly enough to prevent respondents from engaging in similarly illegal practices in future advertisements. . . .

The judgment of the Court of Appeals is reversed and the case remanded for the entry of a judgment enforcing the Commission's order.

Reversed and remanded.

MR. JUSTICE HARLAN, whom MR. JUSTICE STEWART joins, dissenting in part.

. . . The only question here is what techniques the advertiser may use to convey essential truth to the television viewer. If the claim is true and valid, then the technique for projecting that claim, within broad boundaries, falls purely within the advertiser's art. . . .

The faulty prop in the Court's reasoning is that it focuses entirely on what is taking place in the studio rather than on what the viewer is seeing on his screen. That which the viewer sees with his own eyes is not, however, what is taking place in the studio, but an electronic image. If the image he sees on the screen is an accurate reproduction of what he would see with the naked eyes were the experiment performed before him with sandpaper in his home or in the studio, there can hardly be a misrepresentation in any legally significant sense. While the Commission undoubtedly possesses broad authority to give content to the proscriptions of the Act, its discretion, as the Court recognizes, is not unbridled, and "in the last analysis the words 'deceptive practices' set forth a legal standard and they must get their final meaning from judicial construction" . . .

Nor can I readily understand how the accurate portrayal of an experiment by means of a mock-up can be considered more deceptive than the use of mashed potatoes to convey the glamorous qualities of a particular ice cream . . . ; indeed, to a potato-lover "the smile on the face of the tiger" might come more naturally than if he were actually being served ice cream.

It is commonly known that television presents certain distortions in transmission for which the broadcasting industry must compensate. Thus, a white towel will look a dingy gray over television, but a blue towel will look a sparkling white. On the Court's analysis, an advertiser must achieve accuracy in the studio even though it results in an inaccurate image being projected on the home screen. . . .

A perhaps more commonplace example suggests itself: Would it be proper for respondent Colgate, in advertising a laundry detergent, to "demonstrate" the effectiveness of a major competitor's detergent in washing white sheets; and then "before the viewer's eyes," to wash a white (not a blue) sheet with the competitor's detergent? The studio test would accurately show the quality of the product, but the image on the screen would look as though the sheet had been washed with an ineffective detergent. All that has happened here is the converse: a demonstration has been altered in the studio to compensate for the distortions of the television medium, but in this instance in order to present an accurate picture to the television viewer.

In short, it seems to me that the proper legal test in cases of this kind concerns not what goes on in the broadcasting studio, but whether what is shown on the television screen is an accurate representation of the advertised product and of the claims made for it. . . .

Appendix

Excerpts from Federal Antitrust Laws

SHERMAN ACT, 1890[1]

SECTION 1 Every contract, combination in the form of trust or otherwise, or conspiracy, in restraint of trade or commerce among the several States, or with foreign nations, is hereby declared to be illegal: *Provided,* That nothing herein contained shall render illegal, contracts or agreements prescribing minimum prices for the resale of a commodity which bears, or the label or container of which bears, the trademark, brand, or name of the producer or distributor of such commodity . . . Every person who shall make any contract or engage in any combination or conspiracy hereby declared to be illegal shall be deemed guilty of a misdemeanor, and, on conviction thereof, shall be punished by fine not exceeding fifty thousand dollars, or by imprisonment not exceeding one year, or by both said punishments, in the discretion of the court.

SECTION 2 Every person who shall monopolize, or attempt to monopolize, or combine or conspire with any other person or persons, to monopolize any part of the trade or commerce among the several States, or with foreign nations, shall be deemed guilty of a misdemeanor, and, on conviction thereof, shall be punished by fine not exceeding fifty thousand dollars, or by imprisonment not exceeding one year, or by both said punishments, in the discretion of the court.

[1] 26 Stat. 209, 15 U.S. Code 1–7. Amended by Miller-Tydings Act (1937), 50 Stat. 693, 15 U.S. Code 1; and Act of July 7, 1955, 69 Stat. 282, 15 U.S. Code 1.

CLAYTON ACT. 1914[2]

SECTION 2   That it shall be unlawful· for any person engaged in commerce, in the course of such commerce, either directly or indirectly, to discriminate in price between different purchasers of commodities, which commodities are sold for use, consumption, or resale within the United States or any Territory thereof or the District of Columbia or any insular possession or other place under the Jurisdiction of the United States, where the effect of such discrimination may be to substantially lessen competition or tend to create a monopoly in any line of commerce: *Provided*, That nothing herein contained shall prevent discrimination in price between purchasers of commodities on account of differences in the grade, quality, or quantity of the commodity sold, or that makes only due allowance for differences in the cost of selling or transportation, or discrimination in price in the same or different communities made in good faith to meet competition: *And provided further*, That nothing herein contained shall prevent persons engaged in selling goods, wares, or merchandise in commerce from selecting their own customers in bona fide transactions and not in restraint of trade.

SECTION 3   That it shall be unlawful for any person engaged in commerce, in the course of such commerce, to lease or make a sale or contract for sale of goods, wares, merchandise, machinery, supplies, or other commodities, whether patented or unpatented, for use, consumption, or resale within the United States or any Territory thereof or the District of Columbia or any insular possession or other place under the jurisdiction of the United States, or fix a price charged therefor, or discount from, or rebate upon, such price, on the condition, agreement, or understanding that the lessee or purchaser thereof shall not use or deal in the goods, wares, merchandise, machinery, supplies, or other commodity of a competitor or competitors of the lessor or seller, where the effect of such lease, sale, or contract for sale or such condition, agreement, or understanding may be to substantially lessen competition or tend to create a monopoly in any line of commerce.

SECTION 7   That no corporation engaged in commerce shall acquire, directly or indirectly, the whole or any part of the stock or other share capital of another corporation engaged also in commerce, where the effect of such acquisition may be to substantially lessen competition between the corporation whose stock is so acquired and the corporation making the

2 38 Stat. 730, 15 U.S. Code 12–27.

acquisition, or to restrain such commerce in any section or community, or tend to create a monopoly of any line of commerce.

No corporation shall acquire, directly or indirectly, the whole or any part of the stock or other share capital of two or more corporations engaged in commerce where the effect of such acquisition, or the use of such stock by the voting or granting of proxies or otherwise, may be to substantially lessen competition between such corporations, or any of them, whose stock or other share capital is so acquired, or to restrain such commerce in any section or community, or tend to create a monopoly of any line of commerce.

This section shall not apply to corporations purchasing such stock solely for investment and not using the same by voting or otherwise to bring about, or in attempting to bring about, the substantial lessening of competition. . . .

ROBINSON-PATMAN ACT, 1936, AMENDING SECTION 2 OF THE CLAYTON ACT[3]

SECTION 2 (a) That it shall be unlawful for any person engaged in commerce, in the course of such commerce, either directly or indirectly, to discriminate in price between different purchasers of commodities of like grade and quality, where either or any of the purchases involved in such discrimination are in commerce, where such commodities are sold for use, consumption, or resale within the United States or any Territory thereof or the District of Columbia or any insular possession or other place under the jurisdiction of the United States, and where the effect of such discrimination may be substantially to lessen competition or tend to create a monopoly in any line of commerce, or to injure, destroy, or prevent competition with any person who either grants or knowingly receives the benefit of such discrimination, or with customers of either of them: *Provided,* that nothing herein contained shall prevent differentials which make only due allowance for differences in the cost of manufacture, sale, or delivery resulting from the differing methods or quantities in which such commodities are to such purchasers sold or delivered: *Provided, however,* That the Federal Trade Commission may, after due investigation and hearing to all interested parties, fix and establish quantity limits, and revise the same as it finds necessary, as to particular commodities or classes of commodities, where it finds that available purchasers in greater quantities are so few as to render differentials on account thereof unjustly discriminatory or promotive of monopoly in any line of commerce; and the foregoing

[3] 49 Stat. 1526, 15 U.S. Code 13.

shall then not be construed to permit differentials based on differences in quantities greater than those so fixed and established: *And provided further,* That nothing herein contained shall prevent persons engaged in selling goods, wares, or merchandise in commerce from selecting their own customers in bona fide transactions and not in restraint of trade: *And provided further,* That nothing herein contained shall prevent price changes from time to time where in response to changing conditions affecting the market for or the marketability of the goods concerned, such as but not limited to actual or imminent deterioration of perishable goods, obsolescence of seasonal goods, distress sales under court process, or sales in good faith in discontinuance of business in the goods concerned.

(b) Upon proof being made, at any hearing on a complaint under this section, that there has been discrimination in price or services or facilities furnished, the burden of rebutting in prima facie case thus made by showing justification shall be upon the person charged with a violation of this section, and unless justification shall be affirmatively shown, the Commission is authorized to issue an order terminating the discrimination: *Provided, however,* That nothing herein contained shall prevent a seller rebutting the prima facie case thus made by showing that his lower price or the furnishing of services or facilities to any purchaser or purchasers was made in good faith to meet an equally low price of a competitor, or the services or facilities furnished by a competitor.

(c) That it shall be unlawful for any person engaged in commerce, in the course of such commerce, to pay or grant, or to receive or accept, anything of value as a commission, brokerage, or other compensation, or any allowance or discount in lieu thereof, except for services rendered in connection with the sale or purchase of goods, wares, or merchandise, either to the other party to such transaction or to an agent, representative, or other intermediary therein where such intermediary is acting in fact for or in behalf, or is subject to the direct or indirect control, of any party to such transaction other than the person by whom such compensation is so granted or paid.

(d) That it shall be unlawful for any person engaged in commerce to pay or contract for the payment of anything of value to or for the benefit of a customer of such person in the course of such commerce as compensation or in consideration for any services or facilities furnished by or through such customer in connection with the processing, handling, sale, or offering for sale of any products or commodities manufactured, sold, or offered for sale by such person, unless such payment or consideration is available on proportionally equal terms to all other customers competing in the distribution of such products or commodities.

(e) That it shall be unlawful for any person to discriminate in favor of one purchaser against another purchaser or purchasers of a commodity bought for resale, with or without processing, by contracting to furnish or furnishing, or by contributing to the furnishing of, any services or facilities connected with the processing, handling, sale, or offering for sale of such commodity so purchased upon terms not accorded to all purchasers on proportionally equal terms.

(f) That it shall be unlawful for any person engaged in commerce, in the course of such commerce, knowingly to induce or receive a discrimination in price which is prohibited by this section.

SECTION 3 It shall be unlawful for any person engaged in commerce, in the course of such commerce, to be a party to, or assist in, any transaction of sale, or contract to sell, which discriminates to his knowledge against competitors of the purchaser, in that, any discount, rebate, allowance, or advertising service charge is granted to the purchaser over and above any discount, rebate, allowance, or advertising service charge available at the time of such transaction to said competitors in respect of a sale of goods of like grade, quality, and quantity; to sell, or contract to sell, goods in any part of the United States at prices lower than those exacted by said person elsewhere in the United States for the purpose of destroying competition, or eliminating a competitor in such part of the United States; or, to sell, or contract to sell, goods at unreasonably low prices for the purpose of destroying competition or eliminating a competitor.

Any person violating any of the provisions of this section shall, upon conviction thereof, be fined not more than $5,000 or imprisoned not more than one year, or both.

CELLER-KEFAUVER ACT, 1950, AMENDING
SECTION 7 OF THE CLAYTON ACT[4]

SECTION 7 That no corporation engaged in commerce shall acquire, directly or indirectly, the whole or any part of the stock or other share capital and no corporation subject to the jurisdiction of the Federal Trade Commission shall acquire the whole or any part of the assets of another corporation engaged also in commerce, where in any line of commerce in any section of the country, the effect of such acquisition may be substantially to lessen competition, or to tend to create a monopoly.

No corporation shall acquire, directly or indirectly, the whole or any part of the stock or other share capital and no corporation subject to the jurisdiction of the Federal Trade Commission shall acquire the whole or any part of the assets of one or more corporations engaged in commerce, where in any line of commerce in any section of the country, the effect of such acquisition, of such stocks or assets, or of the use of such stock by the voting or granting of proxies or otherwise, may be substantially to lessen competition, or to tend to create a monopoly. . . .

4 64 Stat. 1125, 15 U.S. Code 18.

FEDERAL TRADE COMMISSION ACT, 1914[5]

SECTION 5   (a) (1) Unfair methods of competition in commerce, and unfair or deceptive acts or practices in commerce, are hereby declared unlawful.

(2) Nothing contained in this Act or in any of the Antitrust Acts shall render unlawful any contracts or agreements prescribing minimum or stipulated prices, or requiring a vendee to enter into contracts or agreements prescribing minimum or stipulated prices, for the resale of a commodity which bears, or the label or container of which bears, the trademark, brand, or name of the producer or distributor of such commodity and which is in free and open competition with commodities of the same general class produced or distributed by others, when contracts or agreements of that description are lawful as applied to intrastate transactions under any statute, law, or public policy now or hereafter in effect in any State, Territory, or the District of Columbia in which such resale is to be made, or to which the commodity is to be transported for such resale.

(3) Nothing contained in this Act or in any of the Antitrust Acts shall render unlawful the exercise or the enforcement of any right or right of action created by any statute, law, or public policy now or hereafter in effect in any State, Territory, or the District of Columbia, which in substance provides that willfully and knowingly advertising, offering for sale, or selling any commodity at less than the price or prices prescribed in such contracts or agreements whether the person so advertising, offering for sale, or selling is or is not a party to such a contract or agreement, is unfair competition and is actionable at the suit of any person damaged thereby.

(4) Neither the making of contracts or agreements as described in paragraph (2) of this subsection, nor the exercise or enforcement of any right or right of action as described in paragraph (3) of this subsection shall constitute an unlawful burden or restraint upon, or interference with, commerce.

(5) Nothing contained in paragraph (2) of this subsection shall make lawful contracts or agreements providing for the establishment or maintenance of minimum or stipulated resale prices on any commodity referred to in paragraph (2) of this subsection, between manufacturers, or between producers, or between wholesalers, or between brokers, or between factors, or between retailers, or between persons, firms, or corporations in competition with each other. . . .

5 38 Stat. 717, 15 U.S. Code 41–58. Amended by Wheeler-Lea Act (1938), 52 Stat. 111, 15 U.S. Code 41; and McGuire Act (1952), 66 Stat. 632, 15 U.S. Code 45.